THE INMATE PRISON EXPERIENCE

MARY K. STOHR, Ph.D.
Boise State University

CRAIG HEMMENS, J.D., Ph.D.
Boise State University

PEARSON

Prentice
Hall

Upper Saddle River, New Jersey 07458

Library of Congress Cataloging-in-Publication Data

Stohr, Mary K.
The inmate prison experience / Mary K. Stohr, Craig Hemmens,
p. cm.
Includes bibliographical references.
ISBN 0-13-112345-9
  1. Prison psychology—United States. 2. Prisoners—United States—Attitudes. 3. Imprisonment—United States. I. Stohr, Mary K. II. Title.

HV6089 .H36 2004
365'.6—dc21   2002038163

Editor-in-Chief: Stephen Helba
Executive Editor: Frank Mortimer, Jr.
Assistant Editor: Korrine Dorsey
Production Editor: Mary Jo Graham, Carlisle Publishers Services
Production Liaison: Barbara Martine Cappuccio
Director of Production and Manufacturing: Bruce Johnson
Managing Editor: Mary Carnis
Manufacturing Buyer: Cathleen Petersen
Creative Director: Cheryl Asherman
Cover Design Coordinator: Miguel Ortiz
Cover Designer: Scott Garrison
Cover Image: Terry Eggers, Corbis/StockMarket
Editorial Assistant: Barbara Rosenberg
Marketing Manager: Tim Peyton
Formatting and Interior Design: Carlisle Communications, Ltd.
Printing and Binding: Phoenix Book Tech Park

Pearson Education LTD, *London*
Pearson Education Australia PTY, Limited, *Sydney*
Pearson Education Singapore, Pte. Ltd.
Pearson Education North Asia Ltd., *Hong Kong*
Pearson Education Canada, Ltd., *Toronto*
Pearson Educación de Mexico, S.A. de C.V.
Pearson Education—Japan, *Tokyo*
Pearson Education Malaysia, Pte. Ltd.

10 9 8 7 6 5 4 3 2 1
ISBN 0-13-112345-9

CONTENTS

PREFACE

There has been research on prisons almost since their creation. Prisons were created with a hopeful, reformist zeal, but very quickly degraded into soulless institutions. De Beaumont and de Tocqueville (1997) in the 1700s examined a number of early American penitentiaries and described the decrepit conditions of many of them. Although such early researchers and observers generally confined their examination of prison life to the surface details, such as recounting the daily routine of prisoners, these descriptions uniformly painted a picture of suffering and degradation. Conditions did not improve much, if at all, in the nineteenth century penal systems. Historians have provided detailed and often horrific accounts of life in the work camps and prisons that was prevalent at that time (Oshinsky 1996; Rothman 1980). As David Rothman (1980, 17) notes in his classic work, *Conscience and Convenience:*

> Every observer of American prisons and asylums in the closing decades of the nineteenth century recognized that the pride of one generation had become the shame of another. The institutions that had been intended to exemplify the humanitarian advances of republican government were not merely inadequate to the ideal but were actually an embarrassment and a rebuke . . . the evidence was incontrovertible that brutality and corruption were endemic to the institutions.

As social science developed in the early twentieth century, researchers on social institutions turned a critical eye to the prisons. Modern sociological research on prison life dates from Clemmer's (1940) pioneering work *The Prison Community,* a study described as "[t]he first systematic investigation of the prisoner world" (Marquart and Sorensen 1997, 95). Clemmer examined the manner in which inmates interacted with one another, their surroundings, and the correctional staff in an effort to determine how living in prison affected inmates. Clemmer (1940, 299) developed the concept of "prisonization" to explain how a prisoner becomes assimilated into the informal social structure of the prison.

Clemmer (1940, 299) defined prisonization as "[t]he taking on in greater or less degree of the folkways, mores, customs, and general culture of the penitentiary." According to Clemmer, inmates, suffering from the "[a]lienative effects of the coercive power exercised by prison officials" (1940, 299) grew increasingly anti-social, and learned not only how to commit crimes, but how to adopt a value system in opposition to the prison administration and, supposedly, in opposition to the value system espoused by the general public.

Gresham Sykes, in *The Society of Captives* (1958) and elsewhere (Sykes and Messinger 1960), developed further Clemmer's concept of prisonization, explaining the cause of inmate alienation as a reaction to the "pains of imprisonment" (1958, 63–83). Sykes identified five pains associated with prison life: loss of one's liberty, loss of material possessions, loss of heterosexual contact, loss of personal autonomy, and loss of personal security. Suffering these pains, Sykes believed, caused inmates to become insecure and bitter, and led them to "reject their rejecters" (McCorkle & Korn 1954, 98). The result was that the pains of imprisonment forged an inmate population unified by its shared pains. Prisoners developed their own informal social structure based on their responses to the pains of imprisonment. This subculture reinforced a set of norms and values in opposition to those espoused by the prison staff. This was known as the "inmate code" (Sykes & Messinger 1960, 5–6). Additionally, inmates adopted one of a series of social roles in an effort to mitigate the rigors of prison life. Sykes (1958, 84–108) devised a typology of 11 inmate social roles, including the "tough," "fag," "merchant," and "real man."

The "Big House" with its attendant inmate code and social roles, as depicted by Clemmer and Sykes, has many of the components of Goffman's "total institution" (1961). In his well-known book, *Asylums,* Goffman discussed how life within a variety of institutions, such as mental hospitals, monasteries, military training camps, and prisons is affected by the institution itself. These sorts of institutions are closed worlds in which the inhabitants live highly regimented, ordered lives surrounded by other inhabitants and from which they are unable to leave or escape. Inmates in these institutions suffer a series of what Goffman called "degradations" (1961, 43). A universal characteristic of these institutions is the pervasiveness of their impact—all who live within them face the same problems of adjustment. Goffman (1961, 22) acknowledged that individuals do bring with them into the institution their individual personas and personal characteristics, but he argued that the institution's impact is so strong, so all-encompassing, that it strips them of these characteristics, through the process of "mortification."

The model of prison life developed by Clemmer and reinforced in some respects by Sykes and Goffman, became known as the "deprivation" model. The deprivation model was challenged by researchers who decried its disregard for the effect of the outside world and individual characteristics on how inmates adjust to prison (Irwin and Cressey 1962; Carroll 1974; Jacobs 1977). These writers noted that an inmate did not come into prison a blank slate, but rather brought with him (but now including her) the code of the streets, which he used in modified form within the prison walls. This was referred to as the "importation model."

Scholarship on prisons that has appeared in the last three decades has tended to recognize the interplay between the internal operation and experience for inmates and the outside influences that give the inmates' lives, their imprisonment, and the existence of the prison itself, context. Oshinsky (1996), in his recounting of the operation of the Parchman Prison Farm in Mississippi in the twentieth century, notes that the historical artifact of slavery serves as the framework for understanding this "farm with slaves" for black inmates. "Blacks came to Parchman as field workers and left the same way. That was their lot in life. Anything more was anathema in a culture where white supremacy and unskilled Negro labor went hand in hand. In Mississippi, rehabilitation was a dangerous word" (Oshinsky 1996: 224). Likewise, in the *Stateville* Illinois prison, Jacobs (1977) and in *Hacks, Blacks, and Cons,* Carroll (1974) describe an existence for inmates that is both a part of, and apart from, that of the larger community.

The articles in this book were selected to represent the best and most relevant research on the prison experience. The focus of this book is on what life is like in prison for the prisoners. The amount of research on prison life is tremendous, but much of it is duplicative, ill-conceived, or out of date. We have endeavored to select articles that are current or, even if relatively old, still representative of the best work on a particular issue. We acknowledge that there are other articles that could well have been included, but space constraints preclude the inclusion of every interesting and important article. This book is intended to serve as a starting point for thought and discussion, and for further investigation on the nature of the prison experience for inmates.

The collection is divided into four parts and consists of 18 articles. The first section, "Inmate Adjustment to Prison," includes four articles that examine a variety of issues related to adjustment to prison, including the inmate society, the impact of prison on inmate self-esteem, and acculturation and acceptance of prison as a way of life. The second section, "Individual Adjustment Factors," includes five articles that examine some of the individual factors affecting inmate adjustment, such as race, age, gender, and socioeconomic status. The four articles in section three, "Institutional Adjustment Factors," examine the effect of certain institutional factors, including overcrowding, AIDS policies, and prison gangs. The fourth and final section, "Societal Adjustment Factors," has five articles that examine a variety of current issues, such as education and treatment programs, and the incarceration of women and youthful offenders.

REFERENCES

Carroll, L. (1974). *Hacks, Blacks, and Cons.* Lexington, MA: D.C. Heath and Company.

Clemmer, D. (1940). *The Prison Community.* New York: Holt, Rinehart and Winston.

de Beaumont, G. and A. de Tocqueville (1997, originally published in 1833). On the Penitentiary System in the United States and Its Application in France. In J. W. Marquart and J. R. Sorenson (eds.), *Correctional Contexts: Contemporary and Classical Readings.* Los Angeles, California: Roxbury Publishing Company, pp. 47–55.

Goffman, E. (1961). *Asylums.* Chicago: Aldine.

Irwin, J. and D. R. Cressey (1962). Thieves, Convicts and the Inmate Culture. *Social Problems* 10(2): 142–155.

Jacobs, J. (1977). *Stateville: The Penitentiary in Mass Society.* Chicago: University of Chicago Press.

Marquart, J. W. and J. R. Sorensen (1997). *Correctional Contexts: Contemporary and Classical Readings.* Los Angeles: Roxbury Publishing Company.

McCorkle, L. and R. Korn (1954). Resocialization Within the Walls. *The Annals of the American Academy of Political and Social Sciences* 293(1): 88–98.

Oshinsky, D. M. (1996). *Worse Than Slavery: Parchman Farm and the Ordeal of Jim Crow Justice.* New York: The Free Press.

Rothman, D. (1980). *Conscience and Convenience: The Asylum and its Alternatives in Progressive America.* New York: Harper Collins Publishers.

Sykes, G. (1958). *The Society of Captives.* Princeton, NJ: Princeton University Press.

Sykes, G. M. and S. L. Messinger (1960). The Inmate Social System. In D. Cressey (ed.), *Theoretical Studies in Social Organization of the Prison.* New York: Plenum.

ACKNOWLEDGMENTS

We would like to thank our sweethearts, wife/husband, and co-authors (in other words, each other) for support in this endeavor. We are doubly thankful that we have such a wonderful daughter, Emily Rose Stohr-Gillmore, to dedicate this book to. We are also grateful for the support of Emily's dad, Michael Gillmore; our Prentice Hall editor, Susan Beauchamp; Kim Davies (thanks for the extra resources!); and of course the authors of all these insightful articles for allowing us to enhance this collection with their works. The authors would also like to thank the following reviewers: Joel Allen, Oakland Community College, Auburn Hills, MI; Paul Becker, Morehead State University, Morehead, KY; Alex del Carmen, University of Texas, Arlington, TX; Ron G. Iacovetta, Wichita State University, Wichita, KS; Donna Nicholson, Manchester Community College, Manchester, CT; Robert Rogers, Middle Tennessee State University, Murfreesboro, TN; and Jody L. Sundt, Southern Illinois University, Carbondale, IL.

ABOUT THE EDITORS

Mary K. Stohr is an Associate Professor and the Chair in the Department of Criminal Justice Administration at Boise State University. She holds a Ph.D. in political science from Washington State University. She has an abiding interest in the nature and operation of correctional institutions and her research and teaching has generally been focused in that direction.

Craig Hemmens is an Associate Professor in the Department of Criminal Justice Administration at Boise State University. He holds a J.D. from North Carolina Central University School of Law and a Ph.D. in criminal justice from Sam Houston State University. He has conducted research on the attitudes of prison inmates and staff, and on the operation of prison drug treatment programs.

SECTION 1

INMATE ADJUSTMENT TO PRISON

We begin the book with four articles that examine the "pains of imprisonment" and how inmates adjust to life behind the walls. The authors take varying approaches to their study of this subject, and come to some intriguing conclusions.

In the first reading in this section, by John Irwin and Donald R. Cressey, "Thieves, Convicts and the Inmate Culture," the authors argue that individual background and pre-institutional experiences have a major impact on how an inmate adapts to incarceration. They do not deny that incarceration has an impact, and a significant one, on the inmate, but they assert that the fact of incarceration alone does not explain everything. And while they acknowledge the existence and importance of the inmate subculture, they insist that the norms of this subculture are not formed solely in response to the pains of imprisonment, but in large part reflect the values and norms brought with the inmate from the free world. The source of these free world values may be the criminal underworld, which many inmates have experienced prior to incarceration, or it could be the social background of the inmate, such as whether he lived in an urban ghetto, a suburb, or a sparsely populated rural area. Prisonization, or the rejection of prosocial attitudes, is not a response to the deprivations of incarceration, but merely a reflection of an inmate's preprison experiences and characteristics in the prison setting. The inmate subculture, then, is based on values brought with, or imported by, the inmate from the outside world. The norms are then transmitted to future inmates through social interaction. Proponents of the importation model posit that the pains of imprisonment are mediated by external factors.

The extent to which an inmate embraces the norms, values, and beliefs of a correctional institution, or prisonization, perhaps depends on whether he or she perceives the sentence as "just" and/or of value. Patricia Van Voorhis, Sandra Lee Browning, Marilyn Simon, and Jill Gordon, in their article "The Meaning of Punishment: Inmates' Orientation to the Prison Experience," explore the dynamic between "inmates' identification with sentencing intents" and factors that might influence those orientations among both male maximum and minimum security inmates. They find that some inmates acknowledge a deterrent value for prisons, others think the sentence fits the crime, and still others think that imprisonment suits no reasonable societal or individual purpose. They also find that those who are most disadvantaged, see more rehabilitative potential in prisons than those who were employed, older, and White.

It is not altogether uncommon to hear popular accounts of prisoners who did not want to be released from prison or jail, either for fear they would reoffend or because they had nowhere to go. Sometimes a released offender will commit an offense soon after his or her release, just to get back into a correctional facility. Most inmates, however, profess that they would rather be in the free world. But this does not necessarily mean that soon-to-be released inmates or those facing prison versus probation, do not have some fears of the free world.

In fact, as Ben Crouch reports in his article, "Is Incarceration Really Worse: Analysis of Offenders' Preferences for Prison Over Probation," probation may be more of a deterrent to crime than prison, that is if one considers dread and deterrent to be causally related. He finds in his interview data from Texas inmates that some offenders, particularly African-American males, may prefer prison to probation time.

Castellano and Soderstrom indicate in their article, "Self-Esteem, Depression, and Anxiety Evidenced by a Prison Inmate Sample: Interrelationships and Consequences for Prison Programming," that there is a great deal of anecdotal evidence that inmates preparing to be released to the community suffer from higher levels of stress. Low levels of self-esteem, heightened depression, and anxiety may be part and parcel of the adjustment some inmates make to prison and their imminent departure or "gate fever." In their study of inmates about to exit correctional facilities in Illinois, the authors found that their subjects had a greater degree of anxiety and depression and less self-esteem than the "normal populations" that the measurement instruments had been used with.

THIEVES, CONVICTS
AND THE INMATE CULTURE

John Irwin and Donald R. Cressey

In the rapidly-growing literature on the social organization of correctional institutions, it has become common to discuss "prison culture" and inmate culture" in terms suggesting that the behavior systems of various types of inmates stem from the conditions of imprisonment themselves. Use of a form of structural-functional analysis in research and observation of institutions has led to emphasis of the notion that internal conditions stimulate inmate behavior of various kinds, and there has been a glossing over of the older notion that inmates may bring a culture with them into the prison. Our aim is to suggest that much of the inmate behavior classified as part of the prison culture is not peculiar to the prison at all. On the contrary, it is the fine distinction between "prison culture" and "criminal subculture" which seems to make understandable the fine distinction between behavior patterns of various categories of inmates.

A number of recent publications have defended the notion that behavior patterns among inmates develop with a minimum of influence from the outside world. For example, in his general discussion of total institutions, Goffman acknowledges that inmates bring a culture with them to the institution, but he argues that upon entrance to the institution they are stripped of this support by processes of mortification and dispossession aimed at managing the daily activities of a large number of persons in a small space with a small expenditure of resources.[1] Similarly, Sykes and Messinger note that a central value system seems to pervade prison populations, and they maintain that "conformity to, or deviation from, the inmate code is the major basis for classifying and describing the

Social Problems, Vol. 10 No. 2, April 1962 142–155 © 1962 University of California.
We are indebted to the following persons for suggested modifications of the original draft: Donald L. Garrity, Daniel Glaser, Erving Goffman, and Stanton Wheeler.

[1]Erving Goffman, "On the Characteristics of Total Institutions," Chapters 1 and 2 in Donald R. Cressey, Editor, *The Prison: Studies in Institutional Organization and Change.* New York: Holt, Rinehart and Winston, 1961, pp. 22–47.

social relations of prisoners."[2] The emphasis in this code is on directives such as "don't interfere with inmate interests," "don't lose your head," "don't exploit inmates," "don't weaken," and "don't be a sucker." The authors' argument, like the argument in other of Sykes' publications is that the origin of these values is situational; the value system arises out of the conditions of imprisonment.[3] Cloward stresses both the acute sense of status degradation which prisoners experience and the resulting patterns of prison life, which he calls "structural accommodation."[4] Like others, he makes the important point that the principal types of inmates—especially the "politicians" and the "shots"—help the officials by exerting controls over the general prison body in return for special privileges. Similarly, he recognizes the "right guy" role as one built around the value system described by Sykes and Messinger, and points out that it is tolerated by prison officials because it helps maintain the status quo. Cloward hints at the existence in prison of a *criminal* subculture when he says that "the upper echelons of the inmate world come to be occupied by those whose past behavior best symbolizes that which society rejects and who have most fully repudiated institutional norms." Nevertheless, his principal point is that this superior status, like other patterns of behavior among inmates, arises from the *internal* character of the prison situation. McCleery also stresses the unitary character of the culture of prisoners, and he identifies the internal source of this culture in statements such as: "The denial of validity to outside contacts protected the inmate culture from criticism and assured the stability of the social system," "A man's status in the inmate community depended on his role there and his conformity to its norms," "Inmate culture stressed the goals of adjustment within the walls and the rejection of outside contacts," and "Status has been geared to adjustment in the prison."[5]

The idea that the prison produces its own varieties of behavior represents a break with the more traditional notion that men bring patterns of behavior with them when they enter prison, and use them in prison. Despite their emphasis on "prisonization" of newcomers, even Clemmer and Riemer noted that degree of conformity to prison expectations depends in part on prior, outside conditions.[6] Schrag has for some years been studying the social backgrounds and careers of various types of inmates.[7] Unlike any of the authors cited above, he has collected data on both the pre-prison experiences and the prison experiences of prisoners. He relates the actions of inmates to the broader community as well as to the forces that are more indigenous to prisons themselves.[8] Of most relevance here

---

[2]Richard A. Cloward, Donald R. Cressey, George H. Grosser, Richard McCleery, Lloyd E. Ohlin, and Gresham M. Sykes and Sheldon L. Messinger, *Theoretical Studies in Social Organization of the Prison.* New York: Social Science Research Council, 1960, p. 9.

[3]*Ibid.,* pp. 15, 19. See also Gresham M. Sykes, "Men, Merchants, and Toughs: A Study of Reactions to Imprisonment," *Social Problems,* 4 (October, 1957), pp. 130–138: and Gresham M. Sykes, *The Society of Captives,* Princeton: Princeton University Press, 1958, pp. 79–82.

[4]Cloward, *et al., op. cit.,* pp. 21, 35–41.

[5]*Ibid.,* pp. 58, 60, 73.

[6]Donald Clemmer, *The Prison Community,* Re-issued Edition, New York: Rinehart, 1958, pp. 229–302; Hans Riemer, "Socialization in the Prison Community," *Proceedings of the American Prison Association,* 1937, pp. 151–155.

[7]See Clarence Schrag, *Social Types in a Prison Community,* Unpublished M.S. Thesis, University of Washington, 1944.

[8]Clarence Schrag, "Some Foundations for a Theory of Correction," Chapter 8 in Cressey, *op. cit.,* p. 329.

is his finding that anti-social inmates ("right guys") "are reared in an environment consistently oriented toward illegitimate social norms,"[9] and frequently earn a living via contacts with organized crime but do not often rise to positions of power in the field. In contrast, asocial inmates ("outlaws") are frequently reared in institutions: "The careers of asocial offenders are marked by high egocentrism and inability to profit from past mistakes or to plan for the future."[10]

However, despite these research findings, even Schrag has commented as follows: "Juxtaposed with the official organization of the prison is an unofficial social system originating within the institution and regulating inmate conduct with respect to focal issues, such as length of sentence, relations among prisoners, contacts with staff members and other civilians, food, sex, and health, among others."[11] Garrity interprets Schrag's theory in the following terms, which seem to ignore the findings on the pre-prison careers of the various inmate types:

> Schrag has further suggested that all inmates face a number of common problems of adjustment as a consequence of imprisonment and that social organization develops as a consequence. When two or more persons perceive that they share a common motivation or problem of action, a basis for meaningful interaction has been established, and from this interaction can emerge the social positions, roles, and norms which comprise social organization. Schrag suggests that the common problems of adjustment which become the principal axes of prison life are related to time, food, sex, leisure, and health.[12]

Garrity himself uses the "indigenous origin" notion when he says that "the axial values regarding shared problems or deprivations provide the basis for articulation of the broad normative system or 'prison code' which defines positions and roles in a general way but allows enough latitude so that positions and roles take on the character of social worlds themselves."[13] However, he also points out that some prisoners' reference groups are outside the prison, and he characterizes the "right guy" as an "anti-social offender, stable, and oriented to crime, criminals, and inmates."[14] "The 'right guy' is the dominant figure in the prison, and his reference groups are elite prisoners, sophisticated, career-type criminals, and other 'right guys.' "[15] Cressey and Krassowski, similarly, seem confused about any distinction between a criminal subculture and a prison subculture. They mention that many inmates of Soviet labor camps "know prisons and maintain criminalistic values," and that the inmates are bound together by a "criminalistic ideology,"[16] but they fail to deal theoretically with the contradiction between these statements and their observation that the inmate leaders in the labor camps are "toughs" or "gorillas" rather than "right guys" or "politicians." Conceivably,

---

[9]*Ibid.,* p. 350.

[10]*Ibid.,* p. 349.

[11]*Ibid.,* p. 342.

[12]Donald R. Garrity, "The Prison as a Rehabilitation Agency," Chapter 9 in Cressey, *op. cit.,* pp. 372–373.

[13]*Ibid.,* p. 373.

[14]*Ibid.,* p. 376.

[15]*Ibid.,* p. 377.

[16]Donald R. Cressey and Witold Krassowski, "Inmate Organization and Anomie in American Prisons and Soviet Labor Camps," *Social Problems,* 5 (Winter, 1957–58), pp. 217–230.

head"—with the least suffering and in a minimum amount of time are provided. Of course, the subculture itself is both nurtured and diffused in the different jails and prisons of the country.

There also exists in prisons a subculture which is by definition a set of patterns that flourishes in the environment of incarceration. It can be found wherever men are confined, whether it be in city jails, state and federal prisons, army stockades, prisoner of war camps, concentration camps, or even mental hospitals. Such organizations are characterized by deprivations and limitations on freedom, and in them available wealth must be competed for by men supposedly on an equal footing. It is in connection with the *maintenance* (but not necessarily with the *origin*) of this subculture that it is appropriate to stress the notion that a minimum of outside status criteria are carried into the situation. Ideally, all status is to be achieved by the means made available in the prison, through the displayed ability to manipulate the environment, win special privileges in a certain manner, and assert influence over others. To avoid confusion with writings on "prison culture" and "inmate culture," we have arbitrarily named this system of values and behavior patterns a "convict subculture." The central value of the subculture is utilitarianism, and the most manipulative and most utilitarian individuals win the available wealth and such positions of influence as might exist.

It is not correct to conclude, however, that even these behavior patterns are a consequence of the environment of any particular prison. In the first place, such utilitarian and manipulative behavior probably is characteristic of the "hard core" lower class in the United States, and most prisoners come from this class. After discussing the importance of toughness, smartness, excitement and fate in this group, Miller makes the following significant observation:

> In lower class culture a close conceptual connection is made between "authority" and "nurturance." To be restrictively or firmly controlled is to be cared for. Thus the overtly negative evaluation of superordinate authority frequently extends as well to nurturance, care, or protection. The desire for personal independence is often expressed in terms such as "I don't need *nobody* to take care of me. I can take care of myself!" Actual patterns of behavior, however, reveal a marked discrepancy between expressed sentiments and what is covertly valued. Many lower class people appear to seek out highly restrictive social environments wherein stringent external controls are maintained over their behavior. Such institutions as the armed forces, the mental hospital, the disciplinary school, the prison or correctional institution, provide environments which incorporate a strict and detailed set of rules defining and limiting behavior, and enforced by an authority system which controls and applies coercive sanctions for deviance from these rules. While under the jurisdiction of such systems, the lower class person generally expresses to his peers continual resentment of the coercive, unjust, and arbitrary exercise of authority. Having been released, or having escaped from these milieux, however, he will often act in such a way as to insure recommitment, or choose recommitment voluntarily after a temporary period of "freedom."[24]

In the second place, the "hard core" members of this subculture as it exists in American prisons for adults are likely to be inmates who have a long record of confinement in institutions for juveniles. McCleery observed that, in a period

---

[24]*Op. cit.,* pp. 12–13.

is his finding that anti-social inmates ("right guys") "are reared in an environment consistently oriented toward illegitimate social norms,"[9] and frequently earn a living via contacts with organized crime but do not often rise to positions of power in the field. In contrast, asocial inmates ("outlaws") are frequently reared in institutions: "The careers of asocial offenders are marked by high egocentrism and inability to profit from past mistakes or to plan for the future."[10]

However, despite these research findings, even Schrag has commented as follows: "Juxtaposed with the official organization of the prison is an unofficial social system originating within the institution and regulating inmate conduct with respect to focal issues, such as length of sentence, relations among prisoners, contacts with staff members and other civilians, food, sex, and health, among others."[11] Garrity interprets Schrag's theory in the following terms, which seem to ignore the findings on the pre-prison careers of the various inmate types:

> Schrag has further suggested that all inmates face a number of common problems of adjustment as a consequence of imprisonment and that social organization develops as a consequence. When two or more persons perceive that they share a common motivation or problem of action, a basis for meaningful interaction has been established, and from this interaction can emerge the social positions, roles, and norms which comprise social organization. Schrag suggests that the common problems of adjustment which become the principal axes of prison life are related to time, food, sex, leisure, and health.[12]

Garrity himself uses the "indigenous origin" notion when he says that "the axial values regarding shared problems or deprivations provide the basis for articulation of the broad normative system or 'prison code' which defines positions and roles in a general way but allows enough latitude so that positions and roles take on the character of social worlds themselves."[13] However, he also points out that some prisoners' reference groups are outside the prison, and he characterizes the "right guy" as an "anti-social offender, stable, and oriented to crime, criminals, and inmates."[14] "The 'right guy' is the dominant figure in the prison, and his reference groups are elite prisoners, sophisticated, career-type criminals, and other 'right guys.' "[15] Cressey and Krassowski, similarly, seem confused about any distinction between a criminal subculture and a prison subculture. They mention that many inmates of Soviet labor camps "know prisons and maintain criminalistic values," and that the inmates are bound together by a "criminalistic ideology,"[16] but they fail to deal theoretically with the contradiction between these statements and their observation that the inmate leaders in the labor camps are "toughs" or "gorillas" rather than "right guys" or "politicians." Conceivably,

---

[9]*Ibid.,* p. 350.

[10]*Ibid.,* p. 349.

[11]*Ibid.,* p. 342.

[12]Donald R. Garrity, "The Prison as a Rehabilitation Agency," Chapter 9 in Cressey, *op. cit.,* pp. 372–373.

[13]*Ibid.,* p. 373.

[14]*Ibid.,* p. 376.

[15]*Ibid.,* p. 377.

[16]Donald R. Cressey and Witold Krassowski, "Inmate Organization and Anomie in American Prisons and Soviet Labor Camps," *Social Problems,* 5 (Winter, 1957–58), pp. 217–230.

leadership is vested in "toughs" to a greater extent than is the case in American prisons because the orientation is more that of a *prison* subculture than of a criminal subculture in which men are bound together with a "criminalistic ideology."

It is our contention that the "functional" or "indigenous origin" notion has been overemphasized and that observers have overlooked the dramatic effect that external behavior patterns have on the conduct of inmates in any given prison. Moreover, the contradictory statements made in this connection by some authors, including Cressey,[17] seem to stem from acknowledging but then ignoring the deviant subcultures which exist outside any given prison and outside prisons generally. More specifically, it seems rather obvious that the "prison code"— don't inform on or exploit another inmate, don't lose your head, be weak, or be a sucker, etc.—is also part of a *criminal* code, existing outside prisons. Further, many inmates come to any given prison with a record of many terms in correctional institutions. These men, some of whom have institutional records dating back to early childhood, bring with them a ready-made set of patterns which they apply to the new situation, just as is the case with participants in the criminal subculture. In view of these variations, a clear understanding of inmate conduct cannot be obtained simply by viewing "prison culture" or "inmate culture" as an isolated system springing solely from the conditions of imprisonment. Becker and Geer have made our point in more general terms: "The members of a group may derive their understandings from cultures other than that of the group they are at the moment participating in. To the degree that group participants share latent social identities (related to their membership in the same 'outside' social groups) they will share these understandings, so that there will be a culture which can be called *latent,* i.e., the culture has its origin and social support in a group other than the one in which the members are now participating."[18]

We have no doubt that the total set of relationships called "inmate society" is a response to problems of imprisonment. What we question is the emphasis given to the notion that solutions to these problems are found within the prison, and the lack of emphasis on "latent culture"—on external experiences as determinants of the solutions. We have found it both necessary and helpful to divide inmates into three rough categories: those oriented to a criminal subculture, those oriented to a prison subculture, and those oriented to "conventional" or "legitimate" subcultures.

THE TWO DEVIANT SUBCULTURES

When we speak of a criminal subculture we do not mean to imply that there is some national or international organization with its own judges, enforcement agencies, etc. Neither do we imply that every person convicted of a crime is a member of the subculture. Nevertheless, descriptions of the values of professional thieves, "career criminals," "sophisticated criminals," and other good crooks indicate that there is a set of values which extends to criminals across the

---

[17]Edwin H. Sutherland and Donald R. Cressey, *Principles of Criminology,* Sixth Edition, New York: Lippincott, 1960, pp. 504–505.

[18]Howard S. Becker and Blanche Geer, "Latent Culture: A Note on the Theory of Latent Social Roles," *Administrative Science Quarterly,* 5 (September, 1960), pp. 305–306. See also Alvin W. Gouldner, "Cosmopolitans and Locals: Toward an Analysis of Latent Social Roles," *Administrative Science Quarterly,* 2 (1957), pp. 281–306 and 2 (1958), pp. 444–480.

nation with a good deal of consistency.[19] To avoid possible confusion arising from the fact that not all criminals share these values, we have arbitrarily named the system a "thief" subculture. The core values of this subculture correspond closely to the values which prison observers have ascribed to the "right guy" role. These include the important notion that criminals should not betray each other to the police, should be reliable, wily but trust worthy, cool headed, etc. High status in this subculture is awarded to men who appear to follow these prescriptions without variance. In the thief subculture a man who is known as "right" or "solid" is one who can be trusted and relied upon. High status is also awarded to those who possess skill as thieves, but to be just a successful thief is not enough; there must be solidness as well. A solid guy is respected even if he is unskilled, and no matter how skilled in crime a stool pigeon may be, his status is low.

Despite the fact that adherence to the norms of the thief subculture is an ideal, and the fact that the behavior of the great majority of men arrested or convicted varies sharply from any "criminal code" which might be identified, a proportion of the persons arrested for "real crime" such as burglary, robbery, and larceny have been in close contact with the values of the subculture. Many criminals, while not following the precepts of the subculture religiously, give lip service to its values and evaluate their own behavior and the behavior of their associates in terms relating to adherence to "rightness" and being "solid." It is probable, further, that use of this kind of values is not even peculiarly "criminal," for policemen, prison guards, college professors, students, and almost any other category of persons evaluate behavior in terms of in-group loyalties. Whyte noted the mutual obligations binding corner boys together and concluded that status depends upon the extent to which a boy lives up to his obligations, a form of "solidness."[20] More recently, Miller identified "toughness," "smartness," and "autonomy" among the "focal concerns" of lower class adolescent delinquent boys; these also characterize prisoners who are oriented to the thief subculture.[21] Wheeler found that half of the custody staff and sixty percent of the treatment staff in one prison approved the conduct of a hypothetical inmate who refused to name an inmate with whom he had been engaged in a knife fight.[22] A recent book has given the name "moral courage" to the behavior of persons who, like thieves, have shown extreme loyalty to their in-groups in the face of real or threatened adversity, including imprisonment.[23]

Imprisonment is one of the recurring problems with which thieves must cope. It is almost certain that a thief will be arrested from time to time, and the subculture provides members with patterns to be used in order to help solve this problem. Norms which apply to the prison situation, and information on how to undergo the prison experience—how to do time "standing on your

[19]Walter C. Reckless, *The Crime Problem,* Second Edition, New York: Appleton-Century-Crofts, 1945, pp. 144–145; 148–150; Edwin H. Sutherland, *The Profesisonal Thief,* Chicago: University of Chicago Press, 1937.

[20]William Foote Whyte, "Corner Boys: A Study of Clique Behavior," *American Journal of Sociology,* 46 (March, 1941), pp. 647–663.

[21]Walter B. Miller, "Lower Class Culture as a Generating Milieu of Gang Delinquency," *Journal of Social Issues,* 14 (1958), pp. 5–19.

[22]Stanton Wheeler, "Role Conflict in Correctional Communities," Chapter 6 in Cressey, *op. cit.,* p. 235.

[23]Compton Mackenzie, *Moral Courage,* London: Collins, 1962.

head"—with the least suffering and in a minimum amount of time are provided. Of course, the subculture itself is both nurtured and diffused in the different jails and prisons of the country.

There also exists in prisons a subculture which is by definition a set of patterns that flourishes in the environment of incarceration. It can be found wherever men are confined, whether it be in city jails, state and federal prisons, army stockades, prisoner of war camps, concentration camps, or even mental hospitals. Such organizations are characterized by deprivations and limitations on freedom, and in them available wealth must be competed for by men supposedly on an equal footing. It is in connection with the *maintenance* (but not necessarily with the *origin*) of this subculture that it is appropriate to stress the notion that a minimum of outside status criteria are carried into the situation. Ideally, all status is to be achieved by the means made available in the prison, through the displayed ability to manipulate the environment, win special privileges in a certain manner, and assert influence over others. To avoid confusion with writings on "prison culture" and "inmate culture," we have arbitrarily named this system of values and behavior patterns a "convict subculture." The central value of the subculture is utilitarianism, and the most manipulative and most utilitarian individuals win the available wealth and such positions of influence as might exist.

It is not correct to conclude, however, that even these behavior patterns are a consequence of the environment of any particular prison. In the first place, such utilitarian and manipulative behavior probably is characteristic of the "hard core" lower class in the United States, and most prisoners come from this class. After discussing the importance of toughness, smartness, excitement and fate in this group, Miller makes the following significant observation:

> In lower class culture a close conceptual connection is made between "authority" and "nurturance." To be restrictively or firmly controlled is to be cared for. Thus the overtly negative evaluation of superordinate authority frequently extends as well to nurturance, care, or protection. The desire for personal independence is often expressed in terms such as "I don't need *nobody* to take care of me. I can take care of myself!" Actual patterns of behavior, however, reveal a marked discrepancy between expressed sentiments and what is covertly valued. Many lower class people appear to seek out highly restrictive social environments wherein stringent external controls are maintained over their behavior. Such institutions as the armed forces, the mental hospital, the disciplinary school, the prison or correctional institution, provide environments which incorporate a strict and detailed set of rules defining and limiting behavior, and enforced by an authority system which controls and applies coercive sanctions for deviance from these rules. While under the jurisdiction of such systems, the lower class person generally expresses to his peers continual resentment of the coercive, unjust, and arbitrary exercise of authority. Having been released, or having escaped from these milieux, however, he will often act in such a way as to insure recommitment, or choose recommitment voluntarily after a temporary period of "freedom."[24]

In the second place, the "hard core" members of this subculture as it exists in American prisons for adults are likely to be inmates who have a long record of confinement in institutions for juveniles. McCleery observed that, in a period

---

[24]*Op. cit.,* pp. 12–13.

of transition, reform-school graduates all but took over inmate society in one prison. These boys called themselves a "syndicate" and engaged in a concentrated campaign of argument and intimidation directed toward capturing the inmate council and the inmate craft shop which had been placed under council management. "The move of the syndicate to take over the craft shop involved elements of simple exploitation, the grasp for a status symbol, and an aspect of economic reform."[25] Persons with long histories of institutionalization, it is important to note, might have had little contact with the thief subculture. The thief subculture does not flourish in institutions for juveniles, and graduates of such institutions have not necessarily had extensive criminal experience on the outside. However, some form of the convict subculture *does* exist in institutions for juveniles, though not to the extent characterizing prisons for felons. Some of the newcomers to a prison for adults are, in short, persons who have been oriented to the convict subculture, who have found the utilitarian nature of this subculture acceptable, and who have had little contact with the thief subculture. This makes a difference in their behavior.

The category of inmates we have characterized as oriented to "legitimate" subcultures includes men who are not members of the thief subculture upon entering prison and who reject both the thief subculture and the convict subculture while in prison. These men present few problems to prison administrators. They make up a large percentage of the population of any prison, but they isolate themselves—or are isolated—from the thief and convict subcultures. Clemmer found that forty percent of a sample of the men in his prison did not consider themselves a part of any group, and another forty percent could be considered a member of a "semi-primary group" only.[26] He referred to these men as "ungrouped," and his statistics have often been interpreted as meaning that the prison contains many men not oriented to "inmate culture" or "prison culture"—in our terms, not oriented to either the thief subculture or the convict subculture. This is not necessarily the case. There may be sociometric isolates among the thief-oriented prisoners, the convict-oriented prisoners, and the legitimately oriented prisoners. Consequently, we have used the "legitimate subcultures" terminology rather than Clemmer's term "ungrouped." Whether or not men in this category participate in cliques, athletic teams, or religious study and hobby groups, they are oriented to the problem of achieving goals through means which are legitimate outside prisons.

BEHAVIOR PATTERNS IN PRISON

On an ideal-type level, there are great differences in the prison behavior of men oriented to one or the other of the three types of subculture. The hard core member of the convict subculture finds his reference groups inside the institutions and, as indicated, he seeks status through means available in the prison environment. But it is important for the understanding of inmate conduct to note that the hard core member of the thief subculture seeks status in the broader criminal world of which prison is only a part. His reference groups include people both inside and outside prison, but he is committed to criminal life, not

---

[25]Richard H. McCleery, "The Governmental Process and Informal Social Control," Chapter 4 in Cressey, *op. cit.,* p. 179.
[26]*Op. cit.,* pp. 116–133.

prison life. From his point of view, it is adherence to a widespread criminal code that wins him high status, not adherence to a narrower convict code. Convicts might assign him high status because they admire him as a thief, or because a good thief makes a good convict, but the thief does not play the convicts' game. Similarly, a man oriented to a legitimate subculture is by definition committed to the values of neither thieves nor convicts.

On the other hand, within any given prison, the men oriented to the convict subculture are the inmates that seek positions of power, influence, and sources of information, whether these men are called "shots," "politicians," "merchants," "hoods," "toughs," "gorillas," or something else. A job as secretary to the Captain or Warden, for example, gives an aspiring prisoner information and consequent power, and enables him to influence the assignment or regulation of other inmates. In the same way, a job which allows the incumbent to participate in a racket, such as clerk in the kitchen storeroom where he can steal and sell food, is highly desirable to a man oriented to the convict subculture. With a steady income of cigarettes, ordinarily the prisoners' medium of exchange, he may assert a great deal of influence and purchase those things which are symbols of status among persons oriented to the convict subculture. Even if there is no well-developed medium of exchange, he can barter goods acquired in his position for equally-desirable goods possessed by other convicts. These include information and such things as specially-starched, pressed, and tailored prison clothing, fancy belts, belt buckles or billfolds, special shoes, or any other type of dress which will set him apart and will indicate that he has both the influence to get the goods and the influence necessary to keeping and displaying them despite prison rules which outlaw doing so. In California, special items of clothing, and clothing that is neatly laundered, are called "bonaroos" (a corruption of *bonnet rouge,* by means of which French prison trusties were once distinguished from the common run of prisoners), and to a lesser degree even the persons who wear such clothing are called "bonaroos."

Two inmates we observed in one prison are somewhat representative of high status members of the convict subculture. One was the prison's top gambler, who bet the fights, baseball games, football games, ran pools, etc. His cell was always full of cigarettes, although he did not smoke. He had a job in the cell block taking care of the laundry room, and this job gave him time to conduct his gambling activities. It also allowed him to get commissions for handling the clothing of inmates who paid to have them "bonarooed," or who had friends in the laundry who did this for them free of charge, in return for some service. The "commissions" the inmate received for doing this service were not always direct; the "favors" he did gave him influence with many of the inmates in key jobs, and he reputedly could easily arrange cell changes and job changes. Shortly after he was paroled he was arrested and returned to prison for robbing a liquor store. The other inmate was the prison's most notorious "fag" or "queen." He was feminine in appearance and gestures, and wax had been injected under the skin on his chest to give the appearance of breasts. At first he was kept in a cell block isolated from the rest of the prisoners, but later he was released out into the main population. He soon went to work in a captain's office, and became a key figure in the convict subculture. He was considered a stool pigeon by the thieves, but he held high status among participants in the convict subculture. In the first place, he was the most desired fag in the prison. In the second place, he was presumed to have considerable influence with the officers who frequented the captain's office. He "married" another prisoner, who also was oriented to the convict subculture.

Since prisoners oriented either to a legitimate subculture or to a thief sub-culture are not seeking high status within any given prison, they do not look for the kinds of positions considered so desirable by the members of the convict subculture. Those oriented to legitimate subcultures take prison as it comes and seek status through channels provided for that purpose by prison administrators—running for election to the inmate council, to the editorship of the institutional newspaper, etc.—and by, generally, conforming to what they think administrators expect of "good prisoners." Long before the thief has come to prison, his subculture has defined proper prison conduct as behavior rationally calculated to "do time" in the easiest possible way. This means that he wants a prison life containing the best possible combination of a maximum amount of leisure time and a maximum number of privileges. Accordingly, the privileges sought by the thief are different from the privileges sought by the man oriented to prison itself. The thief wants things that will make prison life a little easier—extra food, a maximum amount of recreation time, a good radio, a little peace. One thief serving his third sentence for armed robbery was a dish washer in the officers' dining room. He liked the eating privileges, but he never sold food. Despite his "low status" job, he was highly respected by other thieves, who described him as "right," and "solid." Members of the convict subculture, like the thieves, seek privileges. There is a difference, however, for the convict seeks privileges which he believes will enhance his position in the inmate hierarchy. He also wants to do easy time but, as compared with the thief, desirable privileges are more likely to involve freedom to amplify one's store, such as stealing rights in the kitchen, and freedom of movement around the prison. Obtaining an easy job is managed because it is easy and therefore desirable, but it also is managed for the purpose of displaying the fact that it can be obtained.

In one prison, a man serving his second sentence for selling narcotics (he was not an addict) worked in the bakery during the entire term of his sentence. To him, a thief, this was a "good job," for the hours were short and the bakers ate very well. There were some rackets conducted from the bakery, such as selling cocoa, but the man never participated in these activities. He was concerned a little with learning a trade, but not very seriously. Most of all, he wanted the eating privileges which the bakery offered. A great deal of his time was spent reading psychology, philosophy, and mysticism. Before his arrest he had been a reader of tea leaves and he now was working up some plans for an illegal business involving mysticism. Other than this, his main activity was sitting with other inmates and debating.

Just as both thieves and convicts seek privileges, both seek the many kinds of contraband in a prison. But again the things the thief seeks are those that contribute to an easier life, such as mechanical gadgets for heating water for coffee and cocoa, phonographs and radios if they are contraband or not, contraband books, food, writing materials, socks, etc. He may "score" for food occasionally (unplanned theft in which advantage is taken of a momentary opportunity), but he does not have a "route" (highly organized theft of food). One who "scores" for food eats it, shares it with his friends, sometimes in return for a past or expected favors, but he does not sell it. One who has a "route" is in the illicit food selling business.[27] The inmate oriented to the convict subculture, with its emphasis on displaying ability to manipulate the environment, rather than on

---

[27]See Schrag, "Some Foundations for a Theory of Correction," *op. cit.,* p. 343.

pleasure, is the inmate with the "route." The difference is observable in the case of an inmate assigned to the job of clerk in the dental office of one prison. This man was known to both inmates and staff long before he arrived at the institution, for his crime and arrest were highly publicized in the newspapers. It also became known that he had done time in another penitentiary for "real crime," and that his criminal exploits had frequently taken him from one side of the United States to the other. His assignment to the dental office occurred soon after he entered the prison, and some of the inmates believed that such a highly-desirable job could not be achieved without "influence" and "rep." It was an ideal spot for conducting a profitable business, and a profitable business was in fact being conducted there. In order to get on the list to see the dentist, an inmate had to pay a price in cigarettes to two members of the convict subculture who were running the dental office. This practice soon changed, at least in reference to inmates who could show some contact with our man's criminal friends, in or out of prison. If a friend vouched for a man by saying he was "right" or "solid" the man would be sitting in the dental chair the next day, free of charge.

Generally speaking, an inmate oriented to the thief subculture simply is not interested in gaining high status in the prison. He wants to get out. Moreover, he is likely to be quietly amused by the concern some prisoners have for symbols of status, but he publicly exhibits neither disdain nor enthusiasm for this concern. One exception to this occurred in an institution where a thief had become a fairly close friend of an inmate oriented to the prison. One day the latter showed up in a fresh set of bonaroos, and he made some remark that called attention to them. The thief looked at him, laughed, and said, "For Christ's sake, Bill, they're *Levi's* (standard prison blue denims) and they are always going to be Levi's." The thief may be accorded high status in the prison, because "rightness" is revered there as well as on the outside, but to him this is incidental to his being a "man," not to his being a prisoner.

Members of both subcultures are conservative—they want to maintain the status quo. Motivation is quite different, however. The man oriented to the convict subculture is conservative because he has great stock in the existing order of things, while the man who is thief oriented leans toward conservatism because he knows how to do time and likes things to run along smoothly with a minimum of friction. It is because of this conservatism that so many inmates are directly or indirectly in accommodation with prison officials who, generally speaking, also wish to maintain the status quo. A half dozen prison observers have recently pointed out that some prison leaders—those oriented to what we call the convict subculture—assist the officials by applying pressures that keep other inmates from causing trouble, while other prison leaders—those oriented to what we call the thief subculture—indirectly keep order by propagating the *criminal* code, including admonitions to "do your own time," "don't interfere with others' activities," "don't 'rank' another criminal." The issue is not whether the thief subculture and convict subculture are useful to, and used by, administrators; it is whether the observed behavior patterns originate in prison as a response to official administrative practices.

There are other similarities, noted by many observers of "prison culture" or "inmate culture." In the appropriate circumstances, members of both subcultures will participate in fomenting and carrying out riots. The man oriented to the convict subculture does this when a change has closed some of the paths for achieving positions of influence, but the thief does it when privileges of the kind that make life easier are taken away from him. Thus, when a "prison reform" group takes over an institution, it may inadvertently make changes which lead to alliances between the members of two subcultures who ordinarily are quite indifferent to each other. In more routine circumstances, the thief adheres to a tight system of mutual aid for other thieves—persons who are "right" and "solid"—a direct application in prison of the norms which ask that a thief prove himself reliable and trustworthy to other thieves. If a man is "right," then even if he is a stranger one must help him if there is no risk to himself. If he is a friend, then one must, in addition, be willing to take *some* risk in order to help him. But in the convict subculture, "help" has a price; one helps in order to gain, whether the gain be "pay" in the form of cigarettes, or a guarantee of a return favor which will enlarge one's area of power.

RELATIONSHIPS BETWEEN THE TWO SUBCULTURES

In the routine prison setting, the two deviant subcultures exist in a balanced relationship. It is this total setting which has been observed as "inmate culture." There is some conflict because of the great disparity in some of the values of thieves and convicts, but the two subcultures share other values. The thief is committed to keeping his hands off other people's activities, and the convict, being utilitarian, is likely to know that it is better in the long run to avoid conflict with thieves and confine one's exploitations to the "do rights" and to the members of his own subculture. Of course, the thief must deal with the convict from time to time, and when he does so he adjusts to the reality of the fact that he is imprisoned. Choosing to follow prison definitions usually means paying for some service in cigarettes or in a returned service; this is the cost of doing easy time. Some thieves adapt in a more general way to the ways of convicts and assimilate the prisonized person's concern for making out in the institution. On an ideal-type level, however, thieves do not sanction exploitation of other inmates, and they simply ignore the "do rights," who are oriented to legitimate subcultures. Nevertheless, their subculture as it operates in prison has exploitative effects.[28]

Numerous persons have documented the fact that "right guys," many of whom can be identified as leaders of the thieves, not of the convicts, exercise the greatest influence over the total prison population. The influence is the long run kind stemming from the ability to influence notions of what is right and proper, what McCleery calls the formulation and communication of definitions.[29] The thief, after all, has the respect of many inmates who are not themselves thieves. The right guy carries a set of attitudes, values and norms that have a great deal of consistency and clarity. He acts, forms opinions, and evaluates events in the prison according to them, and over a long period of time he in this way determines basic behavior patterns in the institution. In what the thief thinks of as "small matters," however—getting job transfers, enforcing payment of gambling debts, making cell assignments—members of the convict subculture run things.

---

[28]See Donald R. Cressey, "Foreword," to Clemmer, *op. cit.,* pp. vii–x.
[29]"The Governmental Process and Informal Social Control," *op. cit.,* p. 154.

It is difficult to assess the direct lines of influence the two deviant subcultures have over those inmates who are not members of either subculture when they enter a prison. It is true that if a new inmate does not have definitions to apply to the new prison situation, one or the other of the deviant subcultures is likely to supply them. On the one hand, the convict subculture is much more apparent than the thief subculture; its roles are readily visible to any new arrival, and its definitions are readily available to one who wants to "get along" and "make it" in a prison. Moreover, the inmate leaders oriented to the convict subculture are anxious to get new followers who will recognize the existing status hierarchy in the prison. Thieves, on the other hand, tend to be snobs. Their status in prison is determined in part by outside criteria, as well as by prison conduct, and it is therefore difficult for a prisoner, acting as a prisoner, to achieve these criteria. At a minimum, the newcomer can fall under the influence of the thief subculture only if he has intimate association over a period of time with some of its members who are able and willing to impart some of its subtle behavior patterns to him.

Our classification of some inmates as oriented to legitimate subcultures implies that many inmates entering a prison do not find either set of definitions acceptable to them. Like thieves, these men are not necessarily "stripped" of outside statuses, and they do not play the prison game. They bring a set of values with them when they come to prison, and they do not leave these values at the gate. They are people such as a man who, on a drunken Saturday night, ran over a pedestrian and was sent to the prison for manslaughter, a middle class clerk who was caught embezzling his firm's money, and a young soldier who stole a car in order to get back from a leave. Unlike thieves, these inmates bring to the prison both anti-criminal and anti-prisoner attitudes. Although it is known that most of them participate at a minimum in primary group relations with either thieves or convicts, their relationships with each other have not been studied. Further, criminologists have ignored the possible effects the "do rights" have on the total system of "inmate culture." It seems a worthy hypothesis that thieves, convicts and do rights all bring certain values and behavior patterns to prison with them, and that total "inmate culture" represents an adjustment or accommodation of these three systems within the official administrative system of deprivation and control.[30] It is significant in this connection that Wheeler has not found in Norwegian prisons the normative order and cohesive bonds among inmates that characterize many American prisons. He observes that his data suggest "that the current functional interpretations of the inmate system in American institutions are not adequate," and that "general features of Norwegian society are imported into the prison and operate largely to offset any tendencies toward the formation of a solidary inmate group. . . ."[31]

---

[30]"But if latent culture can restrict the possibilities for the proliferation of the manifest culture, the opposite is also true. Manifest culture can restrict the operation of latent culture. The problems facing group members may be so pressing that, given the social context in which the group operates, the range of solutions that will be effective may be so limited as not to allow for influence of variations resulting from cultures associated with other identities." Becker and Geer, *op. cit.*, pp. 308–309.

[31]Stanton Wheeler, "Inmate Culture in Prisons," Mimeographed report of the Laboratory of Social Relations, Harvard University, 1962, pp. 18, 20, 21.

BEHAVIOR AFTER RELEASE

If our crude typology is valid, it should be of some use for predicting the behavior of prisoners when they are released. However, it is important to note that in any given prison the two deviant subcultures are not necessarily as sharply separated as our previous discussion has implied. Most inmates are under the influence of *both* subcultures. Without realizing it, inmates who have served long prison terms are likely to move toward the middle, toward a compromise or balance between the directives coming from the two sources. A member of the convict subculture may come to see that thieves are the real men with the prestige; a member of the thief subculture or even a do right may lose his ability to sustain his status needs by outside criteria. Criminologists seem to have had difficulty in keeping the two kinds of influence separate, and we cannot expect all inmates to be more astute than the criminologists. The fact that time has a blending effect on the participants in the two deviant subcultures suggests that the subcultures themselves tend to blend together in some prisons. We have already noted that the thief subculture scarcely exists in some institutions for juveniles. It is probable also that in army stockades and in concentration camps this subculture is almost nonexistent. In places of short-term confinement, such as city and county jails, the convict subculture is dominant, for the thief subculture involves status distinctions that are not readily observable in a short period of confinement. At the other extreme, in prisons where only prisoners with long sentences are confined, the distinctions between the two subcultures are likely to be blurred. Probably the two subcultures exist in their purest forms in institutions holding inmates in their twenties, with varying sentences for a variety of criminal offenses. Such institutions, of course, are the "typical" prisons of the United States.

Despite these differences, in any prison the men oriented to legitimate subcultures should have a low recidivism rate, while the highest recidivism rate should be found among participants in the convict subculture. The hard core members of this subculture are being trained in manipulation, duplicity and exploitation, they are not sure they can make it on the outside, and even when they are on the outside they continue to use convicts as a reference group. This sometimes means that there will be a wild spree of crime and dissipation which takes the members of the convict subculture directly back to the prison. Members of the thief subculture, to whom prison life represented a pitfall in outside life, also should have a high recidivism rate. However, the thief sometimes "reforms" and tries to succeed in some life within the law. Such behavior, contrary to popular notions, is quite acceptable to other members of the thief subculture, so long as the new job and position are not "anti-criminal" and do not involve regular, routine, "slave labor." Suckers work, but a man who, like a thief, "skims it off the top" is not a sucker. At any rate, the fact that convicts, to a greater extent than thieves, tend to evaluate things from the perspective of the prison and to look upon discharge as a short vacation from prison life suggests that their recidivism rate should be higher than that of thieves.

Although the data collected by Garrity provide only a crude test of these predictions, they do support them. Garrity determined the recidivism rates and the tendencies for these rates to increase or decrease with increasing length of prison terms, for each of Schrag's inmate types. Unfortunately, this typology does not clearly make the distinction between the two subcultures, probably because of the blending process noted above. Schrag's "right guys" or "antisocial offenders," thus, might include both men who perceive role requirements in terms of the norms of the convict subculture, and men who perceive those requirements in terms of the norms of the thief subculture. Similarly, neither his "con politician" ("pseudosocial offender") nor his "outlaw" ("asocial offender") seem to be what we would characterize as the ideal-type member of the convict subculture. For example, it is said that relatively few of the former have juvenile records, that onset of criminality often occurs after a position of respectability has already been attained in the civilian community, and that educational and occupational records are far superior to those of "right guys." Further, outlaws are characterized as men who have been frequently reared in institutions or shifted around in foster homes; but they also are characterized as "undisciplined trouble-makers," and this does not seem to characterize the men who seek high status in prisons by rather peaceful means of manipulation and exploitation. In short, our ideal-type "thief" appears to include only some of Schrag's "right guys"; the ideal-type "convict" seems to include some of his "right guys," some of his "con politicians," and all of his "outlaws." Schrag's "square Johns" correspond to our "legitimate subcultures" category.

Garrity found that a group of "square Johns" had a low parole violation rate and that this rate remained low no matter how much time was served. The "right guys" had a high violation rate that decreased markedly as time in prison increased. In Garrity's words, this was because "continued incarceration [served] to sever his connections with the criminal subculture and thus to increase the probability of successful parole."[32] The rates for the "outlaw" were very high and remained high as time in prison increased. Only the rates of the "con politician" did not meet our expectations—the rates were low if the sentences were rather short but increased systematically with time served.

Noting that the origins of the thief subculture and the convict subculture are both external to a prison should change our expectations regarding the possible reformative effect of that prison. The recidivism rates of neither thieves, convicts, nor do rights are likely to be significantly affected by incarceration in any traditional prison. This is not to say that the program of a prison with a "therapeutic milieu" like the one the Wisconsin State Reformatory is seeking, or of a prison like some of those in California, in which group counseling is being used in an attempt to change organizational structure, will not eventually affect the recidivism rates of the members of one or another, or all three, of the categories. However, in reference to the ordinary custodially-oriented prison the thief says he can do his time "standing on his head," and it appears that he *is* able to do the time "standing on his head"—except for long-termers, imprisonment has little effect on the thief one way or the other. Similarly, the routine of any particular custodial prison is not likely to have significant reformative effects on members of the convict subculture—they will return to prison because, in effect, they have found a home there. And the men oriented to legitimate subcultures will maintain low recidivism rates even if they never experience imprisonment. Garrity has shown that it is not correct to conclude, as reformers have so often done, that prisons are the breeding ground of crime. It probably is not true either that any particular prison is the breeding ground of an inmate culture that significantly increases recidivism rates.

---

[32] *Op. cit.*, p. 377.

CHAPTER 2

THE MEANING OF PUNISHMENT: INMATES' ORIENTATION TO THE PRISON EXPERIENCE

Patricia Van Voorhis, Sandra Lee Browning,
Marilyn Simon and Jill Gordon

This article examines inmates' perceptions of sentencing intents (e.g., deterrence, rehabilitation, incapacitation, and retribution). Two prison populations are sampled; 114 minimum security and 111 maximum security federal prisoners. Four months following admission, subjects were surveyed about their perceptions of their prison experience. The authors examine (a) inmates' identification with sentencing intents; (b) the interrelationships among these orientations; and (c) factors associated with the orientations. Results find inmates in both samples either adhered to several orientations, accepting notions of rehabilitation while also finding prison to be a deterrent, deserved, and a reparation, or they saw no purpose to the prison sanction. Multivariate analyses, for penitentiary inmates, found that inmates most likely to focus on rehabilitation were non-White, young, unemployed at the time of their arrest, and not entrenched in crime as a lifestyle. Older, White, inmates, and those employed at arrest, were more likely to observe that no purpose was served. Models were less conclusive for minimum security inmates.

As the federal and state governments implement the latest series of crime control bills, policy makers confidently claim to have achieved punishment strategies that will capture the attention of criminals. Embedded in such legislation is new-found confidence that additional boot camps, "three-strikes-you're-out" laws, "truth in sentencing," intermediate sanctions, and the elimination of Pell Grants, good time, and weight rooms will go far toward solving the crime problem. And, for the time being, these new ideas seem to have achieved unprecedented media attention and vote-getting appeal.

Data for this project were obtained through a grant awarded to the University of Cincinnati by the National Institute of Justice (#85-IJ-CX-0063). The content of this article is attributable to the authors and does not reflect the official position or policies of the U.S. Department of Justice.

THE PRISON JOURNAL, Vol. 77 No. 2, June 1997 135–167

News accounts and political speeches underscore the reasoning behind the new laws: (a) some criminals must be put away for a long time, (b) incapacitation is the only sure way to stop a criminal, and (c) if our current sentences are not solving the crime problem, we must not be administering enough punishment. Thus tougher sentences will incapacitate and deter future criminals better than current sanctions, particularly anything supportive of offender rehabilitation. This line of reasoning seems largely speculative. In the United States Congress, for example, neither the legislation nor the rationales were presented to the scrutiny of correctional practitioners or scholars (Corrections 2000, 1994), and numerous provisions of the new bills, in fact, are not supported by correctional experts *or* extant research (American Correctional Association, 1994).

Although the assumption that the new bills will have an impact on offender perceptions is a weak one, such reasoning illustrates a long tradition of speculating about what offenders will think about their sanction, and history tells us that such assumptions carry a good deal of weight in generating crime control policies. In truth, however, we know very little about how offenders make sense of the punishment experience. We know even less about whether or not offender perceptions have any impact on prison adjustment or future crimes. Simply put, the purpose of corrections is typically the design of lawmakers and less frequently jurisprudential scholars; a current theory or philosophy is almost never supported by evidence that offenders make sense of their punishments in the same way.

This article explores the orientations of two different prison populations, a minimum security federal prison camp and a maximum security federal penitentiary. We examine the extent to which inmates experience traditional correctional purposes (e.g., deterrence, rehabilitation, incapacitation, and retribution). After serving at least 4 months of their prison terms, the subjects of this study were surveyed and asked questions pertaining to how they were making sense of their sentence. Did they see it as deserved? Was it a punishment? Was it a deterrent? Could it be rehabilitative? Was it teaching them a lesson? Alternatively, was no purpose being served? We examine (a) the extent to which inmates perceive traditional sentencing intents, (b) whether or not these perceptions differ across different correctional environments, (c) interrelationships between orientations, and (d) psychological, demographic, and criminal record correlates of correctional perceptions.[1]

REVIEW OF THE LITERATURE

An overview of the literature on the purpose of punishment shows us that inquiry is limited mostly to theoretical and philosophical analysis, public surveys, and policy analyses of the impact of sentencing changes on aggregate crime rates. Scholarly analysis and debate of the most optimal purpose of punishment dates back to the work of Classical scholars Jeremy Bentham and Cesaria Beccaria, proceeds through the time of the positivist criminologists and on to the formation of the Justice Model (American Friends Service Committee, 1971; Fogel, 1979; Morris, 1974) and its critics (Cullen & Gilbert, 1982; Currie, 1985; Palmer, 1983). More recently, the discussion focuses on a renewed interest in punishment as a deterrent (Paternoster, 1987) or as an effective means of incapacitation (Blumstein & Cohen, 1978; Newman, 1978; Sherman & Hawkins, 1982; Zimring

& Hawkins, 1995). Public surveys are numerous. But although these data appear to support the notion that prisons should be punitive (Zimring & Hawkins, 1991), they also support prison rehabilitation programming (Cullen, Skovron, Scott, & Burton, 1990; McCorkle, 1993; Public Agenda Foundation, 1987). Surprisingly, offender viewpoints are seldom sought.

In the absence of the criminals' views, the assertions of scholars, policy makers, activists, and the public are surprisingly presumptuous. Yet such assumptions are well-embedded in American correctional history. They include the Quakers' vision of the penitent inmate who would think about his transgressions while in solitary confinement. From time to time scholars have also maintained that many prisoners are not interested in rehabilitation but rather profess rehabilitative intents in order to impress parole boards (Mitford, 1973; Morris, 1974). Additional assumptions include (a) retributive sentences are overly punitive to inmates (Menninger, 1966), and (b) rehabilitative, indeterminant sentences are overly punitive (American Friends Service Committee, 1971; Fogel, 1979; von Hirsch, 1976). More recently, Hawkins and Alpert (1989) note that given the current overcrowded conditions of most prisons, most correctional goals are severely compromised, if not totally unattainable, and inmates can spot the resulting hypocrisy. Finally, some hold that we can give up on notions of rehabilitation, retribution, and deterrence; a modest level of selective incapacitation is our most realistic hope (Sherman & Hawkins, 1982; Zimring & Hawkins, 1995). In this last instance, it doesn't really matter *what* inmates think.

In sum, most discussions of the purpose of prison, or of any sanction, embody modest to strong suppositions regarding how offenders will perceive (or not perceive) the sanction and how these perceptions might then affect future criminal behavior. Ironically, most of these same discussions omit any empirical evidence of offender viewpoints.

Deterrence Research

One exception to this trend emerges from a body of research pertaining to perceptions of deterrence. Although this research offers very little (Paternoster, 1987) to equivocal (Klepper & Nagin, 1989) evidence of a sanction's severity serving as a deterrent, most studies sample the general population, focusing on the notion of general deterrence. In contrast, empirical studies of prison inmates cast serious doubt on any hopes that prison might be considered by inmates to be a deterrent (Sherman & Hawkins, 1981; Zimring & Hawkins, 1995). Furthermore, studies of the effectiveness of deterrent punishments (e.g., scared straight, shock probation) find these "get tough" strategies to be less effective than alternatives (Gendreau & Ross, 1987).

On a more complex note, the effects of specific deterrent and punitive options are highly idiosyncratic (Bonta & Gendreau, 1990; Gibbs, 1975; McClelland & Alpert, 1985). Even Wilson and Herrnstein (1985), while speaking to the importance of offenders' assessments of the costs and benefits of crime, inform that such calculations are likely to vary from individual to individual. Of course, these observations come as no surprise to the behavioral psychologists who assert that the impact of punishment on future behavior is affected by such individual perceptions as the legitimacy of the punishing agent and one's personal repertoire of instigators and inhibitors (Bandura, 1973). Others tell us that biological and cognitive factors may predispose "unconditionable" individuals to dismiss the severity of a specific sanction (Eysenck, 1977; Quay, 1965).

Rehabilitation Research

Limiting our inquiry to whether or not offenders perceive their sanctions as punitive or deterrent ignores another, albeit less popular, correctional purpose—rehabilitation. Clearly, offender orientations to rehabilitation would appear to be an extremely important notion to examine. Readers will perhaps recall claims of inmates "using" treatment participation not for the intended purposes of self-improvement, but rather to impress parole boards into granting an early release (Mitford, 1973; Morris, 1974). Although the notion of "the parole game" lent powerful support to the "Nothing Works" movement and to shifts in correctional policy that favored punishment over rehabilitation (Cullen & Gilbert, 1982), empirical support for inmates using rehabilitation to manipulate parole boards is difficult to find. Mitford (1973) cites a National Council on Crime and Delinquency (NCCD) survey of inmates conducted 40 years ago, where inmates' lack of enthusiasm was attributable to poor programming as much, if not more, than to their insincerity or lack of interest in self-improvement. Certainly, superficial attempts at programming can breed some level of cynicism among inmates (Hawkins & Alpert, 1989), and research may have difficulty separating inmates' insincerity from the quality of the programming.

In contrast, surveys that tap inmates' opinions about correctional priorities, asking what *should* happen rather than what is happening, offer rather strong support for rehabilitation (Cullen & Gilbert, 1982; Hawkins, 1976; Toch, 1977; Wright, 1989). The most convincing evidence in this regard appears in responses to Toch's Prison Preference Inventory where inmates are asked to rank their main concerns of prison life. Respondents consistently rank "support" (in the form of programming leading to self-improvement or development) as their highest priority, above even safety, privacy, and freedom (Toch, 1977; Wright, 1989).

The Importance of Inmates' Perceptions

Do offender perceptions really matter? Clearly, some would argue that they don't, maintaining that it is for society rather than criminals to determine the purpose or meaning of punishment. Certainly, recent moves to incapacitation suggest that criminals do not really have to think anything about their sanction; it is rather for society to protect itself and to impose sanctions that reflect appropriately the gravity of certain crimes (Zimring & Hawkins, 1995). Most jurisprudential scholars, however, incorporate both the concern and rights of the citizen *and* the perceptions of the criminal. In his legal definition of punishment, for example, H. L. A. Hart (1961) lists five aspects of punishment. The very first one addresses the perspective of the offender: "It (punishment) must involve pain or other consequences normally considered unpleasant." Hart's fifth proposition considers the society: "It must be imposed and administered by an authority constituted by a legal system against which the offense is committed."

But the importance of offender perceptions extends beyond the philosophical intent of a punishment to the practical realm of intended and unintended effects and consequences. The significance of offender perceptions, for example, was revealed in recent discussions of the punitiveness of prison relative to intensive probation. Joan Petersilia posed the question a few years ago, offering the rather surprising suggestion that some inmates might find Intensive Supervision Programs (ISP) *more punitive* than prison (1990). Subsequent research has found this to be the case (Crouch, 1993; Petersilia & Piper-

Deschenes, 1994), even when the respondents were currently serving prison terms. Such findings raise alarming questions about our current prison binge as well as its underlying rationale—punishment. For most of the subjects surveyed in these two studies, the punitive and deterrent potential of prison was weakened by (a) the prospect of early release in order to reduce prison overcrowding; (b) cases where incarceration is normative rather than a mark of shame;[2] (c) the economic marginality of an underclass of Americans, which in turn reduces the attractiveness of life outside of prison (Wilson, 1987); (d) the promise of seeing friends and kindred spirits with similar links to criminal lifestyles; (e) a life that is for some easier than life on the outside; and (f) the intrusiveness of intensive probation (Petersilia, 1990).

In another sense, offender perceptions may affect not only whether the sentence has its desired impact but whether it has desired consequences. With the reemergence of restitution programs in the 1970s, for example, came numerous discussions of the legal intent of restitution. Legal and correctional scholars conceptualized restitution from every possible correctional intent (see Van Voorhis, 1983). Probationers ordered to reimburse their victims, however, held divergent views of the sanction. Some viewed it as an opportunity for reparation; others saw it more instrumentally, as a way to pay one's way out of a harsher sanction. But those who were oriented to the reparative aspects of their court-ordered restitution were significantly more likely to successfully reimburse their victims (Van Voorhis, 1985). Such studies suggest that offender perceptions of a sanction may also have an impact on its effectiveness.

Individual Effects

Nevertheless, offender perceptions of a sanction are highly idiosyncratic. In the studies noted in the previous section, for example, researchers found that only certain inmates diminish the severity of prison or the moral importance of restitution. Prison experience, race, marital status, and age appear to differentiate those who would choose prison from those who would prefer probation. The prison is more likely to be viewed as less punitive than intensive probation by unmarried, African American, and older inmates, as well as those who have longer criminal and prison histories (Crouch, 1993). A similar study, employing a smaller sample, noted that married inmates tended to be more likely to view jail or prison as more severe than probation (Petersilia & Piper-Deschenes, 1994). In another example, probationers classified at higher stages of moral development were more likely to identify the reparative aspects of restitution. Perceiving restitution as a means for buying one's way out of trouble was significantly more likely to characterize probationers classified at lower stages of moral development (Van Voorhis, 1985).

And from the findings that prison experience diminishes one's perceptions of the severity of prison (e.g., McClelland & Alpert, 1985), we could hypothesize that criminal personalities, as defined in a number of offender-based personality typologies and studies of the impact of personality on crime (see Andrews & Bonta, 1994; Caspi et al., 1994; Jesness & Wedge, 1983; Megargee & Bohn, 1979; Quay, 1983; Warren, 1983), might be less likely to perceive their sanction as a deterrent. This is because offenders assessed as asocial aggressive, criminal personality, or as having internalized antisocial values are more likely to have extensive criminal records than those classified into other types on these offender typologies or assessment systems. Because we find them to be comfortable with the criminal label (Van Voorhis, 1994), we may also find them to be more comfortable with the criminal sanction, relative to their peers.

In sum, although prison inmates are a much studied group, few studies have directly asked them about the manner in which they make sense of a sanction relative to the broader array of traditional correctional intents. We have learned a good deal about their adjustment patterns, attitudes toward prisons, behavior while in prisons, and physical and psychological reactions to prison life, but we have not asked them to help us sort out the meaning of punishment. Yet the few exceptions seem extremely relevant to correctional policy. In addition to contributing to how scholars and policy makers might define a sanction, such research may even question the very foundation of some correctional options.

This article will address most of the issues raised in the preceding discussion: (a) Do inmates consider their immediate prison term to be a deterrent? (b) Do they see it as punitive? (c) Is the sentence teaching them a lesson? (d) Do inmates take rehabilitation seriously? (e) Are they conning the parole board? (f) How do the orientations of a maximum security population differ from those among minimum security inmates? (g) What is the relationship among orientations? (h) What are the demographic, psychological, and criminal record correlates of traditional correctional orientations? In contrast to other studies (e.g., Crouch, 1993; Petersilia & Piper-Deschenes, 1994), however, we are not asking inmates to compare their sanction to an alternative option. Neither do we examine the effects of the inmates' orientations on future behaviors.

METHODOLOGY

Data for this study were part of a larger classification study conducted at the United States Federal Penitentiary and the Federal Prison Camp at Terre Haute, Indiana, between 1986 and 1988. On the Federal Bureau of Prison's security system, the penitentiary is considered low maximum security and the prison camp is designated minimum security. We use data collected in a follow-up survey of the prison inmates administered at a minimum of 4 months following their admission to prison.

Sample Characteristics

A total of 179 penitentiary and 190 prison camp inmates participated in the larger classification study. Study participants were selected at prison intake immediately following their sentencing or probation revocation. Data for all participants were collected at similar points during their prison term—at intake and during a 4- to 6-month follow-up period. Criteria for selecting the study participants excluded transferring inmates (or inmates who had already served a portion of their sentence), non-English-speaking inmates, and inmates who were expecting release or transfer within 4 months of intake. Participation was voluntary; response rates were 76% for the penitentiary and 83% for the prison camp.

This article does not focus on the entire sample, but rather 111 (64%) penitentiary inmates and 114 (69%) prison camp inmates who completed a follow-up survey.[3] As might be expected, the penitentiary inmates differed from the prison camp inmates in substantial ways. The prison camp inmates can be portrayed as slightly older than the penitentiary inmates. Their median age was 37 years (mean = 32), whereas the median age for the penitentiary inmates was 33 years (mean = 28). The prison camp inmates were more likely to be married (47%) than were the penitentiary inmates (40%). The prison camp sample was 80% White, and the penitentiary sample was 52% White. Fifty-six percent of the prison camp inmates were employed full time at the time of their arrest, whereas full-time employment characterized only 18% of the penitentiary inmates. Most of the prison camp inmates had at least a high school education or a GED (79%), whereas only 57% of the penitentiary inmates had similar educations.

Prior record and current offense factors differed dramatically between the two samples. Although the majority of inmates in both the prison camp (76%) and the penitentiary (96%) had prior records, inmates serving prior prison terms composed only 14% of the prison camp inmates and a much larger proportion of the penitentiary inmates (67%). In addition, 62% of the penitentiary inmates evidenced prior violent offenses, whereas only 10% of the camp inmates had a violent offense on record. Conviction offenses leading to the current sentence were also different between the two samples. Drug offenses composed the modal category for the prison camp inmates (53%); 26% of the penitentiary inmates were convicted of drug offenses. Bank robberies represented the modal crime conviction category for the penitentiary inmates (31%), whereas only 3% of the camp inmates were convicted of bank robberies. Sixteen percent of the penitentiary and none of the prison camp inmates were convicted of a violent offense. Weapons possession during the conviction offense characterized 8% and 48%, respectively, of the camp and the penitentiary samples.

This section has detailed a number of differences that might be expected to have an impact on inmates' perceptions of the purpose of their prison sentence. In addition to differences in demographic factors noted to affect findings in similar studies (e.g. Crouch, 1993; Petersilia & Piper-Deschenes, 1994), the penitentiary sample is represented by inmates who have far more prison experience, longer criminal careers, and more criminal associates.

Data Collection and Measures

Data pertaining to inmates' orientation to the purpose of their sentence (or dependent variables) were collected in a follow-up survey of the inmates that was administered at a minimum of 4 months into their sentence. We were not able to obtain survey data for all members of the samples because the survey was put into place 9 months into the study when the research staff realized that variability on official disciplinary measures was limited. Implementing the survey late resulted in losing those cases that had been transferred, released, or had been given paid work assignments. Thus data attrition occurred with the earliest participants rather than with a specific type of participant. As a result, it is unlikely that the survey results are biased by sample attrition. In fact, difference of proportions tests between the surveyed inmates and the unsurveyed inmates revealed that the groups were not significantly different on background factors such as age, race, education, urban environment, employment status at arrest, prior record, and psychological classifications.

Another potential problem concerned the amount of time intervening between prison intake and the administration of the survey. Ideally, we wanted all inmates to complete the survey during the fourth to sixth month following intake. We placed a priority, however, on obtaining as many surveys as possible, and this meant that the follow-up time periods were sometimes less than 4 months (especially if the inmate served less than 4 months) or more than 6 months for those early intakes who agreed to complete the survey. Thus the time intervening between intake and administration of the survey ranged from 3 to 36 months for the penitentiary inmates (mean = 7.2 months; median = 6.0 months) and from 2 to 12 months for the prison camp inmates (mean = 5.5 months).[4] To test for any potential biases, we correlated these times with survey measures constructed for use in this study and found no relationships.

Measurement of correctional orientations. The survey measures that represent the focus of this study tap inmates' attitudes on Likert-type scale items ranging from 5 = *strongly agree* to 3 = *neutral* to 1 = *strongly disagree*. Items that were relevant to traditional correctional orientations, and used in the present study, are shown in Table 2.1. Two of the measures, *rehabilitation* and *deserves punishment* are composite indexes. As can be seen in Table 2.1, rehabilitation consists of two items and deserves punishment consists of 3 items. Measures of internal consistency (Cronbach's alpha) for the rehabilitation scale were .72 for the penitentiary sample and .55 for the camp sample. Alpha for the deserves punishment scale was .78 and .86 for the penitentiary and the prison camp, respectively.

It is important to understand the nature of the constructs being measured. We asked inmates for their perceptions of what the prison experience meant to them. We might have asked them to be prescriptive, indicating what prison should be, but we did not.

Measurement of independent variables. A portion of our analyses seeks to identify correlates of correctional orientation—to identify the types of inmates most

Table 2.1
Measures of Correctional Orientation

Name	Corresponding Survey Questions	Type of Measure
Rehabilitation	This experience is helping me to grow.	Index
	I can accomplish something here.	Alpha = .72 (Pen)
		Alpha = .55 (Camp)
Deterrence	This experience has taught me a lesson.	Single item
	I have given up criminal activity forever.	
Retribution	Doing this time makes me feel like I'm paying back society for my offense.	Single item
Deserts	I deserve to do some time.	Index
	I deserve to be in this institution.	Alpha = .78 (Pen)
	I deserve to be punished.	Alpha = .86 (Camp)
Incapacitation	Society is safer with me in here.	Single item
No purpose	No purpose can be served by my doing prison time.	Single item
Impress parole board	Inmates should look for activities that will show the parole board that they have used their time constructively.	Single item
Scam	It is possible to psych the staff out.	Single item

likely to adhere to a given correctional orientation. Our selection of independent variables is guided by both previous research and by a desire to explore psychological precursors of punishment orientations. From the work cited above (e.g., Crouch, 1993; Petersilia & Piper-Deschenes, 1994), we are directed to consider the importance of age, race, marital status, and employment status. In particular, we are reminded that prison is preferred over intensive probation by older, unmarried, non-White inmates, who evidence entrenched criminal histories and experience with incarceration (Crouch, 1993; McClelland & Alpert, 1985). We are also encouraged to test for a possible class or employment effect—that the disadvantaged may see some purpose in prison (see also Wilson, 1987). Finally, examination of these variables is also supported by the more general prison adjustment literature, where age, unemployment prior to arrest, and marital status are frequently cited correlates of prison adjustment (e.g., see Flanagan, 1983; Myers & Levy, 1978; Toch & Adams, 1989).

Demographic and criminal record variables were extracted from presentence reports. Except for the age variable, all demographic and prior record variables are bivariate.

Our literature review also briefly discussed the relevance of personality and psychological factors that may have an impact on inmates' understanding of correctional purpose, such as moral (or conceptual) development (Van Voorhis, 1985), impulsivity (Bandura, 1973; Eysenck, 1977; Quay, 1965), and commitment to a criminal lifestyle (McClelland & Alpert, 1985; Van Voorhis, 1995). Given the impact of personality and other psychological constructs on more general forms of prison adjustment (Van Voorhis, 1994, 1995), we also explore the effects of IQ and neurotic personality styles.

Personality and cognitive development measures were obtained by the Jesness Inventory Classification System (Jesness & Wedge, 1983). This system is an actuarial measure of Interpersonal Maturity Level (I-Level) (Warren, 1983). The I-Level classifications are obtained through a paper and pencil test, the Jesness Inventory (Jesness & Wedge, 1983), which contains 155 items that yield scores on 9 I-level subtype (personality) scales. Construct validity tests of the types revealed that they could be collapsed into four personality types: (a) aggressive (also with criminal values), (b) neurotic, (c) situational, and (d) immature. The I-level types were collapsed in another way to form a cognitive developmental continuum from low to high maturity. The reader is referred to the larger classification study for further details on construct and predictive validity of these measures (Van Voorhis, 1994). Tests were scored by Consulting Psychologists Press in Palo Alto, California.

Measures of IQ were obtained from the Shipley Institute of Living Scale (Shipley, 1940), which is used in many settings to obtain an efficient (60-item) estimate of WAIS-R scores through conversion tables developed by Zachary, Crumpton, and Spiegel (1985).

RESULTS

Table 2.2 shows the frequency and percentage distribution of inmates across the correctional orientation items. Perhaps one of the most surprising findings from this portion of the analysis concerns the similarity of responses between the two groups. Notwithstanding substantial differences in criminal histories, prison experience, and current offenses, difference of proportion tests revealed

Table 2.2
Frequency and Percentage Distribution of Inmates across Correctional Orientations

Orientation	Penitentiary		Prison Camp	
	N	Percentage	N	Percentage
Rehabilitation: This experience is helping me to grow, and I can accomplish something here.				
Strongly disagree	10	9	11	10
Disagree	18	17	15	13
Neutral	27	26	31	28
Agree	34	32	43	38
Strongly agree	17	16	12	11
Total	106	100	112	100
Deterrence: This experience taught me a lesson. I have given up criminal activity forever.				
Strongly disagree	4	4	6	6
Disagree	7	7	5	5
Neutral	23	22	14	13
Agree	28	27	36	34
Strongly agree	41	40	45	43
Total	103	100	106	100
Retribution: Doing this time makes me feel like I'm paying back society for my offense.				
Strongly disagree	25	23	37	33
Disagree	34	31	30	26
Neutral	23	21	15	13
Agree	20	18	24	21
Strongly agree	8	7	8	7
Total	110	100	114	100
Deserts: I deserve to do some time; I deserve to be in this institution; I deserve to be punished.				
Strongly disagree	24	22	33	30
Disagree	32	29	35	32
Neutral	36	33	26	24
Agree	16	15	14	13
Strongly agree	1	1	1	1
Total	109	100	109	100

Table 2.2
Continued

Orientation	Penitentiary		Prison Camp	
	N	*Percentage*	*N*	*Percentage*
Incapacitation: Society is safer with me in here.				
Strongly disagree	65	60	79	71
Disagree	37	34	28	25
Neutral	4	4	3	3
Agree	2	2	1	1
Strongly agree	1	1	1	1
Total	109	100	112	100
No purpose: No purpose can be served by my doing prison time.				
Strongly disagree	8	7	7	6
Disagree	30	27	31	28
Neutral	28	26	26	23
Agree	22	20	18	16
Strongly agree	22	20	29	26
Total	110	100	112	100
Impress parole board: Inmates should look for activities that will show the parole board that they have used their time constructively.				
Strongly disagree	2	2	6	5
Disagree	7	7	5	5
Neutral	23	21	26	23
Agree	42	39	46	41
Strongly agree	34	32	29	26
Total	108	100	112	100
Scam: It is possible to psych the staff out.				
Strongly disagree	6	6	5	5
Disagree	35	33	31	28
Neutral	46	43	51	46
Agree	18	17	21	19
Strongly agree	2	2	2	2
Total	107	100	110	100

NOTE: Percentages may not sum to 100, due to rounding.

no significant differences between groups. Slight differences were noted on two items: (a) *deterrent,* where 10% more prison camp inmates than penitentiary inmates indicated that their sentence was a specific deterrent, and (b) *deserts,* where 10% more of the prison camp inmates than the penitentiary inmates disagreed with the assertion that they deserved to be punished. In the first instance, these differences may reflect the minimum security inmates' lack of experience or familiarity with prison or the criminal justice system—so that relative to the familiar, life in even a minimum-security institution was a deterrent. The second difference also makes sense. Given the less serious nature of the criminal careers and offenses of minimum-security inmates, more may feel that prison is undeserved. Just the same, similarities between the two populations far outweighed any differences.

The notions adhered to by the majority of inmates (in both settings) were rehabilitation, deterrence, the need to impress the parole board, and the idea that the prison experience was serving no purpose. In contrast, far fewer inmates believed that they were "paying back" society, deserved to be incarcerated, or needed to be incarcerated for the safety of society. Similarly, relatively few inmates adhered to a belief that they could scam the staff. The orientations agreed to by the highest proportion of inmates were that their experience was a deterrent (67% penitentiary and 77% prison camp) and that, at some point, they would have to impress the parole board.

For an appropriate interpretation of these responses, one must examine the meaning of the index items carefully. We have made an attempt to differentiate inmates' beliefs and priorities (i.e., what prison should be) from their actual experiences (what prison is). With respect to rehabilitation, for example, subjects were asked not whether they wanted to participate in rehabilitation programs, but whether they were actually finding programs that would help them grow. We don't know whether a negative response to the items means that the inmate was not interested in rehabilitation or that he was not able to find meaningful programs. However, during an intake interview, discussions of the ideal purpose for prison revealed different findings. In the interview, the majority of both the penitentiary inmates (60%) and the camp inmates (58%) indicated that rehabilitation *should* be the priority for corrections. In contrast, none of the remaining options, such as deterrence, incapacitation, retribution, punishment, or "no purpose," received more than 15% of the interview responses.[5]

Interrelationships between Inmate Perceptions of Correctional Intents

An examination of the interrelationships between these notions adds more perspective to the findings discussed in the previous section. A correlation matrix of items for the penitentiary inmates is shown in Table 2.3. The matrix shows considerable agreement among some of the items. In fact, Table 2.3 suggests that attitudes, in a general sense, were either favorable or unfavorable. For example, inmates scoring high on the rehabilitation items *also* indicated that they deserved to do time, were being taught a lesson by the sentence, adhered to the notion of reparation, and believed that some purpose was being served by their sentence. More modest relationships are found between *rehabilitation* and *show board* and between rehabilitation and *scam staff*. Additional strong interrelationships are noted between *deterrence* and *retribution* and *deserts* and between

Table 2.3
Correlation Matrix of Correctional Orientation Measures, Penitentiary

	Rehabilitation	Deterrence	Retribution	Deserts	Incapacitation	No Purpose	Show Board	Scam Staff
Rehabilitation	1.00	.36***	.28**	.42***	.11	−.50***	.21*	.20*
Deterrence		1.00	.26**	.31**	.03	−.23*	.23*	.00
Retribution			1.00	.49***	.12	−.24**	.07	−.25**
Deserts				1.00	.42***	−.36***	.02	−.01
Incapacitation					1.00	−.17	.04	.05
No purpose						1.00	−.13	.03
Show board							1.00	.12
Scam staff								1.00

*$p \leq .05$. **$p \leq .01$, two-tailed. ***$p \leq .001$.

incapacitation and *deserts*. It is also noteworthy that inmates who believed that no purpose was being served were generally not the same inmates who agreed with the more traditional purposes of prison. Finally, a moderate negative relationship between scam staff and retribution finds those inmates who agreed that they were "paying back" for their offense to be less likely to believe that they could scam staff.

Was rehabilitation chosen solely in order to please the parole board? Pearson's *r* for the relationship between show board and rehabilitation, although significant, was modest, indicating that many inmates were not equating rehabilitation with "playing the parole game"—but some were.

The results appear to suggest that inmates either agreed with a package of traditional correctional intentions or they did not. In other words, they either perceived the societal purposes of prison or they did not. In order to fully support this interpretation, however, one must first dismiss the very real possibility that these data instead indicate response biases or the subjects' desire to offer socially desirable responses to researchers. In response, it is not the case that agreement is only between those responses that cast a favorable light on the inmate and those that do not. First, it is apparent from Tables 2.2 and 2.3, for example, that it was not true that these inmates simply examined a list of items and agreed with those that "looked good." For example, they did not agree with an assertion that society was safer with them in prison. In addition, some inmates who agreed with the notion of rehabilitation also thought it possible to scam staff or to look good to the parole board. One would assume that a subject would not choose such options if he wanted to look good on the survey. Moreover, some of the similarities cease as we observe distinct patterns of correlates in the next analyses. At this point, then, we would limit our caution to the observation that surveys are more susceptible to higher intercorrelations than some other type of measure might be, but that response bias is refuted in several instances.

Table 2.4 shows the survey matrix for the prison camp inmates. One sees similar interrelationships between favorable attitudes and generally unfavorable ones as was noted for the survey results of the penitentiary inmates. There are noteworthy exceptions, however. In this environment, specific deterrence is not as consistent with rehabilitation and retribution as it is among penitentiary inmates. Recalling that the prison camp inmates were more likely to perceive the deterrent effects of their sanction, it appears that they viewed deterrence as conceptually distinct from rehabilitation. For these inmates, only the notion of deserts appeared consistent with deterrence. Otherwise, the deterrence item is somewhat conspicuously a response from a distinct group of inmates.

The *no purpose* variable was negatively related to all but one orientation, scam staff and deterrence, where there were no relationships. As with the penitentiary surveys, the inmates responding to the no purpose item were quite consistent in their attitudes and quite distinct from other inmates.

The *show board* item was positively related to *rehabilitation, retribution,* and *deserts items* and negatively related to the *no purpose* and *scam staff* items. In both samples, findings for the *show board items* cast some doubt upon the image of inmates as insincere consumers of rehabilitative programs. Indeed, while the *show board item* is modestly related to *rehabilitation,* inmates responding favorably to this item generally were not manipulators of staff or possessive of cynical orientations to prison (no purpose).

Table 2.4

Correlation Matrix of Correctional Orientation Measures, Prison Camp

	Rehabilitation	Deterrence	Retribution	Deserts	Incapacitation	No Purpose	Show Board	Scam Staff
Rehabilitation	1.00	.17	.47***	.53***	.27**	-.53***	.25**	-.13
Deterrence		1.00	.18	.28**	-.05	-.06	.07	-.14
Retribution			1.00	.53***	.29**	-.34***	.35***	-.24**
Deserts				1.00	.40***	-.50***	.28**	-.11
Incapacitation					1.00	-.38***	.16	.00
No purpose						1.00	-.24**	.09
Show board							1.00	-.25**
Scam staff								1.00

*$p \leq .05$. **$p \leq .01$. ***$p \leq .001$.

Demographic, Psychological, and Criminal Record Correlates of Correctional Orientations

We turn now to a bivariate examination of the psychological, demographic, and criminal record factors associated with the various correctional intents. Table 2.5 presents results of bivariate tests for the penitentiary sample. Understandably, perhaps, one of the orientations, show board, was found to have no correlates. In the case of the rehabilitation measure, however, age, IQ, race, employment, and prison experience were found to be significantly related, indicating that inmates who found the prison experience helpful were younger, non-White inmates, who were unemployed at the time of their arrest and had evidenced no prior prison experience and relatively low IQ scores.

In terms of the other orientations, we note somewhat fewer differentiating factors. But inmates *not* diagnosed as aggressive were more likely to agree that their sentence was deserved (deserts) or could serve as a way to pay back society (reparation), whereas aggressive inmates were more likely to believe that staff could be scammed. All three of these relationships were weak. At the same time, dependent inmates were significantly more likely to feel that their sanction was reparative. As in other studies (e.g., McClelland & Alpert, 1985) experienced inmates (those who had served prior prison terms) were less likely to agree that prison was serving as a deterrent.

There were a few more demographic correlates of the correctional orientations than psychological ones. Most notable, inmates who felt that prison was teaching them a lesson were young and had no previous incarcerations. On the other hand, older, White inmates, and those whose incarceration had interrupted full-time employment, tended to see no purpose to the sanction. Younger inmates were more likely to believe that staff could be scammed. Finally, those who were not married prior to arrest were slightly more likely to orient to the notion of incapacitation—that society was safer with them in prison.

An examination of the same issues among minimum-security inmates reveals four main correlates: (a) IQ, (b) age, (c) race, and (d) prison experience. Inmates with low IQ scores were more likely to believe that prison was incapacitating them and allowing them to repay society; inmates with higher IQs were slightly more likely to believe that no purpose was being served. Younger inmates were significantly more likely to believe that prison was rehabilitating them, offering an opportunity to repay society, deserved, and serving purposes of incapacitation. At the same time, younger inmates were more likely to believe that staff could be scammed. Older inmates and those with prior prison experience were more likely to believe that no purpose could be served by their sentence. Non-White inmates were more likely to agree with the purpose of retribution and incapacitation. Prior prison had an impact on a need to present oneself favorably to the parole board; those without prior terms were more likely to see this as a priority. At the same time, less prison experience also was correlated with the belief that one could achieve something constructive in prison (rehabilitation).

Personality was not a strong factor, except that inmates classified as aggressive on the Jesness Inventory were significantly more likely to believe that one could scam staff.

Table 2.5

Bivariate Relationships between Correctional Orientations Measures and Personality, Cognitive Development, Demographic, and Prior Offense Variables, Penitentiary

	Rehabilitation	Deterrence	Retribution	Deserts	Incapacitation	No Purpose	Show Board	Scam Staff
Psychological Variables								
Aggressive	.02	−.05	−.20**	−.17*	−.08	.09	.00	.16*
Neurotic	.01	.04	.07	.05	.14	−.09	.09	.03
Dependent	−.05	−.02	.23**	.07	.00	.04	.00	−.16*
Situational	.01	.04	−.04	.11	−.03	−.07	−.09	−.09
Cognitive development	.04	.08	−.04	.07	.05	−.13	−.03	.02
WAIS-R	−.19**	−.03	−.12	−.03	−.05	.13	−.17*	.06
Demographic and Criminal Record Variables								
Age	−.34***	−.17*	.08	−.09	−.11	.27***	−.05	−.29***
Race	.26***	−.10	.08	−.02	−.03	−.20**	.03	.06
Urban	−.09	.16	−.10	.10	−.08	.02	−.09	−.05
Marital	.05	−.04	.02	−.03	.17*	.04	−.09	−.02
School fail	−.06	−.12	.07	−.04	−.20**	.00	−.25***	−.01
Employment	−.21**	.00	−.15	−.15	−.11	.19*	−.09	.02
Prior prison	.20**	.20**	.04	.03	−.13	−.14	.10	.02

*$p \leq .10$. **$p \leq .05$. ***$p \leq .01$.

33

Table 2.6

Bivariate Relationships between Correctional Orientations Measures and Personality, Cognitive Development, Demographic, and Prior Offense Variables, Prison Camp

	Rehabilitation	Deterrence	Retribution	Deserts	Incapacitation	No Purpose	Show Board	Scam Staff
Psychological Variables								
Aggressive	.09	−.07	−.15	−.12	−.05	.02	.06	.21**
Neurotic	−.11	−.05	.07	.10	.05	−.05	−.14	−.04
Dependent	.06	.10	.14	.01	.16	.05	.01	−.08
Situational	−.06	−.04	−.04	.03	−.16*	−.02	.06	−.13
Cognitive development	−.12	−.05	−.01	.08	−.14	−.05	−.07	−.13
WAIS-R	−.05	−.13	−.25***	−.03	−.27***	.17*	−.02	.05
Demographic and Criminal Record Variables								
Age	−.15	−.09	−.12*	−.28***	−.19**	.18**	.06	−.19**
Race	.06	.05	.27***	.02	.19**	−.03	.09	.10
Urban	−.03	−.02	.01	.09	−.06	.04	.07	−.22**
Marital	.01	−.04	.04	.05	.11	−.02	.05	.04
School fail	.08	−.14	−.26***	.08	−.18*	−.03	−.03	.12
Employment	−.09	−.06	−.18*	−.03	−.11	.13	−.05	.17**
Prior prison	.15	−.09	−.09	.01	−.05	.19*	.21**	−.06

*$p \leq .10$. **$p \leq .05$. ***$p \leq .01$.

A clearer examination of these profiles is facilitated by the following multivariate analysis. We move to that also in order to explore similarities and differences between the two types of prison populations.

Multivariate Analysis of the Relationship between Demographic, Psychological, and Criminal Record Correlates of Correctional Orientations

Multiple regression of psychological,[6] demographic, and prior record factors on correctional orientations for the penitentiary sample produced several rather strong models. As Table 2.7 shows, R^2 for the rehabilitation, retribution, and no purpose equations were .27, .19, and .21, respectively. Partialing out the effects of interrelationships between variables presents a more accurate profile of the type of inmates who held each orientation.

Turning to the rehabilitation model, for example, inmates oriented to the notion of rehabilitation were (a) young, (b) non-White, (c) unemployed prior to their arrest, and (d) classified Situational by the Jesness Inventory. At the same time, these inmates were not aggressive, subcultural types of offenders, committed to criminal values. One certainly might view this group of inmates as disadvantaged, but not as committed to their criminal careers.[7] For another model, inmates who were *not* diagnosed aggressive, and those who were unemployed prior to arrest, were most likely to see incarceration as a chance to repay society. Such findings are somewhat similar to those observed for the deserts model, although the rather high R^2 for this model was not significant.[8] The latter test also observed an age effect.

Inmates finding no purpose to prison were (a) older, (b) White, and (c) employed at the time of their arrest. Results for other tests would have been clearer with a larger sample and more powerful tests. We see, of course, numerous instances where relatively high betas do not reach significance.

Nevertheless, we observe that psychological factors were somewhat less important than demographic and prior record variables, although in all likelihood at least some would have been found significant in more powerful tests.

Looking at the same tests for minimum-security inmates, Table 2.8 shows weaker models than those observed for the penitentiary sample. Yet effects of age, prior prison, and aggressive personality appear to be similar for those of the penitentiary sample, in many instances. In the main, however, these models do not yield to the clear interpretations found among penitentiary inmates.

In this sample of inmates, many of whom were serving their first sentence, and a short one at that, prior prison produced interesting effects on correctional orientation. Those with no prior incarcerations felt that no purpose could be served by the sanction. Those with prior prison and older inmates were more likely than others to believe that they needed to impress a parole board.

The only significant model, incapacitation, should be viewed with caution due to the variability problems on the dependent variable. Still, inmates who felt society was safer with them in prison were more likely to have low IQ scores.

Table 2.7

Regression of Psychological, Demographic, and Prior Prison Variables on Correctional Orientations, Penitentiary Sample

	Rehabilitation	Deterrence	Retribution	Deserts	Incapacitation	No Purpose	Show Board	Scam Staff
Aggressive	.01	-.16	-.25*	-.14	ref	.19	-.15	.15
Neurotic	ref	ref	ref	ref	.02	ref	ref	ref
Dependent	-.03	.05	.18	.16	.10	.03	-.14	-.01
Situational	.22*	.03	.01	.21	.10	-.11	-.15	.06
WAIS-R	-.07	-.05	.06	.14	-.03	.02	-.17	.15
Age	-.24**	-.21	.06	-.23*	-.26**	.28**	.01	-.35***
Race	.24**	-.06	.07	-.05	-.13	-.20*	.03	.06
Marital	.03	-.07	.03	.05	.17	.09	-.10	-.05
Employment	-.24**	-.04	-.32**	-.25**	-.11	.21**	-.01	.09
Prior prison	.17*	.04	.03	-.05	-.18	-.05	-.13	-.02
R^2	.27	.08	.19	.14	.11	.21	.06	.17
F	3.16**	.75	2.13**	1.50	1.07	2.34**	.57	1.84*
SE	1.10	1.14	1.17	.97	.72	1.17	.99	.84

*$p \leq .10$. **$p \leq .05$. ***$p \leq .01$.

Table 2.8

Regression of Psychological, Demographic, and Prior Prison Variables on Correctional Orientations, Prison Camp

	Rehabilitation	Deterrence	Retribution	Deserts	Incapacitation	No Purpose	Show Board	Scam Staff
Aggressive	.10	.06	−.21	−.25*	−.07	.15	.12	.13
Neurotic	ref	ref	ref	ref	ref	ref	ref	ref
Dependent	.18	.13	.12	.09	.15	.06	.11	−.03
Situational	−.03	.05	−.03	.00	−.12	.05	.11	−.09
WAIS-R	.05	−.06	−.13	.07	−.25**	.17	.03	.07
Age	−.11	−.14	−.08	−.27**	−.14	.03	.22*	−.21*
Race	.00	.01	.17	−.02	.08	.11	.05	.14
Marital	−.11	−.01	−.05	−.06	.10	.00	.05	.00
Employment	−.03	−.06	−.04	.04	.03	.14	−.12	.09
Prior prison	.18	−.09	.16	.03	−.03	−.25**	.28**	−.17
R^2	.09	.05	.17	.12	.18	.12	.15	.14
F	.73	.43	1.64	1.00	1.74*	1.06	1.36	1.28
SE	1.08	1.16	1.30	1.05	.71	1.28	1.07	.87

*$p \leq .10$.   **$p \leq .05$.

37

CONCLUSION

Prior to discussing the implications of these findings, let us first review what it was we measured. We measured actual inmate experiences of the prison environment, rather than prescriptive impressions of what they thought prison should be. There are both limitations and benefits to this approach. One clear limitation occurs as we attempt to differentiate inmates' values and priorities from the effects of the prison environment. The rehabilitation scale, for example, shows us whether inmates felt they could achieve personal growth in the current prison setting. But was a positive response attributable to the inmate's motivation or to his experience in specific treatment programs? Probably both. On the other hand, the advantage of this approach is that these measures have somewhat clearer policy relevance and a greater potential for testing the impact of the prison experience. What, for example, is one to do with a prescriptive measure (e.g., that prison *should be* rehabilitative) when we don't know what experiences would in fact be rehabilitative? At the same time the cognitive psychologists and more recently medical scholars inform us that one's perceptions of experiences can often be more important determinants of outcome than actual experience (Ellis, 1973; Meichenbaum, 1977).

With this context in mind, we highlight what we consider to be the most important observations of this research. First, although the maximum and the minimum security prison settings offered dramatically different living environments and terms of imprisonment, the meaning of the punishment experience was remarkably similar in both settings. A reasonable explanation, of course, is that the similar perceptions may actually be attributable to the differences among samples. A minimum-security setting, for example, may be as much of a deterrent to an inexperienced inmate as the maximum-security facility is to the experienced. Although the differences were not significant, fewer minimum security inmates felt that prison was deserved, and proportionately more prison camp inmates than penitentiary inmates felt that the experience was a deterrent. Future studies may find it beneficial to examine these findings in terms of Andrews and Bonta's (1994) observation that intensive interventions for relatively low-risk inmates are counterproductive. We are also reminded of the often repeated responses of a group of University of Chicago scholars that prisons should be reserved for the most serious offenders (Morris, 1974; Zimring & Hawkins, 1991). More conclusive findings, of course, await research on the impact of offender perceptions on future crimes.

Our analysis of the interrelationships between orientations would typically be performed as a methodological prelude to multivariate analysis. In this case, however, the importance of the findings of the correlation matrix extend beyond measurement issues. We did not anticipate the clustering of orientations that we found. Instead of finding a focus on one purpose, we noted subjects who simultaneously experienced several correctional intentions at once, that is, the prisons' rehabilitative, incapacitative, retributive, *and* deterrent effects. It appeared that one group of inmates accepted several rationales simultaneously, whereas another group was more cynical, believing that no purpose could be served and that staff could be manipulated. We caution, however, that surveys can amplify the magnitude of interrelationships among items. However, in this study, the interitem correlations did not interfere with subsequent bivariate and multivariate analysis. If we take the observation that inmates either adhered to a package of traditional sentencing purposes or they did not on its face value, we can also note that these inmates do not differ substantially from their counterparts in the policy arena. Policy discussions and published agency materials routinely mention numerous goals at once. Historically, some have speculated that corrections suffers from goal confusion or a contradiction of purposes, but the inmates in these samples are not inconsistent with more recent correctional scholars whose writings assert that treatment and control (Palmer, 1992) or treatment and punishment (Andrews & Bonta, 1994; Bonta & Gendreau, 1990) can and perhaps should coexist.

In related research (Crouch, 1993; McClelland & Alpert 1985; Petersilia & Piper-Deschenes, 1994), experienced offenders, African Americans, unmarried, and older inmates tended to view prison as less punitive than certain types of community sanctions. Even though our sample is different (inmates rather than probationers or arrestees) and our questions pertain to the immediate situation rather than to the selection of a preferred sanction, our findings are somewhat consistent. In our study, age, race, prearrest employment status, and the extent of one's criminal career and prison experience were important determinants of how offenders made sense of their sentence. In exploring additional factors, IQ and personality also had an impact on prisoners' orientation to the experience. Marital status, however, had very little influence. Consistent with the earlier research, younger inmates with less prison experience were more likely to view prison as a deterrent. We go beyond the earlier research, however, in observing that not only were older inmates slightly less likely to see prison as a deterrent, in both settings, they saw *no* purpose to prison.

Perhaps the most relevant aspect of these factors is seen in the penitentiary sample in a comparison of those inmates who thought they were getting something out of prison (young, non-White, unemployed, situational, with less prior prison experience) with those who saw no purpose (White, older, and previously employed inmates). We are able to support one of the suggestions put forward by Petersilia (1990), citing Wilson (1987). The profile of the penitentiary inmate who believed that he was getting something out of prison shows a disadvantaged individual, who had no employment prior to his arrest, perhaps had limited opportunities for securing employment, and was non-White. Adding the personality measures to these analyses afforded an opportunity to separate offenders with more entrenched criminal values and experience from those who were less experienced. Interestingly, those who felt they could gain from prison programming were non-White individuals who were not experienced criminals; a significant proportion of these inmates had no prior prison experience, and were classified as Situational personality types. This adds an individual who held to basically prosocial values (rather than to criminal values) to this profile. In contrast, inmates who felt that nothing could be gained from the penitentiary experience were older, White inmates who had been employed prior to prison. We could speculate that these were inmates who had social investments that were interrupted by incarceration; however, the fact that marriage/families were not a correlate discourages us from going too far in this line of interpretation.

Our findings also point us toward a better understanding of specific correctional goals, most notably deterrence and rehabilitation. A substantial group of inmates in both settings noted that prison was not only a deterrent, but that the deterrent influences of the punishment would dissuade them from future criminal activities. Thus, although we did not offer these subjects the opportunity to compare sentencing options, as did and Petersilia & Piper-Deschenes

(1994) and Crouch (1993), it would be most difficult to say that prison is not punitive or a deterrent to one who is actually serving a sanction.

It remains to be seen, however, whether or not inmates' perceptions of deterrence favorably affect criminal behavior upon release. And it is on the matter of its impact on future crimes that deterrence breaks down. Further, any tendency we might have to seize upon our deterrence findings as supportive of "get tough" movements should be viewed with caution. For one thing, these subjects told us that *these* specific environments were deterrents. These findings, in other words, would not generalize to the "get tough" approaches that place a qualitatively different emphasis on deterrence. Furthermore, extant research has shown us, rather consistently, that deterrence, for its own sake, is not effective (Gendreau & Ross, 1987).

In addition, we are interested in the correlations between deterrence and other rationales noted for the penitentiary sample, and the lack of a similar finding among the prison camp inmates. It would have been enlightening to explore further the minimum security inmates' perspectives on deterrence. They did not hold the deterrent aspects of their experience to be consistent with its rehabilitative aspects (as the penitentiary inmates did). We did, however, find a bivariate correlation between deterrence and deserts, suggesting that many of those who were deterred also felt that they deserved their sanction.

With respect to rehabilitation, we have learned that a substantial portion of the inmates express a desire to participate in rehabilitative programming. This is consistent with the research of Toch (1977), Wright (1989), and others. In our study, a somewhat lower proportion of inmates indicated that they are actually experiencing meaningful rehabilitative programming in prison. Were they simply using treatment to "play the parole game"? Probably not. We observed a moderate correlation between the rehabilitation item and the parole board item in the prison camp setting and a weaker but nonsignificant one among penitentiary inmates. Generally, inmates in the prison camp, especially, did not use the prospect of parole as the overriding motive. Those who indicated positive responses on the show board item also scored high on a belief that they were repaying society and deserved to be punished. Further, they stood apart from those inmates who saw no purpose in prison. Our reasons for not questioning the sincerity of the penitentiary inmates are somewhat different. Here the *show board* item was unrelated to any other orientation, suggesting that perhaps these inmates may have been a separate group from those who responded positively to other items. But the most important evidence questioning the validity of the parole game concerns the absence of any positive relationships between show board and the two other measurements of inmate cynicism (*no purpose* and *scam* staff). Perhaps this finding suggests not so much that inmates are exploiting rehabilitation, but that they realistically realize that success will have its payoffs. The findings might be likened to the student who achieves good grades, the employee who secures a stellar work evaluation, the person who faithfully saves money, and the colleague who is trusted by his or her coworkers. These individuals could hardly be expected to ignore the impact of their performances on their futures.

Some might be tempted to conclude on the basis of these observations that rehabilitation's strong relationship with other correctional goals, particularly deterrence, might suggest that the prison experience in itself may be rehabilitative—we don't need specific rehabilitation programs. We would caution against such a conclusion and remind readers of the findings for boot-camps and intermediate sanctions (Cullen, Wright, & Applegate, 1993) or perhaps for correctional programming in general (Gendreau & Ross, 1987). There is no evidence to suggest that sanctions with no treatments are indirectly serving as treatments. In fact, even with the advent of intermediate sanctions, we did not have positive effects on recidivism until the treatment components were added. Our results suggest, instead, that rehabilitation need not be inconsistent from other correctional intentions such as deterrence, retribution deserts, and incapacitation.

Finally, there are some unsettling, but important aspects to the profile of the inmate who thinks he can get something out of a maximum security prison experience. He was young, unemployed, non-White, was not evidencing pro-criminal values or an extensive prison experience, and the somewhat limited programming that this and other institutions are prepared to offer him was seen as a way he could grow. One is reminded of William Julius Wilson's "truly disadvantaged" or perhaps of the earlier words of John Irwin with regard to those who held out hope for the prison experience:

> They were led to believe that they would be able to raise their education level, to learn a trade, to have physical defects corrected, and would receive help in various individual or group therapy programs in solving psychological problems. In effect, they were led to believe that if they participated in prison programs with sincerity and resolve, they would leave prison in better condition than when they entered and would generally be much better equipped to cope with the outside world. (1970, p. 52)

If indeed the prison experience and the participation in prison programs has the potential to foster growth and development on the part of the individual inmate, minority males because of their greater numbers in the system as well as their lack of opportunities elsewhere stand to benefit the most.

Based on data obtained from the Department of Justice Statistics, the 1990 Sentencing Project Report found that 1 in 4 (23%) Black males between the ages of 20 and 29 were under some form of correctional supervision—jail, prison, probation, or parole (Mauer, 1990). In their follow-up study, "Young Black Americans and the Criminal Justice System: Five Years Later," Mauer and Hurling (1995) found that the Black male incarceration rates rose to 1 in 3 (32%), resulting in approximately 827,440 young Black males being involved in the criminal justice system.

Thus, with the growing number of young, non-White, previously unemployed males in the system, the rehabilitative services provided in prison have the potential to serve as an educational and employment training program. Thurston (1993) makes this point with respect to Adult Basic Education Programs. In this light, the prison experience for certain groups of inmates could serve as a resource—an opportunity to improve their lives.

However, as cautioned by Michael Tonry (1995), we should not look to the criminal justice system to solve problems of poverty, unemployment, and an inadequate educational system. At best, the system can "resolve not to exacerbate fundamental social problems and to do as little harm as possible" (Tonry, 1995, p. 163). From a policy standpoint, however, it seems tragic to continually ignore this group of inmates—justifying our neglect perhaps through specious reference to growing crime, decline in values, and assumptions about what may or may not be going on in the minds of offenders.

How these perceptions ultimately determine prison outcomes and future behavior, of course, remains to be seen. We found a number of inmates indicating such favorable responses as "I have learned my lesson," "I deserve to be here," or "I can experience personal growth in here." But we do not know what these orientations mean in terms of either prison adjustment or future criminal behavior. An emerging body of research, however, is beginning to recognize criminogenic attitudes as one of the major predictors of future crimes (see Andrews & Bonta, 1994).

The future directions for this research seem clear. First, the impact of correctional orientations on prison adjustment will be conducted using the same sample. In addition, an assessment of the impact of these orientations on the recidivism of these offenders would be extremely valuable. Finally, we would like to see a similar study conducted among state prison inmates, preferably a maximum security sample.

NOTES

1. Analysis of the impact of correctional orientations on prison adjustment and recidivism will be the subject of a future article. It is beyond the scope of the present article.
2. This may be noted among criminal subcultures.
3. As will be explained shortly, the surveyed groups were not unrepresentative of the larger inmate population.
4. The concern for variable follow-up time frames reflects research findings that show that inmates' responses on a number of psychological and attitudinal measures may be influenced by their current sentence phase (see Bukstel & Kilmann, 1980).
5. We should note, however, that this item was difficult to rate; the percentage interrater agreement for the item was 59%.
6. The cognitive development variable is not entered into the multiple regression models, because of its strong bivariate relationship to IQ and the absence of any bivariate relationships between IQ and correctional orientations (see Tables 2.5 & 2.6).
7. In partialing out separate effects of Situational classification and prior sentences, we note different findings from those reported for Table 2.5.
8. Sample sizes, of course, greatly reduced the power of the multivariate tests.

REFERENCES

American Correctional Association. (1994). ACA issues positions on crime bill. *ACA On the Line, 17*(2), 1.

American Friends Service Committee. (1971). *Struggle for justice.* New York: Hill and Wang.

Andrews, D., & Bonta, J. (1994). *The psychology of criminal conduct.* Cincinnati, OH: Anderson.

Bandura, A. (1973). *Aggression: A social learning analysis.* New York: Prentice Hall.

Blumstein, A., Cohen, J., & Nagin, D. (1978). *Deterrence and incapacitation: Estimating the effects of criminal sanctions on crime rates.* Washington, DC: National Academy of Sciences.

Bonta, J., & Gendreau, P. (1990). Re-examining the cruel and unusual punishment of prison life. *Law and Human Behavior, 14,* 347–372.

Bukstel, L., & Kilmann, P. (1980). Psychological effects of imprisonment on confined individuals. *Psychological Bulletin, 88*(3): 469–493.

Caspi, A., Moffit, T., Silva, P., Stouthamer-Loeber, M., Krueger, R., & Schmutte, P. (1994). Are some people crime prone? Replications of the personality-crime relationship across countries, genders, races, and methods. *Criminology, 32*(2), 163–195.

Corrections 2000. (1994). Federal crime bill in final stages. *Corrections Alert, 1*(1), 1–2.

Crouch, B. (1993). Is incarceration really worse? Analysis of offenders' preferences for prison over probation. *Justice Quarterly, 10*(1), 67–88.

Cullen, F., & Gilbert, K. (1982). *Reaffirming rehabilitation.* Cincinnati, OH: Anderson.

Cullen, F., Skovron, S., Scott, J., & Burton, V. (1990). Public support for correctional treatment: The tenacity of rehabilitative ideology. *Criminal Justice and Behavior, 17*(1), 6–18.

Cullen, F., Wright, J., & Applegate, B. (1993, November). *Control in the community.* Paper presented at a conference of the International Association of Residential and Community Alternatives, Philadelphia, PA.

Currie, E. (1985). *Confronting crime: An American challenge.* New York: Pantheon.

Ellis, A. (1973). *Humanistic psychotherapy.* New York: Julian.

Eysenck, H. (1977). *Crime and personality.* London: Granada.

Flanagan, T. (1983). Correlates of institutional misconduct among state prisoners. *Criminology, 21,* 29–39.

Fogel, D. (1979). *"We are the living proof:" The justice model for corrections* (Vol. 2). Cincinnati, OH: Anderson.

Gendreau, P., & Ross, R. (1987). Revivification of rehabilitation: Evidence from the 1980s. *Justice Quarterly, 4*(3), 349–407.

Gibbs, J. (1975). *Crime, punishment, and deterrence.* New York: Elsevier.

Hart, H. L. A. (1961). *The concept of law.* Oxford: Oxford University Press.

Hawkins, G. (1976). *The prison: Policy and practice.* Chicago: University of Chicago Press.

Hawkins, R., & Alpert, G. (1989). *American prison systems: Punishment and justice.* Englewood Cliffs, NJ: Prentice Hall.

Irwin, J. (1970). *The felon.* Englewood Cliffs, NJ: Prentice Hall.

Jesness, C., & Wedge, R. (1983). *Classifying offenders: The Jesness Inventory Classification System.* Sacramento, CA: California Youth Authority.

Klepper, S., & Nagin, D. (1989). The deterrent effect of perceived certainty and severity of punishment revisited. *Criminology, 27*(4) 721–746.

Mauer, M. (1990). *Young, Black men and the criminal justice system: A growing national problem.* Washington, DC: The Sentencing Project.

Mauer, M., & Hurling, T. (1995). *Young, Black Americans and the criminal justice system: Five years later.* Washington, DC: The Sentencing Project.

McClelland, K., & Alpert, G. (1985). Factor analysis applied to magnitude estimates of punishment seriousness: Patterns of individual differences. *Journal of Quantitative Criminology, 1*(3), 307–318.

McCorkle, R. (1993). Research note: Punish or rehabilitate. *Crime and Delinquency, 39*(2), 240–252.

Megargee, E., & Bohn, M. (1979). *Classifying criminal offenders: A new system based on the MMPI.* Beverly Hills, CA: Sage.

Meichenbaum, D. (1977). *Cognitive-behavioral modification: An integrative approach.* New York: Plenum.

Menninger, K. (1966). *The crime of punishment.* New York: Vintage.

Mitford, J. (1973). *Kind and unusual punishment: The prison business.* New York: Alfred A. Knopf.

Morris, N. (1974). *The future of imprisonment.* Chicago: University of Chicago Press.

Myers, L., & Levy, G. (1978). Description and prediction of the intractable inmate. *Journal of Research in Crime and Delinquency, 15,* 214–228.

Newman, G. (1978). *The punishment response.* New York: Lippincott.

Palmer, T. (1983). The "effectiveness" issue today: An overview. *Federal Probation, 46*, 3–10.

Palmer, T. (1992). *The re-emergence of correctional intervention: Developments through the 1980s and prospects for the future.* Beverly Hills, CA: Sage.

Paternoster, R. (1987). The deterrent effect of perceived certainty and severity of punishment: A review of the evidence and issues. *Justice Quarterly, 4*(2), 173–217.

Petersilia, J. (1990). When probation becomes more dreaded than prison. *Federal Probation, 54*(1), 23–27.

Petersilia, J., & Piper-Deschenes, E. (1994). What punishes? Inmates rank the severity of prison vs. intermediate sanctions. *Federal Probation, 58*(1), 3–8.

Public Agenda Foundation. (1987). *Crime and punishment: The public's view.* New York: Edna McConnell Clark Foundation.

Quay, H. (1965). Psychopathic personality: Pathological stimulation-seeking. *American Journal of Psychiatry, 122*, 180–183.

Quay, H. (1983). *Technical manual for the behavioral classifications system for adult offenders.* Washington, DC: U.S. Department of Justice.

Sherman, M., & Hawkins, G. (1982). *Imprisonment in America: Choosing the future.* Chicago: University of Chicago Press.

Shipley, W. (1940). A self-administering scale for measuring intellectual impairment and deterioration. *Journal of Psychology, 9*(2), 371–377.

Thurston, L. (1993). *A call to action: An analysis and overview of the United States criminal justice system, with recommendations.* Chicago, IL: Third World Press.

Toch, H. (1977). *Living in prison.* New York: Free Press.

Toch, H., & Adams, K. (1989). *Coping: Maladaptation in prisons.* New Brunswick, NJ: Transaction.

Tonry, M. (1995). *Malign neglect: Race, crime and punishment in America.* Oxford: Oxford University Press.

Van Voorhis, P. (1983). Theoretical perspectives on moral development and restitution. In W. Lauffer & J. Day (Eds.), *Personality theory, moral development, and criminal behavior.* Lexington: D.C. Heath.

Van Voorhis, P. (1985). Restitution outcome and probationers' assessments of restitution: The effects of moral development. *Criminal Justice and Behavior, 12*(3), 259–287.

Van Voorhis, P. (1994). *Psychological classification of the adult, male, prison inmate.* Albany, NY: State University of New York Press.

Van Voorhis, P. (1995, November). *Personality and the crime paradigm: Directions from the classification research.* Paper presented at the Annual Meeting of the American Society of Criminology, Boston, MA.

von Hirsch, A. (1976). *Doing justice.* New York: Hill and Wang.

Warren, M. (1983). Applications of interpersonal maturity to offender populations. In W. Lauffer & J. Day (Eds.), *Personality theory, moral development, and criminal behavior.* Lexington: D.C. Heath.

Wilson, J. (1987). *The truly disadvantaged: The inner city, the underclass, and public policy.* Chicago: University of Chicago Press.

Wilson, J., & Herrstein, R. (1985). *Crime and human nature.* New York: Simon and Schuster.

Wright, K. (1989). Race and economic marginality in explaining prison adjustment. *Journal of Research in Crime and Justice, 26*(1), 67–89.

Zachary, R., Crumpton, E., & Spiegel, D. (1985). Estimating WAIS IQ from the Shipley Institute of Living Scale. *Journal of Clinical Psychology, 41*(4), 532–540.

Zimring, F., & Hawkins, G. (1991). *The scale of imprisonment.* Chicago: University of Chicago Press.

Zimring, F., & Hawkins, G. (1995). *Incapacitation: Penal confinement and the restraint of crime.* New York: Oxford University Press.

CHAPTER 3

IS INCARCERATION REALLY WORSE?
ANALYSIS OF OFFENDERS' PREFERENCES
FOR PRISON OVER PROBATION*

Ben M. Crouch

Recent correctional reforms have ameliorated the deprivations of prison and indirectly have caused states to toughen probation because many offenders must be diverted from incarceration to meet court-defined limits on prison crowding. These changes raise the possibility that offenders increasingly may view prison as easier or less punitive than probation. Using interview data from newly incarcerated Texas offenders, this analysis examines the extent to which offenders prefer incarceration when presented with choices between paired prison and probation sentences. Though a number of demographic and experiential variables are examined, multivariate analysis reveals that being African-American is the strongest predictor of a preference for prison. Implications of these results are discussed.

State penal codes, typically involving combinations of retributionist and utilitarian philosophies, represent society's hope of repaying offenders and of deterring crime (Hawkins and Alpert 1989: 86–90; Newman 1978: ch. 10). To these ends, penal codes reflect a hierarchy of punishments ranging downward from death through incarceration, probation, and fines. This hierarchy of sanctions not only is the basis for penal codes but also operates in the minds of citizens on juries or in voting booths and directly affects how prosecuting attorneys apply the law to offenders. Moreover, society holds a broad consensus regarding the correspondence between seriousness of crime and severity of punishment (Hamilton and Rytina 1980; Rossi, Simpson, and Miller 1985).

---

*The larger research project from which data for this analysis are taken was funded by the Texas Commission on Alcohol and Drug Abuse. Comments by Mark Fossett, Kelly Damphousse and three anonymous reviewers from *Justice Quarterly* significantly improved the manuscript and are gratefully acknowledged.

JUSTICE QUARTERLY, Vol. 10 No. 1, March 1993
© 1993 Academy of Criminal Justice Sciences

In this country imprisonment has been the preferred method of punishing serious offenders, and the use of the prison sanction recently has increased significantly. Through the 1980s, the number of persons incarcerated increased by 134 percent, and the rate of incarceration doubled (Dillingham 1991). Theoretically, if this extensive use of prisons is to have the punitive and deterrent effect on offenders that the public and officials desire, a fundamental assumption must consistently be met: that offenders generally share the state's punitiveness ranking of criminal sanctions. For example, offenders sentenced to prison should perceive that sanction as more punitive or more severe than probation.[1]

Recent correctional reforms, however, especially federal court-instigated reforms (Jacobs 1980; Thomas 1988), may affect prisoners' perceptions of the relative severity of sanctions and in turn may challenge the validity of this basic assumption. Litigated reforms, for example, have heightened prisoners' access to courts, have curtailed extreme abuse by prison staff, and have improved living conditions (Crouch and Marquart 1990; Hawkins and Alpert 1989; Jacobs 1980). All of these changes translate into less capricious and less depriving institutions.

In addition, courts have proscribed overcrowding. To prevent prison populations from exceeding legal limits, state correctional officials often have taken the expensive but popular course of building new prisons to meet growing demands. Officials also have sought to control overcrowding by releasing many prisoners after only a short stay in prison to make room for more convicts and by diverting convicted felons from prison into community programs, especially probation (Morris and Tonry 1990). The public often objects to these latter strategies because they "put criminals back on the streets." Legislators typically have reacted to this objection by making nonincarceration sentences tougher. Intensive probation supervision (Clear and Hardyman 1990), for example, subjects offenders to routine reporting, probation fees, and the hassles of frequent drug tests and unannounced home visits.

Taken together, these correctional changes can make prisons less onerous (better conditions and possibly shorter stays) and probation more burdensome. These changes may lead some felons to define the "new," reformed prisons not only as less punitive than probation but even as preferable. Because prison and probation are the most widely used sanctions for serious crimes, such a shift in preference by offenders runs counter to society's hierarchy of sanctions. It tends to undermine the state's presumption that prison is "worse" than probation and thus a greater deterrent.

Evidence of such a shift in perceptions of sanctions is presented by Petersilia (1990) in a paper titled "When Probation Becomes More Dreaded than Prison." She cites a RAND Corporation study in which prison-bound felons were allowed to choose between staying in the community under intensive supervision by the probation department or going to prison. In the first year, one-third of those who initially had opted for probation changed their minds and asked to be sent to prison.

Similarly, in the late 1980s in Texas, probation officers and prosecuting attorneys began to note that prisoners increasingly were requesting prison and trying to avoid probation. One surprised Texas judge stated, "Not in my wildest

---

[1]See Hawkins and Alpert (1989) for a discussion of severity of sanctions.

six years on the bench has this ever come up before . . . I've had (offenders ask) for probation instead of prison, but I've never had one . . . ask me to do away with probation and go to prison" (Bryan-College Station Eagle 1991). Such preferences are surprising because at least through the mid-1980s (Crouch and Marquart 1989), probation always was viewed as a break for the offender, especially in a state such as Texas, with its history of tough prisons.

Unfortunately, beyond these preliminary and anecdotal observations, little is known about how offenders today weigh the relative costs of prison and probation. Although considerable research has addressed perceptions of sanctions in relation to deterrent outcomes (see Hawkins and Alpert 1989:149–50 for review), the possibility that some offenders may prefer prison to probation has not been examined systematically. Yet a clearer understanding of these preferences is relevant to punishment theory as well as to policy; both would benefit from deeper insight into how offenders perceive our major sanctioning options, especially during a time of rapid change in American corrections. In this study I seek to fill a significant gap in the literature by examining perceptions of the relative punitiveness of prison and probation in a large sample of state offenders.

Determinants of Offenders' Perceptions of Sanctions

Although I know of no work beside Petersilia's (1990) thoughtful paper that bears directly on the questions raised here, several lines of research and theory suggest factors that may influence offenders' perceptions of sanctions. The first is a long tradition of research into prison subculture, which demonstrates that variations in experience with crime and the justice system cause offenders to perceive and cope with prison in different ways. Because of their greater involvement, "right guys," "thieves," and "convicts," (for example) would know more about the relative personal costs of various sanctions and thus would be less threatened by the prospect of prison than "square Johns" (Bowker 1977; Hawkins and Alpert 1989: chs. 7,8; Irwin and Cressey 1962). If prisons in some sense are becoming easier in relation to prison conditions of the past and to probation, experienced offenders should be more aware of these changes and should be inclined to introduce them into their calculations of sanction costs.

Factors not tied directly to offending or to experience with the justice system also may affect how offenders weigh sanctions. For example, it may be inferred from both social control theory (Hirschi 1969; Krohn 1990: 301–305) and the "underclass" argument (Jencks and Peterson 1991; Wilson 1987, 1991) that social and economic distance from conventional society may affect how offenders judge the relative punitiveness of probation and of prison.

Social control theory generally holds that weaker involvement in conventional social institutions translates into a greater likelihood of law violation. By extension, persons with weak ties to conventional institutions such as marriage and education might be more likely to reject the state's utilitarian hierarchy of punishment severity and to regard prison as a much less devastating personal experience than penal codes presume.

A similar inference emerges from the "underclass" thesis. Wilson (1987) argues that inner-city persons, especially members of minorities, have become increasingly disadvantaged as their environment has changed economically and technologically. Structural changes weaken both their families (Sampson

1987) and their labor force attachment; these circumstances exacerbate and promote economic marginality. Such changes also undermine the commitment of inner-city dwellers to conventional standards of law and commerce. As a result, they frequently turn to crime and drug sales (Sullivan 1989; Taylor 1990). If marginality results in limited access to and support of middle-class standards among underclass persons, it also may lead to a rejection of the conventional middle-class assumption that even a long probation is less severe than a year in prison.

Inner-city African-Americans are a specific focus in the underclass literature. As a group they are uniquely subject to the disadvantageous conditions caused by structural changes. Perhaps not surprisingly, this minority is incarcerated at a higher rate than other ethnic groups (Christianson 1991; Krisberg et al. 1987) and has constituted a steadily increasing proportion of prison populations for 50 years (Greenfeld and Langan 1987).

Some research suggests that African-Americans, once incarcerated, may adjust to prison more easily than other groups (Carroll 1982; Johnson 1976). Some observers offer a possible explanation for this differential pattern of adjustment: because so many of these inner-city males are imprisoned, they routinely find friends and even relatives already in prison who can provide information, protection, and material goods (Jacobs 1974; Rettig, Torres, and Garrett 1977).

A more fundamental explanation for racial differences in adjustment to prison is that the ghetto experience makes the potential violence and deprivation of a prison term seem less threatening to African-Americans (Carroll 1982; Johnson 1976). Because the ghettos from which many African-Americans come are often unpredictable and threatening environments, they learn to emphasize self-protection and to develop physical and psychological toughness. This toughness protects African-American prisoners and enables them to dominate others behind bars, especially whites. It is suggested that whites are targeted both because they often lack toughness and because they represent the society responsible for the disadvantages African-Americans have experienced (Carroll 1982; Lockwood 1980). This last argument, however, has not been supported consistently by research (Goodstein and McKenzie 1984). Wright (1989), for example, found that prison adjustment among African-Americans was related more strongly to economic marginality than to race.

Though Hispanics also may be affected by the underclass phenomenon (Tienda 1989), less research has concentrated on Hispanics' prison adjustment or perceptions of sanctions. Wright (1989), however, cites research suggesting that Hispanics, like whites, are less able than African-Americans to withstand the stress of incarceration. Though the available evidence is mixed and incomplete, it suggests that race and ethnicity may influence how offenders view the relative costs or punitiveness of criminal sanctions.

Finally, the broad reforms that have altered correctional practices and institutions over the past two decades (see Crouch and Marquart 1989; Jacobs 1977) also should affect offenders' perceptions of sanctions. In Texas, reforms clearly altered both prison and probation experiences. A survey of Texas prisoners in 1987 (Crouch and Marquart 1990) revealed that the litigated reform process made the state's prisons much less threatening than they had been in the late 1970s and early 1980s, expanded prisoners' rights, and reduced privations. At the same time, early release policies had to be instigated to meet court and legislative limits on crowding; the result was a reduction in actual time served.

While prison time was becoming easier in many respects, correlated changes in probation were making community sanctions more onerous across the state. As a result of diversion programs rapidly developed to limit prison crowding, many offenders who would once have gone to prison remained in the community, typically under very close supervision.

Little is known about offenders' perceptions of the relative costs of prison and probation and about how these perceptions may vary. It is also unclear how the factors identified above contribute to this variation. Consequently this analysis addresses two questions: 1) How do felons today perceive the relative punitiveness of prison and of probation? 2) What accounts for variations in perception among offenders?

METHODS

Sample and Data Collection

The research reported here draws on a survey of 1,027 male[2] felons in Texas interviewed between mid-September and mid-December 1988. The respondents represent approximately a 10 percent random sample of all offenders sentenced to incarceration during this period. All interviews were conducted at the state prison's reception center, which processes all newly committed male prisoners. During the two days prisoners typically spend at this center, officials collect information on prisoners for classification and final assignment to a prison unit.

Each evening during the data collection phase, the lead interviewer drew a random sample of 15 names from the 150 to 175 prisoners who had just completed their second day of processing and would depart the next day for a prison unit. The interview team learned quickly that only about 11 or 12 interviews could be completed in an evening. A few more names were drawn daily, however, in case of refusals. Only 36 prisoners refused to be interviewed, and records maintained by the research team revealed no resultant sample bias. The final sample was representative of the population of felons sentenced to prison in Texas in 1988. The percentages of the sample and of the prison population were respectively white, 36 and 35; African-American, 41 and 43; Hispanic, 22 and 21.

A team of six well-trained criminal justice graduate students from Sam Houston State University conducted all interviews.[3] Interviewers began the lengthy instrument after each respondent signed an informed consent form explaining that he would receive no payment, that all information given would be confidential, and that he could stop the interview with impunity at any time. All interviews were conducted in the reception center's visiting room, where

---

[2]Only male prisoners were interviewed in this study. Although females constitute less than 10 percent of the prison population, their presence in this research would have been valuable. Unfortunately, however, female prisoners are processed into the prison system at a site 175 miles away, and funds were not available to conduct research at both reception centers.

[3]The interview team included a native Spanish speaker who used, as required, a Spanish-language version of the interview schedule.

interviewers and respondents were separated by a mesh screen (a standard security measure in Texas prisons). The setting was not crowded; thus respondents had enough distance from each other and from the lone security officer to
facilitate a comfortable interview and to maintain confidentiality. Interviewers
asked each question and recorded answers on the interview schedule, probing
as required. Because the larger study from which these data come involved extensive information on drug use and criminality, the interviews often lasted between one and 1½ hours. So that the research would not conflict with normal
activities in the reception center, all interviews took place after 5:30 PM, and virtually all were completed in one sitting.

Most of the data used in the analysis are self-reported. Some basic information obtained from respondents (e.g., age, race, offense) could have been verified through official records. Most of the information, however, could not be
verified, either because that information is not maintained by prison officials or
because much of the information which officials maintain and which is critical
to this project came initially from prisoners' self-reports.

The Dependent Variable

Respondents cannot be asked to state a preference for prison or probation in
the abstract. At the same time, there is an almost unlimited number of dis-
crete prison and probation terms that respondents can be asked to weigh.
Thus we developed a prison preference index, the dependent variable for this
study.

In the survey, respondents were presented with 11 pairs of hypothetical
criminal sanctions; each pair contained a specific probation term and a specific
prison term. These pairs of sanctions, presented as years on probation versus
years in prison, were 10 versus 1, 5 versus 1, 3 versus 1, 10 versus 2, 5 versus
2, 3 versus 2, 10 versus 3, 5 versus 3, 10 versus 4, 5 versus 4, 10 versus 5. In each
pair, respondents were asked to indicate which sanction they would prefer to
face personally.

Although the specific sanctions included in these pairs appear to be arbitrary gradations of sentences, several pairs reflect realistic possibilities in the
Texas justice system from the late 1980s to the present. Because of limits on
prison bed space, Texas offenders typically spend only about one calendar year
in prison for each 10 years of their sentence. Thus, because the common prison
sentences of 10, 15, and 20 years actually result in only about one, two, or
three years behind bars, and because the most severe probation sentence in
Texas is 10 years, the pairs of sanctions involving 10 years of probation and
one, two, or even three years of prison reflect actual possibilities. We included
other pairs, though less realistic in this sense, to ensure adequate variance in
responses.

The final index was determined both empirically and logically. We ranked
the pairs according to the proportion of respondents choosing prison over probation. For six of the 11 pairs, the proportion choosing prison was less than 16
percent. For the remaining five pairs, however, the proportion choosing prison
ranged from 66 percent (10 vs. 1) to 25 percent (10 vs. 3). These five pairs also
seemed to be logical choices in that they reflect most closely the actual sanctions

that offenders might face in Texas, as noted above. For these reasons we included only five of the 11 pairs of sanctions in the final index.[4]

The following pairs of sanctions were included in the final index: 10 years' probation[5] versus one full year in prison,[6] five years' probation versus one year in prison, 10 years' probation versus two years in prison, three years' probation versus one year in prison, and 10 years' probation versus three years in prison. Probation choices were scored 0; prison choices, 1. I summed choices across the pairs to create the dependent variable. Scores on the preference index ranged from 0 (preferred probation regardless of prison options) to 5 (preferred prison regardless of probation options). See Table 3.1. I did not weigh choices in creating index scores.

Preliminary analysis revealed marked consistency in patterns of choice: respondents who preferred one year in prison when the option was only three years' probation (3 vs. 1) virtually always also chose one year in prison when the options were 10 versus 1 and 5 versus 1. This consistency suggests that an additive variable adequately measures the strength of preference for prison.[7] Constructed in this way, intercorrelations ranging from .76 to .87 between the index and each pair also indicate considerable index validity.

The present analysis is not intended to discover the precise point at which offenders choose one sanction over another, nor does it aim at a fine-grained psychological mapping of attitudes toward particular punishments. In view of the limited amount of research devoted to offenders' perceptions of probation

---

[4]To ensure that restriction of the prison preference index to five pairs of sanctions did not obscure some extreme patterns of choice or orientations of respondents, I regressed an index using all 11 pairs on the model examined here. Results (not reported) did not differ from those based on the five-pair index reported in this paper; signs and statistical significance patterns were virtually the same. Clearly, using the restricted index does not introduce bias into the results. At the same time, results are based on offenders' responses only to relatively realistic options.

I also explored another approach to the dependent variable, using two measures of preference for prison instead of the one reported here. The two measures were defined by dividing the five-item prison preference index into two separate indexes. The first of these indexes included those pairs of items in which a 10-year probation term was constant and was contrasted with prison terms of first one, then two, then three years. The second index contained pairs in which the prison term was constant at one year and was contrasted with probation terms of first 10, then five, then three years. The purpose of examining two separate indexes was to assess the possibility that variations in terms may carry different meanings. That is, preferences for prison might take one pattern when the prison option is always a single year of incarceration and quite another when the prison term rises in relation to a constant probation term. Analysis showed that when these two different indexes were regressed on the model, results were very similar to those reported for the five-item prison preference index, but in several instances somewhat weaker. To maximize reliability and to simplify discussion, I used the five-item index in this analysis.

[5]I made no distinction between intensive supervision and regular probation.

[6]Interviews made clear that the year in prison was a full calendar year, not a one-year sentence reduced (as it frequently is) by parole.

[7]Though questions also were asked about perceptions of the justice system, these appeared in the instrument after the pairs of sanctions. Thus, the questions about changes in the justice system did not color responses regarding preference of sanction.

Table 3.1
Coding of Variables

Prison Preference Index

In each of the five pairs of sanctions, probation choice = 0 and prison choice = 1. Index scores are determined by adding across choices; they range from 0 (never preferred prison) to 5 (always preferred prison).

Demographic Variables

Three race/ethnicity variables: 0 = other, 1 = African-American; 0 = other, 1 = Hispanic; 0 = other, 1 = white
Age: Actual age of respondent
Marital status: 0 = not married; 1 = married when locked up

Economic Marginality Variables

Occupational status: 0 = not working; 1 = working full-time
Education: 1 = 11 years or fewer; 2 = 12 years; 3 = 12 years or more

Criminal Experience Variables

Age at first arrest: 1 = 13 or under; 2 = 14 to 16; 3 = 17 to 18; 4 = over 18
Self-reported criminal offenses: 1 = fewer than 5 offenses; 2 = 5 to 10; 3 = 11 to 20; 4 = 21 to 75; 5 = more than 75
Number of times in state prison: Self-reported

Present Sentence Variables

"Aggravated" sentence: 0 = no; 1 = yes
Current sentence: actual length of sentence

Perceptions of Key Elements of the System

Are "Texas offenders more likely to choose prison over probation today than in the early 1980s?" 0 = no; 1 = yes
"Probation has gotten much stricter." 4 = strongly agree; 3 = agree; 2 = disagree; 1 = strongly disagree

versus prison, the objective here is more modest: I wish to assess the extent of preferences for prison and then to ascertain the relationships between those preferences and relevant variables from existing theory and research. The dependent variable employed here seems appropriate to these tasks.

Other Variables

From the review of factors that may shape offenders' perceptions of criminal sanctions, I developed a number of variables. These variables, which constitute the model examined in this analysis, fall into five categories: demographics, economic marginality, involvement with crime and the justice system, nature of the present sentence, and perceptions of change in the justice system.

Demographic variables. These include race/ethnicity, age, and marital status before this incarceration. Because some research shows that some minorities may experience prison differently (Carroll 1982; Johnson 1976), I hypothesize that African-American offenders would choose prison more often than would other subgroups.

Two other demographic variables are age and marital status. Age is included as a measure of life experience and maturity. Here I assume that being older would be associated with a preference for probation. First, older offenders tend to mature out of crime, in part because of the personal costs of prison for them (Shover 1985). In addition, older offenders may wish to avoid an environment dominated by younger and often aggressive offenders (Alston 1986:218; Shover 1985). Marital status is taken as indicating not only ties to conventionality but also a reason to stay in the community on probation rather than opting for the isolation of prison. Being married should be related to a preference for probation.

Economic marginality. Because detailed data on economic marginality are lacking in this study, I rely on educational and occupational status before incarceration (Wright 1989). Offenders with less education and those who were not working full-time are assumed to be more marginal. As indicators of underclass status, being poorly educated and lacking regular, legal employment should correspond to lower stakes in conformity. I hypothesize that marginality is associated with a greater likelihood of preferring prison.

Involvement with crime and the justice system. The hypothesis here is that greater experience with the justice system and with criminality will be associated positively with a preference for prison. Variables designed to measure involvement in crime are age at first arrest and prior incarcerations. An early beginning to a criminal career has been shown to predict a serious career in crime (Wolfgang, Thornberry, and Figlio 1987: ch. 5). Two additional indicators of involvement in the justice system are the number of times on probation and the number of times incarcerated in a state prison. I expect that as these formal exposures to the justice system increase, so will a tendency to prefer prison.

The final indicator of involvement in criminality is the amount of crime in which the respondent has engaged. The amount of personal crime is measured by self-reports of the number of times respondents committed (regardless of arrest) an array of crimes including breaking into a building or car to steal something, stealing without breaking and entering, using a weapon to get something desired, and physically hurting someone on purpose. I hypothesize that offenders with greater experience in crime will be more likely to prefer prison than will those with less crime experience.

Present sentence. These variables include the actual length of sentence and whether the respondent received an "aggravated" sentence. In Texas, an aggravated sentence requires an offender to serve one-fourth (by the calendar) of the assessed sentence before becoming eligible for parole consideration. I included these two variables to control for the possibility that the conditions of the sentence facing the respondent at the time of the interview could affect the choices of sanction.

Perceptions of change in the Justice System. These perceptions are assessed by two questions: "Do you think Texas offenders are more likely to choose prison over probation today than in the early 1980s?" and "Has probation gotten much stricter in recent years?" In both questions, respondents weigh changes in prison and probation and state their own perceptions of current sanctions. The hypothesis here is that the greater the belief in changes in aspects of the correctional system (more people choosing prison; probation stricter), the greater the likelihood that respondents will indicate a preference for prison. A respondent need not have been on probation to have an opinion on its relative costs.

The model also includes two interaction terms involving race/ethnicity and crime involvement. These terms are included because prior research leaves unclear whether the experience of growing up African-American (or Hispanic) affects perceptions of prison or whether only minority males with long crime histories seem to adjust more easily to the prospect of prison. These interaction terms control statistically for the impact of crime experience combined with race, and thus allow the impact of race/ethnicity to emerge, net of crime experience.

Analysis

Ordinary least squares (OLS) regression is used here. Although respondents' choices in each pair yielded dichotomous data, the dependent variable is not dichotomous. Because the dependent variable is determined by summing responses across all five choices in the index, OLS is the appropriate technique. OLS regression permits us to assess the effects of each independent variable on responses regarding sanction preference while simultaneously holding constant the effect of other independent variables.

Limitations of the Research

Several qualifications should be noted in interpreting these findings. First, because the respondents' choices did not translate into a sanction they actually had experienced, the approach used here is artificial. Second, in a related vein, the fact that the respondents already were in prison when interviewed could have prompted them to choose prison more readily. There is no reason to expect, however, that the reality of incarceration affected respondents differentially or affected results significantly. Third, although statements regarding choices between prison and probation appear throughout the following discussion, this fact is not intended to convey categorical preference. That is, respondents weighed specific prison and probation terms rather than correctional alternatives in the abstract. Moreover, the prison terms in the choices were relatively short—never more than three years. Nonetheless, as indicated above, several of the choices approximate true alternatives that offenders in Texas and other states might face. Fourth, the research was conducted in only one state; thus the generalizability of findings to other offenders and other correctional systems is uncertain. Yet the diversity of crimes and ethnic groups in Texas, as well as the size of the state, argue that insights developed from offenders in Texas might well be paralleled in other states. Finally, although Texas offers much qualitative evidence that offenders' perceptions of prison and probation have been altered markedly by recent correctional reforms, no data are available on perceptions of sanctions before the reforms. Consequently the significance of the reforms for offenders' perceptions cannot be demonstrated directly here.

RESULTS

The first question addressed here concerns the extent to which offenders might prefer prison when asked to choose between various prison and probation terms. The responses (see Table 3.2) demonstrate clearly that prison is a relatively attractive option for many offenders: two-thirds of the respondents would choose one year in prison over 10 years on probation. Almost half still would opt for prison when the probation term is reduced to five years, and nearly one-third persist in preferring prison even when the alternatives are a seemingly light three years on probation and one year in prison. Even when the prison term rises to three full years against 10 on probation, one-quarter of the sample would choose prison. Thus it is evident that many Texas offenders would choose prison over probation, which society typically defines as less punitive.

In an attempt to explain these patterns, I regressed preferences on a number of variables drawn from theory and prior research. Table 3.3 presents the results of zero-order correlations among the index and the variables used in the model; Table 3.4 displays the multivariate results.

Respondent's age is also significant; being older predicts a preference for prison. This finding is contrary to expectations. A positive association between age and a preference for prison may reflect older offenders' desire to be cared for by a prison system which, through court order, recently has become more sensitive to prisoners' needs. Perhaps such offenders also have little community or family support; thus a few years in prison may be preferable, particularly if prison is no longer reputed to be so dangerous or so demanding.

Marital status, the final demographic variable, has a significant negative effect on preference for prison, as expected. Married men opt for probation, whereas unmarried men tend to choose prison. Being married seems to reflect both social and personal support in the community, which the isolation of prison threatens. Apparently the presence of a wife, who can offer at least some stability to a life frequently disrupted by brushes with the law, makes men wish to avoid prison.

Table 3.2
Offenders' Choices among Prison and Probation Terms

Choice of Sanction	Percentage Choosing Prison
1. 10 years probation 1 year prison	66
2. 5 years probation 1 year prison	49
3. 10 years probation 2 years prison	40
4. 3 years probation 1 year prison	32
5. 10 years probation 3 years prison	25

Table 3.3
Zero-Order Correlation Matrix

	Index	Afroamer	Hispanic	White	Age	Married	Educatn	Working	Probatn	Prisons	Agearr	Totcrime	Sentence	Aggsent	Probtuff	Otbrsprf	Afrinter	Hisinter
index|	1.0000																	
afroamer|	0.0489*	1.0000																
hispanic|	-0.0558*	-0.4440*	1.0000															
white|	-0.0045*	-0.6695*	-0.3683*	1.0000														
age|	0.1454*	-0.0368	-0.0158	0.0513*	1.0000													
married|	-0.0751*	0.0083	0.0661*	-0.0634*	0.0838*	1.0000												
educatn|	-0.0162	0.0756*	-0.1227*	0.0234	0.1514*	-0.0103	1.0000											
working|	-0.0400	-0.1156*	0.0396	0.0871*	0.0149	0.1202*	0.0294	1.0000										
probatn|	-0.0299	-0.0017*	-0.0103	0.0104	0.0216	-0.0410	-0.0040	-0.0367	1.0000									
prisons|	0.1646*	0.0353	-0.1009*	0.0471	0.2412*	-0.0402	0.0175	-0.0858*	0.0333	1.0000								
agearr|	-0.0365	0.1040*	0.0133	-0.1189*	0.2074*	0.0531*	0.1553*	0.0918*	-0.0392	-0.1810*	1.0000							
totcrime|	0.0763	-0.1098*	-0.0516*	0.1568*	-0.1638*	0.0046	-0.0674*	-0.0885*	0.0048	0.2512*	-0.4506	1.0000						
sentence|	0.1103*	0.0144	-0.0445	0.0219	0.0727*	0.0746*	-0.0277	-0.0034	-0.0431*	0.2014*	0.0394	0.1018*	1.0000					
aggsent|	0.0448	-0.0473	0.0756*	-0.0136	0.0529	0.0220	-0.0505	0.0578	-0.0358	-0.0667*	-0.0089	-0.0433	0.2952*	1.0000				
probtuff|	-0.0896*	0.0139	0.0416	-0.0489	0.0966*	-0.0101	-0.0487	-0.0409	-0.0028	0.0602*	0.0130	-0.0127	0.0219	-0.0062	1.0000			
othrsprf|	0.1921*	-0.0215	-0.0355	0.0517	-0.0634*	-0.0155	0.1079*	0.0281	0.0416	-0.0686*	0.0223	0.0752*	-0.0128	-0.0139	-0.1158	1.0000		
afrinter|	0.0484*	0.8100*	-0.3597*	-0.5423*	-0.0669*	0.0216	0.0481	-0.1287	-0.0109	0.1136*	0.0692*	0.3113*	0.0533	-0.0533	-0.0481	0.0274	1.0000	
hisinter|	-0.0268	-0.3865*	0.8704*	-0.3206*	-0.0629*	0.0498	-0.1287*	0.0179	0.0092	-0.0433	-0.1009	0.1669*	-0.0259	0.0622	0.0388	-0.0074	-0.3130*	1.0000

*Significant at or beyond .05.

AGGARR = age 1st arrest; TOTCRIME = crime involvement; PROBATN = times on probation; PRISONS = times in prison; SENTENCE = sentence length; AGGSENT = aggravated sentence; PROBTUFF = probation tougher; OTHRSPRF = others are preferring prison; AFRINTER and HISINTER = interaction terms

Table 3.4
Coefficients for Regression of Prison Preference Index on Selected
Independent Variables (Standard errors)

	Prison Preference Index	
Demographics		
Afroamer (a)	.784**	(.356)
Hispanic (a)	.204	(.437)
Age	.040***	(.009)
Married	−.361**	(.145)
Economic Marginality		
Education	−.163	(.105)
Working	−.071	(.136)
Crime Experience		
Age first arrest	−.039	(.064)
Prior Probations	−.025	(.017)
Prior Prisons	.176***	(.064)
Total crime	.145*	(.081)
Present Sentence		
Sentence Yrs.	.009*	(.005)
Aggravated	.193	(.234)
Justice System Views		
Probation tougher	.271**	(.110)
Others prefer prison	.424***	(.072)
Interaction Terms		
Af. Amer. x crime	−.161*	(.098)
Hisp. Amer x crime	−.051	(.125)

NOTE: (a) Reference category is white.

Adjusted R square = .101

*p < .10   **p < .05   ***p < .01

I found only limited support, however, for the hypothesis that economic marginality is related positively to a preference for prison. I expected that full-time employment would give offenders a preference for a sanction that would let them remain in the community and allow them to avoid the disruption of prison. The results, however, show that although the sign is in the expected direction, working full-time does not significantly affect choice of sanction. One reason may be that for most of these men, full-time employment is often menial and short-term (Parker and Horwitz 1986:796). Thus even full-time jobs may not be sufficiently rewarding to affect offenders' choice of sanctions. Similar results obtain for the education variable. A higher level of education was taken to reflect a nonunderclass background and a desire to avoid not only the disruption but the stigma of prison. The analysis reveals that higher education is in the hypothesized direction, but the relationship is not statistically significant.

The third set of variables in the model measures commitment to criminality and experience with the justice system. Four variables—age at first arrest, prior probations, prior incarcerations, and the amount of crime reported by the respondent—were expected to give greater exposure to the street crime and to the personal cost of legal consequences today. Table 3.4 reveals that although age at first arrest is not related significantly to perceptions of sanctions, the total amount of crime reported by the offender is in the hypothesized direction and nears statistical significance ($p < .10$).

I found only partial support for the hypothesis that exposure to formal sanctions would be associated with a preference for prison. As expected, net of other effects, the frequency of incarceration in the past is associated positively and significantly with preferring prison to probation. Yet in the case of probation experience, although the sign surprisingly somewhat is negative (those most often on probation in the past tend to prefer it), the empirical relationship is not significant.

Interaction terms linking race/ethnicity with criminal involvement were included in the model to determine whether minority status combines with extensive criminality to affect perceptions. Theoretically the interaction terms reflect minority "heavies," offenders with a high frequency of crime commission. The analysis explores the possibility that a high percentage of minority heavy offenders might explain African-Americans' general preference for prison over probation. This possibility is reasonable because active African-American offenders may be more likely to be sent to prison, more familiar with what prison may hold in store, and more apt to find "homies" there (Jacobs 1974; also see Davidson 1974; Rettig 1977). Such circumstances would seem to make prison less threatening. Analysis reveals somewhat surprising results, however. First, the signs for both interaction terms are unexpectedly negative, and one interaction—African American by total crime—approaches statistical significance ($p < .10$). The negative sign hints at the intriguing possibility that because these offenders are heavies, they realize that their street activities are attractive and cannot be pursued as well in prison. Though prison is an expected occupational hazard for which they may be prepared, still it is an inconvenience to be avoided, and thus would not be preferred. This point is consistent with Irwin and Cressey's (1962) characterization of the "thief," but it is speculative. The important consideration is that even after controlling for crime involvement, the African-American status variable remains significant. This finding underscores the importance of racial status alone to perceptions of sanctions.

A fourth set of variables in the model involves characteristics of respondents' present sentence. These variables control for situational effects. Although all respondents already are in prison, nonetheless it seems reasonable that if respondents were beginning an "aggravated" or especially long sentence at the time of the interview, they might tend to choose probation. The results are mixed. Having an aggravated sentence has no effect on the choices examined here, but sentence length approaches significance ($p = .06$); respondents with longer sentences tend to prefer prison. Note, however, that although the coefficient is significant, it is relatively small. Therefore it appears that the attributes of respondents' sentences have a limited impact on choice.

The final set of variables in the model taps current offenders' perceptions of the Texas justice system and how offenders might react to it. The first variable, agreement that "probation has gotten much stricter in recent years," is associated positively and significantly with choice of sanction. The second, agreement with the question "Do you think Texas offenders are more likely to choose prison over probation today than in the early 1980s?," has an even more powerful effect on the dependent variable. The belief that other offenders are opting increasingly for prison apparently affects respondents' preferences for prison. This finding points not only to the impact of beliefs about others' sanction preferences, but also to the consequences of a widespread belief that choosing prison over probation is a wise and rational move in view of changes in the correctional system.

DISCUSSION

David Garland (1991) recently drew attention to the importance of the sociology (as opposed to the philosophy) of punishment. He states: "Properly done, the sociology of punishment should inform us about the social forces that condition penal processes and the various social consequences that these processes in turn produce" (Garland 1991:120). The analysis presented here contributes to a sociology of punishment by exploring how offenders judge the relative personal costs of probation and of prison.

In addition to demonstrating a frequent preference for prison, the analysis reveals offender characteristics that shape these preferences. Characteristics reflecting lifestyle, life course, or street experience are particularly important. That is, a preference for prison is more likely among offenders who are African-American, older, unmarried, and widely exposed to crime and institutional corrections, and who share beliefs that probation has grown stricter and that other offenders now prefer prison to probation.

Theoretically, these findings suggest that choosing prison may be related to offender characteristics that result in a relatively low personal cost for going to prison, at least for the terms examined here. If one has few ties either to the community or to the dominant conventionality, one has little to lose by being incarcerated. Older and unmarried men, for example, may risk few relationships by going to prison; in addition, prison offers a rather structured environment.

At the same time, the better-educated offenders tend to prefer probation, a pattern consistent with the notion of personal cost. Persons with more education presumably are more likely to be at risk of losing not only the time they spend in prison but their reputation and status as well. Remaining in the community on probation, where work and family can be maintained, permits a convicted felon to salvage more of a life than does going to prison.

Prison also is preferred by those who already are largely committed to a deviant lifestyle, with its attendant trips to jail and prison. For persons deeply involved "in the life," prison carried only the inconvenience of the sentence, not the added loss of reputation. Indeed, going to prison may even be a badge of honor for some offenders (Petersilia 1990:24). Moreover, as noted above, these would be the very persons to know that today's prisons are less like the isolated plantations or the forgotten warehouses of the past.

In addition, offenders with little to lose should be the most likely to learn through jail and street experience about the system designed to control them.

The analysis showed that the presence of shared beliefs about the relative punitiveness of probation and incarceration is a strong predictor of a preference for prison. Community jails are places where these beliefs are shared. Jails routinely bring together experienced offenders, novices, and a full range of the community's "rabble" (Irwin 1985), who share information about crime and its current consequences. With the spread of the notion that prison is not as bad as probation and may not last as long as in the past, more offenders may wish to avoid probation and to opt for prison, if possible.

Finally, the analysis underscores the significance of race and ethnicity in understanding how offenders relate to the experience of incarceration. Results support the position that being African-American, as a proxy for a broad cultural experience, is singularly important in shaping offenders' views of sanctions (Carroll 1982; Johnson 1976). The significance of race is not weakened by economic marginality, as some research suggests (Wright 1989), or by criminal involvement. Possibly African-Americans tend strongly to feel that they will be subjected proportionately to harassment under strict probation supervision. Under such circumstances, prison may seem more attractive than the pressures of close supervision on probation. Indeed, many African-American offenders feel that because they are incarcerated so frequently, a probation term soon will lead anyway to revocation and a prison term. Thus, with little to lose but the hassles of probation, prison may be the lesser of two evils for many African-American offenders.

The model examined here certainly does not explain sanction preferences. Indeed, it accounts for only 10 percent of the variation in preferences. This finding is a clear indication that factors not included in the model are important. This research, however, sought primarily to determine the significance of variables that literature suggests are theoretically relevant rather than to maximize the percentage of variance explained. The results reflect the contribution of theoretically derived variables; at the same time, they point to a need for additional research on how these and other variables may affect offenders' perceptions of sanctions.

CONCLUSION

The present research bears on the assumption that offenders rather consistently will define prison as more punitive than probation. In view of the public's tendency to regard incarceration as the only means of "getting tough" on crime (Petersilia 1990; Sherman and Hawkins 1981; Zimring and Hawkins 1991), this assumption largely accounts for the importance of incarceration in America's response to crime. As a corollary, citizens often are ambivalent about probation; they believe it allows offenders to avoid the presumed punitive and deterrent effects of prison. This public orientation also prompts resistance to the early release of prisoners and to other diversion programs used by state officials to relieve prison crowding. The present analysis, however, suggests that this assumption is frequently not met among offenders. Results show that many offenders define common prison terms as less punitive than even three or five years on probation. At least in part, this situation inverts the penal code's hierarchy of sanctions thought to control crime.

When this occurs, a fundamental irony emerges in our justice system. That is, the lawbreakers whom middle-class citizens are most likely to fear and want most to be locked away—members of minorities with limited ties to conventionality (see Anderson 1990), the disaffected, the disadvantaged, and the deviant in general—tend to be the very offenders who view prison terms of even two or three years as easier than probation and as preferable. To the extent that these views among offenders are widespread, the contemporary demand for extensive incarceration (but often for limited terms) may foster two unwanted outcomes: less deterrence and more prisoners.

It would be inappropriate to conclude that offenders view prison as pleasant; most probably would try to avoid a truly long stay. Nonetheless, the patterns of perceptions reported here suggest a need to rethink how sanctions affect those for whom they are designed. If offenders often regard probation as more difficult and more burdensome than the prison terms that many actually will face, citizens and legislators might be less inclined to view nonprison sanctions as barely acceptable options to be used only sparingly when prison beds cannot be found.

The results of this study thus encourage efforts to explore nonprison sanctions (Morris and Tonry 1990). If offenders often define probation to be as "tough" as prison, nonprison sanctions not only might meet public expectations (Petersilia 1990), but also might help to reduce the current staggering rate of imprisonment.

REFERENCES

Alston, L. (1986) *Crime and Older Americans.* Springfield, IL: Thomas.

Anderson, E. (1992) *Streetwise: Race, Class and Change in an Urban Community.* Chicago: University of Chicago Press.

Bowker, L. (1977) *Prison Subcultures.* Lexington, MA: Heath.

Bryan-College Station Eagle 1991, "Man Picks Prison over Probation" (March 24. A–1)

Carroll, L. (1982) "Race, Ethnicity and the Social Order of the Prison." In R. Johnson and H. Toch (eds.), *Pains of Imprisonment,* pp. 181–203. Beverly Hills: Sage.

Christianson, P. (1991) "Our Black Prisons." In K. Haas and G. Alpert (eds.), *The Dilemmas of Corrections: Contemporary Readings,* pp. 64–76. Prospect Heights, IL: Waveland.

Clear, T. and P. Hardyman (1990) "The New Intensive Supervision Movement." (*Crime & Delinquency*) 36:42–60.

Crouch, B. M. and J. Marquart (1989) *An Appeal to Justice: Litigated Reform of Texas Prisons.* Austin: University of Texas Press.

——(1990) "Resolving the Paradox of Reform: Litigation, Prisoner Violence and Perceptions of Risk." *Justice Quarterly* 7:103–24.

Davidson, T. (1974) *Chicano Prisoners: The Key to San Quentin.* New York: Holt, Rinehart and Winston.

Dillingham, S. (1991) *National Update.* Washington, DC: Bureau of Justice Statistics, Department of Justice.

Garland, D. (1991) "Sociological Perspectives on Punishment." In M. Tonry (ed.), *Crime and Justice: A Review of Research,* pp. 115–66. Chicago: University of Chicago Press.

Goodstein, L. and D. McKenzie (1984) "Racial Differences in Adjustment Patterns of Prison Inmates—Prisonization, Conflict, Stress and Control." In D. Georges-Abeyie (ed.), *The Criminal Justice System and Blacks,* pp. 271–306 New York: Clark Boardman.

Greenfeld, L. and P. Langan (1987) "Trends in Prison Populations." Paper presented at the National Conference on Punishment for Criminal Offenses, Ann Arbor.

Hamilton, V. L. and S. Rytina (1980) "Social Consensus on Norms of Justice: Should the Punishment Fit the Crime?" *American Journal of Sociology* 85:1117–44.

Hawkins, R. and G. Alpert (1989) *American Prison Systems: Punishment and Justice.* Englewood Cliffs, NJ: Prentice-Hall.

Hirschi, T. (1969) *Causes of Delinquency.* Berkeley: University of California Press.

Irwin, J. (1985) *The Jail.* Berkeley: University of California Press.

Irwin, J. and D. Cressey (1962) "Thieves, Convicts and the Inmate Culture. *Social Problems* 10:142–55.

Jacobs, J. (1974) "Street Gangs behind Bars." *Social Problems* 21:395–409.

_____ (1977) *Stateville: The Prison in Mass Society.* Chicago: University of Chicago Press.

_____ (1980) "The Prisoners' Rights Movement and Its Impacts 1960–1980." In N. Morris and M. Tonry (eds.), *Crime and Justice: An Annual Review of Research, Vol. 2,* pp. 429–70. Chicago: University of Chicago Press.

Jencks, C. and P. Peterson (1991) *The Urban Underclass.* Washington, DC: Brookings Institute.

Johnson, R. (1976) *Culture and Crisis in Confinement.* Lexington, MA: Lexington Books.

Krisberg, B., I. M. Swartz, G. Fishman, Z. Eisikovits, E. Guttman, and K. Joe. "The Incarceration of Minority Youth." *Crime and Delinquency* 33:173–205.

Krohn, M. (1990) "Control and Deterrence Theories." In J. Sheley (ed.), *Criminology: A Contemporary Handbook,* pp. 295–315. Belmont, CA: Wadsworth.

Lockwood, D. (1980) *Prison Sexual Violence.* New York: Elsevier.

Morris, N. and M. Tonry (1990) *Between Prison and Probation: Intermediate Punishments in a Rational Sentencing System.* New York: Oxford University Press.

Newman, G. (1978) *The Punishment Response.* New York: Lippincott.

Parker, N. and A. Horwitz (1986) "Unemployment, Crime and Imprisonment: A Panel Approach." *Criminology* 24:751–73.

Petersilia, J. (1990) "When Probation Becomes More Dreaded Than Prison." *Federal Probation* (March):23–27.

Rettig, R., M. Torres, and G. Garret (1977) *Many: A Criminal Addict's Story.* Boston: Houghton Mifflin.

Rossi, P., J. Simpson, and J. Miller (1985) "Beyond Crime Seriousness: Fitting the Punishment to the Crime," *Journal of Quantitative Criminology* 1:59–90.

Sampson, R. (1987) "Urban Black Violence: The Effect of Male Joblessness and Family Disruption." *American Journal of Sociology* 93:348–82.

Sherman, M. and G. Hawkins (1981) *Imprisonment in America: Choosing the Future.* Chicago: University of Chicago Press.

Shover, N. (1985) *Aging Criminals.* Beverly Hills: Sage.

Sullivan, M. (1989) *Getting Paid: Youth Crime and Work in the Inner City.* Ithaca: Cornell University Press.

Taylor, C. S. (1990) *The Dangerous Society.* East Lansing: Michigan State University Press.

Thomas, J. (1988) *Prisoner Litigation: The Paradox of the Jailhouse Lawyer.* Totowa, NJ: Rowan & Littlefield, Publishers.

Tienda, M. (1989) "Puerto Ricans and the Underclass Debate." *Annals of the American Academy of Political and Social Sciences* 501:105–19.

Wilson, W. J. (1987) *The Truly Disadvantaged: The Inner City, The Underclass and Public Policy.* Chicago: University of Chicago Press.

_____ (1991) "Studying Inner-City Social Dislocations: The Challenge of Public Agenda Research. *American Sociological Review* 56:1–14.

Wolfgang, M., T. Thornberry, and R. Figlio (1987) *From Boy to Man, from Delinquency to Crime.* Chicago: University of Chicago.

Wright, K. (1989) "Race and Economic Marginality in Explaining Prison Adjustment." *Journal of Research in Crime and Delinquency* 26:67–89.

Zimring, F. and G. Hawkins (1991) *The Scale of Imprisonment.* Chicago: University of Chicago Press.

CHAPTER 4

SELF-ESTEEM, DEPRESSION, AND ANXIETY EVIDENCED BY A PRISON INMATE SAMPLE: INTERRELATIONSHIPS AND CONSEQUENCES FOR PRISON PROGRAMMING

Thomas C. Castellano and Irina R. Soderstrom

Relatively little is known about the psychological characteristics of prison inmates and how recent imprisonment policies may affect those characteristics. This article examines levels of self-esteem, depression, and anxiety among a sample of prison inmates who recently completed or were enrolled in prerelease life skills courses. The data reveal these inmates to be a very depressed and anxious group with little self-esteem. Implications for further research and prison programming efforts are highlighted.

Inmate adjustment to the "pains of imprisonment" and the psychological distress evidenced by prison inmates is of paramount concern within the correctional literature. Compared to the mental and emotional states of members of the community at large, the psychopathology of inmates has long been acknowledged as being a "special problem" (Cormier, Kennedy, & Sendbuehler, 1967). A variety of perspectives have been used to explain the high level of distress and maladaptive behaviors exhibited within prison settings. Some have focused on the composition of the inmate population, and suggest that prison inmates tend to be those who experience general problems in living. High levels of psychological distress and maladaptive behaviors are not the result of the prison environment. Rather, they are attributable to the underlying psychological and social characteristics of most prison inmates. Other perspectives tend to locate the cause(s) of psychological distress and negative behaviors within the prison environment itself. The primary causative factor stems from the fact that

This article was originally presented at the annual meeting of the American Society of Criminology, Boston, MA, November 1995.

THE PRISON JOURNAL, Vol. 77 No. 3, September 1997 259–280 © 1997 Sage Publications, Inc.

inmates live in a community based on deprivation of liberty, while members of the community at large live in a community based on liberty and social responsibility. Maladaptive behaviors, psychological distress, and inmates who are changed for the worse are direct by-products of a brutalizing social institution.

Surprisingly, given the importance of the general topic, there is a relative paucity of correctional research that involves the systematic measurement of the mental and emotional states of inmates with standardized psychological inventories, and attempts to identify the correlates and causes of the measurement outcomes (see Adams, 1992, for a review). Especially lacking is research that examines fluctuations in these states as the inmate goes through various stages of the prison experience. For instance, only a few studies have indicated that various events during incarceration (e.g., being notified of upcoming release) actually serve as stressors that trigger or magnify maladjustments in inmates (Cormier et al., 1967; Renzema, 1988; Toch & Adams, 1989).

One such triggering event may be imminent release. In 1967, Cormier et al. discussed the notion of *gate fever,* a term that refers to the preliberation anxiety experienced by soon-to-be released inmates anticipating the sudden passage from imprisonment to freedom. Gate fever is characterized by irritability, anxiety, restlessness, and a variety of psychophysiological symptoms. The notion of gate fever was further supported in Renzema's (1988) study, which measured inmates' stress levels 1 month prior to release and at 1-, 3-, and 6-month intervals after release. The research indicated that the most stressful time for the inmate sample was the period before release from prison. Stress levels were found to decrease dramatically after release from prison, but were back on the increase by the third month out. By the sixth month of release, stress levels were approaching prerelease levels.

An understanding of the effects of the prison environment on offender psychological characteristics can provide useful information regarding the delivery and potential effects of programs implemented within that environment. For instance, if gate fever does exist, logical implications for prerelease programming result. Perhaps prerelease programming should address gate fever directly and attempt to ameliorate some of its symptomatology. These attempts may include attempts to deal with the offender's emotive state (e.g., stress, anxiety, and depression) so that interventions such as life skills training are more likely to have some impact. This concern was the genesis of this article, which derives from a large-scale process and impact evaluation of Illinois' PreStart program.

PreStart, an innovative structure for prerelease programming and postrelease offender assistance and supervision service delivery, was implemented in Illinois in July 1991. The PreStart program intended not to re-create the prerelease and parole supervision practices of the immediate past but to establish a novel structure and approach to inmate reintegration into the community. Illinois introduced a bifurcated system into its mandatory supervised release program. Radically different from most parole supervision structures, PreStart separated the surveillance and supervision functions of parole from integrative social service provision functions. After mandated specialized institutional preparation for release (termed Phase I programming)—which involves the delivery of 30 hours of life-skills-oriented programming—the vast majority of releases would be allowed to voluntarily use community resources brokered through a system of newly developed community service centers. The service centers were designed to be information and resource brokerage facilities, intended to promote the abilities of releases to develop and implement effective employment, residential living, and treatment plans. The focus of the plan was for "PreStart agents" (not "parole agents") to provide releasees with assistance on a voluntary basis in community service centers (not parole offices). Guns, badges, bullying, and threats of revocation for not playing by the rules (e.g., meeting regular reporting requirements) were to be replaced by community resource manuals, referral forms, and a helping hand. Aiding the majority of prison releasees (i.e., those not identified as community risks) in efforts to succeed in the community was to be done without reliance on traditional elements of parole supervision—coercion, active offender supervision, or mandated offender-agent contact. If releasees manifested "dangerous" behaviors, except in the most extreme cases, law enforcement agencies, not corrections officials, were to respond. This structure is premised on a model of the ex-convict as a volitional actor who is given the opportunity to make responsible choices—including the option of refusing assistance.

The research team felt that a desirable aspect of the process and impact evaluation of PreStart would be to characterize the prison environments in which Phase I programming was implemented and ascertain the mental and emotional states of the inmates participating in the prerelease phase of the program. Such an analysis would have implications for the underlying premise of the PreStart program—that the offender is a volitional actor who has the emotional and psychological strength to engage in rational and effective decision-making processes—and could lead to a more informed analysis of why PreStart did or did not have its desired effect on offender transitions to the community.

METHODOLOGY

In 1992 and 1993, attempts were made at each of 14 correctional facilities in Illinois to survey inmates who had completed at least half of the PreStart modules (a total of 10 were mandated) and who were scheduled to be released from the facility to mandatory supervision within 3 months. The goals of these attempts included (a) generating information to enhance an implementation analysis and (b) developing a sample of inmates to be tracked for at least 1 year in the community for purposes of conducting subsequent recidivism analyses.

Initially, up to 50 inmates were randomly selected from each facility based on predetermined eligibility criteria for inclusion within the study. Shortly thereafter, realizing that attrition was proving greater than expected, the target sample size was increased to 65 inmates from each facility, thus further assuring that a minimum of 50 completed questionnaires would be obtained from each facility. This also served to compensate for the relatively small number of residents at community correctional centers (CCCs) who met the predetermined eligibility requirements at any one point in time (on average about 15). Questionnaires were administered to the selected inmates in a group setting. Additionally, to increase response rates and the validity of the responses, attempts were made to preidentify the reading level of inmates and to administer the questionnaire to low-reading inmates in much smaller groups (one staff to one to three inmates). These attempts proved quite successful.

Table 4.1 details inmate response patterns from these visits by facility for 1992 and 1993. Facilities are identified by letters instead of their names. In 1992, a total of 659 inmates were targeted for survey purposes. Of the total,

Table 4.1
Response Rates by Facility

Facility	Year	Initial Subjects	Completed or Attempted	Refusal	Not Accessible	Ineligible	Missing	Effective Response Rate[a]
A	1992	73	47	19	3	3	1	71%
	1993	25	23	1	1	0	0	96%
B	1992	36	21	10	1	3	1	68%
	1993[b]	18	13	2	3	0	0	87%
C	1992	8	4	4	0	0	0	50%
	1993	9	9	0	0	0	0	100%
D	1992	86	49	13	19	2	4	80%
	1993	51	38	10	3	0	0	79%
E	1992	61	38	7	11	5	0	84%
	1993[c]	29	19	9	0	1	0	68%
F	1992	64	51	13	0	0	0	80%
	1993	64	37	24	3	0	0	61%
G	1992	56	39	15	3	0	0	74%
	1993	45	24	13	8	0	0	65%
H	1992	60	46	13	1	0	0	78%
	1993	61	47	14	0	0	0	77%
I	1992	45	42	0	2	0	1	100%
	1993	56	53	0	3	0	0	100%

Table 4.1
Continued

Facility	Year	Initial Subjects	Completed or Attempted	Refusal	Not Accessible	Ineligible	Missing	Effective Response Rate[a]
J	1992	61	22	24	7	8	0	48%
	1993	54	27	21	6	0	0	56%
K	1992	16	9	1	6	0	0	90%
	1993[b]	25	15	10	0	0	0	60%
L	1992	14	8	3	3	0	0	73%
	1993[b]	14	8	6	0	0	0	57%
M	1992	17	15	0	2	0	0	100%
	1993[b]	25	25	0	0	0	0	100%
N	1992	62	34	9	19	0	0	79%
	1993	60	45	8	5	2	0	85%
Total	1992	659	425	131	77	21	0	77%
	1993	536	383	118	32	3	7	76%

[a]The effective response rate is the number of people who agreed to participate divided by the number of those approached who were both eligible and accessible.

[b]At all community correctional centers, the initial subject value is based on the number of residents who attended the survey administration in response to an administrative request to do so. Thus, all eligible persons at the facility did not necessarily attend the survey administration.

[c]At facility E, 40 inmates from the preceding PreStart classes were solicited for the evaluation by institutional staff. Of these 40, 14 were present at the survey administration. These 14 plus the 15 from the current PreStart class constitute the 29 initial subjects.

77 (11.7%) were inaccessible for a variety of reasons and 21 (3.2%) did not meet inclusionary criteria. Of those targeted for inclusion in the study, 424 agreed to participate in the study (64.3%), 131 refused (19.8%), and 6 cannot be accounted for (0.9%). Responses from individuals who attempted to complete the questionnaire resulted in 410 fully usable survey questionnaires.

In 1993, 536 inmates were approached for survey purposes. A total of 383 (71.4%) agreed to complete the questionnaire, while 118 (22.0%) inmates refused participation, and 35 (6.5%) were either inaccessible (e.g., a superseding inmate assignment was in effect) or ineligible (e.g., inmate had not participated in PreStart yet). Of the 383 completed questionnaires, 2 were identified as being unusable. Survey efforts thus yielded 381 usable questionnaires. This article will focus on the results of the 1992 survey efforts.

Because of the voluntary nature of participation in the study, some nonresponse bias is expected. Evaluation team observations indicated that refusal rates were highest among the most alienated and hostile inmates, who also tended to be the youngest inmates. Accordingly, inmate responses discussed in this article will tend to overrepresent the views of individuals who are more likely to perceive their entire correctional experience in a positive light. The effective response rate (calculated by dividing the number of individuals who agreed to complete the questionnaire by all eligible inmates who personally heard the evaluation team's request for participation) was very high (76%) in both years. This suggests that biases found in the data cannot account for more than a small proportion of the variation in the findings reported. These response rates are considered to be very acceptable, and internal reliability and validity checks indicate that the data are of high quality. Whatever biases that exist are likely to be concentrated at the facility level because response rates varied across facilities.

Upon completion of the group-administered questionnaires, mass interviews were conducted with the inmate samples at each facility. Following a standard protocol, inmates were asked to discuss the strengths and weaknesses of PreStart programming, to assess perceived levels of staff and administration commitment to PreStart, to evaluate the quality of instruction, and to make recommendations for improved programming. Discussion was quite animated and telling, with sessions often lasting up to 1 hour. Comments varied but on the whole were quite positive. Also, there was a good deal of variation in inmate responses across facilities, which tended to parallel staff assessments and evaluative staff observations, and which suggested that even very alienated inmates sometimes agreed to participate in the study.

Sample

Table 4.2 presents some basic descriptive information on the inmates who responded to the survey in 1992 and 1993. Generally, the table indicates that the aggregate characteristics of both samples are quite comparable. The average age of the surveyed inmates is roughly 30, which is quite consistent with the average age of all inmates released from IDOC facilities between July and October of 1992 (29.28 years). The inmate samples contained a disproportionate number of females (21.6% in 1992, 23.6% in 1993) compared to their representation in the IDOC exit population (6.4%). Hispanics were also overrepresented in the

Table 4.2

Characteristics of Inmate Samples, by Year

Characteristic	*1992 (N = 425)*	*1993 (N = 381)*
Age		
Mean	29.99	30.87
Standard deviation	8.47	9.33
Race		
White	25.1%	28.6%
Black	54.2%	54.6%
Hispanic	12.7%	11.5%
Native American	3.3%	1.8%
Asian	0.9%	0.8%
Other	1.4%	0.5%
Missing	2.3%	2.1%
Jobs 6 months before prison		
Employed	52.6%	51.2%
Unemployed	45.5%	48.6%
Missing	1.9%	0.3%
Sex		
Male	73.5%	75.6%
Female	21.6%	23.6%
Missing	4.9%	0.8%
Level of education		
Elementary school	6.1%	7.3%
1–3 years high school (no GED)	32.6%	29.1%
1–3 years high school (GED)	24.2%	22.6%
High school graduate	15.5%	15.7%
1–3 years college	15.7%	21.0%
4+ years college	1.6%	3.1%
Missing	4.2%	1.0%
Job set up after release?		
No	44.4%	33.9%
Yes	29.6%	43.8%
Unsure	23.2%	21.5%
Missing	2.8%	0.8%
Place to live when released?		
No	4.2%	4.2%
Yes	87.8%	88.7%
Unsure	5.9%	6.8%
Missing	0.0%	0.3%

(continued)

Table 4.2
Continued

Characteristic	1992 (N = 425)	1993 (N = 381)
Drug use 6 months prior to prison		
No	39.9%	36.0%
Yes	55.6%	56.2%
Missing	4.5%	7.9%
Frequency of drug use		
Not applicable	36.9%	35.7%
Daily	6.2%	18.4%
Almost daily	15.7%	12.3%
Few times/week	15.5%	13.4%
Once a week	1.9%	1.6%
Few times/month	6.3%	7.1%
Once a month	1.2%	0.3%
Once/a few times	2.8%	2.1%
Missing	3.5%	9.2%
Percentage using		
Marijuana	39.2%	41.2%
Opiates	14.8%	14.2%
Cocaine	32.4%	29.7%
Hallucinogens	6.1%	6.3%
Crack		7.3%

NOTE: GED = General Equivalency Diploma

inmate samples (12.7% in 1992 and 11.5% in 1993 vs. 7.4% of the IDOC exits from July to October of 1992). Correspondingly, the sample underrepresents males (73.5% and 75.6% of the respective inmate samples vs. 93.6% of IDOC exits) and Blacks (54.2% and 54.6% vs. 62.5% of IDOC exits).

Inmates in the research samples also clearly represent a group of people exhibiting obvious educational needs. Only 32% of the 1992 inmates and 39.8% of the 1993 inmates achieved a level of education that at least included the completion of high school without reliance on a general equivalency diploma (GED). These figures parallel the percentage of inmates who graduated from high school among all IDOC inmates released from prison between July and October of 1992 (33.9%). Thus, the 1993 inmates seemed slightly better educated than the 1992 inmates, but both groups appear to have achieved similar levels of education as compared to the IDOC exit population. Employment needs were also high among the inmate samples—45.5% of the 1992 and 48.6% of the 1993 inmate samples were unemployed during the 6 months prior to be-

Table 4.3
Inmate Perceptions of Postrelease Problems

Source of Problem	1992		1993	
	Mean	SD	Mean	SD
Finding job	3.27	2.19	3.06	2.24
Medical/dental needs	2.53	2.07	2.57	1.97
Conditions of parole	1.67	1.45	1.67	1.54
Doing drugs	1.83	1.64	2.11	1.99
Place to live	1.72	1.65	1.90	1.79
Family conflict	1.83	1.60	2.08	1.81
Support family	3.50	2.39	3.41	2.25
Bad crowd	2.09	1.89	2.21	1.98
Labeled as ex-con	2.98	2.29	3.21	2.26
Not able to read/write	1.55	1.31	1.81	1.75
Drinking too much	1.71	1.59	1.86	1.85
Being a good parent	1.66	1.49	1.57	1.32
Getting legal help	2.23	1.90	2.29	1.86
Having someone to talk to	2.13	1.92	2.19	1.87
Enough money to start	3.68	2.52	3.55	2.43
Having a plan	1.98	1.52	2.32	1.83
Dealing with temper	2.46	1.87	2.53	2.12
Having good job skills	2.31	1.92	2.39	1.88
Going back to prison	2.27	2.06	2.50	2.29

ing incarcerated. Upon release, reintegrative needs prominently feature the acquisition of a job (only about 30% of the 1992 inmates and 44% of the 1993 inmates had jobs already lined up) and housing (with 10% of the inmates having indefinite or no residential plans).

The fundamental economic nature of reintegrative needs for most offenders is reaffirmed by the data presented in Table 4.3, which presents rankings of self-reported problem areas inmates expect to encounter upon release. The means are based on a scale of 1 to 5, with 1 representing *not a problem at all* and 5 representing *a very serious problem*. The table indicates that the primary concerns and need areas of soon-to-be-released inmates relate to jobs and money. A large percentage of the inmates also reported having used illegal drugs during the 6 months before their incarceration (55.6% and 56.2%, respectively), many of whom used drugs daily or multiple times per week (47.4% and 44.1%, respectively). Further, a significant percentage reported using highly addictive drugs such as cocaine (about 30%) and opiates (over 14%). Thus, it is surprising that the mean scores reported in Table 4.3 for "doing drugs" as a concern of inmates about to be released were relatively low (1.83 in 1992, 2.11 in 1993).

The portrait of these inmates is generally quite compatible with what is known about the characteristics of prison inmates nationwide, as well as within the state of Illinois. The willingness to report on histories of substance abuse (in numbers comparable to other surveys of prison inmates), a positive rapport that was often developed between the evaluation staff and the inmates, and the correspondence of the aggregate characteristics of the inmate samples with the population of IDOC exits are suggestive that these and the following self-reported data are both valid and fairly representative measures of IDOC inmate characteristics and attitudes.

Psychological Characteristics of the Sampled Inmates

To acquire a deeper understanding of the sampled inmates and to ascertain the level of gate fever, a number of standardized psychological inventories were administered to subsamples of the surveyed inmates. The 1992 inmate sample was administered the Coopersmith Self-Esteem Inventory (SEI), the State-Trait Anxiety Inventory (STAI), and the Center for Epidemiological Studies Depression Scale (CES-D). The 1993 inmate sample was administered only the latter scale. Accordingly, the balance of this article will focus on the 1992 sample. All of the inventories are self-administered paper-and-pencil instruments.

Self-esteem. The Coopersmith Self-Esteem Inventory was designed to measure self-evaluative attitudes regarding social, academic, family, and personal areas of experiences (Adair, 1984). The Adult Form, which consists of 25 items and has been found to be valid and reliable for a variety of ethnic groups and many special populations (Coopersmith, 1981), was administered to 285 inmates during the 1992 surveying effort.[1]

Mean scores on the SEI with "normal" populations have tended to range between 70 and 80, with a standard deviation between 11 and 13 (Coopersmith, 1981). In terms of a classificatory level of self-esteem, the upper quartile of scores can be thought of as representing high self-esteem, the lower quartile as representing low self-esteem, and the interquartile range as reflecting medium self-esteem. In the PreStart inmate population, the mean self-esteem score was 54.37 (*SD* = 13.9), well below the range of means typically found for "normal" populations. In fact, even those respondents who scored one standard deviation above the inmate population mean (approximately 68) were still below the "normal" range of means. Accordingly, the upper quartile (representing those with high self-esteem) contained scores of 63 to 100, the interquartile range (reflecting medium self-esteem) contained scores of 44 to 62, and the lower quartile (reflecting low self-esteem) contained scores of 20 to 43. The data were slightly positively skewed (.259), once again reflecting the tendency of the inmate self-esteem scores to be lower than those found in the "normal" populations from which the SEI was originally validated.

Anxiety. Spielberger developed the STAI, Form Y, for use by adults. It is a brief and objective self-reported measure of state and trait anxiety. Form Y of the STAI, which consists of 20 state anxiety and 20 trait anxiety items, has been normed on working adults, college students, high school students, and military recruits. Form Y of the STAI was administered to 280 inmates from the 1992 sample.[2]

In past applications of the STAI to collect norming data from samples experiencing neutral or relatively nonstressful testing conditions, mean State-Anxiety scores were either similar to or slightly lower than the Trait-Anxiety scores for these samples. However, when the testing conditions were stressful (e.g., administering the STAI to military recruits in a highly stressful training program), mean State-Anxiety scores were considerably higher than the mean Trait-Anxiety scores for those samples (Spielberger, 1983).

Typical mean State- and Trait-Anxiety scores for samples experiencing neutral testing conditions have been around 35 (with a standard deviation of approximately 10). In a study reported in the manual for the STAI (Spielberger, 1983), Form X (which typically has similar descriptive statistics as Form Y) was administered to an inmate sample ($N = 212$) at a federal correctional institution in Tallahassee, Florida, as part of the institution's classification and testing program. In this study, the mean age of the prisoners was 21 years, and their mean educational level was tenth grade. The reported mean State-Anxiety score was 45.96 ($SD = 11.04$), and the mean Trait-Anxiety score was 44.64 ($SD = 10.47$), thus reflecting the more stressful testing conditions of incarceration.

With the PreStart inmates, the mean State-Anxiety score was 41.13 ($SD = 12.14$), the mean Trait-Anxiety score was 41.39 ($SD = 10.92$), and both response distributions were slightly positively skewed (.146 and .151, respectively). The obtained mean values were greater than those reported for "normal" populations experiencing neutral testing conditions and were less than those reported for the inmate sample that had been administered Form X.

Part of this result was not surprising because the stressful testing conditions of incarceration would lead one to expect mean anxiety scores above the average typically reported for "normal" populations tested under neutral conditions. The other part of this result was a bit surprising, because it was contrary to the expected outcome. It was hypothesized that the PreStart inmate mean would be higher than that found for other inmate samples because PreStart inmates would be released soon, and it was expected that the fears that accompany reintegration into the community would cause higher levels of anxiety than the levels found in the general inmate population (gate fever). On further consideration, however, it seemed reasonable that the PreStart mean level of anxiety would be lower than the level of anxiety found in a sample of inmates involved in the classification stages of incarceration (fear of what is to come) in a federal institution.

However, with regards to the "normal" populations for which normed data exist on the STAI, the PreStart inmate sample indicated considerably higher levels of both state anxiety and trait anxiety. Further, little distinction can be made between the two subscales' response distributions, meaning that both State- and Trait-Anxiety score levels were above "normal" levels.

Depression. The Center for Epidemiologic Studies Depression (CES-D) scale was designed to measure *state* (current) levels of depressive symptomatology for use in research applications within a "normal" (i.e., nonpsychiatric) adult population aged 18 and older (Devins & Orme, 1985). The instrument was developed through a process based on factor analytic techniques and face validity judgments involving the selection of items from previously validated depression scales (e.g., Beck, Ward, Mendelson, Mock, & Erbaugh, 1961; Dahlstrom & Welsh, 1960; Gardner, 1968; Raskin, Schulterbrandt, Reatig, & McKeon, 1969; Zung, 1965).

Thus, key items relevant to depressive symptomatology that were extracted from existing depression instrumentation constitute the 20-item CES-D.

The CES-D was administered to all of the inmates in the 1992 and 1993 samples, resulting in 306 usable response sets from the 1992 inmates (72% of the total) and 253 usable response sets from the 1993 inmates (66% of the total). Inmates were asked to respond to the CES-D by indicating the frequency at which each of the 20 items were felt during the past week.[3]

Radloff (1977) suggested using a cutoff score of 16 to indicate case levels of depression. Barnes and Prosen (1984) suggested using the following classifications for interpreting CES-D composite scores: 0–15.5 (*not depressed*), 16–20.5 (*mild depression*), 21–30.5 (*moderate depression*), 31–60 (*severe depression*).

Most studies using the CES-D with large samples (1,000+) have yielded total score means ranging from 7.5 to 12.5, with modal values around 8.5 and standard deviations ranging from 7.5 to 9.8 (with a considerable tendency for positive skewness ranging from 1.5 to 1.69; Devins & Orme, 1985). For the 1992 PreStart inmate population, the mean CES-D score was 17.62, with a standard deviation of 10.35 and a slight positive skewness of .468. For the 1993 PreStart inmate population, the mean CES-D score was 24.225, with a standard deviation of 10.12 and a slight positive skewness of .333. Because the mean depression scores were considerably higher than the cutoff score (16) defining case depression, and because 52.3% of the 1992 inmate sample and 75.9% of the 1993 inmate sample scored above the cutoff score, the PreStart inmate sample was determined to have depressive symptoms to a much greater degree than the "normal" populations for which the instrument was developed.

In terms of the levels of depression defined by Barnes and Prosen (1984), 47.7% of the 1992 PreStart inmate sample showed no indication of case depression, 14.4% showed mild depression, 25.2% showed moderate depression, and 12.7% showed severe depression. When the range of scores that fell within one standard deviation of the mean were examined, 68% of the sample scored between 7 and 28, which covers the classifications of not depressed to moderate depression. For the 1993 inmate sample, even higher levels of depression were found, with 21.3% indicating no depression, 17.8% showing mild depression, 35.2% showing moderate depression, and 25.7% showing severe depression. The main conclusion drawn from these results was that the PreStart inmate sample indicated higher state levels of depression (as might be expected) than previously tested samples from the general (nonincarcerated and nonpsychiatric) population.

Relationships between Self-Esteem, Anxiety, and Depression

The intercorrelations of the self-esteem, anxiety, and depression scales were examined for the 1992 inmates to test the discriminant validity of each and to assess the degree to which self-esteem, anxiety, and depression may be overlapping psychological constructs as measured by these instruments. If a great deal of overlap exists, additional empirical support for the concept of gate fever would be established.

Validity of the measures.   In his manual for the STAI (Form Y), Spielberger (1983) provided evidence to support several types of validity for the original instrument, Form X, and for Form Y. Although much of the validity evidence was derived from studies using Form X, it should be noted that Form X and Form Y are highly correlated (typically, $r = .70-.75$) versions of the same instrument, and thus the evidence found for Form X can be generalized to apply to Form Y.

The construct validity of the Adult Form (Form Y) was reported as having been demonstrated by both scales' abilities to discriminate between neuropsychotic persons and "normal" persons. It was also reported that the concurrent validity of the Trait-Anxiety subscale of Form X was established through high correlations with other trait-anxiety type measures. Finally, it was reported in the STAI manual (1983) that convergent and divergent validities of Form X had been established through high correlations with related measures of constructs like emotional disturbance and psychopathology, and through low correlations with unrelated constructs.

In Chaplin's (1984) report on the development and technical aspects of the STAI, it was reported that the State-Anxiety subscale has been shown repeatedly to have construct validity. However, the author reported that the Trait-Anxiety subscale has yet to be shown to have construct validity, although the subscale has been shown to demonstrate some discriminant validity in its ability to differentiate between "normal" adults and different diagnostic groups of psychiatric patients.

One other study that offers evidence of the STAI's validity is really a validation study of the CES-D, which was conducted by Orme, Reis, and Herz (1986). The authors used the STAI as a criterion for testing the discriminant validity of the CES-D upon administering the instrument to 116 individual parents participating in family support programs designed to prevent child abuse and neglect. Because the authors found that the CES-D correlated highly with the Trait-Anxiety subscale and that the CES-D correlated moderately with the State-Anxiety subscale, they concluded that at the very least, the CES-D and the Trait-Anxiety subscale were measuring from a similar construct domain.

A considerable amount of evidence has been provided by a number of authors to establish the validity of the SEI. However, most of the results are specific to the original School Form of the SEI, with only a couple of studies establishing the validity of the shortened and revised form for adults. Many of the studies cited in Coopersmith's (1981) manual for the SEI were conducted using the School Form, and they established the construct validity (Kimball, 1972; Kokenes, 1974, 1978), concurrent validity (Simon & Simon, 1975), predictive validity (Donaldson, 1974), and convergent and discriminant validities (Cowan, Altmann, & Pysh, 1978; Drummond & McIntire, 1977; Fullerton, 1972; Goodstadt & Kipnes, 1971).

With regards to establishing the construct validity of the Adult Form of the SEI, support seems to be more favorable for its discriminant validity than its convergent validity. Bedeian and Zmud (1977) reported that the convergent validity of the short School Form was "weak" when 257 university students' responses to the SEI were assessed and compared to their responses on the Adjective Check List. However, Coopersmith (1981) indicated that Crandall, in a 1973 study, reported a validity coefficient of .59 between the Adult Form and the Rosenberg Self-Esteem Inventory, and thus concluded that, at least for that particular sample of 300 college students, the convergent validity of the SEI was supported.

In a study of the SEI's construct validity, Ahmed, Valliant, and Swindle (1985) experimentally manipulated 154 college psychology students' levels of self-esteem by providing bogus positive and negative feedback regarding their IQ scores. Observations were then made of the effect of the provided IQ knowledge on SEI retest scores. The results of this part of the study indicated that the bogus feedback had no significant effect on the retest scores. However, when the total SEI scores were correlated with subscale scores on a Guilt Scale and with the Minnesota Multiphasic Personality Inventory (MMPI) Psychasthenia Scale, the obtained coefficients were negative and statistically significant. Thus, it was concluded that the construct validity, and specifically the discriminant validity of the SEI, was supported.

Reiter and Costanzo (1986) also conducted a study of the construct validity of the Adult Form of the SEI. After administering the SEI and the Guilford-Zimmerman Temperament Survey (GZTS) to 28 volunteer adults (average age = 22), the authors concluded that similar relationships were observed between GZTS subscales and the total SEI score as those identified by Coopersmith in 1967.

To test the construct validity of these measures for the PreStart inmate sample, the discriminant validity coefficients were computed between the State-Anxiety and Trait-Anxiety subscales of the STAI, the CES-D, and the SEI. It was expected that the two subscales of the STAI would correlate moderately and positively with the CES-D (i.e., high levels of anxiety would be somewhat associated with high levels of depression). It was also expected that the two subscales of the STAI would correlate moderately and negatively with the SEI (i.e., high levels of anxiety would be somewhat associated with low levels of self-esteem).

As can be seen in Table 4.4, all of the hypothesized relationships were supported. The State- and Trait-Anxiety subscales were moderately and positively correlated with the CES-D composite scores, indicating that high levels of anxiety were associated with high levels of depression. Also, as hypothesized, the two anxiety subscales were moderately and negatively correlated with the SEI composite scores, indicating that high levels of anxiety were associated with low levels of self-esteem.

Because correlations around .60 are frequently used to support an instrument's convergent validity, the validity coefficients for the two subscales' relationship, as well as their relationships to the CES-D, seem rather problematic. It appears that a great deal of overlap occurred between the two anxiety subscales. Additionally, it appears that the STAI measures content from the depression construct domain as well as from the anxiety construct domain.

After correcting these validity coefficients for attenuation due to the unreliability of the various instruments (for formula, see Allen & Yen, 1979), the maximum possible measurement-error-free validity estimates were obtained (see

Table 4.4
Validity Coefficients

	State-Anxiety	Trait-Anxiety	CES-D	SEI
State-Anxiety	1.00			
Trait-Anxiety	.80	1.00		
CES-D	.68	.69	1.00	
SEI	−.47	−.58	−.53	1.00

NOTE: $p < .001$ for all coefficients. CES-D = Center for Epidemiological Studies Depression Scale; SEI = Coopersmith Self-Esteem Inventory.

Table 4.5
Validity Coefficients Corrected for Attenuation Due to Unreliability

	State-Anxiety	*Trait-Anxiety*	*CES-D*
State-Anxiety			
Trait-Anxiety	.88		
CES-D	.77	.78	
SEI	−.64	−.79	−.74

NOTE: CES-D = Center for Epidemiological Studies Depression Scale; SEI = Coopersmith Self-Esteem Inventory.

Table 4.5). The problems of convergence between the instruments became even more evident once these adjustments were made to the validity coefficients.

In fact, all of the validity coefficients increased to strong levels of association once measurement errors were removed. Thus, although the internal consistency reliability measures obtained for the two subscales supported their unidimensionality, the failure to demonstrate discriminant validity for the two subscales lent support to the conclusion that the two anxiety subscales tend to measure the same anxiety construct, and that anxiety construct appears to overlap with depression and self-esteem constructs as well. Thus, at least with respect to this "special population" sample of inmates, the construct validity of the STAI could not be established. In fact, all of the scale intercorrelations fell within the moderate to strong association levels. The CES-D was moderately correlated with the self-esteem measure (SEI); however, the CES-D was associated more strongly with *both* the state and trait anxiety measures (which is not surprising, because the State- and Trait-Anxiety subscales correlated very strongly with each other).

Thus, the results lead to the conclusion that the CES-D could be somewhat distinguished from the SEI but not from the STAI. Therefore, very little support has been provided in this current, and very limited, study of the construct validity of the CES-D when used with the PreStart inmate sample. Further, it appears that the CES-D taps into other noncognitive constructs such as self-esteem and anxiety instead of just limiting itself to the content domain of depressive symptomatology.

SUMMARY, CONCLUSIONS, AND DISCUSSION

The CES-D, SEI, and STAI are instruments commonly used to measure depression, self-esteem, and anxiety, respectively. Each has been considered to exhibit strong psychometric properties and to have high levels of reliability and validity. Each has been formed with general populations. Each was administered during the summer of 1992 to a sample of inmates who were participating in PreStart, an innovative community reintegration program implemented in Illinois in July 1991. The purpose of this study was to test the reliability and validity of these instruments when used with a sample drawn from this special population of inmates, and to assess whether the inmate sample suffers from gate fever.

Because the PreStart sample's mean CES-D score was considerably higher than the typical mean range, as well as above the cutoff score defining case depression (16), and because 52.3% of the inmates scored above that cutoff score, it was concluded that the PreStart sample displayed depressive symptoms to a much greater degree than the "normal" populations for which the instrument was developed. The PreStart sample also evidenced much lower levels of self-esteem and much greater levels of anxiety than "normal" populations.

This study set out to further assess the construct validity of the above measures through the use of interscale correlations. Because all of the validity coefficients fell into the moderate to strong association ranges, it was concluded that strong support for the various instruments' construct validity could not be established in this, albeit limited, cross-validation study.

In particular, the fairly high correlations between the CES-D and the State- and Trait-Anxiety scales seemed rather problematic. However, a plausible explanation exists for the lack of distinction between the CES-D scores and the STAI scores. In 1967, Cormier et al. discussed the notion of gate fever, a term that refers to the preliberation anxiety experienced by soon-to-be-released inmates anticipating the sudden passage from imprisonment to freedom. Gate fever is characterized by irritability, anxiety, restlessness, and a variety of psychophysiological symptoms.

Because much of the symptomatology of gate fever is similar to the symptomatology of depression (both are characterized by irritability, anxiety, hopelessness, and restlessness), there is reason to believe that the inflated depression levels observed among the PreStart inmate sample were reflective of the inmates' gate fever, because these inmates were about to be released into the community at large. Gate fever would also account for the inability to discriminate between CES-D scores and STAI scores. Clearly, more research is needed to determine if the current findings are an artifact of gate fever, or if the CES-D simply does not distinctly measure depressive symptomatology in prerelease inmates.

Thus, it was concluded that the findings obtained for the PreStart inmate sample were uniquely different from findings presented in previous cross-validation studies of the CES-D, STAI, and SEI. Although some aspects of the study did confirm the appropriateness of using these inventories with an inmate sample, there were other indications that the instruments could not be cross-validated for use with inmates participating in a prison release program. The unique mental and emotional experiences of inmates participating in a prerelease program suggest that the use of these inventories, particularly the CED-D and STAI, developed for nonincarcerated and nonpsychiatric populations may be problematic.

Overall, it appears that the PreStart inmates, as a group, exhibit much higher levels of anxiety and depression than persons in the "normal" population, as well as much lower levels of self-esteem. Moreover, these characteristics seem to be concentrated among certain inmates. That is, inmates who suffer from low self-esteem are also more likely to exhibit high levels of depression and anxiety. Although the PreStart prerelease program directly attempts to promote higher levels of esteem among its clients, and may indirectly affect anxiety levels, these data suggest that consideration should be given to the development of prerelease programming that directly addresses levels of inmate anxiety and depression.

Clearly, however, more cross-validation research needs to be conducted with these instruments in the future so that a more thorough understanding can be acquired as to the instruments' stability and utility across populations, circumstances, and time. Specifically, more research needs to be conducted concerning the unique mental and emotional states of inmates as they move through the stages of incarceration. This would aid in determining when it would be inappropriate to administer inventories developed for nonincarcerated populations. Moreover, the consequences of delivering services to a highly depressed and anxious population suffering from low levels of self-esteem warrant greater consideration in the development of program interventions.

NOTES

1. In scoring the Adult Form of the Coopersmith Self-Esteem Inventory (SEI), positive items were considered "correct" (i.e., given a value of 1) if answered "like me" and negative items were considered "correct" if answered "unlike me." A total self-esteem score was obtained by multiplying the raw score summation across all 25 items by 4, thus allowing for a maximum total score of 100 points. The scale should be considered as a composite score only, because no subscales were intended on the shorter forms of the SEI. High scale scores correspond to high self-esteem, and scores have tended in the past to be skewed in the direction of high self-esteem among "normal" populations.

   For the sample of PreStart inmates, Cronbach's alpha of .60 resulted in a test of the scale's internal consistency reliability. This alpha level is considerably lower than has been found in other applications of the SEI. Because deletion of any singular item would only raise the alpha value to a level not exceeding .62, the value of .60 was considered to be stable and realistic for this special inmate population. Correlations of single items with the total test score ranged from .06 to .48, and the average interitem correlation was .06. Because the obtained reliability coefficient was of a moderate level, and because the item to total correlations and the average interitem correlation tended to be in the moderate to low range, one may conclude that the total index must be thought of as a multidimensional and heterogeneous measure of a self-esteem construct.

   A principal components analysis was conducted on the PreStart inmate data to examine the internal structure of the SEI scale. It revealed that the SEI is a multidimensional instrument that broadly samples the self-esteem content area. The analysis provided further support for the consistent finding inferred across other factorial studies of the Adult Form of the SEI that the instrument is not the homogeneous scale it was originally intended to be. Instead, all the measures of homogeneity (i.e., Cronbach's alpha, interitem and item-total correlations, components analysis) show the scale to be heterogeneous and the concept of self-esteem measured by the composite score on the instrument to be general.

2. In scoring the State-Trait Anxiety Inventory (STAI), each item was given a weighted score ranging from 1 to 4, corresponding to the amount of presence or absence felt by the respondent for each item. The State-Anxiety subscale assesses how respondents felt at the moment they were taking the self-evaluation questionnaire, whereas the Trait-Anxiety subscale assesses to what level respondents "generally" felt anxious. Total scores for the two subscales of the STAI were obtained by summing across the weighted item scores, thus resulting in a possible scoring range of 20 to 80 for each subscale (Spielberger, 1983).

All of the internal consistency reliability coefficients reported in the past for the STAI have been exceptionally high, indicating a great deal of homogeneity and unidimensionality in the two subscales. In fact, all of the Cronbach's alpha coefficients reported by Spielberger (1983) for both anxiety subscales either approximated or exceeded .90. In the sample of PreStart inmates, alpha values also exceeded .90. The standardized item alpha for the State-Anxiety subscale was .91, and was considered quite stable, because deletion of any one of the subscale's items failed to lower the alpha value below .90, nor would it raise the alpha value. The standardized item alpha for the Trait-Anxiety subscale was .90, and was also considered quite stable.

3. A score of 0 was given for each response of *rarely or none of the time*, a score of 1 for each response of *some or a little of the time*, a score of 2 for each response of *occasionally or a moderate amount of time*, and a score of 3 for each response of *most or all of the time*. The instrument was then objectively scored by reversing the scores of positive items (4, 8, 12, 16) and then adding the raw scores across all 20 items, yielding a total scoring range of 0 to 60. High Center for Epidemiological Studies Depression Scale (CES-D) scores reflected high levels of depression.

Tests of internal consistency reliability have repeatedly provided evidence supporting the homogeneity of the CES-D. For example, Radloff (1977) reported a coefficient alpha of .85 for a general population sample and a coefficient alpha of .90 for a patient sample. Barnes and Prosen (1984) reported an alpha of .89 for a volunteer sample of family practitioner clients. In the 1992 sample of PreStart inmates, a Cronbach's alpha of .86 resulted. Because deletion of any singular item on the CES-D would only lower the alpha of the total CES-D, but not to an alpha value below .82, the value of .86 was considered to be stable and realistic for this special inmate sample. Similar findings were found for the 1993 inmate sample (Cronbach's alpha = .84).

To investigate the structural stability of the CES-D when used with a special population such as the PreStart sample, a principal components analysis was conducted with the 1992 data. The results of a principal components analysis of the PreStart sample's responses to the CES-D supported previously reported findings concerning the structural makeup of the CES-D. The conclusions drawn from the analysis were that the scale displayed a great deal of homogeneity and that the responses obtained from this special inmate sample reflected an underlying structure identical to those obtained from "normal" (i.e., nonincarcerated and nonpsychiatric) samples.

REFERENCES

Adair, F. (1984). Coopersmith Self-Esteem Inventories. In D. J. Keyser & R. C. Sweetland (Eds.), *Test critiques* (Vol. 1, pp. 226–232). Kansas City, MO: Test Corporation of America.

Adams, K. (1992). Adjusting to prison life. In M. Tonry (Ed.), *Crime and justice: A review of research* (Vol. 16, pp. 275–359). Chicago: University of Chicago Press.

Ahmed, S. M. S., Valliant, P. M., & Swindle, D. (1985). Psychometric properties of Coopersmith Self-Esteem Inventory. *Perceptual and Motor Skills, 61,* 1235–1241.

Allen, M. J., & Yen, W. M. (1979). *Introduction to measurement theory.* Monterey, CA: Brooks/Cole.

Barnes, G. E., & Prosen, H. (1984). Depression in Canadian general practice attenders. *Canadian Journal of Psychiatry, 29,* 2–10.

Beck, A. T., Ward, C. H., Mendelson, M., Mock, J., & Erbaugh, J. (1961). An inventory for measuring depression. *Archives of General Psychiatry, 4,* 561–571.

Bedeian, A. G., & Zmud, R. W. (1977). Some evidence relating to convergent validity of Form B of Coopersmith's Self-Esteem Inventory. *Psychological Reports, 40,* 725–726.

Chaplin, W. F. (1984). Strait-Trait Anxiety Inventory. In D. J. Keyser & R. C. Sweetland (Eds.), *Test critiques* (Vol. 1, pp. 626–632). Kansas City, MO: Test Corporation of America.

Coopersmith, S. (1981). *Self-esteem inventories.* Palo Alto, CA: Consulting Psychologists Press.

Cormier, B., Kennedy, M., & Sendbuehler, M. (1967). Cell breakage and gate fever. *British Journal of Criminology, 7,* 317–324.

Cowan, R., Altmann, H., & Pysh, F. (1978). A validity study of selected self-concept instruments. *Measurement and Evaluation in Guidance, 10,* 211–221.

Dahlstrom, W. G., & Welsh, G. S. (1960). *An MMPI handbook.* Minneapolis: University of Minnesota Press.

Devins, G. M., & Orme, C. M. (1985). Center for Epidemiologic Studies Depression Scale. In D. J. Keyser & R. C. Sweetland (Eds.), *Test critiques* (Vol. 2, pp. 144–160). Kansas City, MO: Test Corporation of America.

Donaldson, T. S. (1974). *Affective testing in the Alum Rock voucher schools.* Santa Monica, CA: RAND.

Drummond, R. J., & McIntire, W. G. (1977). Evaluating the factor structure of self-concept in children: A cautionary note. *Measurement and Evaluation in Guidance, 9,* 172–176.

Fullerton, W. S. (1972). *Self-disclosure, self-esteem and risk taking: A study of their convergent and discriminant validity in elementary school children.* Doctoral dissertation, University of California, Berkeley.

Gardner, E. A. (1968). *Development of a symptom checklist for the measurement of depression in a population.* Unpublished manuscript.

Goodstadt, B., & Kipnes, D. (1971). *Report on achievement instruction materials.* Philadelphia: Research for Better Schools.

Kimball, O. M. (1972). Development of norms for the Coopersmith Self-Esteem Inventory: Grades four through eight. *Dissertation Abstracts International, 34,* 1131–1132.

Kokenes, B. (1974). Grade level differences in factors of self-esteem. *Developmental Psychology, 10,* 954–958.

Kokenes, B. (1978). A factor analytic study of the Coopersmith Self-Esteem Inventory. *Adolescence, 13,* 149–155.

Orme, J. G., Reis, J., & Herz, E. J. (1986). Factorial and discriminant validity of the Center for Epidemiological Studies Depression (CES-D) Scale. *Journal of Clinical Psychology, 42*(1), 28–33.

Radloff, L. S. (1977). The CES-D Scale: A self-report depression scale for research in the general population. *Applied Psychological Measurement, 1*(3), 385–401.

Raskin, A., Schulterbrandt, J., Reatig, N., & McKeon, J. (1969). Replication of factors of psychopathology in interview, ward behavior, and self-report ratings of hospitalized depressives. *Journal of Nervous and Mental Disease, 148,* 87–96.

Reiter, H. H., & Costanzo, D. (1986). Relation between personality variables and the Coopersmith Self-Esteem Inventory. *Mankind Quarterly, 27*(2), 161–165.

Renzema, M. (1988). The stress comes later. In R. Johnson & H. Toch (Eds.), *The pains of imprisonment* (pp. 147–164). Prospect Heights, IL: Waveland.

Simon, W. E., & Simon, M. G. (1975). Self-esteem, intelligence and standardized academic achievement. *Psychology in the Schools, 32,* 97–100.

Spielberger, C. D. (1983). *Manual for the State-Trait Anxiety Inventory (Form Y).* Palo Alto, CA: Consulting Psychologists Press.

Toch, H., & Adams, K. (1989). *Coping: Maladaptation in prisons.* New Brunswick, NJ: Transaction.

Zung, W. W. K. (1965). A self-rating depression scale. *Archives of General Psychiatry, 12,* 63–70.

SECTION ONE: INMATE ADJUSTMENT TO PRISON

DISCUSSION QUESTIONS

1. Why do Irwin and Cressey argue that the prison code is influenced by environmental factors?
2. Which inmates in the Van Voorhis, Browning, Simon, and Gordon study were most likely to focus on rehabilitation and why would that be?
3. If, as Crouch finds, some inmates fear probation more than prison, what does that tell us about prisons and probation in this country?
4. What do Castellano and Soderstrom think affects the depression levels of inmates in their study?

SECTION 2

INDIVIDUAL ADJUSTMENT FACTORS

Early prison researchers tended to view inmates as a homogenous group— prisoners versus guards in the deprivation model, or Black inmates versus White inmates in the importation model. Later researchers began to examine cracks in this unified portrayal, focusing on characteristics such as race, gender, age, socioeconomic status, and place of origin. The authors of the articles in the following section examine the literature that focuses on the impact of specific demographic characteristics on inmate adjustment to prison.

While earlier studies made passing reference to racial differences and their potential impact on the prisoner subculture, the picture generally painted was one of inmate homogeneity. Regardless of whether such a picture was accurate then, indications are that it certainly is not accurate today. Several participant observation studies conducted in the 1970s detailed the changing inmate population, focusing particularly on racial differences. Later empirical studies validated these participant observation studies of racial polarization, but did not completely endorse their view of the impact of racial polarization on the prison environment.

Kevin N. Wright, in his article "Race and Economic Marginality in Explaining Prison Adjustment," finds that the Black and the White male inmates in the New York facilities he studied tended to adjust somewhat similarly to their imprisonment. From his measures of the "distress" and "aggressiveness" that inmates experience and practice, he found that when prior incarceration and economic marginality were controlled for, the effect of race on inmate adjustment was nil.

In addition to race and economic marginality, age is frequently cited as an important explanatory variable in criminal justice. A number of studies of violence in prison suggest that age is an important factor in inmate adjustment patterns. Age has been closely linked to the likelihood of aggressive behavior in prison. As inmates increase in age, there is a linear decline in the number of aggressive acts toward other inmates and/or correctional staff. A study by Doris Layton MacKenzie of age and aggressive behavior in prison, titled "Age and Adjustment to Prison: Interactions with Attitudes and Anxiety," revealed a slightly more complex picture, however. Rather than a linear decline with age, she found that aggressive behavior rose until the late twenties, then declined. Additionally, interpersonal conflicts with other inmates remained high for a longer period of time than did interpersonal conflicts with correctional officers.

Angela S. Maitland and Richard D. Sluder also explore the effect of age in their article, "Victimization in Prisons: A Study of Factors Related to the General Well-Being of Youthful Offenders." They note that several factors influence the sense of well-being, and thus the adjustment, of the male inmates they studied in a midwestern state prison. Those who had less fear about being a victim, those who had not been a victim, those who had less of a sense of anomie, and those who felt they had friends who would support them if they were threatened, experienced a greater degree of well-being in the prison.

Craig Hemmens and James W. Marquart, in their article "Friend or Foe? Race, Age, and Inmate Perceptions of Inmate-Staff Relations," note that race and age also influence how inmates view correctional staff. After interviewing Texas "exmates" (those inmates just released from prison) they found that the younger inmates had more problems with staff and were more likely to believe that staff treated them poorly. They found, too, that Black and Hispanic inmates also perceived staff in a more negative light in that they believed that staff treated them less fairly and with more force than White inmates believed they were treated.

Of course, the most neglected area of inmate adjustment and degrees of prisonization is that of the women inmates' prison experience. In Barbara Owen's book-length study of the largest women's prison in California, titled *In the Mix: Struggle and Survival in a Women's Prison* (Chapter 6 "The Mix: The Culture of Imprisoned Women" is included here), she chronicles just how different that experience is from men's and how it has been misrepresented by researchers in the past. It is not that the women don't import a culture and adhere to a prison culture to lessor and greater degrees, just as men do. It is that the culture they import and the culture they create, is based on a differential life experience that reflects patriarchy, cultural determinism of gender roles, and biological differences. They don't have to worry as much as men do about violence on the inside; that is more often their lot on the outside in self-destructive relationships. But they must negotiate the travails of a prison system that is shaped by the larger culture; their prison experience is both similar to and different from men's.

CHAPTER 5

RACE AND ECONOMIC MARGINALITY IN EXPLAINING PRISON ADJUSTMENT

Kevin N. Wright

A common theme found in the prison literature suggests that blacks, because of their experience in the modern urban ghetto, are more resilient to the pains of incarceration. Ghetto life supposedly socializes the individual to engage in self-protection against the hostile social environment of the slum and the cold and unpredictable prison setting. Two images of the male black inmate are found in the literature: Carroll describes the black prisoner as tough, domineering, and aggressive, while Johnson suggests that he is strong, stoic, and unmoved by pressure. A review of the empirical research about race and adjustment reveals that support for either of these images is mixed. Using multiple indicators of distress and aggressive behavior, this study finds that, with the exception of self-inflicted injury, blacks and whites experience incarceration similarly. Outcome results were corroborated by findings that blacks and whites have similar environmental needs and rate their prison settings similarly. Some support for the claim that a more economically marginal life-style before incarceration is related to successful adjustment was found, yet this was true independent of race. These findings lead to the conclusion that racial distinctions are not universal, and the practice of suggesting that blacks adapt one way and whites another leads to inappropriate conclusions about patterns of prison adjustment.

The prison literature generally supports the proposition that blacks are more resilient to the pains of incarceration than members of other ethnic groups. Previous research suggests that blacks may be more immune to the degradation that accompanies confinement and better able to stave off serious threats to their self-esteem (Carroll, 1982). They appear to feel significantly safer in prison and have fewer symptoms of psychological distress than whites or Hispanics (Johnson, 1976; Oldroyd and Howell, 1977; Fagan and Lira, 1978). They suffer

This research was supported by a grant from the National Institute of Justice, 83-IJ-CX-0011.

JOURNAL OF RESEARCH IN CRIME AND DELINQUENCY. Vol. 26 No. 1, February 1989
67–89 © 1989 Sage Publications, Inc.

psychological crises and breakdowns less often and rarely resort to self-injury to relieve intense stress (Johnson, 1976). Blacks have been characterized as having more control and influence of the day-to-day activities of the prison than members of other ethnic groups (Irwin, 1980; Bartollas, Miller, and Dinitz, 1976).

Surprisingly, as Goodstein and MacKenzie (1984a, pp. 272–274) point out, the relationship between race and individual patterns of adjustment has only recently been identified. Rather than describing the variety of inmate behaviors that occur, early studies sought to depict a common culture. Inmates were characterized as having a rigid set of norms, a well-defined informal organization, and a system of sanctions to ensure conformity. The purpose of the informal inmate organization was perceived to be resistance to formal authority and protection of inmates' senses of self-worth (Clemmer, 1940; Sykes, 1966; Sykes and Messinger, 1960; Wellford, 1967; Thomas, 1970; Thomas and Peterson, 1977). It was not until the 1970s that race emerged as an important variable in determining prison behavior. The works of Jacobs (1974, 1976, 1977), Carroll (1974), Johnson (1976), and Irwin (1980) questioned the unidimensional image of the inmate subculture and argued that racial differences play a significant role in individual and institutional activities.

Research since the 1970s indicates that race is related to both aggression and distress, but in reviewing this literature, one finds contradictory findings, descriptions, and interpretations. In this article, research concerning race and patterns of prison adjustment will be reviewed with particular attention given to the discrepancies in the literature. From this review, several research questions will be posed and tested.

INTERRACIAL DIFFERENCES

The explanation given most often for the perceived greater resiliency among black inmates is that their experience in the subculture of the black ghetto prepares them to respond better to the pains of incarceration. As Carroll (1982, p. 188) suggests, "having been raised to be cunning and tough, they feel less vulnerable, and through their extensive involvement in peer groups they are able to monopolize the available goods and services and, to some degree, can counter the power of the guards."

The literature identifies two additional factors as playing a role in determining interracial differences in adjustment: ethnic solidarity and prior prison experience. Ethnic solidarity is related to the common ghetto experiences of many black inmates. Robert Johnson (1976, p. 18) notes that "ghetto survival is characterized by emphasis on self-protection in a cold, unpredictable, often hostile world, where the most reliable source of support can be found among similarly circumstanced peers." Yet many white inmates come from a ghetto background, so black solidarity in prison is promoted by more than common living experiences. According to Carroll (1982, pp. 187–188), blacks develop defense mechanisms to discrimination, debasement, and degradation. Black nationalism, unity, and mutual support against white oppression strengthen their resistance to the stresses of confinement. As Goodstein and MacKenzie (1984a, pp. 274–275) point out, there is greater cultural diversity among white inmates caused by ethnic and social class heterogeneity and urban and rural social differences.

The third factor suggested to be related to adjustment is the inmate's prior experience with imprisonment. Goodstein and MacKenzie (1984a, p. 5) suggest that, "It stands to reason that an environment which is unknown to an individual is likely to engender higher levels of stress." The new inmate must cope with the rigors of incarceration and learn how to adapt but must also deal with his fears of victimization by other inmates and the brutality of the guards. This factor is important since the national prisoner survey found that black inmates served more time and have longer sentences than white inmates (see Goetting and Howsen, 1983, p. 24). This finding leads us to expect blacks to be able to survive imprisonment better than whites; however, research by Goodstein and MacKenzie (1984a, pp. 285–286) failed to establish the relationship between time served and adjustment.

Greater resiliency among blacks in prison is considered to be manifest in two ways, in terms of distress and conflict. Whites are considered to be more likely to suffer distress; blacks are believed to be more aggressive. Both propositions have been tested empirically, yet results do not clearly support either proposition. Johnson (1976) found white inmates to be overrepresented among those who suffer psychological breakdowns while incarcerated. Among these inmates, whites were more likely to attempt suicide and engage in self-mutilation. Johnson (1976, p. 143) properly noted that his findings did not allow him to conclude anything about the prevalence of psychological crises within the population but that the inmates suffering crises make up a very small proportion of the population.

Three studies since Johnson, by randomly selecting inmates for study and then determining who had suffered psychological distress, have attempted to reach some conclusion about the prevalence of problems within prison. Fagan and Lira (1978) found that white inmates reported greater mood disturbances, more depression, and higher levels of tension and anxiety than black inmates. Similarly, Oldroyd and Howell (1977) found greater levels of depression among white inmates than black. In contrast, Goodstein and MacKenzie (1984a, p. 292) found no difference in the scores of black and white inmates on an anxiety scale and exactly the opposite to what was expected about inmate depression. Black inmates indicated that they were more depressed than whites.

Given these findings what can be concluded about the relationship of race to distress is ambiguous. Johnson found that whites appear to be more susceptible to severe crises than blacks. This finding has not been contradicted by further research but severe psychological distress appears to affect only a small proportion of the inmate population. Conclusions about other forms of distress—anxiety and depression—are less clear.

Similar disparity is found in the research regarding differential involvement in conflict and aggressive behavior among the races. In their study of the intractable inmate, Myers and Levy (1978) found blacks to be chronic disciplinary problems more frequently than whites. Bartollas, Miller, and Dinitz (1976) discovered that black juveniles exerted more control of the day-to-day activities and social life in the institution than did whites.

Several studies found blacks to be overrepresented among the assailants and whites overrepresented among the victims. This is particularly true for sexual victimization (Carroll, 1974; Scacco, 1975; Jones, 1976; Lockwood, 1980; Wooden and Parker, 1982) where blacks are less often the targets and more likely to be the aggressors. This pattern was also observed by Fuller and

Orsagh (1977) in their study of interracial violence in general. In 82% of the incidents examined, black inmates were the assailants and whites were the recipients of attacks.

In research that looked at violent acts that became recorded as official misconduct (Poole and Regoli, 1980; Flanagan, 1983; Ramirez, 1983), black inmates are found to be charged more frequently with assaultive behavior than whites. However, there are contradictory findings. Studies by Ellis, Grasmick, and Gilman (1974), Petersilia (1983), Goetting and Howsen (1983) report no difference in the frequency among blacks and whites. This lack of difference was also found in self-reports of involvement in violence that led Poole and Regoli to conclude that prison officials discriminate against blacks in the application of sanctions. This suggestion may explain the disparity in findings in that researchers have defined and measured aggression and conflict differently. Findings of Goodstein and MacKenzie (1984a, p. 285) may help explain the discrepancy in discovering that blacks claim to be in conflict with guards more often than whites, while whites claim to be in conflict with other inmates more than blacks. Results and subsequent conclusions may also be confounded by facility-to-facility variations.

Despite the discrepant findings, two different characterizations of the "typical" black inmate have emerged in the literature. The first is perhaps best articulated in the work of Leo Carroll (1974, 1982) who describes black inmates as aggressive. Carroll suggests that the ghetto experiences of blacks who end up in prison breeds cunningness and toughness. Consequently, these individuals are more likely to act out, take advantage of others, and control goods and services within the inmate culture. Carroll suggests that as a defense against discrimination, blacks achieve unity and provide mutual support. This strengthens the black inmate's resistance to the pains of incarceration and the authority of the administration. From Carroll's perspective, black inmates are more likely to be the aggressors in violent and exploitive incidents and to disobey prison rules more frequently than whites.

A second related, but in important ways different, perspective is proposed by Robert Johnson (1976) who views maintaining one's "cool" as more characteristic of black inmates than assertiveness. According to Johnson (1976, p. 16), "Survival techniques developed in response to slave and caste status involved the maintenance of a defensive, self-protectively vigilant posture, coupled with the concealment of feelings (particularly anger and fear) behind a facade of obsequiousness or serenity." Rather than acting out, a more likely response of the black inmate would be to "remain unmoved by pressure." In control, smooth, and together characterize the black inmate according to Johnson. Strength is another component of the black inmate's persona as he gives the impression of being cold, uncaring, and potentially explosive. Johnson indicates that "both facades are meant to put people off, to avoid victimization, and to hide self-revealing ("uncool") feelings of anger and fear."

Like Carroll, Johnson recognizes the importance of the injustice of the ghetto experience and racial discrimination in preparing black inmates for subsequent feelings of powerlessness and resentment encountered during incarceration. Johnson also recognizes that peer support is endemic to black inmates. Like Carroll, he claims whites suffer greater stress than blacks. What does not follow from Johnson's perspective is that blacks are more aggressive; self-control and the avoidance of emotional or aggressive outbursts characterize the black inmate.

Whites may find it necessary to fight to protect themselves or their identity as "manly" men. They may also confront official authority for this same reason.

RESEARCH QUESTIONS

From this review, it is clear that while there may be considerable agreement among prison researchers that adjustment to prison is different for blacks than whites, the exact nature of these differences remains unclear. Four research questions seem to emerge. First, do blacks and whites differ in their patterns of adjustment? Two hypotheses have been tested in the past: that white inmates suffer greater stress and that black inmates are more aggressive. The review of the literature revealed inconsistent findings regarding both hypotheses. Two confounding methodological factors cloud the conclusions that can be drawn: the way in which stress or conflict are operationally defined and whether official or self-reported indicators are used. To overcome these problems, multiple indicators of adjustment should be examined for the same sample and their results compared.

If there are differences between blacks and whites in the way they adapt to prison, these patterns should be manifest in ways other than behavioral outcomes. Hans Toch (1977, pp. 1–9) argues that because perception of environment is not objective, people define social and physical qualities in terms of their own needs and values. A given setting can be evaluated in different ways by two individuals with significantly different concerns. According to Toch, transactions between people and their environments may be either congruent (the milieu corresponds to the individual's needs) or incongruent (where attributes are in conflict with individual concerns). Drawing on Toch's conceptualization, a second research question asks whether black and white inmates have different environmental needs and whether they evaluate the attributes of the prison environment differently.

If differences are observed between blacks and whites, the next question to be considered is to what extent these differences can be explained by previous experience in prison. Inmates who have been incarcerated should cope with the pressures of confinement better than inmates who are experiencing incarceration for the first time. There are two related questions to be considered: whether blacks and whites differ in their previous incarceration and to what extent experience is related to adjustment outcomes.

A fourth, and perhaps the most important research question, is whether there is any empirical justification for experience in the urban ghetto as an explanation of adjustment differences. As noted above, this post hoc explanation is suggested to account for what researchers observe and has not been tested. It is possible that inmates from impoverished backgrounds, irrespective of race, should arrive at prison differentially prepared for what faces them. If this is true, within racial groups variations in outcomes should be observed across socioeconomic backgrounds.

METHODS

The design to evaluate the relationship of race and prison adjustment consisted of selecting a sample of inmates, obtaining information about each subject's race, prior incarceration, needs and perceptions of the environment, and socioeconomic background, and comparing those variables to several indicators of adjustment. To control for variations from facility-to-facility, which may have influenced past studies, this research was conducted in several New York State facilities. Site visits in which four questionnaires (three of which are pertinent to this study) were administered to inmate research subjects were made during July, August, and September 1983. To coincide with this collection period, information from computerized records of the corrections department was taken for August 15, 1983.

Adjustment problems were conceptualized in two ways: as distress and as aggressiveness. Seven measures were used, four associated with the first conceptualization and three with the latter. Four variables were obtained from official records and three from a questionnaire administered to the subjects.

Indicators of disruptive and assaultive behavior were collected from the disciplinary records of each prison. These measures identify individuals officially recognized as difficult to control and who posed security problems. Whether an inmate had attempted suicide or injured himself was also obtained from these records and used as one of the indicators of distress. Information was coded into the three categories for the three years prior to the research, from August 15, 1980, to August 15, 1983.

Sick-call information was obtained from another set of official records as an indicator of emotional distress. A variable record was recorded for each inmate for the same three-year period used for disciplinary information. To create a measure of distress, only those diagnoses associated with stress were selected and summed. Because some facilities did not provide current and complete information, these data were not as reliable as desired.

Since past research (O'Leary and Glaser, 1972; Flanagan, 1980; Zink, 1958; Poole and Regoli, 1980; Johnson, 1966) suggests that official records may be racially biased, somewhat ambiguous, and subjective, inmates were also asked if they had problems in relating to other inmates and the staff or were experiencing personal distress. The Prison Adjustment Questionnaire (PAQ) was developed to measure inmate self-perceptions of these adjustment problems. The questionnaire consists of 20 questions that explore nine problems inmates experience during incarceration. Inmates are asked to compare how they are doing in prison with how they did in the free world. If their adjustment is worse in prison, then they are asked to indicate how severe or frequent the problem occurs.

Factor analyses revealed that the items formed three well-defined dimensions. One dimension, Internal, indicates to what extent the individual is experiencing adjustment problems and internalizing them. The individual suffering in this way will feel uncomfortable with the people around him, be angry, and will have trouble sleeping. A second dimension, External, characterizes those individuals who externalize their distress by fighting and arguing. A final dimension, Physical, characterizes inmates who experience physical adversities including sickness, injury, and being taken advantage of by other inmates. Indicators of internal consistency varied between .50 and .74, which for scales with few items more than meets acceptable standards. The three scales were slightly correlated, between .30 and .40. Table 5.1 lists the correlations among all outcome measures with the exception of self-injury for which the variance was too small for inclusion.

Indicators of the predictor variables were taken from the automated background files of the corrections department. Race was recorded as a bivariate

Table 5.1
Correlation Matrix (N = 913)

Variable	1	2	3	4	5
(1) Aggressive Disciplinary Infractions					
(2) Assaultive Disciplinary Infractions	.01				
(3) Sick-Calls	.25*	−.04			
(4) Internal PAQ	.0001	.05	.01		
(5) External PAQ	−.004	.11*	.0001	.29*	
(6) Physical PAQ	.06	.03	.008	.39*	.38*

*Significant at alpha < .05.

measure. Whites, Hispanics, and Native Americans were classified as white, blacks were classified as blacks, and orientals were dropped from the sample. Prior prison experience was also recorded as a bivariate variable with the value determined by whether the subject had a previous adult incarceration.

Within the department's background data, there was no indications of whether inmates had grown up in a ghetto setting or the degree to which they had internalized the values of the ghetto culture, so it was necessary to use proxy measures for this attribute. Preincarceration employment and educational history were used to identify individuals more likely to have experienced the socializing forces of the impoverished community. Employment was measured as a bivariate variable of whether the individual was employed at the time of his arrest. Educational achievement was classified into four groups: no high school, some high school, high school graduate, and beyond high school.

Two questionnaires were used to measure inmates' contextual needs and perceptions of their environmental settings within prison. The questionnaires were completed in two, two-hour sessions. Inmates were not financially compensated for their participation but were told a letter of appreciation would be placed in their institutional files. Inmates could elect to take a paper and pencil test in English, or if they preferred, taped versions, in English and Spanish, were available.

Toch's Prison Preference Inventory was given to determine each subject's environmental preferences regarding eight dimensions: Privacy, Safety, Structure, Support, Emotional Feedback, Social Stimulation, Activity, and Freedom. This 58-item, forced-choice instrument provides a ranking of environmental concerns as well as a numerical weight for each dimension. A new instrument for measuring perceptions of the prison setting, the Prison Environment Inventory, was developed for use in this study. Since they are the environmental conditions found to be of greatest concern to inmates, Toch's eight environmental factors were used as dimensions. Based upon an elaborate array of item and dimension analyses to test internal validity, a final, 48-item

Table 5.2
Analysis of Sample Representativeness

Background Variable	Sample N = 913	Population N = 11,725
Chi-Square Value and Significance		
(1) Ethnicity		324.15 .0001
(2) Occupation		.015 .9022
(3) Crime		21.98 .1085
(4) Second Time Felon		3.53 .1714
(5) Education		20.28 .0001
(6) Previous Adult Record		14.23 .1629
(7) Marital Status		5.27 .3826
T-Value and Significance		
(8) Age		1.03 .3019
(9) Age Entering System		.70 .4848
(10) Minimum Sentence		− .01 .9917

version of the questionnaire was formed (see Wright, 1985, for a discussion of the psychometric properties of the instrument).

Data were collected from randomly selected samples of inmates at five medium- and five maximum-security New York State prisons. The ten prisons were randomly selected from all institutions within each security classification. A list of inmates incarcerated in the facilities was used to generate random samples. Populations were oversampled to allow for attrition. Some inmates were unavailable for survey sessions because they were confined for disciplinary action or protection, or had sick-calls, visits, or court hearings. Other inmates preferred not to participate. Inmates were notified they had been randomly selected and a brief description of the study was given by prison staff. In some facilities, the call-out to the study was mandatory but participation was voluntary. In other facilities both the call-out and participation were voluntary. In one prison, the facility first determined if the inmates were willing to participate, then placed them on the call-out. The total sample consisted of 942 subjects.

To test for bias, the sample was compared to its population on 10 background variables. Except for ethnicity and education, the analyses revealed no differences in the two groups (Table 5.2). The degree of similarity probably indicates that the sample is adequate; however, given that black and less educated inmates are underrepresented in the sample there may be bias. The implications of this problem are discussed in the context of the results later in this manuscript.

FINDINGS

In posing the first research question, we were interested in whether whites suffer more distress and whether blacks are more likely to be aggressive. Different measures of these behavioral responses were used to see if some of the discrepancies in past research could be clarified. The results of the analyses of variance are shown in Table 5.3.

Looking first at the indicators of distress, we note that blacks and whites do not report significantly different levels of Internal or Physical problems. Blacks report for stress-related sick-calls slightly more frequently but not at a rate statistically different from whites. Where we find differences is in the rate of self-injury. This finding is consistent with Johnson's study. Whites engage in this extreme form of adaptation more frequently than blacks. It is clear that self-injury is a form of adaptation selected by very few inmates of either race.

We must ask what these findings mean in contrast to earlier studies that found racial differences in levels of depression. Obviously, something different from depression has been measured in this study. We have attempted to determine if blacks and whites differ in the way they physically experience prison.

Table 5.3
Mean Differences Between White and Black on Distress and Aggressive Outcome Variables

Outcomes	White (N = 409)	Black (N = 501)	F Value	Significance
Distress				
Self-reported internal problems	6.13	5.77	1.59	.21
Self-reported physical problems	1.53	1.51	.01	.90
Stress-related sick-calls	0.77	0.88	.49	.49
Self-injury	0.01	0.001	4.46	.04
Aggressiveness				
Assault infractions	0.06	0.06	.05	.82
Disruptive infractions	1.92	2.71	14.82	.0001
Self-reported external problems	1.15	1.28	.80	.37

The Internal dimension of the PAQ measured if inmates were more uncomfortable, angry, and fearful, less able to sleep, and sick more often in prison than in the free world. The Physical dimension assessed levels of victimization according to whether the inmate was taken advantage of or hurt.

Differences among racial groups on measures of depression can possibly be explained in several ways. Since many psychological inventories have been developed and normed using predominantly white subjects, error may be introduced when the instruments are used with blacks. Second, there may be culturally different patterns of socialization that lead individuals to interpret their experiences differently, so whites may describe themselves as depressed whereas blacks do not.

Turning to the second set of findings in Table 5.3, we observe that blacks and whites have exactly the same average number of assaults on staff and other inmates. This finding contradicts Carroll's contention that suggests that blacks are more aggressive and hostile, willing to strike out at staff, and take advantage of other inmates.

Noting the second row of aggressiveness findings in Table 5.3, one might be tempted to conclude that the significantly greater number of disruptive infractions among black inmates suggests that they defy prison authority more frequently than whites and are not in control of themselves as suggested by Johnson. However, in the third row of findings, we note no statistical differences between blacks and whites in self-reports of disruptive behavior (fights and arguments). This disparity can be interpreted in two ways. It may support earlier claims of racial bias in the application of charges of disturbance by correctional staff. As such, the differences may be an officially created distinction rather than a behavioral one. Alternatively, there may be racial differences in interpretation of what constitutes a "fight" or "argument."

The outcome findings of this study alone do not completely clarify the role race plays in determining adjustment success. For this reason, we decided to test the relationship further by seeing if other variables were affected as theory would predict. Specifically, we tested for differences in environmental needs and evaluations of black and white prisoners. We hypothesized that inmates from different backgrounds would have different sets of environmental needs and that inmates who were experiencing incarceration differently would rate their environmental situations differently. Table 5.4 presents the results of the analyses of variance.

First, looking at environmental concerns, we note that both black and white inmates rank Support as their highest need and Emotional Feedback as their second highest. There are significant differences in the average rankings among blacks and whites on both variables. Blacks express a higher need for tangible assistance and services, while whites have a greater need for emotional sustenance.

Following Support and Emotional Feedback, we continue to observe similar patterns of contextual need expressed by prisoners of both races. Activity is the third ranked concern, and Structure is the fourth. Safety is the fifth ranked need for both blacks and whites, and they do not statistically differ in the average level of need expressed. If inmates come to prison with background experiences that differentially prepares them for the pains of imprisonment, we would not expect such similar lists of concerns, and, in particular, we would not expect Safety concerns to be ranked so similarly.

Table 5.4
Mean Differences and Rankings of Environmental Concerns and Evaluations Between Black and White Inmates

Environmental Variables	*Environmental Concerns*								*Environmental Evaluations*							
	White (N = 405)		Black (N = 487)		F Value	Significance			White (N = 404)		Black (N = 497)		F Value	Significance		
	x̄	(Rank)	x̄	(Rank)					x̄	(Rank)	x̄	(Rank)				
Activity	7.5	(3)	7.3	(3)	1.41	.23			18.0	(2)	17.5	(2)	7.96	.005		
Emotional feedback	8.2	(2)	7.8	(2)	7.38	.007			14.4	(7)	14.6	(7)	0.59	.44		
Freedom	5.2	(8)	5.7	(6)	7.48	.006			16.4	(3)	15.8	(4)	9.60	.002		
Privacy	5.9	(6)	5.4	(8)	10.08	.002			14.7	(6)	14.8	(6)	0.02	.90		
Safety	6.6	(5)	6.9	(5)	2.82	.09			16.0	(4)	16.1	(3)	0.08	.77		
Social stimulation	5.7	(7)	5.4	(7)	3.32	.07			15.8	(5)	15.7	(5)	0.73	.39		
Structure	7.0	(4)	7.1	(4)	.08	.78			19.6	(1)	12.5	(1)	2.58	.11		
Support	9.8	(1)	10.3	(1)	17.65	.0001			12.7	(8)	12.5	(8)	1.98	.16		

It is only with the sixth and eighth rank variables that we observe significant differences in contextual needs. For blacks, who are more oppressed in the free world, there is greater need for freedom. Privacy, as determined culturally, may be as important to whites in the free world as it seems to be in prison.

Turning to the way in which blacks and whites evaluate their contextual situation, we would expect, if they experience incarceration differently, that the two groups would assess their situations differently. That is not the pattern seen in Table 5.4. The rankings are almost identical. The only real difference is that whites believe there is more freedom in prison than blacks. Importantly, Safety is rated almost identically by blacks and whites and is ranked relatively high among the attributes provided.

These analyses fail to confirm the thesis that blacks and whites arrive at prison differentially prepared to deal with the pains of incarceration and experience incarceration differently. Instead, they are consistent with outcome findings that the two groups experience incarceration similarly.

One explanation that has been advanced for racial differences found in past research is that institutional experience may enable an inmate to survive prison better and that blacks are more likely to have a prior incarceration. When race and prior experience were entered into a model to predict the seven outcome variables using ordinary least squares (OLS) regression, some support for this explanation was obtained. For one of the distress variables, self-reported Physical problems, and two of the aggressiveness variables, self-reported External problems and disruptive infractions, the models as a whole and experience were significant. For disruptive infractions, race also was a significant predictor of number of charges. Given this finding, we can speculate that some past findings of differences among black and white prisoners may be attributable to the fact that blacks have been previously incarcerated.

Both Carroll and Johnson explain the differences in the way blacks and whites adjust to prison as resulting from their experience in the urban ghetto. From Carroll's perspective, we hypothesize that there will be a positive relationship between aggressiveness and experience with poverty. From Johnson's ideas, we hypothesize that there will be a negative relationship between distress and experience with poverty.

Proxies of educational level and employment before incarceration were used to identify inmates who may have experienced the socializing forces of an impoverished background. The results of the analyses of differences in adjustment outcomes of inmates distinguished by categories associated with these two variables are shown in Tables 5.5 and 5.6.

As with prior incarceration, we find some support for the theory that background is related to adjustment. Looking at the results of the analyses for all inmates in Table 5.5, we see significant differences in adjustment for three variables, and in all three cases, the differences are in the direction predicted by theory. Inmates who have gone beyond high school in their education are more likely to report experiencing Physical problems, that is, being taken advantage of or hurt. These individuals are less likely to be experienced in institutions or on the "streets," and are the type of inmates referred to as "lambs."

Statistical differences are noted for two aggressiveness variables: assaultive and disruptive infractions. In both cases, there is an inverse relationship with education. These findings are consistent with Carroll's claims.

Table 5.5

Mean Differences Among Inmates with Different Educational Backgrounds on Distress and Aggressive Outcome Variables

Outcomes		No High School	Some High School	High School Grad.	Beyond High School	F Value	Significance
All Inmates	n =	215	408	246	24		
Self-reported internal problems		5.6	5.9	6.3	5.5	1.12	.34
Self-reported physical problems		1.4	1.6	1.3	2.9	4.75	.003
Stress-related sick-calls		0.5	1.0	0.8	1.4	1.87	.13
Self-injury		0.01	0.003	0.0	0.0	2.04	.11
Assault infractions		0.09	0.06	0.04	0.0	2.54	.05
Disruption infractions		2.8	2.7	1.5	1.4	11.20	.0001
Self-reported external problems		1.1	1.4	1.0	1.4	1.53	.20
Black Inmates	n =	92	261	137	11		
Self-reported internal problems		5.9	5.7	5.9	5.8	0.07	.97
Self-reported physical problems		1.3	1.7	1.2	2.0	2.62	.05
Stress-related sick-calls		0.4	1.1	0.7	0.9	1.72	.16
Self-injury		0.0	0.002	0.0	0.0	0.31	.82
Assault infractions		0.1	0.1	0.1	0.0	0.83	.48
Disruption infractions		3.4	3.0	1.8	0.9	6.40	.0004
Self-reported external problems		1.4	1.4	0.8	1.4	2.60	.05
White Inmates	n =	143	144	109	13		
Self-reported internal problems		5.5	6.3	6.8	5.2	2.26	.08
Self-reported physical problems		1.5	1.4	1.4	3.7	4.28	.006
Stress-related sick-calls		0.7	0.7	0.8	1.7	1.32	.27
Self-injury		0.02	0.01	0.0	0.0	1.50	.21
Assault infractions		0.1	0.1	0.03	0.0	1.83	.14
Disruption infractions		2.4	2.1	1.1	1.4	6.67	.0003
Self-reported external problems		1.0	1.2	1.2	1.5	0.56	.65

Table 5.6

Mean Differences Among Employed and Unemployed Inmates on Distress and Aggressive Outcome Variables

Outcomes		Unemployed	Employed	F Value	Significance
All Inmates	n =	254	655		
Self-reported internal problems		6.5	5.7	5.41	.02
Self-reported physical problems		1.8	1.4	6.34	.01
Stress-related sick-calls		0.6	0.9	2.19	.14
Self-injury		0.004	0.005	.04	.84
Assault infractions		.09	.05	8.16	.004
Disruption infractions		4.1	1.7	132.44	.0001
Self-reported external problems		1.8	1.0	27.51	.0001
Black Inmates	n =	149	350		
Self-reported internal problems		6.4	5.5	4.27	.04
Self-reported physical problems		2.0	1.3	9.45	.002
Stress-related sick-calls		0.5	1.0	3.37	.07
Self-injury		0.0	0.001	0.43	.51
Assault infractions		0.1	0.05	3.21	.07
Disruption infractions		4.8	1.8	93.93	.0001
Self-reported external problems		1.9	1.0	16.93	.0001
White Inmates	n =	104	303		
Self-reported internal problems		6.6	6.0	1.57	.21
Self-reported physical problems		1.6	1.5	0.10	.75
Stress-related sick-calls		0.8	0.8	0.04	.84
Self-injury		0.01	0.01	0.02	.89
Assault infractions		0.1	0.05	5.20	.02
Disruption infractions		3.2	1.5	35.94	.0001
Self-reported external problems		1.7	1.0	9.78	.002

These results hold within racial groups. For both black and white inmates, individuals with more than a high school education are more likely to report experiencing Physical problems and less educated inmates have more disruptive infractions. The relationship of assaultive infractions and education did not hold up within racial groups.

In looking down the column of significance values in Table 5.6, it is clear that employment status before incarceration is also related to adjustment. For all inmates and within racial groups, indicators of aggressive behavior are related to whether the individual had a job before prison. As Carroll's thesis implies, unemployed inmates are more aggressive than those who live a less economically marginal life before incarceration.

Findings that are inconsistent with theory are found for two distress variables: self-reports of Internal and Physical problems. Both variables are significantly different for all inmates, but are in the opposite direction from what would be expected. These findings suggest that inmates from a poor background suffer more. When we examine these findings within racial groups, we note that the relationship is not found for whites but holds for blacks. Unemployed blacks, that is, black men who were more economically marginal in the free world, suffer greater distress upon incarceration.

To evaluate the relationship of race, prior incarceration, and poverty to the different adjustment outcomes, covariance analyses of all variables were performed using OLS regression. The purpose of this assessment was to try to separate the effects of race and experience to see what contributes to the way prisoners adapt to incarceration. The results are shown in Table 5.7.

A particularly revealing finding is that, while the models for all six adjustment variables are significant, the amount of variance explained is extremely low. These results indicate that race, prior incarceration, and experience play a role in determining how inmates will adjust to prison, but that role is relatively minor. These findings should not be surprising. Race, prior incarceration, and experience are but three variables that might influence how someone would adjust to prison. Personality and intelligence, reputation and presence of friends, support from home, and physical strength may also affect adjustment patterns. Contextual effects also determine how one will adjust. Whether the prison setting meets the inmate's environmental needs is important.

Another important finding to be noted in Table 5.7 is that race is not a significant predictor of any adjustment indicator except disruptive infractions and self-injury, for which the model itself explains little variance. What this means in the context of a covariance analysis is that when the effects of prior incarceration and economic marginality are statistically controlled, the influence of race is not apparent. The fact that education and employment are significant in some cases gives some credence to the theory.

It is important to note that in the literature most authors refer to experience in the "black" urban ghetto as differentially preparing individuals to deal with the pains of incarceration. Both the culture of poverty and discrimination are considered as contributing factors. But it should be recognized that these are post hoc explanations given by researchers who observe what they perceive to be differences in the ways blacks and whites adjust to prison. What these findings appear to suggest is that economic marginality, whether experienced by a black or a white, will effect how the individual adjusts to prison.

Table 5.7
Covariance Analysis Predicting Adjustment Outcomes

Outcome	Source	F	Sign	R^2
Self-reported internal problems	Model	3.05	.02	.01
	Race	1.81	.18	
	Experience	2.01	.16	
	Education	1.88	.17	
	Employment	6.48	.01	
Self-reported physical problems	Model	3.53	.01	.02
	Race	0.02	.87	
	Experience	9.14	.003	
	Education	0.55	.46	
	Employment	4.41	.04	
Self-injury	Model	2.38	.05	.01
	Race	4.48	.03	
	Experience	0.00	.96	
	Education	4.59	.03	
	Employment	0.45	.50	
Assault infractions	Model	3.26	.01	.01
	Race	0.06	.81	
	Experience	0.00	.99	
	Education	7.45	.007	
	Employment	5.53	.02	
Disruption infractions	Model	40.55	.0001	.15
	Race	17.11	.0001	
	Experience	18.02	.0001	
	Education	34.35	.0001	
	Employment	92.71	.0001	
Self-reported external problems	Model	8.86	.0001	.04
	Race	0.82	.37	
	Experience	14.71	.0001	
	Education	0.28	.60	
	Employment	19.64	.0001	

Given the implications of these findings, the representativeness of the sample must be reconsidered. Recall that black and less educated inmates were underrepresented in the sample. Bias would be present if those inmates in the underrepresented group not found in the sample differ on the outcome variables from those in the sample. For example, if blacks are underrepresented because a particularly aggressive subgroup was held in special housing and consequently could not participate in the study, then the observed rate of assaults for black inmates would be lower than the true rate of assaults. Conversely, blacks could be underrepresented because less aggressive inmates are held in protective custody and could not participate. The same sampling problem is true for education. Inmates with less education may have been unable to complete the survey instruments and more likely to have adjustment problems. These issues cannot be directly considered. However, the consistency of the findings of this study with one theoretical position may suggest that there is no sampling problem; only subsequent studies can substantiate this possibility.

CONCLUSION

In early studies of prison adjustment, researchers sought commonalities in the way inmates experienced incarceration. Out of this era, the importance of the informal inmate culture was recognized. Then, through the influence of Irwin (1970), Jacobs (1977), and others, it was realized that global experiences alone do not capture the prison experience, that differences among subgroups influenced how people ultimately fared during their period of incarceration. But just as early researchers oversimplified adjustment patterns by examining the commonalities of the experience, so have others by looking at racial groups as distinct and intact entities.

If we look at Irwin's (1970) early work, we see that he recognizes two types of black inmates: The hustler, who was characterized as a strong individual, conscious of not being taken advantage of, and in control, much like the individual described by Johnson. In contrast, the disorganized criminal, of which there are also many white inmates, is not at all "together," but pursues a chaotic life in and outside of prison. Because of his weak self-concept, he may be passive and withdraw from the prison social life or he may be drawn into the prison culture. In reviewing Megargee and Bohn's (1979) ten personality types, we find blacks overrepresented among a group of inmates described (pp. 221–223) as cold and bitter individuals who will become hostile and violent when they perceive themselves to have been insulted. But we also find a group with a large proportion of blacks that are extremely passive and try to avoid conflict (pp. 211–213). So while experience prior to incarceration may lead some black inmates to a posture of strength, it may lead others to a position of weakness. This may be the reason, we found that black inmates who were unemployed before incarceration suffered greater distress while imprisoned than black inmates who were employed. Sweeping generalization about racial groups allow us to overlook within-group differences and to reach inappropriate conclusions.

It is undeniable that some blacks and some whites act differently and fit the stereotypes found in the literature described above. But there are weak, passive, and victimized black inmates and strong, aggressive, and exploitive white inmates. Overall, the distinction is not clear, and simplification of causal factors to a bivariate relationship muddles rather than clarifies our understanding.

We found support for the hypotheses that economic marginality, regardless of the race of its residents, influences prison adjustment, but we found this relationship not to be a strong one. Other individual and contextual effects surely go into determining how successfully one will survive prison.

REFERENCES

Bartollas, C., S. Miller, and S. Dinitz. 1976. *Juvenile Victimization: The Institutional Paradox.* New York: Halstead.

Carroll, L. 1974. *Hacks, Blacks and Cons: Race Relations in a Maximum Security Prison.* Lexington, MA: D. C. Heath.

_____ 1982. "Race, Ethnicity, and the Social Order of the Prison." In *The Pains of Imprisonment,* edited by R. Johnson and H. Toch. Beverly Hills, CA: Sage.

Clemmer, D. 1940. *The Prison Community.* New York: Holt, Rinehart & Winston.

Ellis, D., H. G. Grasmick, and B. Gilman. 1974. "Violence in Prisons: A Sociological Analysis." *American Journal of Sociology* 80:16–43.

Fagan, T. J. and F. T. Lira. 1978. "Profile of Mood States: Racial Differences in a Delinquent Population." *Psychological Reports* 43:348–350.

Flanagan, T. J. 1980. "Time Served and Institutional Misconduct: Patterns of Involvement in Disciplinary Infractions Among Long-Term and Short-Term Inmates." *Journal of Criminal Justice* 8:357–367.

_____ 1983. "Correlates of Institutional Misconduct Among State Prisoners." *Criminology* 21:29–39.

Fuller, D. and T. Orsagh. 1977. "Violence and Victimization Within a State Prison." *Criminal Justice Review* 2:35–55.

Goetting, A. and R. M. Howsen. 1983. "Blacks in Prison: A Profile." *Criminal Justice Review* 8:21–31.

Goodstein, L. and D. L. Mackenzie. 1984a. "Racial Differences in Adjustment Patterns of Prison Inmates—Prisonization, Conflict, Stress, and Control." In *The Criminal Justice System and Blacks,* edited by D. Georges-Abeyie. New York: Clark Boardman.

_____ and R. Wu. 1984b. "Institutional Racial Balance and Patterns of Adjustment Among Black and White Prisoners." Paper presented at the annual meetings of the American Society of Criminology, Cincinnati, OH, November 7–11.

Irwin, J. 1970. *The Felon.* Englewood Cliffs, NJ: Prentice-Hall.

_____ 1980. *Prisons in Turmoil.* Boston: Little, Brown.

Jacobs, J. 1974. "Street Gangs Behind Bars." *Social Problems* 21:395–409.

_____ 1976. "Stratification and Conflict Among Prison Inmates." *Journal of Criminal Law and Criminology* 66:476–482.

_____ 1977. *Stateville, the Penitentiary in Mass Society.* Chicago: University of Chicago Press.

Johnson, E. 1966. "Pilot Study: Age, Race, Recidivism as Factors in Prisoner Infractions." *Canadian Journal of Corrections* 8:268–283.

Johnson, R. 1976. *Culture and Crisis in Confinement.* Lexington, MA: D. C. Heath.

Jones, D. A. 1976. *The Health Risks of Imprisonment.* Lexington, MA: Lexington.

Lockwood, D. 1980. *Prison Sexual Violence.* New York: Elsevier.

Megargee, E. I. and M. J. Bohn. 1979. *Classifying Criminal Offenders.* Beverly Hills, CA: Sage.

Myers, L. and G. Levy. 1978. "Description and Prediction of the Intractable Inmate." *Journal of Research in Crime and Delinquency* 15:214–228.

Oldroyd, R. J. and R. J. Howell. 1977. "Personality, Intellectual and Behavioral Differences Between Black, Chicano, and White Prison Inmates in the Utah State Prison." *Psychological Reports* 41:187–191.

O'Leary, V. and D. Glaser. 1972. "The Assessment of Risk in Parole Decision Making." In *The Future of Parole,* edited by D. J. West. New York: International Publication Service.

Petersilia, J. R. 1983. *Racial Disparities in the Criminal Justice System.* Santa Monica, CA: Rand.

Poole, E. P. and R. M. Regoli. 1980. "Race, Institutional Rule Breaking and Disciplinary Response: A Study of Discretionary Decision Making in Prison." *Law and Society Review* 14:931–946.

Ramirez, J. 1983. "Apprehension of Inmate Misconduct." *Journal of Criminal Justice* 11:413–427.

Scacco, A. M. 1975. *Rape in Prison.* Springfield, IL: Charles C. Thomas.

Sykes, G. 1966. *The Society of Captives.* New York: Atheneum.

_____ and S. L. Messinger. 1960. "The Inmate Social System." In *Theoretical Studies in the Social Organization of the Prison,* edited by R. Cloward. New York: Social Science Research Council.

Thomas, C. W. 1970. "Toward a More Inclusive Model of the Inmate Contraculture." *Criminology* 8:251–262.

_____ and D. M. Peterson. 1977. *Prison Organization and Inmate Subcultures.* Indianapolis: Bobbs-Merrill.

Toch, H. 1977. *Living in Prison: The Ecology of Survival.* New York: Free Press.

Wellford, C. 1967. "Factors Associated with Adoption of the Inmate Code: A Study of Normative Socialization." *Journal of Criminal Law, Criminology, and Police Science* 58:197–203.

Wooden W. S. and J. Parker. 1982. *Men Behind Bars: Sexual Exploitation in Prison.* New York: Plenum.

Wright, K. N. 1985. "Developing the Prison Environment Inventory." *Journal of Research in Crime and Delinquency* 8:257–277.

Zink, T. M. 1958. "Are Prison Troublemakers Different?" *Journal of Criminal Law, Criminology and Police Science* 48:433–434.

CHAPTER 6

AGE AND ADJUSTMENT TO PRISON INTERACTIONS WITH ATTITUDES AND ANXIETY

Doris Layton MacKenzie

Interpersonal conflict and major misconducts indicative of aggressive behavior were examined as a function of age for a homogeneous set of prison inmates. In contrast to previous studies, a direct linear decline in these behaviors did not occur with age. The pattern of change over age varied for the aggressive behaviors. Furthermore, age differences in anxiety and attitudes were found. There was no indication that the age differences in conflicts and misconducts were due to age differences in the ability to cope with the environment. However, there was some evidence that attitudes may differentially effect the behavior of inmates of different ages. Stronger attitudes reflecting either fear or victimization or the need to assert oneself in interactions with others led to more interpersonal conflicts at any age but only the youngest responded in manner leading to punishment by the institution.

Aggression and violence are serious problems in male prisons. Interinmate conflicts, threats of violence, victimization, and staff-inmate clashes are common occurrences (Adams, 1985; Ellis, 1974; Gaes & McGuire, 1985; Lombardo, 1982; Sykes, 1966). Research examining violence in prison almost invariably indicates a strong inverse association between age and such behavior. Younger inmates are found to be involved in more disciplinary infractions (Porporino & Zamble, 1984), inmate-inmate assaults (Ekland-Olson, Barrick, & Cohen, 1983), inmate-staff assaults (Wright & Smith, 1985), and they report more conflicts with others (Wright & Smith, 1985).

AUTHOR'S NOTE: This investigation was supported in part by Grant #80-NI-AX-006 from the National Institute of Justice. Requests for reprints should be sent to Doris L. MacKenzie, Assistant Professor of Criminal Justice and Experimental Statistics, Louisiana State University, Baton Rouge, LA 70803. An earlier version of this work was presented at the annual meeting of the Academy of Criminal Justice Sciences, St. Louis, 1987.

CRIMINAL JUSTICE AND BEHAVIOR, Vol. 14 No. 4, December 1987 427–447
© 1987 American Association for Correctional Psychology

The youth-aggression relationship for males is a continual and consistent finding in the literature on inmate adjustment to prison. This is in agreement with the research relating age and violent criminal behavior outside of prison (Greenberg, 1985; Hirschi & Gottfredson, 1983; Wolfgang & Weinger, 1982). However, the finding of an association between youth and aggression does not give us an explanation for the relationship. Thus although we know there is a relationship between age and aggressive behavior, there are few extant theories that can be used to explain this relationship (Greenberg, 1985; Hirschi & Gottfredson, 1983; Wright & Smith, 1985).

Various possible reasons for the aggression-age relationship have been proposed. Younger individuals are thought to be less aware of the consequences of their actions. According to this perspective the costs of aggression and the likelihood of punishment are learned in the process of aging (Wilson & Herrnstein, 1985). Aging has been proposed to bring with it a cautiousness, or loss of nerve, resulting in a fear to act aggressively (Ellis, 1984; Wallach, Kogan, & Bem, 1962). Another view is that as people mature they accept a new normative orientation that is prosocial; they are less apt to consider violence an acceptable method of interacting with others. A factor thought to influence this prosocial orientation is the fact that the older person has made obvious social commitments, such as marriage, children, and careers (Greenberg, 1985). These involvements are hypothesized to be endangered by aggressive behavior and, therefore, act as inhibitors.

As is true of the outside world, there are many reasons for conflicts and aggression within prison. Aggression can be instrumentally motivated and serve as a means to some end (Magaree, 1982).[1] Violent acts may also represent impulsive responses to high levels of stress.[2] That is aversive stimulations (stress) may cause the emotional reactions of rage and anger. Aggressive responses are the outward manifestations of these emotions (Toch, 1982). In such instances the reaction is assumed to occur without thought or plan and have no instrumental motivation. Although two people may act in an identical manner, the reason for each act may be very different. One individual may be performing a well-planned act aimed at accomplishing some end. The other may be reacting without objective, to a stressful situation. The former may be threatening a guard to intimidate, the latter is lashing out only in an attempt to release tension. The appropriate way of handling or punishing such individuals would certainly depend upon the reason for the aggressive act. Some would benefit from stress management; others would more adequately be deterred by punishment.

There are numerous possible causes for age differences in aggression. One possibility is that young people are more impulsive. As has been hypothesized by others, younger people may fail to recognize the costs of aggression or there may be less cost for them (Wilson & Herrnstein, 1985). As a result, when angry, the young person may react with physical aggression. In contrast, the older person who may be equally angry may respond with verbal aggression or express anger in other more subtle ways. This "controlled" aggressive behavior of the older person may be less costly to oneself.

The young and the old may also differ in the problems that lead to aggressive behavior. One group may find an environment or situation more hostile, bothersome, or stressful than the other. For example, younger inmates might find the prison environment more alienating and, thereby, have difficulty coping with the situation. As a result of this extreme stress the young inmate experiences rage and anger. In this case, aggression would not be effective in helping the inmate reach some goal but rather would be manifestation of an impaired coping ability (Toch, 1969). Both young and old would assumedly "act out" when stressed, but the higher level of stress experienced by the young inmate in prison would result in more aggression. From this perspective, the higher levels of aggression of young inmates would be a function of their higher level of stress. Such aggressive responses might be expected to occur in conjunction with high levels of anxiety.

Adams (1985) found prison inmates who had mental health problems had more disciplinary infractions involving violence. The author concludes that disruptive behavior is a manifestation of an inability to cope. The infraction rate for these inmates declined with increased age. However, the age differences varied depending on whether or not the inmate received mental health services. There was little difference between young inmates and older inmates if they have been hospitalized for a mental health problem. However, when those who had not received mental health services were compared, the infraction rates were very different. In this case, younger inmates had substantially higher infraction rates than older inmates. If increases in infraction rates reflect a diminished ability to cope, these results suggest that younger inmates may be less able to cope than older inmates.

One factor that has been found to be related to stress in prison is crowding of the institution. There is some evidence of age differences in the effect of crowding. Inmate assaults and misconducts have been shown to increase as density increases in juvenile and youth institutions; this relationship is weaker or nonexistent in the adult institutions (Ekland-Olson et al., 1983; Nacci, Teitelbaum, & Prather, 1977). Crowding may be more stressful for the younger inmate who responds by lashing out at others. However, other research suggests that assaults against staff increase with crowding in institutions with older inmates but institutions with younger inmates are not affected (Gaes & McGuire, 1985). Thus crowding may exacerbate aggression or certain types of aggression at some ages but have little or no effect on the same individuals at a different age.

Another possible explanation for the age difference in aggression is a difference in internal motivations at different ages. There is some research suggesting that the relevance of the specific internal factors that motivate an individual to respond aggressively may change with age. Older inmates have been found to prefer an environment with structure and caring responses (Toch, 1977). For the older inmate conflict or aggression might result from attempts to remove bothersome or annoying inmates and thus secure quiet or privacy for oneself. This may not be an important motivating factor in a young person's aggressive behavior.

For the younger inmate aggression may be a way to gain status. In a study examining prison inmates, Ellis, Brasmick, and Gilman (1974) asked male inmates why some inmates were more aggressive than others. Most often the inmates gave an instrumental reason for aggression, such as acquiring a sexual partner or retrieving a debt. Far fewer listed unprovoked stress responses. There was an interesting difference between adult and youth prisons, however. In adult prisons an inmate who is constantly fighting with others was feared, despised, and regarded as stupid. In the youth prisons such an individual was feared but, in contrast with the adult prisons, the individual was also given status for being strong and capable of protecting himself.

In summary, there is a strong inverse relationship between age and aggressive behavior in prison. This may be because older inmates have learned to express anger in a different manner. If this is so then the type of assertive or aggressive behavior may vary with age. Another possibility is that aggression is the outward manifestation of rage caused by stress. Younger inmates may be less able to cope and, therefore, their aggression is a reflection of an impaired coping ability rather than serving some instrumental purpose. It is also possible that aggression and conflict have instrumental purposes such as to remove a bothersome inmate or to gain status. Although both of these examples of aggression serve instrumental purposes the goals are widely different. From this perspective the relevance of the specific internal factors or goals that motivate an individual to respond aggressively may change with age.

The purpose of the present study was to examine the aggressive behavior of prison inmates as a function of age. Three measures of aggression were examined: conflicts with other inmates, conflicts with guards, and major misconduct tickets received per month in prison. If older inmates learn to express their anger in a different manner than younger inmates they may have conflicts with others but they may not behave in a manner warranting major misconduct tickets.

The second goal of the study was to examine the relationship among anxiety, aggression, and age. Younger inmates may experience more stress in prison than older inmates. On the other hand, the level of stress may be identical but the response to stress may differ as a function of age. If anxiety is used as a measure of stress then age differences in anxiety would be indicative of differences in stress. A positive relationship between anxiety and aggression would suggest increased aggressive behavior associated with increased stress. However, an interaction between age and anxiety would suggest that the relationship between aggressive behavior and stress depends upon the age of the inmate. For example, increases in stress might be associated with aggressive behavior in young inmates but may not have the same effect in older inmates.

Internal factors have been hypothesized to differ as a function of an inmates' age. For example, the need for isolation from others is expected to be more important to older inmates. In contrast, younger inmates are expected to believe that one must "stand one's ground" in interactions with others. Younger inmates are also expected to have more fears, possibly justified, of being victimized in prison (Bowker, 1982). Previous research suggests that there may be age differences in the factors that influence aggression at different ages. The third aim of this study was to examine whether the internal factors differentially affected the aggression of inmates of varying ages. There may be no age differences in the desire to be isolated. Yet for older inmates these attitudes may be associated with aggression while for younger inmates the attitudes would not. The internal factors examined in this study were (1) isolation attitudes representing the desire of the inmate to serve time in prison without being bothered by others, (2) attitudes about the appropriate way of interacting with others, and (3) how fearful the inmate is about being victimized by others while in prison.

METHOD

Subjects and Procedure

Random samples of inmates in four prisons were drawn from prison records on three successive visits, separated by at least six months. At each visit approximately 250 names were drawn. Inmates were asked to complete a written questionnaire. If an inmate's name was drawn at a successive visit his questionnaire was dropped from this analysis. In all, 2,140 inmates completed the questionnaires once. From the total sample of inmates a subset was used for the present study. This subset included only the 755 inmates who had served less than a year in prison. Inmates were asked to attend questionnaire sessions in groups of approximately 30. After completing consent forms, inmates attending questionnaire sessions worked individually and required about one hour to complete the questionnaire. Inmates received a small monetary sum for their participation.

Institutions

The four institutions studied are large close-security prisons for adult male felons. Somers (Connecticut) and Stillwater (Minnesota) are both mixed (medium and maximum) security-level institutions, as is Logan (Illinois). However, Stateville, a maximum security facility, houses more of the serious offenders incarcerated in Illinois. Comparison of the sample to the populations of the prisons revealed no major differences in age or nonwhite composition except at Stillwater, where the average of the sample was approximately 2 years older than that of the general population.

Age and Time Served

In order to have a homogeneous subset of inmates, only data from those who had served less than one year in the prison studied and on the present conviction were included in this study (see Goodstein & Hepburn, 1985, for a study using the total sample). A subset was used in order to eliminate the confounding of time served with age. Inmates who have served more time in prison are generally older. Therefore, an analysis of age differences would be confounded with time served if all inmates in the prison were included in the study. Since prior research has shown evidence of inmate change over time in prison the decision was made to restrict the research to only those who had served a short time in prison (MacKenzie & Goodstein, 1985).

Instruments

The questionnaire included questions regarding demographic information such as age, education (highest grade completed in school), size of city or town in which the inmates lived immediately before incarceration (large cities, suburbs, medium or small cities, and rural areas), involvement in work or school activities before incarceration (none, part time, full time), and marital status (single-never married, married, divorced, widowed).

Indicators of criminal behavior were the number of prior convictions reported by the inmates and the estimated sentence length. The sentence length was determined by calculating the amount of time from the date of entry until the inmate's self-reported release date. In addition, the inmates were asked to report the offense(s) for which they were currently serving time. These offenses were classified on a 7-point scale for severity using state statutes (most severe = 1).

Involvement in institutionally sanctioned activities was measured by asking inmates to list all the programs and activities in the prison (such as education, sports, or counseling) that they had attended within the past three months.

Two summated scales were used to measure the interpersonal conflicts of the inmates. The first scale, *Inmate Conflicts,* was designed to measure the amount of conflict the respondent had with other inmates in prison (MacKenzie & Goodstein, 1986; Shoemaker & Hellery, 1980). The scale is made up of six statements written to indicate progressively more severe conflict. Response choices ranged from never (1) to daily (6). High scores indicate frequent and severe conflicts with other inmates. The second scale, *Guard Conflicts,* was identical to the first except the items referred to situations involving conflicts between the respondent and guards in the institution.

Misbehavior was measured by the number of major *Misconduct* tickets received by the inmate per month in the institution.

Anxiety was measured using the state version of the State-Trait Anxiety Scale (Spielberger, Gorsuch, & Lushine, 1970), a 20-item summated rating scale with four response choices (high score = high anxiety).

Three summated scales, *Fear of Others, Assertive Interactions,* and *Isolation,* developed through a factor analysis procedure using a large number of individual prisonization items, were used to measure attitudes (Goodstein & Hepburn, 1985; Goodstein & MacKenzie, 1984). The *Fear of Victimization* (4 items) measured the degree to which the respondent was afraid of being injured or attacked by other inmates while in prison (high = high fear) (MacKenzie & Goodstein, 1985). How strongly the inmate felt about keeping up a strong front, fighting if someone pushed him around, and not backing away from trouble was measured with the *Assertive Interactions Scale* (9 items, high = strong assertiveness) (Goodstein & MacKenzie, 1984). The *Isolation Scale* (6 items) measured inmate concern for keeping to himself while in prison, not trusting others, or minding his own business (high = strong attitude of isolation) (see Appendix).

RESULTS

Age Groups

Inmates were categorized into 8 age groups, beginning with the category 19 years of age or less and ending with those 50 years of age or older. The categories between these were in 5-year intervals (see Table 6.1). On the average, the inmates were 28.3 years old (SD = 7.6).

A comparison of the eight age groups revealed no significant differences in mean time served, overall M = 5.8 months (SD = 3.2). Thus age was not confounded with time served in prison.

No significant differences were found for the age groups on the number of prior convictions or estimated sentence length. On the average, the inmates had 1.6 prior convictions (SD = 2.9) and expected to serve 31.3 months in prison (SD = 35.9). The groups did differ on crime severity, $F(7,616)$ = 2.92, $p < .01$. However, as shown in Table 6.1 there was no consistent pattern with age.

While in prison the inmates participated in an average of 1.5 (SD = 1.4) different institutionally sanctioned activities (no age group differences).

Table 6.1
Mean Differences in Attitudes, Behavior, and Past Experiences of Prison Inmates as a Function of Age

	Age in Years (n)							
	19 or less (31)	20-24 (235)	25-29 (196)	30-34 (139)	35-39 (52)	40-45 (30)	45-49 (12)	50+ (21)
Crime Severity	2.2_a	2.9_b	2.9_b	3.1_b	2.4_a	3.0_b	4.1_c	
Education	10.6_b	10.9_{bcd}	11.4_{cd}	11.6_d	11.5_{cd}	10.7_{bc}	10.7_{bc}	9.1_a
Anxiety	54.3_a	55.7_a	55.1_a	53.8_a	54.2_a	46.2_b	55.8_a	47.2_b
Assertive Interactions	28.7_{ab}	32.7_c	31.7_c	31.1_c	31.0_{bc}	29.6_{abc}	29.6_{abc}	26.8_a
Fear of Victimization	12.7_{ab}	14.2_c	13.7_{bc}	13.4_{abc}	13.3_{abc}	12.4_a	13.2_{abc}	12.5_{ab}
Prisoner-Prisoner Conflicts	11.4_{bcd}	13.0_d	12.3_{cd}	11.2_{bc}	11.3_{bc}	9.2_{ab}	8.7_{ab}	7.6_a
Prisoner-Guard Conflicts	9.6_{ab}	11.9_c	10.3_b	9.2_{ab}	8.6_{ab}	8.6_{ab}	7.9_{ab}	6.8_a
Major Misconducts/ Time in Institution	$.45_a$	$.27_b$	$.14_c$	$.08_c$	$.07_c$	$.04_c$	$.01_{bc}$	$.03_c$

NOTE: Age group means followed by the same letter are not significantly different ($p < .05$) from each other.

Significant differences were also found in the age groups for education, $F(7,705) = 6.34$, $p < .001$. differences suggested a curvilinear relationship with age (Table 6.1). Those who were in the youngest age groups and those who were in the oldest group had completed fewer years of school than had those in their late twenties or thirties.

No differences were found in the groups' involvement in work or school activities before incarceration. Of the total, 61.4% had been employed or in school full time, 13.1% had been involved in these activities on a part-time basis, and 25.6% had been neither employed nor in school. Nor were there age group differences in the size of the town in which the inmates lived immediately before incarceration. Those from large cities made up 53.3% of the sample, 10.5% came from the suburb of a large city, 24.6% came from medium or small cities, and the remaining 11.7% came from rural areas.

The groups did differ in their marital status $\chi^2(21) = 132.6$, $p < .01$. The direction of this difference was a change from single (86.7% for those under 20 years old to 9.5% for those over 50 years of age) to married (10% for those under 20 to a peak of 50% for those between 45 and 49). There was also a change from single and married to divorced (from 3.3% for those under 20 to a peak of 38.1% for those over 50) and widowed (from 0 under age 20 to 19.1% for those over 50).

Overall, the age groups were similar on their experiences with the criminal justice system except for differences in crime severity. On the whole, the groups were also quite similar in their experiences prior to prison (e.g., employment experience and city size). As would be expected, changes in marital status did occur with age. Also the groups differed slightly in their level of education.

Behavior in Prison

Means for Prisoner Conflicts and Guard Conflicts for each age group are shown in Table 6.1. As can be seen for these inmates, both Prisoner Conflicts (F(7,697) = 4.72, $p < .001$) and Guard conflicts ($F(7,693) = 6.07$, p < .001) peaked in the early twenties and declined with age.

Examination of the mean differences for the age groups of Misconducts revealed a rapid decline from teenage years through the twenties and, thereafter, a more gradual decline, $F(7,559) = 5.77, p < .001$.

Anxiety and Attitudes

There were no significant differences on anxiety for the age groups under forty (Table 6.1). Those between 40 and 44 and those over 50 were significantly lower than any other age group in anxiety, $F(7,676) = 4.44, p < .001$.

As shown in Table 6.1, the age groups did differ in Assertive Interactions and Fear of Victimization, $F(7,706) = 5.41, p < .001$ and $F(7,708) = 2.42, p < .02$, respectively. Assertive Interactions and Fear of Victimization increased from the first to the second age group. Both peaked during the twenties and declined thereafter. No differences were found for the age groups on Isolation, overall $M = 21.4, SD = 4.3$.

Covariance Analyses

Separate analyses were run to examine whether the number of Guard Conflicts, Prisoner Conflicts, and/or Misconducts changed as a function of the inmates' attitudes and anxiety. To examine whether this change was similar for all ages, analyses of covariance with heterogeneous slopes were performed. In these analyses Inmate Conflicts, Guard Conflicts, and Misconducts were the dependent variables; attitude (or anxiety), age, and the interaction (Age × Attitude) were the independent variables. If the slopes were found to be homogeneous then the interaction term was deleted from the model and the covariance model with homogeneous slopes is reported. On the other hand, if the interaction term in the analysis was significant it was concluded that the slopes were heterogeneous. This would mean that the effect of the attitude (or anxiety) differed depending upon the age of the inmate. In such cases, analyses with separate slopes for each group were run in order to examine the relationship between the attitude and the dependent variable for the age groups.

The results of these analyses are presented in Table 6.2. There were no interactions for the analyses using Fear of Victimization, Assertive Interactions, or Isolation as the covariates and either conflict scale as the dependent variable. Fear of Victimization and Assertive Interactions had positive and significant relationships with Inmate Conflicts and Guard Conflicts. The more the inmate felt it was important to stand up for his own rights in interactions with others, the more conflicts he had with inmates (beta = .26) and with guards (beta = .29). Similarly, the more fearful the inmate was the more interpersonal conflicts he

Table 6.2

F-Ratios for Analyses Examining Interpersonal Conflicts and Misconducts as a Function of Age, Attitudes, and Anxiety

	Dependent Variable		
	Inmate Conflicts (F-ratio)	*Guard Conflicts (F-ratio)*	*Misconducts (F-ratio)*
Fear of Others	55.04**	45.37**	3.90
Age Group	3.34**	4.66**	5.38**
Interaction	—	—	2.52*
Total	9.80**	9.75**	3.95
r^2	.10	.10	.10
Assertive Interactions	61.87**	86.87**	19.78**
Age	2.78**	3.70**	5.20**
Interaction	—	—	2.06**
Total	10.17**	14.10**	4.70**
r^2	.11	.14	.11
Isolation	.41	.03	1.41
Age	4.44**	5.81**	5.56*
Interaction	—	—	2.24*
Total	3.94**	5.09**	3.74**
r^2	.6	.04	.10
Anxiety	46.31**	39.83**	3.82
Age	3.69**	5.01**	5.23**
Interaction	2.52*	—	—
Total	5.98**	9.37	5.06**
r^2	.12	.11	.08

*$p < .05$ **$p > .01$

had (beta = .41, inmates; beta = .35, guards). Isolation was not significant in its relationship to the interpersonal conflict scales.

For the three analyses using these attitudes as covariates with Misconducts as the dependent variable there were interactions. In order to examine the different relationships, analyses with separate slopes for each age group were run with Misconducts as the dependent variable. For those under 20 years old the analyses revealed that Fear of Others was significant in predicting the number of Misconducts ($t = 4.28$, beta = .08, $p < .001$). Fear was not significant in predicting Misconducts for any other age group. Only for inmates under 20 years old is increased fearfulness related to an increase in the number of misconducts.

In the Age × Isolation interaction analyses no differences in the effect of isolation were found for any of the age groups except in the case of those under 20. For these inmates an increase in the desire to be isolated from others was accompanied by a greater number of Misconducts ($t = 4.04$, $p < .001$, beta = .08).

The analyses of separate slopes for age groups with Assertive Interactions as the independent variable and Misconducts as the dependent variable revealed that this attitude was significant for those under the age 20 ($t = 4.16$, $p < .001$, beta = .06) and for those between 20 and 24 ($t = 2.9$, $p < .01$, beta = .02), borderline for those in their late twenties ($t = 1.92$, $p < .06$, beta = .01) and non-significant for the other groups. Thus for inmates under thirty, the stronger the inmate feels he must not be pushed around or back away from trouble, the more major misconducts he has. This increase in the number of misconducts with stronger assertiveness attitudes is greater for the younger age groups (comparison of betas). An increase in these attitudes is not related to misconducts for inmates over thirty.

Anxiety was significant in the analysis with Guard Conflicts (beta = .11) as the dependent variable (Table 6.2). There was a significant Age × Anxiety interaction for inmate conflicts. Anxiety was not significant when Misconducts were the dependent variable. There were no interactions when either Guard Conflicts or Misconducts were the dependent variables.

In the analysis using Anxiety as the covariate and Inmate Conflicts as the dependent variable there was a significant interaction. Analyses with separate slopes for the age groups showed that anxiety was significant in predicting Inmate Conflicts for those under 20 ($t = 2.38$, $p < .05$, beta = .25), and for the two groups in their twenties ($t = 4.12$, $p < .001$, beta = .14; $t = 2.94$, $p < .01$, beta = .12, respectively). As the level of anxiety increased in inmates under the age of 30 the number of conflicts with other inmates increased. Anxiety level did not have this effect on inmates over 30 years of age. Anxiety was not significantly related to inmate conflicts for any of the older age groups.

DISCUSSION

As expected, there was a strong relationship between age and problem behavior in prison. However, in contrast with previous studies of aggressive behavior, the relationship was not a direct linear decline. Interpersonal conflicts with inmates and guards increased from the teens until sometime in the twenties. For both conflict scales the peak was during the twenties, however, conflicts with other inmates remained high for a longer period of time. The pattern for major misconducts by age differed from interpersonal conflicts in that the youngest age group had substantially more misconducts in comparison to other groups and the number of misconducts declined rapidly during the twenties. Thus misconducts peaked during the teenage years while conflicts with others was at a peak for those in their early twenties. After thirty there was no significant change in the number of misconducts; conflicts with prisoners continued to decline over the ages measured. These results do support the hypothesis that the expression of anger may differ over the lifespan. Although inmates in their twenties report more interpersonal conflicts than the younger inmates, they are less apt to have received major misconducts.

It had been hypothesized that one reason for the difference in behavior for the age groups may be due to the difficulties and stress experienced by the youngest groups. If the younger inmates experienced a high level of stress their aggressive behavior might reflect an inability to cope with the environment. However, there was no indication that the age groups who were highest in conflicts with others or in misconducts were more anxious than those of different ages. At any age, increased anxiety was accompanied by increased conflicts with guards. This was not true for conflicts with other inmates. Only for those under thirty was increased anxiety accompanied by increased conflicts with other inmates. One possible interpretation of these results is that during this difficult period of adjustment inmates direct their anger at the people who are seen as the "oppressors" or provokers of their difficulties (Zillmann, 1983). For all inmates these oppressors may be institutional staff, and, therefore, increases in anxiety are related to interpersonal conflicts with guards at all ages. Younger inmates who are at a different stage in life are confronted by a different set of problems. These problems may be related to interactions with other inmates. For example, they may have come to terms with homosexual advances, or territorial concerns. Those who have difficulty coping with these inmate-inmate problems may get into clashes with other inmates. Such inmate difficulties may not be as problematic for older inmates.

If this interpretation is correct then conflicts with others is a function of the difficult situation. The responses by the inmate is to react against those who are perceived as causing the difficulties. Inmates of any age suffer from the "pains" of imprisonment, hence anxiety levels do not differ that much over age (Toch, 1977). Those, of any age, who have difficulties in adjusting to institutional rules and regulations have interpersonal conflicts with the enforcers of the rules—the guards. Inmates also have problems with other inmates. These inmate-inmate difficulties are most relevant to younger inmates. Younger inmates, when stressed by such interpersonal problems, have conflicts with other inmates— the perceived cause of the stress.

Surprisingly, increases in anxiety had no influence on misconducts for any age group. Thus the results do not suggest these inmates have an inability to control their own impulses when in a stressful situation (see Adams, 1985). They appear to have interpersonal clashes with the perceived cause of their difficulties. The lack of relationship between anxiety and misconduct suggests that these interpersonal conflicts may not be of a level to result in severe punishment. Thus although there are conflicts they are not disruptive enough to evoke institutional punishment.

Previous findings of increases in assaults and misconducts in crowded juvenile institutions may be an indication of the inmate-inmate problems that develop when the population increases (Ekland-Olson et al., 1983; Nacci et al., 1977). In contrast with Gaes and McGuire's (1985) finding of increased staff assaults in crowded adult institutions, the present results suggest that conflicts with staff would increase in both youth and adult institutions. However, there is no indication that increased anxiety would lead to serious misbehavior.

The results from the attitude scales were very different from that of anxiety. The desire to be isolated from others did not change as a function of age nor was this attitude related to interpersonal conflicts. Those under twenty years old did receive more misconducts if they were stronger in their desire to be isolated. However, this was the only age group so affected.

Inmates who were afraid of being victimized did have more conflicts with both other inmates and guards. Fear of others was highest for those in their twenties. However, only those under twenty had more misconducts if they were afraid of being victimized by other inmates.

An attitude of assertiveness toward others rose from the teenage years until the early twenties. This assertiveness remained high until the late thirties when it began to decline. Inmates high on this attitude took the position that they would not be pushed around nor would they back away from trouble. This would appear to be an attitude more typical of the young male with a "macho" image. However, the attitude remained fairly consistent throughout the ages of twenty and thirty and did not show a high peak at any age as had conflicts and misconducts. Thus there was no evidence of a new prosocial orientation arising during the twenties or thirties. One expectation has been that the need to assert oneself early in a relationship might change with age.

Assertive attitudes had a strong positive relationship with interpersonal conflicts. A strong assertiveness had been expected to be associated with misbehavior by youth. However, an assertive attitude was accompanied by increased conflicts for all ages. The interaction of age and assertiveness indicated that only at younger ages was increased assertiveness associated with a rise in the number of misconducts.

The youngest age group stands out as anomalous in comparison to the other age groups. They are the only ones who receive more misconducts as a function of their desire for isolation from and their fear of other inmates. They have received substantially more misconducts than others, although they do not report a greater number of interpersonal conflicts. There are a small number of inmates this young. It may be that they are different from others in unmeasured ways, although this was not revealed in the demographic comparisons. It is also possible that radical changes take place from the late teen years into the twenties. The demographic characteristics, including age distributions, of the inmates studied appear representative of similar prisons for adult male felons, however, in the future it would be beneficial to examine juvenile institutions to increase the number of inmates in the youngest age group.

Possibly maturity brings some type of impulse control (Wilson & Herrnstein, 1985). The youthful inmates appear to "get in trouble" as a result of their attitudes much more so than the other inmates. For other inmates, only greater assertiveness results in more misconducts. And, the relationship between assertiveness and misconducts is limited to those under age 30. The older inmates may learn to control their impulses. It is not that the young inmates are more stressed or do not have the ability to cope when stressed, as evidenced by the results of the anxiety analyses. Rather, the younger inmate responds as a function of their attitudes without the inhibitions of the older inmates.

From this perspective, interpersonal conflicts may act as a mechanism for tension release and also have instrumental motivations. When anxious, inmates lash out in anger at the perceived cause of their suffering whether this is the guards or other inmates. There are also instrumental motivations for interpersonal conflicts, such as status, protection of oneself or property, or intimidation. The attitude scales may represent such instrumental motivations for aggressive behavior in prison. Therefore, the inmate who fears others has interpersonal conflicts with them in order to protect himself. Additionally, the inmate who believes he must assert himself in interactions with others also has conflicts to intimidate others or gain status. Conflicts are, in these cases, a means to some end (e.g., self-protection, status). At any age, inmates who are afraid of others or believe they must be assertive may have conflicts for self-protection, status, sexual favors, lenient treatment by staff, and so on.

Age differences arise in how carefully controlled behavior is. When motivated to respond aggressively the older inmate does so with more caution than the younger inmate. This inhibition of behavior might have many causes. Older inmates may be more cautious or circumspect in their clashes with others. Younger inmates may not be as aware of the costs of such behavior or they may be more willing to take risks (Ellis, 1984). In any case, the results suggest that increased fear or assertiveness might lead to more interpersonal conflicts at any age, but only the youngest will respond in a manner to be punished by the institution.

NOTES

1. According to Social Learning Theory this would reflect aggression prompted by anticipated positive consequences (Bandura, 1983).
2. This would be similar to what Bandura (1983) terms emotional arousal (rage, anger) caused by aversive experiences (external or internal stressful stimulation).

REFERENCES

Adams, K. (1985). *Pathology and disruptiveness among prison inmates.* Paper presented at the annual meeting of the American Society of Criminology, San Diego, CA.

Bandura, A. (1983). Psychological mechanisms of aggression. In R. G. Green & E. T. Donnerstein (Eds.), *Aggression: Theoretical and empirical reviews* (Vol. 1). New York: Academic Press.

Bowker, L. H. (1982). Victimizers and the victims in American correctional institutions. In R. Johnson & H. Toch (Eds.), *The pains of imprisonment.* Newbury Park, CA: Sage.

Ekland-Olson, S., Barrick, D., & Cohen, L. E. (1983). Prison overcrowding and disciplinary problems: An analysis of the Texas prison system. *Journal of Applied Behavioral Science, 19*(2), 163–176.

Ellis, D. (1984). Crowding and prison violence: Integration of research and theory. *Criminal Justice and Behavior, 11*(3), 277–308.

Ellis, D., Brasmick, H., & Gilman, B. (1974, July). Violence in prisons: A sociological analysis. *American Journal of Sociology, 80,* 16–34.

Gaes, G. G., & McGuire, W. J. (1985). Prison violence: The contribution of crowding versus other determinants of prison assault rates. *Journal of Research in Crime and Delinquency, 22,* 41–65.

Goodstein, L. I., & Hepburn, J. (1985). *Determinate sentencing and imprisonment: A failure of reform.* Cincinnati, OH: Anderson.

Goodstein, L. I., & MacKenzie, D. L. (1984). Racial differences in adjustment patterns of prison inmates: Prisonization, conflict, stress and control. In D. Georges-Abeyie (Ed.), *The criminal justice system and blacks.* New York: Clark Boardman.

Greenberg, D. F. (1985). Age, crime, and social explanation. *American Journal of Sociology, 91*(10), 1–27.

Hirschi, T., & Gottfredson, M. (1983). Age and the explanation of crime. *American Journal of Sociology, 89,* 552–584.

Lombardo, L. X. (1982). Stress, change, and collective violence in prison. In R. Johnson & H. Toch (Eds.), *The pains of imprisonment.* Newbury Park, CA: Sage.

MacKenzie, D. L., & Goodstein, L. S. (1985). Long-term incarceration impacts and characteristics of long-term offenders: An empirical analysis. *Criminal Justice and Behavior, 12,* 395–414.

MacKenzie, D. L., & Goodstein, L. S. (1986). Stress and the control beliefs of prisoners: A test of three models of control-limited environments. *Journal of Applied Social Psychology, 16*(3), 211–230.

Magaree, E. I. (1982). Psychological determinants and correlates of criminal violence. In M. E. Wolfgang & N. A. Weinger (Eds.), *Criminal violence,* Newbury Park, CA: Sage.

Nacci, P. L., Teitelbaum, H. E., & Prather, J. (1977). Population density and inmate misconduct rates. *Federal Probation, 41,* 26–31.

Porporini, F. J., & Zamble, E. (1984). Coping with imprisonment. *Canadian Journal of Criminology, 26*(4), 403–422.

Shoemaker, D. J., & Hellery, Jr., G. A. (1980). Violence and commitment in custodial settings. *Criminology, 18,* 94–102.

Spielberger, C. D., Gorsuch, R. L., & Lushine, R. E. (1970). *Manual for the state-trait anxiety inventory.* Palo Alto, CA: Consulting Psychological Press.

Sykes, G. (1966). *The society of captives.* New York: Atheneum.

Toch, H. (1969). *Violent men: An inquiry into the psychology of violence.* Chicago: Aldine.

Toch, H. (1977). *Living in prison: The ecology of survival.* New York: Free Press.

Toch, H. (1982). Studying and reducing stress. In R. Johnson & H. Toch (Eds.), *The pains of imprisonment.* Newbury Park, CA: Sage.

Wallach, M. A., Kogan, N., & Bem, D. (1962). Group influence on individual risk taking. *Journal of Abnormal and Social Psychology, 65,* 76–86.

Wilson, J. Q., & Herrnstein, R. J. (1985). *Crime and human nature.* New York: Simon & Schuster.

Wolfgang, M. E., & Weinger, N. A. (Eds.). (1982). *Criminal violence.* Newbury Park, CA: Sage.

Wright, K. N., & Smith, P. (1985). *The violent and the victimized in prison.* Paper presented at the annual meeting of the American Society of Criminology, San Diego, CA.

Zillman, D. (1983). Arousal and aggression. In R. G. Geen & E. J. Donnerstein (Eds.), *Aggression: Theoretical and empirical reviews* (Vol. 1). New York: Academic Press.

APPENDIX

Isolation Scale

	Adjusted Item to Total Correlation
1. There are no *real* friends in prison.	0.44
2. There are few inmates I really trust.	0.29
3. The best way to do time is to mind your own business and have as little as possible to do with other inmates.	0.64
4. In the institution I keep pretty much to myself.	0.51
5. There is no group of men in this institution that I am close with.	0.48
6. It's a good idea to keep to yourself here as much as you can.	0.68

Response choices: Strongly Disagree (1) to Strongly Agree (2).

VICTIMIZATION IN PRISONS: A STUDY OF FACTORS RELATED TO THE GENERAL WELL-BEING OF YOUTHFUL INMATES

Angela S. Maitland and Richard D. Sluder, Ph.D. *

Prison violence has increased dramatically over the past decade (McCorkle, 1993b). Rapes, beatings, and killings have become routine in many prisons (Scharf, 1985). In 1992, state and federal facilities reported 66 prison murders, with an additional 10,181 inmate-on-inmate attacks requiring medical treatment (Camp & Camp, 1993). These statistics do not accurately reflect the extent of actual victimizations, for violence among inmates is customarily under-reported (Reid, 1991).

Given the nature of the typical inmate population, continuous and consistent interpersonal problems, attempted breaches of security, and illegal activities are expected (Wright, 1994). It is thus not unrealistic to anticipate violent, dangerous behavior from prisoners (Reid, 1991). Due to the propensity for violence, prison administrators have reason for concern about this form of behavior.

Although there are many factors related to inmate safety, some (see, e.g., DiIulio, 1987) have suggested that higher custody prisons organized and operated in a bureaucratic fashion will have less violence than those managed more permissively. The reliance on inmates to control their peers presents not only serious security risks, but exacerbates levels of violence in the correctional environment. Practicing this method of control contributes to higher levels of disorder, illicit activities, and, ultimately, loss of custodial control (DiIulio, 1987).

*Both authors are with the Criminal Justice Department at Central Missouri State University. Ms. Maitland is a graduate research assistant and Dr. Sluder is a professor. A version of this article was presented at the Annual Meeting of the Academy of Criminal Justice Sciences, March 1996, Las Vegas, Nevada.
FEDERAL PROBATION, Vol. 60 No. 2, March 1996 24–31 © 1996 Administrative Office of the United States Courts.

Despite the pervasiveness of violence in correctional institutions, administrators are responsible for the maintenance of a safe and secure environment within the prison (Harris, 1993). From moral, ethical, and legal perspectives, administrators have an obligation to ensure that the staff maintains control and provides inmates with an environment free from the constant threat or occurrence of violence (Wright, 1994). Prison officials must be aware of an unsafe environment and take appropriate measures to abate it, as they may be held liable for the violent actions of inmates toward their peers (see, e.g., *Farmer v. Brennan*, 1994).

The stress of continually being alert to the possibility of victimization, and the victimizations themselves, can result in psychophysiological disturbances for inmates (McCorkle, 1993a). Psychophysiological disturbances are physical symptoms, or diseases, caused or exacerbated by stressors in the institutional environment. Indigestion, constipation, nervous stomach, and headaches are but a few examples of psychophysiological symptoms. Physical ailments emanating from these disturbances include hypertension, asthma, ulcers, and colitis (Davidson & Neale, 1990).

The sources of stress—physical and psychological aggression—are inescapable in many prison environments. The prison environment often defines status and becomes a threat to manhood (Wright, 1991b). The status of inmates is often derived from ritualistic tests of strength in which weaker inmates are identified (Wright, 1991a). Weak, young, and effeminate inmates are especially susceptible to being targeted, pursued, and victimized by aggressive inmates (Irwin, 1980).

Victimized prisoners are characterized as inexperienced "lambs," unable to cope with predator inmates (Wright, 1991a). Nonviolent offenders in prison often experience high victimization rates and are prime targets since they do not express a potential for violence or retaliation (McCorkle, 1993b). Reid (1991) notes that new inmates are also prime targets for violence and intimidation. Upon arrival, new inmates may be attacked suddenly and unexpectedly by their more aggressive peers. Although victim characteristics vary according to situational factors, victims are often white, young, and smaller than their aggressors (Toch, 1977).

The effects of victimization are numerous and can be devastating to an inmate. Some of these negative effects include withdrawing from prison activities, depression, feelings of helplessness, economic difficulties, physical injury, disruption of social relationships, and low self-image. Psychological victimization is routine and considered commonplace in these environments. Often, the greatest fear an inmate faces is the ever-present potential for physical victimization (Kappeler, Blumberg, & Potter, 1996).

The degree to which an inmate fears being the victim of prison violence is the strongest predictor of his mental health. Research by McCorkle (1993a) shows that fearful inmates experience a multitude of psychophysiological disturbances. The inmate has difficulty working and satisfying the few practical demands of his environment. He is frequently anxious and depressed and has a low level of energy. Fearful inmates are also more likely to report physical health problems and to express an overall concern about their physical well-being (McCorkle, 1993a). The complexities of managing inmates effectively are thus amplified when offenders suffer from even minor mental health problems.

Despite an emerging body of literature on inmate victimization experiences and the psychophysiological manifestations of related prison stressors, few efforts have been made to study these issues as they relate to youthful prison inmates. Most published research has examined fear, victimization experiences, and the mental health status of older, more institutionally adept inmates housed in maximum security prison facilities (see, e.g., McCorkle, 1993a). Yet research concerning youthful inmates seems especially important since they comprise a significant proportion of inmates incarcerated in state prisons. In 1991, 54.7 percent of all prisoners admitted to state prisons were 29 years of age or younger (Maguire & Pastore, 1994); in 1992, 54.1 percent of all admissions were 29 years of age or younger (Maguire & Pastore, 1995). It would therefore seem especially important to examine dimensions of the prison experience for youthful offenders.

The purpose of this study was to describe and assess the general well-being of youthful inmates in a medium security prison, as measured by the General Well-Being Scale. The study explores the relationship between general well-being and related institutional, social, psychological, and individual variables. More specifically, the study focuses on the relationship between inmate well-being, fear of victimization, victimization experiences, prison stresses, demographic variables, correctional experience, and social support.

METHODOLOGY

For this study, a nonprobability incidental sample of inmates was selected from a prison located in a midwestern state. The prison, which has an average daily population of about 1,100 inmates, has been designated by the state to house younger offenders. The facility is rated as a medium security institution. Survey instruments were presented to inmates attending classes in the education facility at the prison. Inmates were advised of the nature and purpose of the study and informed that it would take about 15 minutes to complete survey instruments. Inmates were assured that confidentiality procedures were in place and that neither corrections officials nor researchers could attribute information provided to any particular individual. Inmates who volunteered for the study were presented with surveys. Upon completion, inmates returned the survey to their classroom instructors. The surveys were then collected from all instructors. Altogether, 111 inmates completed survey instruments.

Dependent Measure

The dependent measure for this study was the General Well-Being (GWB) Scale. The GWB Scale was developed for the National Center for Health Statistics in 1970 to assess self-representations of subjective well-being. It is comprised of 19 items that, when combined, produce an overall score measuring well-being. Cumulative scale scores range from 19 (highest well-being) to 130 (lowest well-being). In addition, six subscales can be derived from the GWB Scale that measure an individual's health worry, energy level, the extent to which one believes he or she has a satisfying and interesting life, depression/cheerfulness, the extent of emotional-behavioral control, and whether a person is relaxed or tense/anxious. The subscale elements ensure that a diversity of content is included in the score (Robinson, Shaver, & Wrightsman, 1991).

Multi-item scales of subjective well-being, such as the GWB Scale, generally have higher levels of validity and reliability because random measurement errors that may affect one item are likely to be at least partially canceled by opposite errors in other items. Furthermore, the broad base of information provided by a multi-item scale enhances the ability to reflect more of the different elements of subjective well-being. A substantial body of literature exists on the relationship between GWB scores and other indicators of mental health (Robinson et al., 1991). In addition, the scale has been used previously to assess the well-being of prisoners (McCorkle, 1993a).

The GWB Scale has been used extensively in previous research on a variety of populations with strong evidence of convergent validity and reliability (Robinson et al., 1991). In this study, Cronbach's Alpha, computed at .865, suggests the scale has an acceptable level of internal consistency. A copy of the scale is included in the appendix.

Independent Measures

Several independent measures were contained within the survey including victimization experiences, fear of victimization, prison stresses, social support, anomie, demographic variables, and correctional experience.

Victimization experiences were measured by a 14-item scale. The participants were asked if they had encountered specific victimization experiences during their current sentence. Inmates were queried, for example, as to whether they had been hit, kicked, punched, or slapped; scratched; pushed or shoved; physically hurt in any way; threatened; sexually assaulted; had money extorted from them; or had any property stolen from them. The participants answered "yes" (0) or "no" (1) to items on the victimization scale.

An index to measure fear of victimization was created by summing the responses to three items. The three items inquired about inmates' perceived safety in prison and about being attacked during their sentences.

Individual perceptions of prison stresses were measured by an 11-item Likert scale. Respondents were asked to rate the degree of difficulty (not hard to very hard) they experienced regarding problems and stresses inmates often face in prison.

There were several indicators of social support. Questions with respect to social support within the prison, as well as external support, were included. The indicators consisted of questions concerning the presence and role of family and friends within and outside the prison.

A scale, designed to measure anomie (Srole, 1956), consisted of five general statements about society. Inmates rated the extent to which they agreed or disagreed with each statement.

The Department of Corrections for the state provided information from computer files on demographics and correctional experience for each inmate. Demographic information included age, race, height, weight, IQ score, education level, and marital status. Correctional experience included the number of times incarcerated, the number of times on probation, length of current sentence, and offense classification.

Table 7.1
Personal Characteristics of Sample

Variable	N	%	Mean	Standard Deviation
Age	102		21.21	2.32
Race				
White	49	48.0		
Nonwhite	53	52.0		
Marital Status				
Single	94	93.1		
Married	7	6.9		
Height in Inches	102		69.69	2.81
Weight	102		162.76	26.83
Highest Level of Education Completed				
7 or less	5	4.9		
8–10	71	69.5		
11–12	26	25.5		
IQ Score	88		86.39	10.05

FINDINGS

Description of Subjects

Table 7.1 presents the general characteristics of the sample (N = 111). Inmates were primarily single and in their early 20s with a mean age of 21.21 years. The racial composition was approximately equal with 48.0 percent white and 52.0 percent nonwhite. The mean IQ score of the sample was 86.39. In terms of educational backgrounds, 74.5 percent of the subjects had completed tenth grade or below.

Table 7.2 depicts the correctional experience of the participants. The data show that the group studied is relatively young and, although most had past involvement in the criminal justice system, few had been incarcerated previously. The mean age at the time of conviction was 19.59 years. Most offenders (86.3 percent) were serving sentences for nonviolent offenses. The mean sentence length for offenders was 60.07 months. The current sentence was the first imprisonment for 95.1 percent of the respondents, with the remaining 4.9 percent having been imprisoned once before. Of the respondents, 59.9 percent had been on probation at least once.

Classification information was obtained from the Department of Corrections for inmates in the study. The department uses the Adult Inmate Management System (AIMS) for classification purposes (see, e.g., Quay, 1984). Under this scheme, inmates are classified into one of three categories: Alphas, Kappas, and Sigmas. Alphas are the "heavies" or aggressors; conversely, Sigmas

Table 7.2
Correctional Experience

Variable	N	%	Mean	Standard Deviation
Age at Time of Conviction	102		19.59	2.25
Felony Class				
A	3	4.5		
B	15	22.7		
C	45	68.2		
D	3	4.5		
Type of Offense				
Violent	14	13.7		
Nonviolent	88	86.3		
Sentence in Months	102		60.07	33.7
AIMS Classification				
Alpha	73	74.5		
Kappa	1	1.0		
Sigma	24	24.5		
Total Times Imprisoned				
0	97	95.1		
1	5	4.9		
Total Times on Probation				
0	41	40.2		
1	38	37.3		
2	17	16.7		
3	6	5.9		
Gang Member				
No	85	79.4		
Yes	22	20.6		

are the "lights" or passives. Kappas are, generally, inmates who fall into the middle of the spectrum and thus are considered neither aggressive nor passive. In this sample, the majority of inmates (74.5 percent) were classified as Alphas, 24.5 percent classified as Sigmas, and 1 percent as Kappas.

One item in the survey instrument asked inmates if they belonged to a gang. The majority of the sample, 79.4 percent, indicated that they did not belong to a gang, while 20.6 percent marked that they were affiliated with some form of gang.

Analysis of Data

Cronbach's Alpha was computed for each scale used as an independent variable in the analysis to test for internal reliability. Alphas for prison stress (.7796), fear of victimization (.7243), victimization experiences (.7852), general well-being

(.8650), and anomie (.5860) were all within acceptable limits for social science research. Each scale appears to provide consistent information.

Bivariate analysis.   To begin the analysis, zero-order correlations were computed for each independent variable thought to be related to inmates' General Well-Being scores. Table 7.3 presents 11 of the strongest zero-order correlations between the GWB Scale and institutional, psychological, and social variables. Fear of victimization, victimization experiences, and classification level are all significantly correlated with general well-being. The strongest correlation is between fear of victimization and general well-being (r = .62). This suggests that the level of fear is a strong predictor of general well-being, with fearful inmates reporting lower well-being. There is a strong negative correlation (r = −.49) between victimization experiences and general well-being. The more victimization incidents an inmate experiences, the more his general well-being suffered. The zero-order correlations further show a relationship between clas-

Table 7.3
Zero-Order Correlations between GWB and Institutional, Psychological, and Social Variables

Variable	Correlation	p-Value
Fear of Victimization	.62	<.0001
Victimization Experiences	−.49	<.0001
AIMS Classification		
Alpha = 0		
Sigma = 1	−.26	.029
Number of Friends in Prison	−.23	.007
Free Time with Friends		
Alone = 0		
With Friends = 1	−.34	<.0001
Friends to Confide in About		
Personal Problems		
No = 0		
Yes = 1	−.26	.007
Could Count on Friends to Help		
if Attacked		
No = 0		
Yes = 1	−.16	.101
Times Attended Religious		
Services in Past Month	−.19	.048
Prison Stress	.27	.007
Anomie	.28	.004
Gang Member		
No = 0		
Yes = 1	−.18	.061

sification level and general well-being (r = −.26). Alphas, the aggressors, reported better well-being.

Five measures of social support were also significantly related with general well-being scores, with the strongest correlations appearing between measures of social support within the prison and general well-being. Inmates who had friends in prison, spent time with friends in prison, could count on friends to help if attacked, and had inmates to confide in about personal problems reported higher levels of general well-being.

As shown by Table 7.3, there is also a relationship between prison stress and general well-being. Inmates having difficulties adjusting to prison stresses, including missing family, conflicts with other inmates, and lack of proper facilities, reported lower levels of general well-being. Table 7.3 shows a relationship between gang membership and general well-being (r = −.18); those who reported being a member of a gang had higher levels of general well-being. Table 7.3 further shows a relationship between the number of times religious services were attended in the past month with general well-being (r = −.19). Inmates attending more religious services had higher levels of general well-being.

In sum, bivariate analysis suggests that inmates appearing to adapt best to the prison environment were those who had few victimization experiences, had less fear of being victimized, had social support systems in place in the prison, more frequently attended religious services, were able to cope better with the pains of imprisonment, had lower levels of anomie, were classified as "aggressors," and, ironically, were affiliated with some form of gang.

Multivariate analysis. In the second stage of the analysis, multiple regression analysis was employed to examine determinants of inmates' general well-being scores. As a check for multicollinearity, zero-order correlations were calculated between each of the predictor variables. The highest correlations were between fear of victimization and victimization experiences (r = −.34) and prison stresses and victimization experiences (r = −.31). The risk of multicollinearity does not appear severe since there are only moderate correlations between a few of our predictor variables.

Each of the significantly correlated independent variables were regressed on the General Well-Being Scale to examine their independent effects in explaining well-being scores (Table 7.4). All of the significantly correlated variables were included in the equation using forced entry. As shown in Table 7.4, significant variables in the equation included fear of victimization, victimization experiences, and anomie scores. With all variables included in the model, 55 percent of the variance in General Well-Being scores is accounted for.

In the third phase of the analysis, separate regression equations were computed by deleting independent variables from the model that were not statistically significant. Variables that were not statistically significant were eliminated one at a time by forced removal. The final model is presented in Table 7.5.

Table 7.5 shows that fear of victimization is the variable most strongly related to general well-being (beta = .420). This suggests that the level of fear is a strong predictor of general well-being, with fearful inmates being least psychophysiologically healthy. Victimization experience remains significant, as do counting on others to help if attacked, anomie, and free time spent with others. The final model shows that prison stresses and indicators of external social

Table 7.4
Multiple Regression of Independent Variables Significantly Correlated with GWB

Variable	Beta	t	p-Value
AIMS Classification	−.092	−.997	.324
Victimization Experiences	−.329	−2.93	.005
Gang Member	−.029	−.301	.765
Free Time Spent With Friends	−.111	−1.15	.257
Anomie	.190	2.05	.046
Count on Friends to Help if Attacked	−.036	−.399	.692
Prison Stresses	.052	−.552	.583
Friends to Confide in About Personal Problems	−.0001	−.008	.993
Times Attended Religious Services	−.133	−1.40	.165
Number of Friends in Prison	−.039	−.380	.706
Fear of Victimization	−.332	2.56	.014

Method = Forced Entry With Listwise Deletion
R-Squared = .63; Adjusted R-Squared = .55
F = 7.395; df = 12, 52; p < .00001

Table 7.5
Determinants of Inmate GWB Final Regression Model

Variable	Beta	t	p-Value
Count on Friends to Help if Attacked	−.159	−2.31	.023
Fear of Victimization	.420	5.42	<.00001
Anomie	.212	3.01	.003
Free Time Spent With Friends	−.191	−2.63	.01
Victimization Experiences	−.316	−4.33	<.00001

Method = Forced Entry With Listwise Deletion
R-Squared = .57; Adjusted R-Squared = .55
F = 24.74; df = 5, 91; p < .00001

support are not independent predictors of general well-being. Differences in general well-being are largely due to the level of fear regarding victimization and actual victimization experiences. With five statistically significant variables included in the final model, 55 percent of the variance in General Well-Being scores is accounted for.

CONCLUSION

Given the nature of the sampling procedures employed, this study is best characterized as exploratory. Yet our findings raise important questions pointing to the need for researchers and criminal justice officials to consider more thoroughly the prison experience for young offenders.

In the present study, five variables were identified as important independent predictors of inmate general well-being. The degree to which an inmate fears being a victim of prison violence is the strongest predictor of his general well-being, which is consistent with previous research on offenders housed in maximum security prisons (McCorkle, 1993a). This finding suggests that an inmate experiencing a high level of fear suffers physically and psychologically. He is often tense, anxious, and unsure of himself. He is often bothered by his "nerves" and feels pressured. He has a low level of energy, is sad and discouraged, and may suffer from illness or physical pain. In sum, the inmate with a high level of fear regarding personal safety reports more problems and has prominent concerns for his overall well-being.

The second most influential predictor of well-being for youthful inmates was related to victimization experiences. Here, our findings suggest that the more victimization incidents an inmate experiences, the more his general well-being suffers. The trauma of actual victimization, coupled with the stress of constant fears of the possibility of victimization, can result in psychophysiological disturbances, lowering an inmate's general well-being (McCorkle, 1993a).

Unlike previous research in this area, we included a measure designed to determine the extent to which inmates perceived the disintegration of social bonds—or *anomia* (see, e.g., Babbie, 1992; Srole, 1956)—in the prison environment and broader society. Our findings suggest that inmates who perceive general normless conditions also have lower levels of general well-being.

Finally, consistent with our anomia finding above, we found that inmates having an internal support system in the prison environment reported higher levels of general well-being. The more free time an inmate spent with friends, the better his well-being. We also found higher levels of well-being among inmates who believed that friends would come to their aid if they were attacked.

At least as important as those findings mentioned above, we found no statistically significant relationships between general well-being and several other variables believed to be related to the way young inmates handle prison incarceration. Inmates general well-being was little affected by several factors commonly called the "pains of imprisonment" (e.g., missing family or friends, possessions, freedom; boredom; lack of privacy; excessive noise; lack of proper facilities). The level of external support an inmate reported (e.g., visits one receives, how often one writes or phones those in the free world) also had little influence on general well-being. Finally, we failed to find relationships between general well-being and several individual level variables including age, race, height, weight, marital status, education level, IQ score, number of prior incarcerations, sentence length, and offense category.

Are there differences in general well-being and, concomitantly, the prison experience between youthful inmates assigned to medium security institutions and older offenders housed in maximum security facilities? To answer this question, it is instructive to compare findings in the present study with research focusing on prisoners housed in maximum security prisons. McCorkle's (1993a) study analyzed determinants of general well-being for inmates housed in a Tennessee maximum security prison. Employing multiple regression analysis, he found relationships between general well-being scores and education level, regrets expressed by inmates about their pasts, boredom, and fear of victimization. Although in many cases we conceptualized and measured constructs slightly differently than McCorkle, our findings are similar in the sense that we found that fear of victimization is the strongest predictor of inmates' general well-being scores. Our findings diverge, however, in the sense that we found actual victimization experiences, the presence and reliance on friends in the prison, and anomia are all related to the general well-being of youthful offenders. Our final model also accounts for more explained variance in general well-being scores; using 13 variables, McCorkle obtained an R-Square of .374. The five variables in our final model accounted for 55 percent of the variance in general well-being scores.

Although findings in the present study should be considered tentative, they nonetheless suggest several factors that corrections officials who manage facilities designated for youthful offenders may wish to consider. To begin, our study suggests a profile of youthful inmates who seem to cope best with the psychophysiological stresses of incarceration. The most healthy inmate is one who believes other inmate friends would come to his defense if he is attacked, has little fear of being victimized, has inmate friends to confide in about personal problems, has experienced few victimizations while in prison, and does not embrace anomic ideologies. Conversely, the inmate most susceptible to the rigors of incarceration has few inmate friends, does not believe that others would aid him if he is attacked, has been victimized while in prison and thus has a high fear of further victimization, and is likely to be anomic.

At a minimum, both custody and program staff may find these profiles of interest in identifying inmates who are likely to have difficulties in adjusting to the prison environment. The profiles may be useful to medical and counseling staff to begin to explore whether inmate complaints are tied to individual and social factors rather than physiological problems. Inmate education and reception programs are suggested, in which inmates are more fully informed of the peculiarities of institutional life and afforded opportunities to develop ties within their social settings. The prison staff has absolute control over vital decisions that directly impact inmates. Properly informed of the effects of various factors on inmate general well-being, corrections officials should be better positioned to make decisions involving inmate needs. Theoretically, this should help reduce the level of fear in inmates, increasing general well-being.

At a broader level, the study reconfirms the necessity of providing inmates with an environment free from physical and psychological victimization. The issues of whether an inmate has a right to be protected from violence and whether prison officials are liable if an inmate is victimized have legal, philosophical, and practical implications. Prison administrators enjoy an obligation to ensure that inmates housed in correctional facilities suffer no further harm during their terms of incarceration.

We close by acknowledging that the findings reported here are not without their limitations. Our study, employing nonprobability sampling techniques, focused on youthful inmates in one prison in a midwestern state. The study's utility for generalization is clearly limited, but as an exploratory effort points to the need for further examination of the prisonization experience for younger inmates. While our model accounted for a relatively large proportion of the explained variance in general well-being scores, much room remains for identifying and testing other variables related to the prison experience for youthful offenders across jurisdictions. It is also worth noting that the present study is based on cross-sectional data. To more fully explore the effects of incarceration on general well-being, the collection and analysis of longitudinal data is obviously needed. The results presented here nonetheless suggest variation in the prison experience by both offender age and institutional security classification.

REFERENCES

Babbie, E. (1992). *The practice of social research* (6th ed.). Belmont, CA: Wadsworth Publishing.

Bowker, L.H. (1980). *Prison victimization.* New York: Elsevier North Holland, Inc.

Camp, G., & Camp, G. (1993). *Corrections yearbook.* South Salem: Criminal Justice Institute.

Davidson, G.C., & Neale, J.M. (1990). *Abnormal psychology.* New York: John Wiley & Sons.

DiIulio, J. (1987). *Governing prisons: A comparative study of correctional management.* New York: The Free Press.

Farmer v. Brennan, No. 92-7247 (1994).

Harris, J.W. (1993). Comparison of stressors among female vs. male inmates. *Journal of Offender Rehabilitation, 19*(1/2), 43–56.

Irwin, J. (1980). *Prisons in turmoil.* Boston: Little, Brown and Company.

Kappeler, V., Blumberg, M., & Potter, G. (1996). *The mythology of crime and criminal justice.* Prospect Heights, IL: Waveland Press.

Maguire, K., & Pastore, A.L. (Eds.). (1995). *Sourcebook of criminal justice statistics 1994.* Washington, DC: U.S. Department of Justice, Bureau of Justice Statistics.

Maguire, K., & Pastore, A.L. (Eds.). (1994). *Sourcebook of criminal justice statistics 1993.* Washington, DC: U.S. Department of Justice, Bureau of Justice Statistics.

McCorkle, R.C. (1993a). Fear of victimization and symptoms of psychopathology among prison inmates. *Journal of Offender Rehabilitation, 9*(1/2), 27–41.

McCorkle, R.C. (1993b). Living on the edge: Fear in a maximum-security prison. *Journal of Offender Rehabilitation, 20,* 73–91.

Quay, H.C. (1984). *Managing adult inmates: Classification for housing and program assignments.* College Park, MD: American Correctional Association.

Reid, S. (1991). *Crime and criminology* (6th ed.). Chicago: Holt, Rinehart and Winston, Inc.

Robinson, J. P., Shaver, P.R., & Wrightsman, L.S. (1991). *Measures of personality and social psychological attitudes* (Vol. 1). New York: Academic Press, Inc.

Scharf, P. (1985). Violence and the crisis of meaning in the prison. In M. Braswell, S. Dillingham, & R. Montgomery (Eds.), *Prison violence in America* (pp. 133–147). Cincinnati: Anderson Publishing Co.

Srole, L. (1956). Social integration and certain corollaries: An exploratory study. *American Sociological Review, 21,* 709–716.

Toch, H. (1977). *Living in prison: The ecology of survival.* New York: The Free Press.

Williams, F.P., III, & McShane, M.D. (1988). *Criminological theory.* Englewood Cliffs, NJ: Prentice Hall.

Wright, K. (1991a). A study of individual, environmental, and interactive effects in explaining adjustment to prison. *Justice Quarterly, 8*(2), 217–242.

Wright, K. (1991b). The violent and victimized in the male prison. *Journal of Offender Rehabilitation, 16*(3/4), 1–25.

Wright, K. (1994). *Effective prison leadership.* Binghamton, NY: William Neil Publishing.

APPENDIX

Prison Stresses Scale

Items preceded by the following statement/question: Listed below are problems inmates often face in prison. How hard has each of the following been for you? (response options ranging from "not hard" = 1 to "very hard" = 5)

a. missing family or friends
b. missing certain activities
c. conflicts with inmates
d. regrets about the past
e. concerns about the future
f. missing personal possessions
g. boredom
h. lack of privacy
i. excessive noise
j. lack of proper facilities
k. missing freedom

Indicators of Internal and External Social Support

1. In the past month, how many times did you attend religious services?
2. During the past month, how many times have you written letters to family or friends?
3. During the past month, how many times have you phoned family or friends?
4. How many times during the past 3 months have you been visited by family or friends?
5. How many friends do you have in this prison?
6. Are there inmates in this prison you feel you can talk to about personal problems? ("no" = 0, "yes" = 1)
7. Do you spend most of your "free time" in this prison alone or with friends? ("alone" = 0, "with friends" = 1)
8. If you were going to be attacked, could you count on friends to help? ("no" = 0, "yes" = 1)

Fear of Victimization Scale

1. How safe do you feel in this prison? (response options ranging from "very safe" = 1 to "very unsafe" = 4)
2. How much do you worry that you'll be attacked during this sentence? (response options ranging from "very little" = 1 to "a great deal" = 3)
3. Do you feel the chance of being attacked in this prison is . . . (response options ranging from "low" = 1 to "high" = 3)

Victimization Experiences Scale

Items preceded by the question: During this sentence, has anyone *tried to, or done,* any of the following things to you? ("yes" = 0, "no" = 1)

a. used any sort of weapon on you
b. hit, kicked, punched, or slapped you
c. scratched you
d. pushed or shoved you
e. bit you or tried to bite you
f. physically hurt you *in any way*
g. made a threat that scared or worried you
h. said that they would hurt you if you didn't give them some of your property
i. called you names or said mean things to you
j. played games with your mind
k. forced sexual activity on you
l. made sexual comments to you that made you feel uncomfortable
m. made you give them money
n. stolen any property that belonged to you

General Well-Being Scale

The following items were preceded by the phrase: During the past month . . .

1. How have you been feeling? (response options ranging from "excellent" = 1 to "very low" = 6)
2. Have you been nervous or bothered by your "nerves"? (response options ranging from "not at all" = 1 to "extremely so, to the point where I could not work or take care of things" = 6)
3. Have you felt in control of your thoughts and emotions? (response options ranging from "yes, definitely so" = 1 to "no, and I am very disturbed" = 6)
4. Have you felt in control of your behavior? (response options ranging from "yes, definitely so" = 1 to "no, and I am very disturbed" = 6)
5. Have you felt as if you were losing your memory? (response options ranging from "not at all" = 1 to "yes, very much so, and I am very concerned" = 6)
6. Have you felt sad, hopeless, or depressed? (response options ranging from "not at all" = 1 to "extremely so, to the point where I could not work or take care of things" = 6)
7. Have you felt you were under stress? (response options ranging from "not at all" = 1 to "yes, almost more than I could bear or stand" = 6)
8. How happy have you been with your personal life? (response options ranging from "extremely happy" = 1 to "very unhappy" = 6)
9. Have you been anxious, worried, or upset? (response options ranging from "not at all" = 1 to "extremely so, to the point of being sick or almost sick" = 6)
10. Have you felt rested when you wake up? (response options ranging from "every day" = 1 to "none of the time" = 6)

11. Have you been bothered by any illness or physical pain? (response options ranging from "none of the time" = 1 to "all the time" = 6)
12. Have you felt tired, worn out, or exhausted? (response options ranging from "none of the time" = 1 to "all the time" = 6)
13. Do you worry about your health? (response options ranging from "none of the time" = 1 to "all the time" = 6)
14. Has your daily life been full of things that are interesting to you? (response options ranging from "all the time" = 1 to "none of the time" = 6)
15. How do you feel now? (response options ranging from "excellent" = 1 to "very low" = 6)

For the following items, inmates were instructed to: Circle the number on the scale which comes closest to how you have generally felt during the past month . . .

16. How concerned or worried have you been about your health? (10-point scale ranging from "not concerned" = 1 to "very concerned" = 10)
17. How relaxed or tense have you been? (10-point scale ranging from "very relaxed" = 1 to "very tense" = 10)
18. How much energy have you had? (10-point scale ranging from "very energetic" = 1 to "no energy" = 10)
19. How depressed or cheerful have you been? (10-point scale ranging from "very cheerful" = 1 to "very depressed" = 10)

Anomie Scale

Items preceded with the statement: For each of the following items mark whether you strongly agree (5), agree (4), are unsure (3), disagree (2), or strongly disagree (1) . . .

a. In spite of what some people say, the lot of the average man is getting worse.
b. It's hardly fair to bring children into the world with the way things look for the future.
c. Nowadays a person has to live pretty much for today and let tomorrow take care of itself.
d. These days a person doesn't really know who he can count on.
e. There's little use writing to public officials because they aren't really interested in the problems of the average man.

CHAPTER 8

FRIEND OR FOE? RACE, AGE, AND INMATE PERCEPTIONS OF INMATE-STAFF RELATIONS

Craig Hemmens* and James W. Marquart

ABSTRACT

The correctional research literature is rife with studies of inmate adjustment patterns. Early studies assumed inmates were part of a monolithic whole, though later research suggested factors such as race, age, and socioeconomic status affect inmate adjustment to prison life. This research focused on the relationship between age and race/ethnicity and perceptions of one aspect of the institutional experience, inmate-staff relations. A survey of recently released Texas inmates revealed that race and age have a major impact on inmate perceptions of staff. © 2000 Elsevier Science Ltd. All rights reserved.

INTRODUCTION

The prison experience has historically been meant to be unpleasant, and prisoners have been expected to suffer to some degree. There is, however, some dispute in the correctional research literature as to whether prison has any impact whatsoever on today's inmates. There is a general consensus in the correctional literature that institutionalization is a dehumanizing and demoralizing experience (Goffman, 1961; Irwin, 1980), but some research suggests that some inmates prefer prison to probation (Crouch, 1993), and that some inmates fare better in prison than others (Goodstein & Wright, 1989; Goodstein & MacKenzie, 1984; Wright, 1991). Some research indicates sociodemographic characteristics such as race and age may affect adjustment to prison, as well as perceptions of the institutional experience.

*Corresponding author *E-mail address:* chemmens@boisestate.edu (C. Hemmens).

JOURNAL OF CRIMINAL JUSTICE, Vol. 28 No. 4, July 2000, 297–312 © 2000, Administrative Office of the United States Courts.

This article builds upon prior research on inmate adjustment patterns. A total of 775 recently released Texas inmates, or "exmates," were surveyed about several aspects of the inmate-staff relationship. Their responses were examined and compared with a host of sociodemographic and criminal history variables. This article isolates and examines the effect of race and age on inmate perceptions of inmate-staff relations.

PRIOR RESEARCH

There is a substantial body of literature on inmate adjustment to prison (much of it focusing on race and age) as well as on inmate-staff relations. Each of these is examined in turn.

Inmate Adjustment

Research on inmate adjustment to incarceration dates from the pioneering study by Clemmer (1940) in which he developed the concept of "prisonization" to explain how prisoners become assimilated into the informal social structure of the prison. Some subsequent researchers built upon Clemmer's work, focusing on the inmate subculture that developed around shared "pains of imprisonment" (Sykes, 1958), which unified the inmate population and created a subculture based on a set of norms and values in opposition to those espoused by the prison staff. This portrayal of prison life became known as the "deprivation" model, and received mixed empirical support. Grusky (1959), Wheeler (1961), Schrag (1961), Garabedian (1963), Wellford (1967), Berk (1968), Wilson (1968), Tittle (1968), and Street (1970) examined the deprivation model in a variety of correctional institutions and found at least some support for it, although the degree of support varied by institution type.

Other researchers (Irwin & Cressey, 1962; Jacobs, 1976; 1977; Thomas, 1977) decried the focus on the so-called pains of imprisonment and institutional factors as the key to understanding inmate adjustment. They examined, instead, attributes and experiences that inmates brought with them to prison. They also argued that inmates brought into prison values learned on the street, in the inner city (Carroll, 1974; 1982). This was referred to as the "importation model." There is empirical support for the importation model (Carroll, 1974; Faine, 1973; Jacobs, 1974; 1977; Lawson et al., 1996, Thomas, 1970; 1977; Wood et al., 1968). Researchers have studied a variety of extra-prison variables, including race, age, socioeconomic status, and criminal history, a number of which have been found to be related to inmate adjustment patterns. Race and age are prominent among these variables. The focus of this article is on the impact of race and age on inmate perceptions of one aspect of the institutional experience, inmate-staff relations.

RACE AND INMATE ADJUSTMENT

Several studies have examined the racial heterogeneity of the inmate population. Earlier studies made passing reference to racial differences and their potential impact on the prisoner subculture (Sykes, 1958), and the picture generally painted was one of inmate homogeneity. Regardless of whether such a picture was accurate then, indications are that it certainly is not accurate today.

Carroll (1974; 1982) and Jacobs (1974; 1976; 1977) both detailed the changing nature of the inmate population, focusing particularly on racial differences.

Jacobs's description of Stateville prison portrayed Black inmates as much more cohesive and unified than White inmates. He argued that this racially-based group unity was a direct consequence of the Black inmates' shared preprison experiences with racism and discrimination in their lives in general and the criminal justice system in particular (Jacobs, 1976; 1977). Carroll posited that Blacks were successful in adjusting to prison not only because of their shared history of discrimination on the basis of race, but also because so many of them came to prison from the urban ghetto, where "making it" on the streets required a greater degree of toughness (Carroll, 1982).

Goodstein and MacKenzie (1984) found that White and Black inmates did vary on the degree of prisonization and time spent in the criminal justice system. White inmates with multiple convictions were more highly prisonized than Whites with one conviction, while Black inmates remained at the same level of prisonization regardless of the number of convictions (Goodstein & MacKenzie, 1984). Black inmates were also more "radicalized" than were White inmates, regardless of the length of confinement. These findings suggest there are significant differences between Black and White inmates, possibly because Blacks have suffered discrimination at the hands of criminal justice actors at all levels of the system.

Several studies of racial differences in prison indicated that Black inmates are significantly more likely than White inmates to be involved in conflicts with both staff and other inmates. Fuller and Orsagh (1977) found that Black inmates were more likely than White inmates to be aggressors. Other studies have also found that interracial conflict most often involves a Black aggressor and a White victim (Bowker, 1980; Lockwood, 1980; Wooden & Parker, 1982). The evidence of racial differences on aggressive behavior is mixed, however. A number of other studies have found little or no support for the hypothesis that non-White inmates are in fact more aggressive or violent than are White inmates, when controlling for other factors such as age, number of prior arrests, and drug and alcohol dependency (Ellis et al., 1974; Goodstein & MacKenzie, 1984; Wright, 1988; Zink, 1957;). In addition, while a number of studies have found that Blacks are much more likely to be involved in conduct that results in official condemnation by the prison administration (Flanagan, 1983; Ramirez, 1983), it has been suggested that racial discrimination on the part of prison administrators or correctional officers may account for this differential (Flanagan, 1983; Howard et al., 1994; Poole & Regoli, 1980; Wright, 1988).

Other studies of racial differences in adaptation to prison indicated that White inmates may suffer from higher levels of stress and fear than Black inmates. One study found that White inmates are more likely than Black inmates to injure themselves intentionally (Wright, 1988). Other studies showed that White inmates had more psychological problems, including breakdowns (Johnson, 1987), and depression. There may be, however, alternative explanations for the difference in adjustment by race. Goodstein and MacKenzie (1984) found no differences in the level of anxiety or the likelihood of depression between Black and White inmates.

Age and Inmate Adjustment

Age is frequently cited as an important explanatory variable in criminal justice (Gottfredson & Hirschi, 1991). A number of studies of violence in prison suggested that age is an important factor in inmate adjustment patterns. Age has been closely linked to the likelihood of aggressive behavior in prison. As inmates become older, there is a linear decline in the number of aggressive acts toward other inmates and/or correctional staff (Ekland-Olson et al., 1983; Porporino & Zamble, 1984), which mirrors the age-crime relationship in the free world (Gottfredson & Hirschi, 1991; Nagin & Farrington, 1992).

A study of age and aggressive behavior in prison by MacKenzie (1987) revealed a slightly more complex picture, however. Rather than a linear decline with age, she found that the rate of aggressive behavior rose until the late twenties, then declined. In addition, interpersonal conflicts with other inmates remained high for a longer period of time than did interpersonal conflicts with correctional officers. Recent research suggests that age is related not only to the likelihood of being involved in violent activity in prison, but also to perceptions of prison as safe or dangerous. Hemmens and Marquart (1999b) found that younger inmates were more likely to perceive prison as a dangerous place than were older inmates.

Inmate-Staff Relations

Living in prison means losing control over much of one's life. Personal autonomy is replaced by the requirement that the individual obey the commands of correctional staff. Inmate-staff relations thus comprise a crucial aspect of the institutional experience, and have been the subject of correctional research since the 1930s. Early researchers assumed that inmates had different norms and values than guards, and that guards and inmates distrusted one another. This research on the prison experience also tended to dichotomize the prison setting, with inmates on one side, guards on the other (Clemmer, 1940; Sykes, 1958).

It was taken for granted by these early researchers that inmates would have different norms and values than guards, and that guards and inmates would distrust one another. Later research has suggested that such a picture is overly simplistic. The Ramirez (1983) research indicated that staff and inmates share similar attitudes concerning a variety of issues. The Marquart (1986a, 1986b) participant observation research indicated that correctional officers who are involved in daily interaction with inmates can establish a rapport with and an understanding of inmates.

Historically, correctional officers have been White males with relatively low education levels, drawn in large part from rural areas, where many prisons were first located (Clemmer; 1940; Jacobs; 1977; Lombardo, 1982). Only recently has the presence of minorities and females in the correctional officer pool become noticeable. Studies of the impact on corrections of the changing correctional officer work force have produced mixed findings. Some studies indicated that minority officers have more punitive attitudes toward inmates than White officers (Jacobs & Kraft, 1978), while other studies found just the opposite (Jurik, 1985) or no difference (Crouch & Alpert, 1982).

In regards to female correctional officers, several studies indicated that female officers do not hold substantially different attitudes toward inmates than male officers (Cullen et al., 1985; Jurik, 1985; 1988; Jurik & Halemba, 1984). In addition, research suggests that while sexist attitudes still exist among inmates and male officers (Crouch, 1985; Zimmer, 1986), in general both inmates and male officers believe female correctional officers can do their jobs as well as male officers (Kissel & Katsampes, 1980; Walters, 1993).

The focus of the research presented in this article was on inmate attitudes towards and perceptions of correctional officers, a relatively understudied aspect of the inmate-staff equation. Much of the prior research has focused on staff attitudes toward inmates. The composition of the Texas correctional officer force has moved from what was characterized by Marquart (1986b) as a "good old boy" system dominated by White males from rural areas, to one with a substantial number of minority and female correctional officers, many from more urban areas. How have inmates perceived this shift in the demographic makeup of the Texas correctional officer force? This research sought to answer this question by examining inmate perceptions of female correctional officers, inmate-staff relations, and the use of force by correctional staff.

METHODS

The data for this study were obtained from a survey, administered over a six-week period, to 775 men released from incarceration in the Texas Department of Corrections—Institutional Division (TDCJ-ID). These former inmates, or "exmates," were interviewed at the bus station in Huntsville, located two blocks west of the Walls Unit. There are over one hundred prisons in TDCJ-ID, though virtually all inmates are processed and released through the front entrance of the Walls Unit, located in the center of Huntsville. They are provided with their personal belongings, a small amount of cash, and a voucher for a bus ticket to their destination. State law requires that releasees must return, via the bus, to the place where they were convicted and sentenced—this requirement ensures that virtually all exmates will in fact go to the bus station upon release.

As the exmates approached the bus station to purchase their tickets, the interviewers approached and asked them to participate in the survey. No material inducements were offered, and confidentiality was assured. Some exmates agreed to submit to the interview at this time, others agreed to be interviewed after obtaining their bus ticket, and still others agreed to be interviewed after first going to a nearby store or restaurant. Some exmates initially refused to cooperate, but later changed their minds and were interviewed while they waited for the bus to arrive. It was not uncommon for exmates to initially refuse to participate, but then change their minds once they observed other exmates participating.

Some exmates refused to be interviewed, or were not approached by the interviewers. Those who refused to be interviewed provided a variety of reasons for their refusal, ranging from distrust to apathy. Interviewers did not approach every single exmate because there were times when there were too many exmates and not enough interviewers. In addition, there were days when no interviewers were available to conduct interviews with released inmates. The selection of who to interview was random in that interviewers simply attempted to contact as many exmates as possible, given the limited number of interviewers and the large number of exmates.

According to TDCJ-ID data, 1,900 inmates were released during the interview period, and 775 inmates submitted to interviews. Assuming that virtually all of these 1,900 inmates passed through the bus station on their way home, as required by law, this generated a response rate of 41 percent. No data were collected on precisely why inmates refused to participate. Care was taken to create a research design that would yield accurate responses and generalizable results, though there are areas of concern, which may limit the usefulness of this study and which should be noted. These include the issues of selection and response bias.

Selection Bias

A simple random sample provides, in theory, the best approximation of the population (Maxfield & Babbie, 1995). In this study, there was no attempt to collect a simple random sample, but rather the interviewers approached as many members of the population under study (defined as all inmates released during the six-week period of study) as possible and sought to interview them. According to TDCJ-ID data, 1,900 inmates were released during this six-week time period, and 775 inmates were in fact interviewed. This represents a response rate of 41 percent. This is an acceptable level, but the question remains whether those who did not respond were systematically different from the whole population. If so, then selection bias would exist, limiting the generalizability and accuracy of the survey results (Maxfield & Babbie, 1995).

Steps taken to limit selection bias in this research project included: (1) contacting exmates as soon as possible after their release from prison, so as to contact as much of the population as possible; (2) employing interviewers of differing ages, races, and genders, in an effort to match as closely as possible the demographic characteristics of the exmate population and thus foster a sense of commonality and trust; (3) employing an interviewer who communicated with Spanish-speaking exmates, so as not to exclude non-English speaking members of the population; (4) reading the survey to exmates, so as not to exclude members of the population with nonexistent or negligible reading skills; and (5) making the survey short and easy to respond to, so as to encourage exmates to participate. The survey was five pages in length, and contained less than one hundred questions. The portion of the survey from which the data for this article was obtained contained fifty Likert-scale questions. A copy of the entire survey is included in the Appendix. These measures should have reduced the amount of selection bias to a level that does not render the results meaningless.

Response Bias

Related to selection bias is the problem of response bias, which may occur when a portion of the sample chooses not to participate in the survey (Fowler, 1993). Where selection bias involves the exclusion of possible respondents by the interviewer, response bias involves the exclusion of possible respondents by the potential respondents themselves. Nonresponse may bias a sample if nonrespondents are systematically different from the sample that is surveyed (Babbie, 1995).

There were exmates in this survey who were contacted by the interviewers, but who chose not to participate. Some gave no reason for their refusal. Reasons given for refusing to participate included general disinterest in the project ("What do I care about some survey?"), suspicion of the interviewers' motives

("How do I know you don't work for the state?"), and a lack of time ("I just got out of prison and I want to have some fun not sit around and answer some stupid survey"). Specific numbers for reasons given for refusing to participate were not collected. Interviewers noted no apparent similarity among those who refused to participate—no one racial or ethnic group or age category seemed more likely to refuse to participate. Sometimes men in a group would not participate; sometimes men in a group would all participate. There was no appreciable pattern of nonresponse based on how, where, or when exmates were approached.

It was not possible to determine if certain groups of exmates having similar but unobservable characteristics refused to participate. Examples may include sex offenders in general who chose not to participate, or Catholic offenders who chose not to participate. As the characteristics of "sex offender" and "Catholic" are not visible to the naked eye, and no information on offense type or religious affiliation was collected from offenders who did participate, there was no way to know if members of these groups (or others) chose not to participate.

Statistical Procedures

The data analysis included two steps. First, responses to individual items were examined using analysis of variance (ANOVA). Second, a logistical regression was conducted, incorporating all of the sociodemographic variables collected to determine which individual variables remained in the equation when controlling for the effects of other variables.

Analysis of Variance

Analysis of variance (or ANOVA) is a statistical procedure by which the ratio of variance between group means is examined to determine the likelihood that a difference in mean scores occurred by chance alone. A more precise name for the procedure, it has been suggested, would be "analysis of means" (Iverson & Norpoth, 1987). ANOVA allows the researcher to identify relationships between variables, even if the observations are not all independent of one another, or the variables interact, occurrences that violate the assumptions of multiple regression (Kachigan, 1991).

In this research, exmate responses on each of the individual survey items were compared on the basis of sociodemographic and criminal history variables. Sociodemographic variables included race, age, education level; criminal history variables included age at first arrest, number of prior incarcerations, and number of years spent in prison. Selection of these variables was based on prior research (Goodstein & MacKenzie, 1984; MacKenzie, 1987; Wright, 1989; 1991). ANOVA was used to determine whether the difference in the mean scores of the various groups (race/ethnicity and four age categories) occurred through chance variation or whether there is a statistically significant relationship between the sociodemographic/criminal history characteristic and responses to the survey items.

It should be noted that while information concerning a host of sociodemographic and criminal history variables was collected, in this article the focus is exclusively on race and age. This is because, in most instances, the other variables failed to reveal a statistically significant relationship between the variable and perceptions (Hemmens, 1998). These have therefore been excluded from the presentation of results. Information concerning other aspects of the institutional experience, including perceptions of AIDS policies, race relations, and violence, was also collected. The relationship between various sociodemographic and criminal history characteristics and perceptions of these issues was discussed elsewhere (Hemmens, 1998; Hemmens & Marquart, 1998; 1999a; 1999b).

The possible range of scores on each item was from 1 (strongly agree) to 4 (strongly disagree). A lower mean score indicated that an exmate group tended to agree with the statement; a higher mean score indicated that an exmate group tended to disagree with the statement. Items were reverse scored when necessary to achieve consistency of interpretation.

Logistic Regression

Logistic regression, or logit, is useful for analysis of dichotomous variables that are not normally distributed, and where the relationship between the dependent and independent variables is not linear. Logistic regression allows the researcher to perform a regression-like analysis of data when the dependent variable is dichotomous rather than continuous. Multiple regression is not robust against the assumption of the continuous linearity of the dependent variable (Menard, 1995).

Logistic regression was chosen for these data because the narrow range of answers (1 to 4 on a modified Likert scale) tended to produce very clear response patterns—exmates either agreed or disagreed with most statements. Exmate responses were recoded into two categories (agree/disagree), and logistic regression was performed. A backward elimination procedure was run, to determine which variables remained in the equation. Backward regression prevents the exclusion of variables involved in suppresser effects. A suppresser effect is when a variable appears to be statistically significant only when another variable is controlled. With backward elimination, since both variables are already in the model, there is less risk of failing to find a relationship when one in fact exists.

FINDINGS

Sociodemographic Characteristics of the Exmate Sample

First, the demographic characteristics of the exmate sample were analyzed and compared with state and national data. Descriptive statistics for the sociodemographic and criminal history characteristics of the 775 male exmates who comprised the sample are summarized in Table 8.1. Sample characteristics were similar to national level data regarding sociodemographic characteristics of male inmates in 1994 (Gilliard & Beck, 1996).

Blacks made up the largest racial/ethnic group in the exmate sample, comprising almost one-half (48 percent) of all respondents. Whites accounted for approximately one-third (33.7 percent) of all respondents, while Hispanics made up just 17.2 percent of the sample. The racial/ethnic composition of the sample was similar to that of inmates nationally. National statistics indicate 45.6 percent of inmates are White, and 48.2 percent are Black/minority (Gilliard & Beck, 1996).

Table 8.1

Sociodemographic and Criminal History Characteristics of the Exmate Sample

Characteristic	Frequency	Percent	Mean
Race/ethnicity			
White	261	33.7	
Black	363	46.8	
Hispanic	133	17.2	
Other	17	2.2	
Age			32.98
19–29	289	37.3	
30–39	326	42.1	
40–49	119	15.4	
50–72	36	4.6	
Education level			10.96
No high school degree	429	55.4	
High school degree	223	28.8	
Some college	87	11.2	
College degree	28	3.6	
Prior incarcerations			2.44
0	351	45.3	
1	61	7.8	
2	215	27.7	
3 or more	148	19.1	
Years in prison			6.08
1–3	112	26.9	
4–5	141	33.8	
6–9	164	39.3	
Age at first arrest			19.37
under 17	379	48.9	
18	88	11.4	
19–21	111	14.3	
22–29	128	16.5	
30 or older	56	7.2	

The average age of the exmate sample was 33 years. White exmates were slightly older, with a mean age of 33.8 years, compared with a mean age of 32.7 years for Black exmates, and 32.2 years for Hispanic exmates. The difference in mean ages was not statistically significant. Precise national statistics on age are not kept, but estimates of the number of inmates by age category complied by the U.S. Bureau of Justice Statistics suggests the mean age of the exmate sample is in line with national statistics. Approximately 55 percent of all inmates nationally are age 32 or younger, while 45 percent are age 33 or older (Snell, 1995). In addition, the median age of inmates on admission (a figure that is available), was 29 years in 1992 (Perkins, 1994).

The mean years of education completed for the exmate sample was just less than eleven years, or less than a high school degree (twelve years). Over one-half (55.4 percent) of all the exmates had not completed high school. Slightly over one-quarter (28.8 percent) of the exmates had a high school degree or GED, while 15 percent had at least some college experience. National statistics on inmate education levels indicate that roughly 40 percent of all male inmates do not have so much as a high school degree, while slightly less than 47 percent have a high school degree, and slightly more than 13 percent have at least some college experience (Snell, 1995). The median education level nationally of inmates at admission in 1992 was eleven years (Perkins, 1994). This closely mirrors the exmate sample. Comparison of the exmate and national samples revealed exmates as a whole were somewhat less educated than inmates nationally, with a greater percentage of exmates having failed to graduate from high school.

Perceptions of Inmate-Staff Relations

Next, the responses to questions dealing with inmate-staff relations were examined. The exmates were divided into three racial groups: White, Black, and Hispanic. Responses by racial/ethnic group were compared to determine whether exmates of different racial/ethnic groups held different perceptions of inmate-staff relations.

Four age-group categories were also created: 19–29 years, 30–39 years, 40–49 years, and 50 and older. Responses by age category were compared to determine whether exmates of different ages held different perceptions of inmate-staff relations. Age categories were created to highlight age differences. Tracking responses by individual years tended to mask differences as the changes between one year and the next were very slight.

Exmates were asked their level of agreement with eight statements regarding correctional staff. ANOVA was then conducted to determine statistically significant differences based on race and age. The eight statements and the responses to each statement are displayed in Table 8.2.

Exmates appeared to share similar feelings about correctional officers and inmate-staff relations. Mean scores on the eight questions regarding perceptions of correctional staff did not often vary significantly based on most of the selected sociodemographic and criminal history characteristics, such as education level, socioeconomic status, and criminal history. The results for these items were thus excluded for ease of presentation here. Only two variables revealed statistically significant results. These were exmate age and race (discussed following).

Age and Perceptions

These results indicate that younger exmates tend to have more problems with correctional staff, believe staff treat inmates in an inhumane fashion, feel new guards are less qualified than in the past, and feel that they were not well-treated in prison. They are also more likely to believe there are not enough guards to ensure inmate safety, and that correctional officers use more force than is necessary.

Table 8.2
Perceptions of Inmate-Staff Relations Using Analysis of Variance

I had very few problems with guards in TDC.

Race/ethnicity	White	Black	Hispanic	
N	260	363	132	
Mean	2.408	2.532	2.561	
SD	.867	.867	.822	

F ratio = 2.055;
   F probability = .1288

Age	19-29	30-39	40-49	50+
N	289	325	118	28
Mean	2.640	2.498[***]	2.246[**]	2.143[a]
SD	.887	.891	.703	.524

F ratio = 7.744;
   F probability = .000

Female guards do their job as well as male guards.

Race/ethnicity	White	Black	Hispanic	
N	259	359	130	
Mean	2.398	2.320	2.346	
SD	.792	.723	.723	

F ratio = .8188;
   F probability = .4413

Age	19-29	30-39	40-49	50+
N	287	318	119	28
Mean	2.317	2.393	2.387	2.143
SD	.758	.749	.678	.705

F ratio = 1.370;
   F probability = .2506

There are enough guards to provide safety and security for inmates.

Race/ethnicity	White	Black	Hispanic	
N	259	362	130	
Mean	2.568	2.547	2.592	
SD	.776	.773	.723	

F ratio = .1785;
   F probability = .8366

Age	19-29	30-39	40-49	50+
N	287	322	119	28
Mean	2.711	2.528[*]	2.437[**]	2.214[a]
SD	.787	.745	.721	.568

F ratio = 7.085;
   F probability = .0001

(continued)

Table 8.2
(Continued)

The quality of new guards entering TDC today is as good as it ever was.

Race/ethnicity	White	Black	Hispanic	
N	224	333	125	
Mean	2.808	2.796	2.856	
SD	.711	.690	.631	
F ratio = .352; F probability = .7034				

Age	19–29	30–39	40–49	50+
N	260	295	105	28
Mean	2.869	2.820	2.781	2.464[a,b]
SD	.691	.669	.679	.637
F ratio = 3.145; F probability = .0247				

TDC staff often act unfairly toward inmates.

Race/ethnicity	White	Black	Hispanic	
N	255	359	132	
Mean	2.835	2.894	2.924	
SD	.696	.701	.561	
F ratio = .917; F probability = .4003				

Age	19–29	30–39	40–49	50+
N	286	319	119	27
Mean	2.923	2.871	2.849	2.593
SD	.671	.722	.591	.752
F ratio = 2.097; F probability = .0992				

Overall, they treated me pretty good in TDC.

Race/ethnicity	White	Black	Hispanic	
N	260	360	133	
Mean	2.300	2.386	2.300	
SD	.623	.711	.623	
F ratio = 1.3431; F probability = .2617				

Age	19–29	30–39	40–49	50+
N	288	324	118	28
Mean	2.493	2.318[*]	2.220[**]	2.036[a]
SD	.703	.654	.572	.429
F ratio = 8.483; F probability = .000				

Table 8.2
(Continued)

Most guards in TDC treat inmates like they are less than human.

Race/ethnicity	White	Black	Hispanic	
N	260	362	133	
Mean	2.873	3.008	2.985	
SD	.737	.700	.627	
F ratio = 2.936;				
F probability = .0537				

Age	19-29	30-39	40-49	50+
N	288	325	119	28
Mean	3.101	2.932[*]	2.773[**]	2.714[a]
SD	.699	.691	.657	.810
F ratio = 8.180;				
F probability = .000				

Prison guards often use too much force on inmates.

Race/ethnicity	White	Black	Hispanic	
N	255	358	133	
Mean	2.576	2.821[*]	2.752	
SD	.784	.746	.690	
F ratio = 8.317;				
F probability = .0003				

Age	19-29	30-39	40-49	50+
N	285	322	116	28
Mean	2.853	2.683[*]	2.612[**]	2.571
SD	.778	.723	.695	.742
F ratio = 4.437;				
F probability = .0042				

In this table, the following notations indicate statistical significance at the .05 level between groups: 1,2 (*), 1,3 (**), 2,3 (***), 1,4 ([a]), 2,4 ([b]). TDC = Texas Department of Corrections.

On the item "I had very few problems with guards in TDC" the difference in the mean score for exmates in the 19–29 age category and exmates age 30 or older was statistically significant at the .05 level. In addition, the difference in mean scores for exmates in the 30–39 and 40–49 age category was statistically significant at the .05 level. This indicates that younger inmates had more problems with correctional staff, and that as exmates age, the likelihood of trouble with staff declines steadily, in a linear fashion. This finding is in accord with research that indicated younger inmates generally have more disciplinary infractions than do older inmates (Ellis, et al., 1974; Howard, et al., 1994; Zink, 1957).

Related to this finding is the observation that younger exmates were more likely to agree with the statement "Prison guards often use too much force on inmates" (this item was reverse coded). The difference in mean scores for exmates in the 19–29 age category and exmates in the older categories was statistically significant at the .05 level, with exmates in the 19–29 age category more likely to agree with the statement. A possible explanation for this finding is that younger inmates are more likely to be involved in altercations with staff, and therefore be the subject of use of force by correctional officers.

In accord with the finding that younger exmates believe staff use excessive force, younger exmates also were more likely to believe that guards treat inmates in an inhumane fashion. On the item "Most guards in TDC treat inmates like they are less than human" the difference in the mean score for exmates in the 19–29 age category and the other three categories was statistically significant at the .05 level (this item was reverse coded). On the item "Overall, they treated me pretty good in TDC," the difference in the mean score for exmates in the 19–29 age category and the other three categories was statistically significant at the .05 level. Younger exmates were clearly more likely than were older exmates to feel they were not well treated. This may be because correctional staff are harder on younger prisoners, or because younger prisoners are less willing to accept what happens to them in prison as proper, or because younger prisoners are involved in more disciplinary infractions and resent being punished by correctional staff.

The differences in mean scores for the various age categories on the item. "TDC staff often act unfairly towards inmates" were not statistically significant, although younger exmates did tend to agree with the statement more than their older counterparts. Taken together, responses to these three items suggest that younger exmates think they are treated *poorly,* but not *inappropriately.* It is unclear whether this is a reflection of low self-esteem or simply a statistical artifact. In addition, it is worth noting that age is related to perceptions in the free world as well. Younger citizens have less positive attitudes toward police than do older citizens (Huang & Vaughn, 1996; Walker, 1992).

Given the tendency of younger exmates to feel that they are poorly treated by correctional staff, they were nonetheless more likely to feel that there are not enough correctional officers to ensure safety and security in prisons. The difference in the mean score of the 19–29 age group and each of the older age groups was statistically significant at the .05 level. In addition, as exmate age increased, belief that there were enough guards increased steadily, which suggests perhaps, that older exmates think there are too many officers getting into their business.

Related to the perception of whether there were enough correctional officers was the perception of the quality of new officers. The mean scores for exmates in the 19–29, 30–39 age categories, and exmates in the 50 and older age category were statistically significant at the .05 level, with the younger exmates tending to disagree with the statement "The quality of new guards entering TDC today is as good as it ever was." This finding suggests that the oldest exmates think new officers are not as qualified as officers hired in the past, an interesting finding given that TDCJ-ID preservice training has increased rather than decreased in recent years.

Exmates were also asked whether they believed that female correctional staff do their jobs as well as male officers. The mean scores for the four age groups did not reveal any statistically significant differences. In this case, a finding of no difference is perhaps as interesting as a finding of some difference. Exmates were fairly unified in their estimation of the ability of female guards vis-à-vis male guards. The mean scores for the age categories fall around 2.3, indicating a slight tendency towards agreement with the statement "Female guards do their jobs as well as male guards." This finding is in accord with prior research on inmate attitudes (Kissel & Katsampes, 1980; Walters, 1993). Inmates seem to hold more positive opinions of female correctional officers than do many male staff. Prior research indicated male officers often resent the introduction of female officers into their male world (Owen, 1985; Zimmer, 1986), and frequently denigrate the job performance of female offices (Jurik, 1985; Zupan, 1992).

Race and Perceptions

The relationship between race and perception of inmate-staff relations turned up as statistically significant on only one item: "Prison guards often use too much force on inmates." On this item (which was reverse coded), the mean score for Black exmates was 2.8, while for White exmates it was 2.6. Black exmates, therefore, were more likely to agree with the statement than White exmates. The Hispanic exmate group had a mean score close to the Black exmates, but this was not statistically significant relative to White exmates. This finding is in accord with research conducted on attitudes of nonincarcerated populations. Black citizens appear to both trust the police less (Cole, 1999; Lasley, 1994), and believe that police use excessive force more often than White citizens (Huang & Vaughn, 1996).

Black and White exmates had different perceptions of use of force by correctional officers, though they did not have substantially different perceptions of whether correctional officers acted unfairly, or treated inmates as "less than human," which might be expected.

Logistic Regression Analysis

Logistic regression was conducted, to determine the impact of the various sociodemographic and criminal history variables when controlling for the effect of other variables. Table 8.3 displays the results of the logistic regression equations for the eight items regarding exmate perceptions of inmate-staff relations. Race and age appeared as significant variables in several items. They were also the only variables to remain in any equation.

These results suggest race/ethnicity is related to perceptions of inmate-staff relations, a fact obscured by the ANOVA procedure. Race/ethnicity and age both play important roles in the logistic regression models for the items regarding perceptions of inmate-staff relations. Differences between White and Black exmates remained in all but two of the eight equations, indicating White and Black exmates have very different perceptions of the inmate-staff relationship. Differences between White and Hispanic exmates remained in several equations as well, suggesting that race is a powerful predictor of perceptions of this aspect of the institutional experience.

White exmates were somewhat more likely than Black exmates to agree with the statement "Overall they treated me pretty good in TDC." White exmates

e² **Table 8.3**
Logistic Regression on Perception of Inmate-Staff Items

Group	B	Wald	Σ	R	Odds ratio
I had very few problems with guards in TDC.					
Age (B/W)	−.3412	11.467	.0007	−.1063	1.41
Age (H/W)	−.3137	5.320	.0211	−.0799	1.39
Age (H/B)	−.4962	16.672	.0000	−.1494	1.64
Female guards do their jobs as well as male guards.					
Race (B/W)	.4125	5.879	.0153	.0698	1.51
There are enough guards to provide safety and security for inmates.					
Race (B/W)	−.3412	11.465	.0007	−.1055	1.40
Age (H/W)	−.3599	8.960	.0028	−.1150	1.43
Age (H/B)	−.3976	11.436	.0007	−.1198	1.50
The quality of new guards entering TDC today is as good as it ever was.					
Age (H/B)	−.2878	5.323	.0210	−.0776	1.33
TDC staff often act unfairly toward inmates.					
Race (H/W)	−.6414	5.868	.0154	−.0939	1.90
Overall, they treated me pretty good in TDC.					
Race (B/W)	−.3944	4.608	.0318	−.0550	1.48
Age (B/W)	−.4496	14.812	.0001	−.1308	1.57
Age (H/W)	−.3691	6.280	.0122	−.0955	1.45
Age (H/B)	−.5681	18.573	.0000	−.1637	1.76
Most guards in TDC treat inmates like they are less than human.					
Race (B/W)	−.6260	10.984	.0009	−.1135	1.87
Age (B/W)	−.4003	13.253	.0003	−.1271	1.49
Race (H/W)	−.7344	8.023	.0046	−.1142	2.08
Age (H/B)	−.4918	13.060	.0003	−.1511	1.64
Prison guards often use too much force on inmates.					
Race (B/W)	−.8832	25.778	.0000	−.1713	2.42
Age (B/W)	−.2550	6.0157	.0142	−.0704	1.29
Race (H/W)	−.6960	9.756	.0018	−.1216	2.00
Age (H/B)	−.3512	8.434	.0037	−.1030	1.42

TDC = Texas Department of Corrections; B = black; W = white; H = hispanic.

were almost twice as likely as Black or Hispanic exmates to disagree with the statement "Most guards in TDC treat inmates like they are less than human." White exmates were more than twice as likely as Black or Hispanic exmates to disagree with the statement "Prison guards often use too much force on inmates." In addition, White exmates were 1.5 times more likely than Black exmates to agree with the statement "Female guards do their jobs as well as male guards," and 1.5 times more likely than Black exmates to agree with the statement "There are enough guards to provide safety and security for the inmates." Finally, White exmates were almost twice as likely as Hispanic exmates to disagree with the statement "TDC staff often act unfairly towards inmates." All of this suggests that White exmates have a higher opinion of correctional staff than minority exmates.

Age also plays an important role in shaping perceptions of inmate-staff relations. Exmates were more likely to agree with the statement "I had very few problems with the guards in TDC," as they get older. For each increase in age category, exmates were approximately 1.5 times more likely to agree with the statement. The same was true in regard to the statement "Overall, they treated me pretty good in TDC." Older exmates were also more likely to disagree with the statement "Most guards in TDC treat inmates like they are less than human." Older exmates were also more likely to disagree with the statement "Prison guards often use too much force on inmates." These findings suggest that older exmates are significantly more likely than younger exmates to have positive opinions of correctional staff, feeling that staff treat inmates decently. This corresponds with the ANOVA findings.

CONCLUSION

Examination of the exmate responses by race and age revealed some significant relationships between race, age, and perceptions of the institutional experience. Other factors (such as criminal history variables) consistently failed to show up as statistically significant in the ANOVA and do not remain in the logistic regression model, though two factors consistently showed up in both the ANOVA and logit procedures: race/ethnicity and age. Age remained in virtually every equation, while racial differences between White and Black exmates remained in several equations as well.

Regarding age, younger exmates also differed from older exmates in their perceptions of correctional staff and inmate-staff relations. Younger exmates reported having more problems with staff, and were more likely to believe that correctional staff treats them poorly: younger exmates tended to agree that staff often acted unfairly, treated inmates as less than human, and used too much force on inmates. All of this suggests that age is closely related to perceptions of staff behavior and inmate-staff interactions. Whether younger exmates feel this way because they are more often engaged in activity that is likely to be the subject of staff reprisals, or because staff treat older exmates with more care and respect, or because younger exmates come into prison with different beliefs about how they should be treated by staff is unclear. Further research on these differences in perception is clearly warranted.

Regarding race/ethnicity, the logistic regression analysis indicated that both Black and Hispanic exmates are more likely than White exmates to feel correctional staff treat inmates unfairly and/or poorly, and use excessive force. This finding is not altogether surprising, given the long history of poor race relations in Texas prisons (Marquart, 1986a, 1986b). It also mirrors research findings in the free world, which indicate that minority populations have a more negative perception of the criminal justice system in general and the police in particular than do Whites (Cole, 1999; Huang & Vaughn, 1996; Walker, 1992).

These findings are in accord with prior research, which found that individual, extra-institutional variables such as race play a major role in inmate adjustment patterns. In addition, this research added to the literature a clearer picture of the impact of age, an understudied variable, on inmate perceptions. Younger and older inmates differ in their perceptions of prison and this difference is often linear in nature, but particularly pronounced when the youngest and oldest inmate age groups are compared.

APPENDIX

 Parolee Attitudes and Expectations Questionnaire

I. Attitudes toward prison and parole

I am going to read you some statements and I would like for you to tell me which response you would agree with: strongly agree, agree, disagree, or strongly disagree.

	Strongly Agree	Agree	Disagree	Strongly Disagree
1. Doing time in Texas Department of Corrections (TDC) is pretty easy today.	1	2	3	4
2. I might be back in prison within the next year or two.	1	2	3	4
3. Offenders in Texas today know they won't do much time.	1	2	3	4
4. Making it on parole today is easy.	1	2	3	4
5. Texas is tougher on offenders today than it used to be.	1	2	3	4
6. Prison is a good way to deal with most offenders.	1	2	3	4
7. I plan to follow most of my parole rules.	1	2	3	4
8. Prison work programs will help me get a job in the free world.	1	2	3	4
9. Being in the free world again is pretty scary.	1	2	3	4
10. I had very few problems with the guards in TDC.	1	2	3	4
11. I support the death penalty for people convicted of murder.	1	2	3	4
12. All inmates should be tested for the AIDS virus.	1	2	3	4
13. Female guards do their jobs as well as male guards.	1	2	3	4
14. The chances of getting the AIDS virus in TDC are very low.	1	2	3	4
15. I worried a lot about getting beaten up or attacked while I was in TDC.	1	2	3	4
16. Race is a big problem in TDC.	1	2	3	4
17. TDC made me more responsible.	1	2	3	4
18. TDC's educational programs prepared me for the free world.	1	2	3	4
19. I almost never had any problems with other inmates while in TDC.	1	2	3	4
20. There are enough guards to provide safety and security for the inmates.	1	2	3	4
21. Inmates will change only if they are motivated to, no matter what TDC does.	1	2	3	4
22. My family thinks less of me since I've been in prison.	1	2	3	4

	Strongly Agree	Agree	Disagree	Strongly Disagree
	1	2	3	4
23. The quality of new guards entering TDC today is as good as it ever was.	1	2	3	4
24. All AIDS-infected inmates should be separate from the general population.	1	2	3	4
25. TDC staff often act unfairly toward inmates.	1	2	3	4
26. Overall, they treated me pretty good in TDC.	1	2	3	4
27. People with three felony convictions should be sentenced to life without parole.	1	2	3	4
28. I feel bad about going to prison.	1	2	3	4
29. Allowing inmates of different races to live in separate living areas is a good idea.	1	2	3	4
30. I plan to work with my parole officer to follow the terms of my parole.	1	2	3	4
31. Parolees like me will have a tough time in the free world.	1	2	3	4
32. Inmates in TDC do not have enough privacy.	1	2	3	4
33. Drugs/alcohol played a big role in landing me in prison.	1	2	3	4
34. Right now, it is too crowded in TDC.	1	2	3	4
35. The prison administration uses parole as a weapon against inmates.	1	2	3	4
36. Inmates have the right to know which other inmates in TDC have AIDS.	1	2	3	4
37. I think it will be harder on parole than it was to do time in TDC.	1	2	3	4
38. The standards used to evaluate me for parole are fair and objective.	1	2	3	4
39. Inmates attack other inmates very often.	1	2	3	4
40. Most guards in TDC treat inmates like they are less than human.	1	2	3	4
41. It is hard to maintain my own identity and be myself in prison.	1	2	3	4
42. Overall, it is pretty safe in TDC.	1	2	3	4
43. I generally feel that I am at least equal to others.	1	2	3	4
44. I take a positive attitude toward myself.	1	2	3	4
45. What happens to me is my own doing.	1	2	3	4
46. I find that one day I have one opinion of myself and on another day I have another opinion.	1	2	3	4
47. It is easier to make a living by doing crime than it is by obeying the law.	1	2	3	4
48. I consider myself a law-abiding citizen most of the time.	1	2	3	4
49. Prison guards often use too much force on inmates.	1	2	3	4
50. Inmates have a lot of control over what other inmates do today.	1	2	3	4

CHAPTER 9

THE MIX: THE CULTURE OF IMPRISONED WOMEN

Barbara Owen

Women sentenced to the Central California Women's Facility found many ways to adapt to their life in prison. The complex and diverse histories of the women incarcerated in this prison community produced a prison culture that is itself complex and diverse across numerous dimensions. These "axes of life" (Schrag, 1944) shape the group design as to how individual women live their own lives and how they live in relation to other women in this prison world.

Three critical areas of life were observed in this study: negotiating the prison world, which involves dimensions of "juice," respect, and reputation; styles of doing time, which include a commitment to the prison code; and one's involvement in trouble, hustles, conflicts, and drugs, known as "the mix" to the women at CCWF. These different dimensions of prison life are not embraced evenly by all members of the prison's population. In fact, they may not shape the liferound of any given prisoner. But taken together, these dimensions comprise the general prison culture among women, and thus shape action and meaning within the prison community.

These dimensions are informed by the liferound of the female prisoner as she seeks to find meaning and rhythm in her time in prison. Participation in prison culture, among the women studied, is dynamic, fluid, and often situational. A woman's participation is determined by a number of factors, including time spent in prison, previous imprisonment, her commitment to a deviant identity, and time left to serve. Immersion in the prison culture is also determined by one's pre-prison experience, one's relationship to time and place, and the range of personal relationships she develops in the prison community. These factors, in turn, shape daily life within the prison and lead to differences in meaning structure, particularly in terms of the prison code of "do your own time." Defining culture as "a group design for living," this final chapter describes the ways a complex strata of women contribute to and participate in this culture.

Owen, Barbara. (1998). *In the Mix*. New York: State University of New York Press.

NEGOTIATING THE PRISON WORLD

Entering the prison world, like any new experience, involves learning a unique set of strategies, behaviors, and meanings. Women negotiating this world are dependent on two key factors. First, access to information about prison and its culture through prior prison experience, having a relative or friend in prison, one's experience in jails, commitment to a deviant identity, and a woman's street culture provides useful indications of what she expects to find in prison. Second, interpersonal coping skills, cleverness, and an understanding of the prison bureaucracy also determine a woman's success in negotiating this new terrain. Women entering prison may or may not have the experiential background or knowledge necessary to interpret or predict their day-to-day life in confinement. Interestingly, both women who are street-smart or prison-smart and women who are organizationally smart do well in negotiating this world. The prison-smart woman has learned through experience how to manage the prison community's resources and members in a way that allows her to "do her own time." The organizationally smart woman, in contrast, is skilled at interpersonal relations, managing bureaucracies, and recognizing reciprocity in terms of "common courtesy." She also carves out a social existence that meets her needs and minimizes the deprivations of imprisonment.

Becoming Prison-Smart: Gaining Respect and Reputation

Through past incarcerations, continuing contact with the criminal justice system, and a commitment to knowing "what is happening," the prison-smart woman negotiates the prison world on her own terms. The prison-smart woman can turn this specialized knowledge to her advantage, cultivating relationships with both staff and other prisoners that allow her some measure of freedom and autonomy in her everyday life, operating narrowly within the prison's rules and regulations, but often outside their specific intent. Through "prison smarts," a woman builds a personal world in which her prison program, including living situation, job, and other activities, are relatively satisfying and devoid of the ongoing aggravation that prison life can bring. A successful prisoner stays out of the "the mix," maintains personal relationships that are constructive and unlikely to bring trouble, and creates a daily program that meets her personal and material needs without drawing any negative attention to herself and her activities. Most lifers, once they have gone through their disruptive adjustment period, fit this profile, but other long-termers and those returning for subsequent terms have learned this lesson. Marlisse, a lifer, offers this observation:

> The prison world has changed since 1977 when I started my term. There are a lot more youngsters, indigent women and game-players that do not know how to do time. They are rude, loud, and cause more fights, more homo-secting. There is no longer any place to have solitude here. I used to be that obnoxious. In my first four or five years, I let all the bitterness and anger out. I took it out on the officers and my peers. I did not know the damage that it would do to me seventeen years later. Now I know how to play the game, how to format my time. I can manipulate staff to do what I want without them knowing about it.

All I want is respect. I just want to do my time. I have my job, a list of rules for the room that says "no homosexuality in here, no drugs, and wash your hands after you go to the bathroom." It is that simple. I keep to myself—I used to have a girlfriend that was in the mix. No more. I know how to do my time, what I need to make it easy, and how to please myself. If I like you, and you need something, then I will tell you how to get it. But mostly I keep to myself.

One key aspect of "prison smarts" is the ability to "get things done." Some women attain a reputation for being able to get things done. Other prisoners will come to her with questions and requests for advice because of this reputation. Like in male prisons, this person is known as having "juice," possessing information and influence that come through a job or relationships with authority figures. Juice, in both male and female prisons, is the ability to get things done, often circumventing the rules or avoiding the delays experienced by the "nobody" or the "nondescript." The prisoner with juice knows what is happening and how to make it happen, whether the need is legitimate or illegitimate. Randi is well known as someone who can get things done. During one evening in the unit, I observed a young woman who was very tentative and hesitant, possibly somewhat confused, approach Randi with a medical problem. She did not think that she could ask the officer for help herself. Asking Randi to intercede on her behalf, she said, "I don't know who to ask or what to say and no one else will help me." Randi considered the problem, approached the sergeant on duty and, in minutes, the woman in need was out the door to the medical staff. Randi explains her juice comes from working for the yard sergeant: "He knows me and is willing to give me a break or someone else if I ask it. Now if I need something, and it is serious enough, I can go to them, and tell them 'I need this now, it is important' and I have got it." Having such relationships and influence did not appear to be disdained by the other women, unlike Sykes's (1958) "centerman," who was seen as more staff-identified than prisoner-identified.

Divine, ending a three-year sentence for cocaine sales, also has juice. She describes her ability to get things done and the advantages she has over other prisoners in getting paperwork (chronos) signed prior to her release:

> If I was just an ordinary person on the yard crew, it would take me three months to get all these chronos cleared—now I can get it done the next day. What if I did not have this access? Here I can walk around the corner and get it done. Staff will sign things for me because they know me. I can talk to the staff, especially the COs.

Critical aspects of "prison smarts" are respect and reputation. The notion of respect is one of the few values held in common with the male prison culture. Also found on the street, the idea of respect, and its opposite, disrespect, shape interaction as well as reaction across most prison communities. However common, respect is a difficult concept to define. In Sykes's 1958 view, the "right guy" is the archetype of respect. He earns this respect by adhering to the prison code and making inmate interests a priority in all relationships. Respect is the cornerstone of doing time. Irwin (1980) argues that the prison code may never have truly represented "right guy" ideals and may have diminished significantly as correction's philosophy shifted from punishment to rehabilitation. In an essay of the contemporary prison code, Renaud (1995) wonders if an ideal form ever existed. In the female prison, the prison code has always been more fluid and flexible, based more on interpersonal relationships than abstract principles (Ward & Kassebaum, 1965). Still, some vestiges of the code, particularly applicable to respect and reputation, remain in the daily life of the female prison.

Respect appears to be based on personal behavior and known history, typically in terms of offense and interaction with staff and prisoners alike. Respect can also be gained through positive as well as negative means. Being able to stand your ground and maintain a positive reputation in dealing with other prisoners seems to be a key to respect in the women's prison. This group interview illustrates some of the critical aspects of respect among the women at CCWF:

TRACY: You respect others for different reasons. It really depends on what you are talking about. If you are talking about the drug scene, and you are holding the bag, you can get respect. If you are into being tough and aggressive, if you beat somebody's ass good enough you have respect.

RANDI: But that is only respect from some people. It totally depends on what you are into here. You can get respect from some people here if you are the bad little girl—the one that is always in trouble. Oh, they respect the hell out of you for that. That is scary. You cannot be good and be respected. You have to be bad.

TRACY: But who the hell wants that kind of respect, anyway?

One way to get respect is to earn a reputation for fairness in your dealings with other prisoners. This respect is cumulative. Randi tells why Divine is a highly respected "Original Gangster":

Divine is respected because she is a convict. She is not an inmate. She does what she can for us. Not because the cops tell her to. If she has something she can change for us in general, she will do it. Without even asking. If we go to her and ask for something, and she can do it, it is done. If you really need to see someone, and you ask Divine to deliver a message to them, she will do it. Because she is a convict.

The concept of reputation is directly related to that of respect. For women invested in the prison culture and lacking attachments to the outside world, reputation in the closed culture of the prison becomes a highly desired commodity. Status in the prison world can be conferred in a variety of ways. Parallel to the male prison culture, women take some pride in adhering to some form of the convict code. The need to be respected was clear among the women at CCWF, but not to the exaggerated extent found in male prison. Having a reputation, being known and being recognized, lifts an individual out of the faceless crowd and gives a woman an elevated prison identity. For those tied to the mix and its values, this type of reputation becomes a centerpiece to prison identity and survival. Of the women interviewed in this study, those most attached to the mix seemed to be the most concerned with this question of reputation and respect. For old-timers, their past behaviors, including earning the appellation "OG" is sufficient. Newcomers, on the other hand, may have to prove themselves in the subtle stratification system. As this repeat offender remarks, "I have many friends in prison but it isn't about being seen and being recognized anymore. It used to be important to be important, but I did not come here to be famous on the yard." Reputation, as in the free world, is based on one's actions but can also be based on public opinion. Randi suggests that reputation may be based on image as well as action:

> I find that a lot of people when they get here have these images that they try to uphold. You know what I am saying. At a time, I had an image that I was trying to uphold about three or four years ago, but I had to drop that and stop trying to save my god damn face and not put it out there. So right now I don't have a problem with being honest with nothing, nothing that I do or say.

Tracy adds that the closeness of the prison world makes public opinion important:

> A lot of times you do care. You think that what people say about you cannot hurt you. But it can. In confined spaces like this, someone puts you down, it can bring you to tears in a heart beat. Everything can hurt you here. And that is sad, because on the streets you can take just about everything and walk away. But you can't walk away in here. You have to take it and listen to what they have to say about you, even if it is not true.

Recognizing Reciprocity

"Learning the ropes" and the skills to apply this knowledge is especially valuable in the prison. While much of this knowledge is context-specific and derived from experience with the prison world, many women are able to become skilled at managing the prison bureaucracy by relying on cleverness and ability, without having a commitment to a prison identity. The more-educated women learn early on to apply skills obtained in their pre-prison life through schooling, employment, experience, or intelligence. Women who have clerical, organizational, computer, and additional work skills also gravitate toward better jobs in the institution and become valued workers, thus gaining juice. Women unattached to the deviant aspects of the prison world have added value in these job situations. Once these women overcome the shock of their incarceration, they learn that application of their middle-class skills and values may go a long way in negotiating the prison environment, at least that part controlled by conventional authority. The middle-class woman also depends on the officers in negotiating the world, but in a way different from having juice. The middle-class woman relies on officers' legitimate authority and applies middle-class standards of social interaction to these interchanges. Ellen, a newly arrived, college-educated woman, offers this view:

> This is a new environment I am in and it will take a little time to get used to it. But I can go to Mrs. S or to Mr. C and the other COs if we have a problem. Or we can go to the sergeant. You have to adjust to the lifers because they have been in a long time and I am a newcomer coming in. But I try not to listen to the women in here. The only ones I listen to are the officers. They are in charge of me, they are the ones taking care of me while I am here. I only trust the officers. I don't really listen to the inmates. I only listen to those in charge.
>
> Some women don't understand that you have to go by their rules. I do. It doesn't make any sense to me (that) these women think they have more authority than the COs over them. The COs will tell you, if you are bitchy to me, then I will be bitchy to you. If you talk to me on an intelligent level, then I will talk to you on an intelligent level. The officers have never been disrespectful to me. The only time they are disrespectful is when people are disrespectful to them. You need to be courteous to them.

Both middle-class and prison-smart women rely on the social skills of courtesy and civility in their interactions with officers and staff. As Victoria, a lifer who has done fifteen years, says, "Why these young girls cuss out the staff and then expect them to lift a finger for them is beyond me."

Many women learn that getting along with officers is a key to negotiating the prison world. Recognizing that officers tend to reciprocate attitudes and behavior, Suzie stated:

> To get respect in here, you have to give them respect. And he (staff) is pretty good about that. There are some people in here that go off, start cussing at you, or start cussing at the cops and shit like that. Of course, the cop is going to treat you like shit. Yeah, and write you a 115. Then if you be nice to them and don't give them no hassle and talk to them with respect, they are pretty good about talking to you with respect. It is simple: they show you respect, you show them respect; they are nice, no harassment.

Taking Someone under Your Wing

Some newcomers learn to negotiate the prison world by being mentored by someone who "knows what is happening." Most of the OGs discuss the fact that "in the old days, someone would take you under their wing and tell you how to do time. Not anymore; these youngsters don't listen to anybody. I guess they have to learn the hard way." Other women develop nonromantic but close relationships with their roommates and feel that it is their responsibility to set them straight, as Tootie tells it:

> Like when Marta moved into our room, I told her how it was and I took more to her and I just got real honest with Marta and ran things down about me and told her things about certain people that she should know to open her eyes. She was nineteen years old. At the end of that, she started seeing the real for what it is. She still wants to go to the yard, and rip and run, but I know she would get tired of that. I tell her, "Why you got to go out to the yard every day?"

Divine gives her perspective on respect:

> There are people here who are older and people who are younger. But I still have to earn respect. I just don't get automatic respect because I am forty-seven years old. I have to act like I am forty-seven years old. And act like I have some sense. If you act like an ignorant youngster, you get treated like an ignorant youngster. And there are youngsters that act like they are forty-seven. I did not know these things when I first started doing time. When I first started doing time, we had people who would take care of us. We had older people who had been in the system a while, who took you under their wing and we listened. Nowadays, these youngsters, they don't listen. But now you have people you don't even want to be bothered by telling them because they will come off at you (like you are) crazy. You try to avoid conflict wherever you can, because that is the best way to do your time, just avoid conflict. If I see somebody that is really acting stupid, wants to be loud and boisterous and act a fool, I stay out of their way. Nothing I can say to them is going to change that; they are going to have to learn the hard way. I can just look at people and tell how they are going to be. Most people you just leave alone.

Left to their own devices are women who do not possess the skills for negotiating a bureaucracy, the prison smarts to work the system, nor a "protector" who watches out for them. These women spend much of their day disorganized and frustrated at their inability to get anything done, or choose to "run the yard and stay in trouble." Rory, a woman with one more year to go on a three-year term, offers this advice to a newcomer:

> The biggest thing that I will tell them is to keep to yourself. And to stay out of everybody else's mess. You have to do your own time. You came here alone and you will go home alone. The only way you are going to get home is to take care of yourself. You are number one. And a lot of people, especially youngsters in here, get involved with other bitches, the yard, or other mess and they are not thinking about themselves.

As another prisoner explained, "Some women are way out of their territory here; they need help from someone who knows what is happening." Due to their lack of experience with the prison world, their lack of juice and overall lack of understanding of the way things work, and their overall inability to organize and develop a strategy for managing the bureaucracy, these women are likely to stumble through their first weeks or months in the prison, lacking the knowledge of the prison-smart woman, the know-how of the bureaucratic operator, or the advice, guidance, or protection of another prisoner.

STYLES OF DOING TIME

Allegiance to the prison code is stratified. The prison social order is based on the stage in one's prison career (youngsters and old-timers), commitment to convict or conventional identity, length of sentence, and level of commitment to prison culture. Styles of doing time are based partially on this stratification but, as Irwin and Cressey (1962) have argued, they are also based on dimensions of pre-prison experience. These styles are further dependent on the in-prison experience, related to the personal relationships previously described. As a woman learns to negotiate the prison culture, she is also exposed to a variety of styles of doing time. At CCWF, there was considerable evidence that these styles of doing time constituted elements of a career, with different behaviors and attitudes at the beginning, middle, and end of the prison term. In some sense, doing time is related to the day-to-day business of developing a program and settling into a satisfying routine. The construction of an approach to doing time is also dependent on the types of systems adopted to give shape and meaning to these activities. Descriptions of male prisons discuss these meaning systems in terms of argot roles, as well as prison culture. In the women's world, there are few static roles used in the everyday interaction—a fact also suggested by Ward and Kassebaum (1965).

Two of the most significant contributions to one's style of doing time are somewhat related: commitment to a deviant identity, particularly a criminal identity, and stage in one's criminal and prison career. This section discusses the "convict code" and the conflicts between old-timers and youngsters.

The Convict Code

Although the convict code among women is not nearly as important as that among men, prison culture is found in the female version of the convict code. Within the male code, described by Sykes and Messinger (1960) and others, the primary rules are "do your own time" and "protect the convict interest," with their implications for group solidarity. This code has carried over to the female prisons with some significant modifications. Although Ward and Kassebaum (1965) did not find a monolithic code that promoted group cohesion, the women at CCWF use the ideal of the convict code in setting and discussing standards of behavior. When asked to described the convict code, the following terms were mentioned throughout the course of this study:

"Mind your own business."
"The police is not your friend: stay out of their face."
"If asked something (by staff), you do not tell."
"Do not allow rat-packing—fight one on one only."
"Take care of each other."

There was universal agreement among the old-timers, specifically the OGs, that the code has changed. Victoria, a lifer in her late forties, suggested:

You used to know that your back was covered. With all these young kids, these gang-bangers, there is less code now. But there is no support for gang behavior in prison. When the gangs first came, I thought, "This is my home and you are not going to come in here and ruin what we have done." These kids are so young, coming in with so much time. They have no upbringing from the streets, no values, no foundation to build on. They have no remembrance of anything. The kids are crude, rude, and loud. Sometimes you have to say to them: "What the fuck do you think you are doing?" And then the next thing you know you have a (prison) kid—I have gotten tired of taking someone under my wing and now I keep to myself.

This feeling of disapproval of the younger generation was held by many women:

There is a difference between the younger generation and the older generation. These youngsters are rude, disrespectful, and inconsiderate. They have never been taught. Even when they get locked up, they are back on the yard, harder than before. They always say, "We [are] the babies here." Well, when I first came, I didn't even know how to act. So many youngsters come to prison and they think they are going "to kick it on the yard." Youngsters want to be noticed, to put their stuff out. They can be loud and obnoxious. I used to tell them (the rules, the code), like not to tell on nobody but I have given up doing that. Years ago, you just didn't tell; I was taught the old way. It's not like the old days. I learned from the old school, in the sixties. Then the convicts stuck together. If you went down, you just took it. You didn't bring nobody down with you. "Do your own time." That was the rule.

A few women have borrowed elements of the male code and avoid interaction with officers at all times. Toni, a forty-eight-year-old woman who has served almost twenty years, commented:

> I still go by the code. I won't have a position where I have to work next to an officer. Now people tell (inform to staff): they don't have common sense; they think they have street knowledge and don't realize that it is different than prison knowledge. The conflict here is age, not race like with the men. Most of the youngsters are gang-bangers. With the male prison gangs: a life or death situation, a power struggle. With women, it is an emotional struggle. Women are weaker, I guess.

Related to this idea is the distinction between "inmates" and "convicts." This repeat prisoner, Misti, offers the perspective of the old-time convict:

> It is how you carry yourself. A lot of women carry themselves like a bunch of wimps. There are a lot of inmates here, but you have to realize that there are a lot of convicts here too. I don't understand what an inmate is because I have never been an inmate. I have always been a straight-up convict. I don't give a fuck. You tell me what to do and I am not going to do it. The judge sent me here to do my time and that is all I am going to do for you guys. Yeah, I got your W number, I belong to the state, but I am telling you like this, I am coming here to do my time, I am not coming here to program, to do what you want me to do. My name is Misti and if you got anything else to ask me, ask me. That is just how I am. But a lot of other people, as an inmate, they will get all scared and stuff and run and tell the police this and that. You don't run to the police. If you have a problem, then you take it to your fellow inmate, or your fellow convict. Don't go to the police with your problem. I would take it to my family—the first place I would go—to my dad or to my brother.

One central aspect to the code and styles of doing time is a perspective on informing on other prisoners to the staff, also known as "telling," "ratting," or "snitching." While severely censored in male prison culture, contemporary female prison culture seems to tolerate a higher level of "telling" than in the past. Randi adds:

> Now we have a lot of stupid people in here—people who don't know the code. It used to be, you snitched, you got cut. It was strict about stealing and ratting. Now the "ho's" can rat all day long and no one will kick their ass. Before you would get a chance if you messed with my woman, but no chance for stealing or ratting. In '89, it started to change.

However, there was some support for certain types of informing, a finding that opposes any descriptions of male prison culture. Blue describes the ambivalence women feel over a strict interpretation of the "code":

> One of the main thing about the code is "don't snitch." It is good to tell for certain things, like if someone gets jumped or somebody got stabbed. But it is just little things that people tell. If you have a fight in your room, let it stay in your room. Why do you want it to get out so you can end up going to jail? Not too long ago, two people were doing some dope in my room and the cops came in. When the

cops came in, the girl threw the outfit behind my locker but they knew (it wasn't mine) because in my record from day one, I am not into drugs. I don't use drugs on the street either.

In some ways, respect can mean adhering to the convict code, but it also concerns one's behavior toward other prisoners and staff. A respected prisoner does not cause trouble for other prisoners and is not "messy." Being messy generally involves gossip and less than truthful behavior, but it can be extreme and involve more serious trouble too.

A minor dimension of respect involves responding to physical challenges. While fights are not an everyday occurrence, being ready to defend yourself contributes to such a reputation, as Birdy describes:

> Respect means you can stand up for yourself. You can lose respect if you lose a fight in the open but you can fight in the room and lose without losing respect. If others call you a bitch, or test you out in the open. Being tested can be like "Come on, bitch, you want me, here I come."

Jackie, a younger woman with many years' experience in doing time, offers this perspective:

> Although I am young, I have experience with older people. I am in the old school. [We are] the OGs in society—we just look at these youngsters and shake our heads. Some people see prison as fun, as a vacation. People get homey in here; their life is here; they get scared when they get close to the gates. They are not willing to break the bad habits from the street that got them here.

And these habits from the streets become "the mix" at CCWF.

The Mix

The final dimension of prison culture found at CCWF is the amorphous concept of "the mix." For the vast majority of the women interviewed and observed, "the mix" is generally something to be avoided. As Mindy tells us, "The mix is continuing the behavior that got you here in the first place." Few women claimed to be presently involved in the mix, but many stated previous involvement. Throughout the interviews these behaviors (and, in a sense, this state of mind) was an important dimension of prison life, something to be aware of and to be avoided. In giving their advice to newcomers, almost everyone interviewed suggested: "Stay out of the mix." In its briefest definition, the mix is any behavior that can bring trouble and conflict with staff and other prisoners. A primary feature of the mix is anything that can "have your days taken" (meaning reducing "good time" credits) or result in going to "jail" (SHU or Ad Seg). A variety of behaviors can put one in the mix. The most frequently mentioned issues were related to "homo-secting," involvement in drugs, fights, and "being messy," that is, being involved in conflict and trouble.

Staff are also aware of the trouble inherent in being in the mix. Randi recalls her wild days: "Staff told me I'd be alright when I got out of the mix; they said once you get into the groove of things; you'll be alright." Being in the mix also involves "being known," in a negative sense. As Roxy, a newcomer serving time for violating her drug offense probation, says, "The mix can be anything that gets you in trouble and causes you to lose time. It can be the dope fiend mix, the homosexual mix, the fighting mix, and the 'working for the cops mix.' "

Most of the women interviewed stated that going home is their first priority, but suggested that some women are more at home in prison and do not seem to care if they "lose time." It appears that those involved in the mix do not act out of an outside orientation, instead devoting their time (and risking their days) for in-prison pursuits, such a drugs, girlfriends, and fighting. Lily, a middle-class woman serving time for embezzlement, remarks on those "in the mix":

> The majority of people who run things in here never had anything in their life—their mothers were whores. Not that I have anything against that. At least they are not stealing. I was fortunate that I had a structure in my life. These people have no values, no convictions. They run the street all their lives. Here they are big because they get $140 draw, and get a box every quarter. Where else in the world can that be the top of life? They have it going on. Then they parole, and it is not so good anymore, and on the streets, they are not running shit. So then they get a case, come back and hey, they are big daddy now (snaps fingers). Well, where else can a very large woman with bad skin and no teeth come and have a haircut and be daddy? And have all the little girls running after them?

Cherry offers that the term "the peoples" also describes those in the mix:

> You hear (the term) the peoples. You will say, "Well who, girl, who is doing all this?" And they will say, "The peoples." Just watch. There are a lot of them who are rolling [in material goods]. They got dope, gold and stuff; the earnings—one woman has seventeen pairs. They are not going to do nothing—they don't do the transactions, the fights, they don't hold the drugs. They are just going to receive everything. It happens in my room: they order others around—[they says things like] "Wash my clothes, wash my shoes off, light my cigarettes, make my coffee; go and get this from so and so. So and so, I doubled on them, I want you to go kick their ass and open their locker and take all their shit. You ain't going to do that for me?" It is so ugly. These are people who have never had love. It has been proven that negative attention is more acceptable than no attention. (Sarcastically) It is wonderful to be in prison and know these things exist.

Tabby adds that the mix is the only way to support yourself if you have no material support from the outside:

> The mix here is the loud types, selling drugs but the mix is really in you, you are like that on the streets. The homegirls know how things are and [tell you] I have to sell this. Some people don't have people on the streets to take care of them, to send them anything. You have to do something in here to survive, [whether it's] to sell dope or steal.

Tootie indicates that she has been on the edges of the mix in the past:

> People in the mix want to be seen. They care about being on the yard more than anything else. I have always been around the mix people, but ever since I got here, no way. I have done cool way down. And now I shoot out there every blue moon and holler at everybody but I shoot right back here. When I first got here, they told me to do this and that, and I said I don't want to go with you. I don't want your coat. I would rather freeze than get all caught up in that. When I ain't got, I will go without.

The mix also involves not minding your own business, violating a tenet of the old convict code:

> The girls that go out here and want to hang with their little groups, get involved in situations that they don't need to get involved in. They start stuff. Some women are messy. Instead of letting things be, they like to make things keep going and going. Instead of just kicking back and don't cause yourself any problems, and just go on and do the program like you put yourself into. You need to get it out of the way so you can go home. I have a friend who was supposed to go home in November, and she just lost her date; now she don't know when she is supposed to go home. It is from being in the mix—being with the wrong crowd. Doing what she feels like doing and not programming. Me, I get the impression that people in the mix don't want to go home. That they have nothing to look forward to on the streets. They like being here with their buddies. Clowning and talking about people. Then problems start when women run to the deputy and tell them what is going on. It doesn't call for that.

There was a general consensus that the yard was the primary location for activities composing the mix. A good majority of the women in this study stated that they avoided the yard as much as possible. Observations over time and the survey responses support this contention. Even on beautiful spring days or evenings, the yard rarely has contained a significant proportion of women. At least two thousand of the women housed at CCWF would be eligible to go to the yard in the evenings or the weekends. Observations and interviews with both staff and prisoners suggest the yard rarely has more than four hundred women at any one time. Special events are an exception. Most women spend time in their units, particularly their rooms, avoiding the mix in the yard. Less than 5 percent of the women interviewed in the survey indicated that they spent their free time on the yard.

Judy, a middle-class disabled prisoner, agrees that many women, particularly newcomers, are leery about going to the yard:

> I have never, ever been afraid, but I get along with all sorts of different people and I am that way out on the streets. I have worked in construction in the worst part of Sacramento and I have never been afraid. I agree that it is pretty safe here, but there are a lot of girls with low self-esteem who are afraid to leave the housing unit to go out to the rec area, where the library is. I guess they are afraid in here of what they call "in the mix," the drug culture—all that goes on in the yard so if a girl is trying to be good, trying to stay clean or whatever, trying to do her time, she is afraid to go out there. I think that is a shame to be afraid to go to the library. They look at me and think I am crazy. They ask me if I go out there alone and I say, of course. And I have taken young, twenty-year-old girls with me to the library, who were afraid to go out there and tell them, you will be okay with me, I promise. They afraid of the unknown. They know the mix is going on out there. They are afraid that someone might start a fight out there and they might get involved in this fight and go to 504. I think they want to be good so they stay away from anything (that will get them in trouble). You do see that kind of fear in here.

As suggested above, the mix has various components. Three of these are discussed: the drug mix, the homosexual mix, and the fighting mix.

The drug mix. For many women, the drug mix is the embodiment of trouble. The risks involved in obtaining and using drugs, the expense of drug use in the inflated market of the prison, and the ultimate loss of time due to sanctions attached to this use are the damages that result from drug use in prison. The drug mix is "continuing the behavior that brought you here." The use of drugs and the risk attached to this use are also related to changes in the content of prisoner culture, as this group conversation suggests:

CANDY: When I was at CIW, I was in the mix. I used to deal when I worked in the mailroom. But then it was a whole different breed of convicts. You have convicts and inmates. I dealt for two and a half years and never got caught. I would not do that here. You can't.

TORY: You can't. The minute you get a load in, somebody is out there going, "Hey, I know she got drugs in on her visit."

VALERIE: They come out of visiting and twenty people rush to get to her. That is not too obvious. Or they will come in front of the unit and wait for you, holler down the hall for you. And you know certain police are up on it and they still do it. They don't give a damn. Ms. R—she sees everybody who is loaded and if you slip up one minuscule of an inch, she will get you. This is her house as well as ours. She knows who is loaded and she is going to bust you. She doesn't have to say anything to you. And then we have other cops who don't give a shit. They know. It makes the rest of us get caught up in something that we don't want to get involved in.

The dynamics of the drug mix are described by Randi:

I am an addict. A garbage can addict. So for me, I can't really be around none of it. I don't want it in my face. I ain't well. But I can try my damndest to stay clean. On the 26th of this month, I will be clean a whole year. There was a time that I wouldn't mind going in with the rat race but when they started taking time, uuhuh, I got out. The pressure of being in the mix starts to get to you. Hell, that's what sent me to prison.

When you are in the mix, you are always in debt. You are always strung out, always scared, (worrying) is your money going to get here on time, am I going to get doubled on? You have to rely on friends (from the streets) for money. Once I needed $350 in street money, quick. I told them that I was strung out and I needed it.

I got strung out when I moved from one unit to another. I was more in check in the other unit—it was more relaxed, and then I moved down here, it was, like Oh my god, it was so tense and I got lassoed in and once I got in to it, they had me. It is like preying on old weaknesses. An old homegirl came down and told me, "I got this great shit; just try it for me and tell me how you like it so I can tell everybody how it is." I pushed it off and pushed it off and one day she caught me at an extremely weak moment and I said, "Fuck it, I don't care, give it here." I took it and I did it and it was like, YEAH, HEY NOW. It didn't take much at all to get back in the mix.

Then I was always on a constant hustle, like if I could move three or four bags, I could have two for me. It was a constant hustle to get everyone else to shoot up so I could have mine. And not get in debt. I would hit up all the dope fiends—all the dope fiends. I knew who they were. It feels good to be out of it now.

Tracy argues that some women begin to use drugs while in prison:

> Anybody can get in the mix. You can get new inmates that have come in here and never used heroin on the streets. They hang around the wrong people and they are $300 to $400 in debt before they even know it. And then they start taking it out of your butt. You know what I mean? You don't have the money to pay them off and you can't get your people to send it in to you. Then you get your ass beat and you still have to pay it. Then they will double on you. You get a week before they double on you. You are paying $100 for an $8 piece on the street.

Money to buy drugs comes from a variety of places. Most women report that cash money is rarely used. Instead, the most common approach is that money is placed on the dealers' books by someone from the outside. This is known as "placing money on the wire." Women will also sell their jewelry, clothes, canteen, and the box (quarterly package). One woman appraised a small necklace I was wearing, saying, "You have got $300 right there," noting that if I was in the drug mix, I would "lose my jewelry in a heart beat."

Those involved in the mix generally traffic in merchandise as well as drugs. These women possess an inside orientation and seem to show little regard for returning to the streets, as Cherry observes:

> The ones moving the merchandise around here are the ones who you got into debt in the first place. The rich and famous people around here (laughs). The big ballers are the people who came here doing two or three years and they are stuck with eight, nine, ten, twelve years because they can't stay out of the mix. They don't care enough about themselves to want to go home, to stay out of trouble here, that is what it is.

Some women mentioned the risk of AIDS as deterring their drug use, as Tootie offers:

> I saw that Magic Johnson video at work. After I saw that, I felt sick to my stomach because of what they were saying in the video (about risk factors). I have not been using no protection, using no rubber every time when I was out there. My mama says, I would have known it by now, but I need to know myself. Here, you have people running around, using the same syringes, knowing they have it. You use the same syringe from one yard to another. There are not that many syringes here. A syringe will run you a hundred dollars. Cash money, or a hundred dollars' groceries, or cash to the books.

The drug mix, then, works against the features that create stability in one's life at CCWF. For women wanting to go home, drug use and its accompanying dangers become "not worth it."

The "homosexual mix." Most women, those involved in same-sex relationships and those not participating, agreed that the "homosexual mix" was a place of trouble. While drugs and fighting seem to make up a good proportion of the mix, some women see that having same-sex relationships makes up the "homosexual mix." This woman describes herself as an "assertive lesbian on the streets":

Most of the femmes are confused (about this) in here. They want that touch, that feeling. But girlfriends can get you in trouble. You have to be careful. It took me a long time to learn this. Now this place scares me. It used to be fun, a playground. No more. When I was involved with women, I used to beat them, and talk trash to them. In lesbian life you do it to get affection. I am still hurt about the way I treated them in the past. (I acknowledge that) I did all those things, my crimes, hurting my woman, but it is all over now. I have been evil.

But most of these women are used to being misused by a man. They don't understand anything but being treated bad. I think there is some abuse in the homosexual culture on the streets. Now it is too hard to get sexually involved with someone in here—there is so much switching.

Lexi, a young black woman, details her stabbing by her intimate partner several years ago at NCWF:

I was stabbed by my roommate at NCWF. She was my homosexual partner and she started getting involved with heroin and I didn't use in there so I told her I was moving out. I tried to move out but the regular staff was on vacation—most of the regular staff can tell when there is going to be trouble. They are real observant. They are familiar with the inmates. They watch which ones are troublemakers, which ones are helpful. And they can tell by watching, even if you are not doing anything right then—your conversation, the way you carry yourself, if you respect staff, if you respect inmates. I had been on that unit for a year and a half and I had a good relationship with the staff. I still helped my staff—he never did no favors or nothing, he was nice, but just watched us. When this started to happen, one officer saw me start to withdraw; he noticed it, he picked it up. My roommate wanted me to be with her always. That staff asked me if I was having a problem. I knew he could tell. I wanted to tell him that I really was having a problem, but I didn't want to get a rat jacket. I was planning to move when Mr. S came back from vacation—I was looking for a way out of the situation. He said that if I was still having the problem when he came back from vacation, then we would talk about it.

I told her I wanted to move, but she thought I was playing. I wanted to go home on my date and I didn't want to fight anybody. I was trying to get myself out of that situation. She was selling my stuff to pay for her dope. I had hoped to move that night. They told me I had to wait until tomorrow to move me. We starting fighting about 10 P.M.—I was yelling, "You have used me, you have taken advantage of my kindness," telling her she was a dirty bitch. In a way I loved her because she was a good person.

I think women's relations are intensified—to be a woman and to know what you want in a relationship and your life. Say you have a man, they run all over the place and do this and do that. You be really loving this person. I was real nice to her; it was like a man/woman relationship with me and her. I was nice to her, just the same way I would do my man. I would cook for her, clean the room. She was more of the aggressive type. A lot of women are not actually just gay. They go with girls that look like boys because they are accustomed to being with men, so they be with them.

I went to the room and we were yelling. We were throwing stuff around. I grabbed her and we started fighting. The scissors were in the room, the blade was 8 inches long. They were just there; we had taken them from the PIA laundry—it was not planned. I was beating her and she said, "I am going to stab you, you whore." The officers could hear us fighting but they could not open the door.

I was stabbed all over—she almost pierced my heart. She stabbed me seven times; she bit me. I blacked out. I didn't realize that I was stabbed until I stood up. I had blood all over me and then I stood up to catch my breath and I seen the blood on my gown. See, when you first get stabbed, the wound closes up and they were afraid there was internal bleeding. All I remember is her telling me, "I am going to stab you, ho."

I was angry and I was hurt that she could do this to me. She was telling me that she loved me after the stabbing. We were both taken to Ad Seg. It was my word against hers about who started it. There was no witnesses. I did thirty-one days in Ad Seg. She got one year in the SHU at CIW. The unit officer came to see me when I was in Ad Seg.

When I got out of Ad Seg, I was real scared; she (the perpetrator) had friends on the yard and a sister in law. I could not sleep, I wouldn't talk to nobody; I never knew who could be plotting against me. My roommates knew how hard it was on me. I was dreaming about the stabbing. The lieutenant called me in because my roommate told him that I was jumpy and not sleeping. It was a real emotion trip. I kept dreaming that she was stabbing at me. I didn't talk to nobody for almost two years. I didn't go into detail (and) discuss it with my family or anyone.

We are supposed to be separated, but I eventually ran into her in the clinic. She was talking to me, saying, "Hey, how have you been?" I was just looking at her; she acted like it didn't happen, then she said, "You hate me" and I said no, but I have asked the Lord to forgive us. My friends have given her a hard time. She also called me on the streets, asking me to forgive her. At one time, she was going to be transferred here, but my counselor interviewed me and told me that my C file said we were enemies. I told her I didn't have a problem with her and then she went to Avenal and not here. We were scared of seeing each other. But now I think that it would be okay if she were here. I have never felt that I should get her back. I just have never understood how she could do that to me. I did not testify against her, so there was no DA filing. She is out now, back with her husband and doing good. She has five kids. I didn't want to see anything bad happen to her.

I was really trying to sort out "why." Why did she have to stab me? She could have beat me up, hit me with anything, but why stab me? The seriousness of it started to get to me because she could have killed me. That made me realize that my daughter would have been by herself. That is where the bitterness came in.

The fighting mix and being messy.   A third feature of the mix at CCWF over-laps both the drug mix and the "homosexual mix." Like Sykes's (1958) goril-las, few women take the role of enforcer, collecting drug debts, or "evening the score" for others. But conflict can exist apart from these activities as well. Conflict may be either verbal or physical. The wide majority of conflict is ver-bal: these conflicts are likely to be interpersonal, a disagreement over behav-ior, an interpretation of bad will, or a personality clash. Such conflicts are likely to arise in face-to-face interactions among roommates or workmates. Women in the "fighting mix" often use force or coercion as a way of bullying other prisoners. Related to the styles of doing time discussed earlier, some women feel they have a right to take advantage of a woman if she can't "stand for her own." The typical conflict relationship rarely accelerates into outright fighting and may often be "cooled out" through talking or intercession by a third party, typically a roommate, homegirl, or family member. Sometimes overlapping with the drug and homosexual mixes, the fighting mix may surface in enforcing the standards of a drug deal (collecting debts or retribution for failed promises to deliver) or intimates may engage in verbal conflict, arguing with each other.

Fighting, the physical form of conflict, occurs in several ways: "lovers' quarrels" accelerating beyond the verbal, drug deals or other form of contraband trade gone sour, insults magnified beyond the verbal sparring of everyday life at CCWF, or, most rare, assaults on strangers or acquaintances. Another form of the conflict mix is being "messy," usually interpreted as one who gossips or instigates conflicts among inmates. Also known as "he said, she said," gossiping and rumor-mongering leads to many hurt feelings and open conflicts within the prison population. "Cutting up" is another feature of being messy and involves making derogatory remarks about another woman, both behind her back and to her face. Mindy describes this process:

> They can cut you up so bad, it makes the next person dislike you. Let's say us three are sitting here. I could tell you so much, cutting her up; cutting up means talking bad, talking negative, talking against her to you, that the next time you see her you would not even want to speak to her. Now, you wouldn't have any reason not to speak to her because you don't know her, but if you listen to what the next person told you, you may want to not speak to her, or fight her, or something harmful. When there isn't any call for it. That's how the mix is up in here. You have to watch what kind of crowd you get in. The messy people that like a lot of "he say, she say." That likes to fight, likes to gang-bang—that have nothing better to do. They are institutionalized. There is some that likes to fight.
>
> But there is some that are not messy. They mind their own business and they know there is a time to be a kid, time to act rowdy and a time to act civilized. Some just like to act rowdy and uncivilized, starting a lot of mess. They either love going to Ad Seg or they figure they won't get caught. They will fight you because you got a new pair of tennis shoes and they don't.
>
> Jealousy here starts a lot of fights. Jealousy, gossip, people who don't care start a lot of mess. There is jealousy over jobs, pay slots, getting a box. You see somebody who don't get a box. They feel offended because they don't get one. You can get really nice stuff in your box. They get nice clothes that they never even thought about in the streets because then they were so much into drugs and doing crime that they ain't got time to think about looking halfway decent. And that envies a person. Especially if it is one of their homeys (who think) you are dressing (up) now. You think you are too good for us. But I guess when you put on clothes from the streets, you do feel different. But not that different. Or they will take you for granted. And want to be better than the other one. Just because they can run this person, they want to run you too. And if you don't do what they say, then they want to fight. It is a trip.

CONCLUSION

The majority of women at CCWF serve their sentences, survive the mix, and return to society, resuming their lives in the free community. Many return to circumstances not of their making, such as abuse and economic marginality, which re-create the conditions of their original offense. Others continue making self-destructive choices of drug use and other criminal behavior. While it is beyond the scope of this monograph to assess the impact of imprisonment on the future of women prisoners, many women wanted to comment on the immediacy of the impact of their imprisonment. Some women argued that prison was

> the best thing that ever happened to me. I know I would be dead if I hadn't been sent here. It has made me stop and think about what I was doing to myself and my kids.

Other women interviewed agreed: prison gave them a "time out" from their self-destructive behavior on the streets and provided an incentive not to return to their previous lives. As Blue suggests:

> In prison, I found out who I was. Because on the streets I was trying to be somebody that I wasn't. While I was in prison, I was trying to fit in where I wasn't welcome, but I tried to make an impression, just to fit in the crowd. To be kicking back and laughing. And I found out that that wasn't really even true on the streets. I did try to impress somebody to be with them. If I didn't fit in, I didn't. It was like, in here, when I got here, seeing that I had to be around so many women and my roommates, I used to sit there and think. Then I started going to church. And I found out who I am and what I want to do in life. I know it is not easy, but can't nobody do it but you. You know, you can't change yourself unless you want to change. And I wanted to change.
>
> I probably would have been dead if I had not come to prison. I probably would have ended up dead. I was living too fast and I was too young to be living that fast. I should have been already getting my degree from college, and I should have been getting my life together where I had my own apartment and my own job. And having a little car—not no fancy car or nothing—just something to get around in. But I didn't. I had it—but it wasn't because I had a job. It was because I had dirty money.
>
> Last year when I made my decision that I was ready and I had come to know myself. I have been through a lot. The experiences I have been through, I don't want anyone else to go through because it is not good. I have been stabbed, I have been shot. I got raped when I was in the eighth grade. There are things that you can walk around once you know yourself.
>
> I try to be calm. There are days where I get in arguments, but it does not end up to nothing. Like I tell them, if you want to sit down and talk to me, woman to woman, then we can. But if you want to stand here and argue with me because I learned that from years ago. It is not going to lead nowhere. And the first thing they say is, "Come on, let's fight. Let's go." And I will look at them and say, "No, I want to go home. I don't know what you want to do."

These convictions notwithstanding, it is important to emphasize the damage of imprisonment, as conveyed in these comments by Morgan, a long-termer serving both time for violence and a SHU term for continued violence inside.

> Prison makes you very bitter. It makes you bitter, and you become dehumanized. I've been in prison since I was seventeen, I have been abandoned by my family

members, and anyone else who knew me out there. Being in prison forces you to use everything that you have just to survive. From day to day, whatever, you know it's very difficult. It's difficult to show compassion, or to have it when you haven't been extended it.

Being in prison all this time, I didn't feel like I belonged, I didn't feel adequate enough to deal with the inadequacies I felt were inside. A person looking at me would not have known that.

But I am finally to a point that I am really in tune with myself. I detached myself as far as socializing, and being in crowds and different things that made me very uncomfortable or paranoid. I was aware of it, so I was able to fight it within myself. It's not very easy for people to do that. You get so caught up in a fantasy that it becomes real. You be caught up and put in a situation right again repeating the same thing. You can't break it cause you don't recognize it. And you know the bottom line is that this is no rehabilitation, no one comes here and gets rehabilitated. Society puts so much effort and money and energy into building institutions, and for what? I feel like mothers make the whole universe. And you know rapists, baby-killers, killers, serial killers, all come from somewhere and it starts in a child at a young age—and if you are neglected, if you are abandoned, different emotional trips as a child, and you grow up, then how are you a perpetrator when you were a victim?

I feel that, in society as a whole, women are subject to being made the victim. I was a victim that turned perpetrator but everybody has an instinct of survival for themselves. You understand what I'm sayin'. Because I was a woman in society, I was put in the situation where it was a do or die thing, and I did. And the courts don't understand it, the State of California, there's no self-defense laws, there's no laws that says, hey, you're a woman. Tough luck.

Yeah, I would consider myself just playin' the hand that I was dealt. And in life no one asks for the hand that they're given. Now that I'm older, I can change it or stay with the situation or complain about my present situation, or whatever, but you know I don't choose to do that, I choose to say, hey, okay, yeah, and so now it's time for me to take responsibility, I'm not a seventeen-year-old—you know I say hey, I recognize what has happened and I recognize what I want to happen in the future. It is up to me.

Yeah, it comes from reading, exploring, and whatever. Mainly, just a lot of reading. When they kept me back here (in SHU) for a period of time, for three years and then the two years, they kept me back here (in SHU), you know you have nothing but self. And it's easy for someone to try to take your dignity or whatever, take the things that are inside, to take from you, like they took my clothes, they took my hair products, they took my makeup, they took the things that I like about myself. The physical things that people see. They took those things.

But that's when I had to build on what was inside of me. And still grow and still let a person see that hey, you know I'm still the same person. You can't see the things that you would see if I was afforded my personal things but hey, I'm still alright. And I fought it, man, I fought it—just fighting it within, cause I knew what they were doing to me, I knew what they were trying to do. You know they came and they counseled me with medication, different psychiatric evaluations. And, no, I'm not going to let you do it, because I'm not going to take what I know is in me, and I know that I have a problem, of course, everyone in prison has a problem. But my problem is not more extreme; it's nothing that can not be dealt with at a young age. You can't throw your hands up at me and I'm only twenty-six. And so many people have. You know what I mean, and it just makes you fight even more.

Once a woman organizes her program and life in the prison, some women begin to think about their lives and what brought them to prison. Divine, ending her third term in prison, makes this statement:

See, when you come in here, you deal with exactly who you are. You become who you really are and you deal with feelings that you have not had to deal with in years. All this is coming out. You are gaining your weight back, you are getting pretty again. I was not pretty when I was out there. I think I am pretty now and you feel good about yourself. And then you start remembering all this shit that you did to all these people and it hurts. You become who you are. Right now I am Divine but my real name is Shelly. Out there I was Moms—the dope dealer. They come in here on A Yard and they look at me and they do not know who I really am because on the streets I did not look even remotely like this. I even acted different out there because I was under the influence. Not only of drugs, but of the lifestyle. You come in here and become who you really are.

Randi, listening to this heartfelt statement, echoes her sentiments:

Here you can become you. And you can get what is inside really out. And sometimes that is not really pretty. And for some people that can be very scary. You have to learn to be honest with yourself here. You can't hide behind a bunch of lies like maybe you did on the streets. It is not what you made (dealing). In here it can be about who you are and what you are if you are honest about yourself. It is the hardest thing in here and it is the step that hurts everybody the most. You have to realize what you have done to people and the things you have done wrong.

This study is an initial attempt to describe and understand the prison community as lived by the several thousand women who come to make a life in prison in contemporary society. As argued in the introduction, imprisonment in this state affects a disproportionate number of women of color and those marginalized by circumstances of family background, personal abuse, and destructive individual choice. Women in prison represent a very specific failure of conventional society—and public policy—to recognize the damage done to women through the oppression of patriarchy, economic marginalization, and the wider-reaching effects of such short-sighted and detrimental policies as the war on drugs and the overreliance on incarceration as social control. The story of the women at CCWF, however, is not hopeless. Many women have survived circumstances far more damaging than a prison term and most will continue to survive in the face of insurmountable odds. As Barbara Bloom and I have suggested elsewhere (Owen & Bloom, 1995b), there are in fact solutions to these problems that challenge assumptions about the criminality and disposability of these women. This description of the lives of women in prison then is offered as a starting point for constructive dialogue and public policy concerning the lives and experiences of women on their own terms.

SECTION TWO: INDIVIDUAL ADJUSTMENT FACTORS

DISCUSSION QUESTIONS

1. Did Wright find that Blacks and Whites tend to experience prison differently or similarly?
2. What does the general literature indicate is the relationship between age and aggression in prisons? Do Layton MacKenzie's findings support this relationship?
3. What connection do Hemmens and Marquart find between age and attitudes toward staff. How strong is the connection between race and such attitudes?
4. What role does prior victimization play in affecting a sense of general well being for the inmates in the study by Maitland and Sluder?
5. What does Owen mean when she talks about female inmates being "the mix?" How is "the mix" different for female inmates than male inmates?

SECTION 3

INSTITUTIONAL
ADJUSTMENT FACTORS

Clearly, what you think about your world depends on who you are and where you are when asked, or in the case of these inmates, studied. The immediacy of issues, the adjustment required to the pains of imprisonment, and the sense of fear one feels in prison, as alleviated or distorted by degrees of prisonization, forges opinions, perceptions, and behaviors. Of course, such attitudes and action might be entirely different for a White man versus a Black man, an old woman versus a young woman, a person just released from prison and one housed in maximum security, a man incarcerated in Ohio and one just released from Texas or whether you perceive your environment as ultramasculine or not. In this section's articles the authors explore the perceptions, fears, and subsequent behavior of men incarcerated, or just released from prison.

John Wooldredge, in his article "Explaining Variation in Perceptions of Inmate Crowding," explores inmate perceptions of crowding in three Ohio prisons. He is able to disaggregate from his data the distinguishing preincarceration demographic, background, and institutional characteristics that shape inmate attitudes towards crowding. Perceptions of crowding differ among these inmates, despite the fact that all are in institutions that haven't exceeded their design capacity for incarceration.

Similarly, Craig Hemmens and James W. Marquart, in their article "Fear and Loathing in the Joint: The Impact of Race and Age on Inmate Support for Prison and Policies," find that ones demographics colors the prism through which policies on AIDS in prison are viewed. Their sense is that the inmate subculture, as chronicled by those just exiting it, does not uniformly homogenize. But instead, that subculture is fractured by preincarceration characteristics; in this study it is the race and age of its members that divides.

If demographics and institutional factors influenced attitudes of the inmates and exmates in the Wooldredge, and the Hemmens and Marquart research, they also were an impetus for behavior adjustment in Richard C. McCorkle's article, "Personal Precautions to Violence in Prison." Older, socially isolated inmates and those who expressed more fear in this Tennessee prison, were more likely to avoid circumstances where violence might erupt or to engage in "passive precautions." Interestingly enough, some of the more proactive and "aggressive precautions" by younger inmates, might constitute their own form of adjustment or manifestation of fear to the real and perceived dangers of incarceration in this maximum-security facility.

One form of this adjustment to fear that Robert S. Fong documents in his article "The Organizational Structure of Prison Gangs: A Texas Case Study," is the resort to gangs. He notes that a power vacuum existed in Texas prisons after they were forced to abandon the brutal authoritarian building tender system in the 1980s. As the prisons scrambled to adjust to the destabilizing exit of the corrupt, but predictable, superstructure provided by the building tender system, prison gangs found fertile ground for recruiting inmates fearful of random violence.

Faith E. Lutze and David W. Murphy, in their article "Ultramasculine Prison Environments and Inmates' Adjustment: It's Time to Move Beyond the 'Boys Will Be Boys' Paradigm," note that ultramasculine prison environments can be related to negative adjustment behaviors. What they find in their comparison of perceptions of male inmates incarcerated in both a shock incarceration and a minimum security prison is that the relative perceptions of ultramasculine characteristics of a prison environment and the associated sex-role stereotypes may inhibit treatment initiatives in correctional environments.

CHAPTER 10

Explaining Variation
in Perceptions
of Inmate Crowding

John D. Wooldredge

The impact of population crowding on an individual's mental well-being has important implications for the goals of institutional corrections, making it worthwhile to understand what influences inmate perceptions of crowding. This study examined possible influences on these perceptions for 581 inmates of 3 Ohio facilities that operated at their design capacities at the time of data collection. Both preinstitutional variables (age, race, and whether an inmate was incarcerated for a sex-related offense) and institutional variables (victimization experience, visitation, and a facility's architectural design) were significant predictors of the perception of crowding. The implications of these results are presented.

The potential problems with crowded prisons have been well documented, such as how they contribute to feelings of anxiety and stress among inmates (Bonta & Gendreau, 1990; Ruback & Innes, 1988), how they interfere with the successful treatment of inmates (Champion, 1988; Skovron, Scott, & Cullen, 1988), and an increased difficulty with controlling large inmate populations (Cobb, 1985; Ellis, Grasmick, & Gilman, 1974; Gaes & McGuire, 1985). Understanding the significant contributors to inmate crowding is clearly important from a policy standpoint.

There no longer seems to be consensus regarding the most appropriate method of measuring inmate crowding (Klofas, Stojkovic, & Kalinich, 1992). Objective measures of crowding (e.g., total population, square feet per inmate, ratio of inmates to design capacity) have been criticized because inmates might perceive similar environments quite differently (Bleich, 1989; Paulus, McCain, & Cox, 1985). Conversely, subjective measures (e.g., inmate perceptions of crowding) have been criticized from the standpoint that the policy implications

THE PRISON JOURNAL, Vol. 77 No. 1, March 1997 27–40

of studies incorporating such measures are unclear because the variables of interest are not easily manipulated (Klofas et al., 1992). This seems to be a valid argument, particularly when considering such practical concerns as the loss in economic efficiency when operating a facility that holds a larger population than that for which it was designed. Yet it is possible that inmates who *perceive* a crowded environment may be more likely to undergo greater psychological stress, engage in deviance, and so forth compared to inmates who do not maintain such a view. Therefore, from the standpoint of the effectiveness of treatment, the prevention of violence and victimization inside prison, and the reduction of psychological stress among inmates, it may be more fruitful to understand the factors that influence inmate *perceptions* of crowding. Understanding the influences on inmate perceptions of crowding may provide insight into ways to alter these perceptions. Using a sample of 581 inmates from three Ohio correctional facilities for adult males, the study presented here examined several possible correlates to inmate perceptions of crowding. All three facilities were operating at their design capacities during the time of data collection.

THEORETICAL FRAMEWORK

Relationships between the density of human populations and an individual's psychological well-being have been explored extensively by psychologists (e.g., Cox, Paulus, McCain, & Karlovae, 1982; Dye, 1978; Freedman, 1979; Galle, Gove, & McPherson, 1972; Levy & Herzog, 1974; Manton & Meyers, 1977). Many researchers have supported the idea that higher levels of population crowding (both inside and outside the home) are related to a greater prevalence of psychological stress and anxiety among members of the population (e.g., Booth & Cowell, 1976; Dye, 1978; Gove, Hughes, & Galle, 1979; Levy & Herzog, 1974). This has important implications for the effective control of correctional facility populations. If crowding is related to an inmate's mental well-being, then crowded conditions within a facility pose a security threat because of the closer physical proximity of any one inmate to other inmates combined with the psychological discomfort an inmate feels as a result of more limited personal space.

Objective Versus Subjective Definitions of Inmate Crowding

Many researchers of inmate crowding, including myself, have defined crowding in terms of some objective criterion such as whether a facility's population exceeds its rated or design capacity, the total number of inmates in a facility on a given day, and so forth (see Klofas et al., 1992, for a review of these definitions). The difficulty with such measures is that inmates may perceive similar environments quite differently based on their unique personalities and definitions of personal space (Paulus et al., 1985). Although the policy implications of studies focusing on objective (versus subjective) measures of crowding may be more clear regarding what can be done to reduce the problem (Klofas et al., 1992), studies of the influences on inmate perceptions of crowding can also yield realistic implications for policy if support is found for relationships between these perceptions and the characteristics of institutionalization that can be controlled (e.g., architectural design of a facility, program participation, victimization experiences, etc.). Further, an inmate's perception of crowding may be more important to understand (versus objective measures of crowding) in terms of the possible *consequences* of crowding mentioned earlier. If a situation defined as real is real in its consequences, then it is possible that inmates who perceive their environment to be crowded may be more likely to undergo stress, perceive inequity, and engage in deviance compared to inmates who do not maintain such a perception.

Cox, McCain, and Paulus have conducted the most extensive research to date on inmate reactions to crowding (McCain, Cox, & Paulus, 1980a, 1980b; Paulus, McCain & Cox, 1973, 1981, 1985). These researchers have examined interrelationships between objective definitions of crowding, inmate reactions to their environment, and the mental well-being of inmates. They have studied a variety of institutions with broad variation in total inmate populations, number of inmates per cell, architectural design, and so forth. Their research has been very important for establishing support for the idea that inmates who perceive closer physical proximity to other inmates are more likely to be anxious, fearful, and frustrated compared to inmates who perceive larger amounts of personal space. These findings imply that architectural designs that enhance perceptions of privacy may help to reduce the negative effects of crowding, regardless of the actual square footage of space available.

Although the findings of Cox, McCain, and Paulus indicate that perceptions of crowding vary significantly across institutions with varying designs and capacities, the logic of their research suggests that there could be significant variation in inmate perceptions of crowding even within the same facility. Examining variation in inmate perceptions of crowding *within* a facility provides the opportunity to study the possible influences on these perceptions while holding constant variation in objective definitions of crowding (such as the ratio of inmates to the design capacity of a facility), which may correlate with inmate perceptions of crowding. The importance of such variables as inmate participation in institutional programs (such as education, vocational training, recreation, counseling, and work) as well as inmate experiences during incarceration (frequency of outside visitors, victimization by inmate crime, etc.) for predicting these perceptions could be examined more reliably. Further, if the ratio of inmates to the design capacity of a facility could be controlled *across* institutions that vary in architectural design, then the relationship between a facility's design and perceptions of crowding could also be examined more reliably.

Possible Influences on Inmate Perceptions of Crowding

One of the major themes underlying the literature on inmate adaptation to imprisonment is that the background characteristics of inmates as well as their routines and experiences during incarceration may influence their mental well-being as well as *how they perceive their environment and other inmates.* For this reason, the literature on inmate adaptation to imprisonment is directly relevant to a study of inmate perceptions of crowding.

Researchers of prisonization have supported the idea that several preinstitutional characteristics of inmates as well as their unique experiences and contacts during incarceration influence how inmates adapt to imprisonment (e.g., Akers, Hayner, & Gruninger, 1977; Berk, 1966; Glaser, 1964; Porporino & Zamble, 1984; Thomas, 1977, 1978; Tittle, 1972; Toch, 1977; Wellford, 1967). Various demographic and background characteristics of inmates (i.e., preinstitutional characteristics) as well as particular types of experiences during incarceration may help to lessen the pains of imprisonment. In turn, inmates who are better able to cope with imprisonment tend to maintain less negative views toward their environment.

A few of the demographic and background variables that could be important predictors of an inmate's ability to cope with imprisonment include age, race, education, and the type of offense incarcerated for. Inmates with preinstitutional characteristics that are atypical in a facility's population may have a more difficult time adjusting to incarceration (Thomas, 1977, 1978). Specifically, adaptation to imprisonment may be more difficult for inmates who are older, White, have higher levels of education, and who are incarcerated for sex-related crimes because (a) they are less similar to the mainstream population and may, therefore, possess greater "social distance" between themselves and other inmates, (b) they may be ostracized by other inmates, or (c) some of these characteristics (such as higher levels of education) may actually inhibit an inmate from interacting with other inmates and becoming integrated into an inmate social system. These types of individuals, in turn, may feel the pains of incarceration more intensely and perceive their environment more negatively.

A few of the characteristics of inmate lifestyles and experiences that could be important predictors of inmate adaptation include the number of visitors an inmate receives in a given period, the number of hours an inmate spends each day in "structured" activities (i.e., education, a job, vocational training, counseling, and legitimate recreational activities provided by the facility's administration), whether an inmate has been victimized by other inmates, time spent in segregation, and the physical environment of a facility. Regarding program participation, perceptions of a facility's environment may be less negative among inmates who are more involved in institutional programs because greater involvement (a) helps to pass time more constructively, (b) increases an inmate's freedom of movement within a facility, and (c) insulates an inmate from potentially negative interactions with other inmates. Also, perceptions of a facility's environment may be less negative if inmates have not had recent experience(s) with victimization by other inmates, receive more visitors during a given period, have spent less time in segregation, and are incarcerated in a facility with a podular design that may enhance inmate perceptions of more personal space (as opposed to a linear architectural design with ranges of cells set perpendicular to long corridors).

The ability to control one's environment and know what to expect from day to day is very important to some inmates (Goodstein, MacKenzie, & Shotland, 1984; Toch, 1977). Goodstein et al. (1984) argued that adaptation to imprisonment may be more difficult for inmates with less "personal control" over their environment because these inmates may possess more intense feelings of depression, anxiety, and stress. Pertinent to this study, institutional routines and experiences that enhance an inmate's ability to control his environment and reduce his fear of the unknown may generally correspond with a healthier state of mind and less negative perceptions of a facility's environment. Specifically, inmates who spend more time each day in institutional programs may perceive greater personal control over their environment because these types of activities probably do not vary much in structure and routine from day to day. The ability to predict their experiences from day to day may enhance feelings of security among inmates.

Along similar lines, if victimization by other inmates increases an inmate's fear of the unknown, then inmates who have *not* been victimized may feel more secure compared to inmates who have been victimized. Regarding visitation, the frequency of visits by outsiders might affect the degree to which inmates feel they have the opportunity to make choices. According to Averill (1973) and Steiner (1979), the opportunity to make choices constitutes an important element of personal control. Inmates who receive more visits during a given period may perceive more "freedom" through the regular maintenance of ties to the outside world. All of this suggests that the logic underlying the link between personal control and inmate adaptation could be used to provide another theoretical justification for the hypothesized relationships between inmate perceptions of crowding and program participation, victimization, and visitation.

RESEARCH METHODS

Three Ohio correctional facilities for adult males were targeted for sample selection. They consisted of a high-close facility with a podular design holding roughly 1,150 inmates, a high-close facility with a linear design (i.e., ranges of cells set perpendicular to long corridors) holding 500 inmates, and a medium-security podular facility with approximately 450 inmates. Each facility houses one inmate per cell. All three facilities were operating at their design capacities at the time of the study. The warden of each facility determined the percentage of inmates that would be permitted to participate in the study. These percentages consisted of 33% from the high-close podular facility (all inmates from one of the three campuses), 25% from the high-close linear facility (all inmates from the first tier of each wing), and 50% from the medium-security facility (all inmates in 5 of the 10 living units).

Self-report data were collected for the study given the need to tap inmate perceptions of crowding and my belief that, regarding inmate victimization in a correctional facility, self-report data are more reliable than official data. Inmates targeted for the study were handed surveys when confined to their cells during a count. At the end of the count, all of the inmates sealed the surveys in envelopes (whether completed or not) and placed them in an enclosed box to guarantee their anonymity. Eighty-one percent of the inmates surveyed at the high-close podular facility completed the surveys ($n = 312$), as did 75% from the high-close linear facility ($n = 99$), and 76% from the medium-security facility ($n = 170$). The final sample consisted of 581 inmates, excluding all illiterate inmates and those in psychiatric units (meaning that the results should not be generalized to these groups).

Based on the demographic and sociodemographic variables examined, each subsample was representative of a facility's population. This was determined by comparing the aggregate-level parameters for each population (provided by the administration of each facility) with the aggregate-level statistics for each subsample.

Table 10.1 presents the measures and univariate descriptives for all of the variables in the complete model. Information tapping an inmate's perception of crowding was collected by asking inmates whether they *strongly disagreed, agreed,* or *strongly agreed* with the statement "This place is too crowded." This categorical scale was dichotomized into whether inmates agreed or disagreed with the statement so that logit regression could be used for the statistical analysis.

Table 10.1
Variables and Univariate Descriptives

Variables	Categories	Frequencies
Dependent variable		
Whether or not an inmate perceives his environment to be crowded	0 = no; 1 = yes	217; 364
Preinstitutional variables		
Age	range: 16–61	$M = 28.65; SD = 7.18$
African American	0 = no; 1 = yes	333; 248
Education (before arrival)	0 = < high school degree; 1 = > high school	366; 215
Incarcerated for sex offense	0 = no; 1 = yes	538; 43
Institutional variables		
Number of visits last month by family/friends	range: 0–8	$M = 1.30; SD = 1.83$
Program participation (hours per day in structured activities)	range: 0–16	$M = 8.51; SD = 4.86$
Victimized by crime during past 6 months	0 = no; 1 = yes	421; 160
Days in segregation during past 6 months	range: 0–180	$M = 9.17; SD = 27.06$
High-close linear design	0 = no; 1 = yes	482; 99

NOTE: $N = 581$.

(Ordinary least squares regression could not be used on the ordinal outcome measure because the assumptions of linearity and normal population distributions of the dependent variable around fixed values of the independent variables were violated.) The distribution of responses to the original ordinal measure consisted of 98 inmates strongly disagreeing with the statement, 119 disagreeing, 80 agreeing, and 284 strongly agreeing. The distribution of scores on the dichotomous measure consisted of 93 inmates disagreeing and 219 inmates agreeing in the high-close podular facility, 18 and 81 inmates (disagreeing and agreeing, respectively) in the linear facility, and 106 and 64 inmates disagreeing and agreeing, respectively, in the medium-security facility.

With the exception of program participation and experience with victimization, the measure of each independent variable is fairly straightforward (see Table 10.1). The measure of program participation consisted of the number of hours, on average, an inmate spent per day in each of the following activities: education classes, vocational classes, studying in the library, counseling, working at a job, and active and inactive forms of recreation provided by the institution (aside from watching television and listening to the radio). Inmates indicated how many hours they spent engaged in each of these activities.

Rather than create separate measures reflecting the extent of participation in each activity, the numbers of hours across all activities were summed to more adequately reflect the concept of time spent each day in "structured" activities provided by the facility's administration.

Several survey questions were used to tap victimization experiences during incarceration. Experience with victimization was measured as a dichotomy tapping whether an inmate was victimized by aggravated assault, robbery, and/or theft of personal property at least once during the 6 months immediately preceding the survey. The survey questions pertinent for constructing this variable included the following:

Please indicate how many times each of the following things happened to you since January 1, 1991 (during the past 6 months):

1. Was hit or kicked by an inmate for a reason other than because you tried to hurt him first;
2. Was stabbed by an inmate for a reason other than because you tried to hurt him first;
3. Someone took something that belonged to you when you were not around and without your permission to do so;
4. Someone took something that belonged to you by using force or threatening to use force if you did not give it to him.

It should be noted that very few inmates indicated that they had been victimized by robbery (question 4) during the period in question. Even when considering all of the victimization questions, a ratio measure tapping the degree of victimization could not be examined because of limited variation in such a measure.

Checks for multicollinearity revealed that it was not a problem for the analysis. None of the predictors, individually or as a group, accounted for more than 38% of the variation in any one predictor. This falls below the criterion of 0.49 ($r = .70$) for establishing multicollinearity (Hanushek & Jackson, 1977).

RESULTS

Table 10.2 presents the results from the logit analysis predicting inmate perceptions of crowding. The results indicate that the complete model does fairly well in "explaining" variation in the dependent variable, with six of the nine independent variables being statistically significant at the .05 level (model $\chi^2 = 95.077$, $df = 10$).

Three of the preinstitutional variables and three of the institutional variables are statistically significant in the complete model, suggesting that each group of variables is just as important as the other for predicting inmate perceptions of crowding. Regarding the preinstitutional variables, it appears that inmates who are older, White, and who are incarcerated for a sex-related crime are more likely to perceive that their environment is too crowded compared to inmates who are younger, African American, and who are not incarcerated for a sex-related offense (respectively). Findings for the institutional variables reveal that inmates are more likely to perceive a crowded environment if (a) they

Table 10.2
Results of Logit Model Predicting Inmate Perceptions of Crowding ($N = 581$)

Predictors	Coefficient	Standard Error
Constant	−1.702	.583
Preinstitutional variables		
Age	0.079*	.019
African American	−0.637*	.210
Education (before arrival)	0.405	.228
Incarcerated for sex offense	1.126*	.560
Institutional variables		
Number of visits last month by family/friends	−0.192*	.054
Program participation (hours per day in structured activities)	0.036	.023
Victimized by crime during past 6 months	0.539*	.237
Days in segregation during past 6 months	0.002	.004
High-close linear design	1.390*	.408
Model χ^2	95.077*	

*Significant within a .05 critical region.

received fewer visits during the month prior to the study, (b) have been recently victimized by crime, and (c) reside in the high-close facility with the linear architectural design. The directions of the statistically significant relationships are in the hypothesized directions for both groups of variables.

The nonsignificant predictors of inmate crowding include an inmate's level of education prior to being incarcerated, the number of hours each day an inmate spends in structured activities, and the number of days an inmate has recently spent in segregation. It should be noted that a separate chi-square analysis revealed that education prior to incarceration and an inmate's level of program participation maintain significant zero-order relationships with the dependent variable. Further, both relationships are in the hypothesized directions. Yet controlling statistically for the other exogenous variables in the complete model renders these relationships statistically nonsignificant.

To explore the magnitude of differences in inmate perceptions of crowding for various types of inmates, the logit equation was used to calculate the probability that an inmate would perceive a crowded environment for two specific groups of inmates. The first group consisted of inmates with the following characteristics: aged 36 (one standard deviation above the mean age for the sample), White, incarcerated for a sex-related crime, received no visitors during the month prior to data collection (one standard deviation below the mean number for the sample), was victimized recently by crime, and resided in the high-close linear facility at the time of the study. The second group included inmates aged 21 (one standard deviation below the mean age for the sample), who were African American, incarcerated for an offense other than a sex-related crime, received three visits during the month prior to data collection (one standard deviation above the mean number for the sample), and did not reside in the high-close linear facility. (For both calculations, either median or mean values were used for the nonsignificant independent variables, depending on their levels of measurement.) The probability for the first group was .99, and the probability for the second group was .28. This appears to be a dramatic difference in probabilities, and it provides support for the idea that the complete model is fairly powerful in its ability to predict inmate perceptions of crowding.

DISCUSSION

The results of the study presented here suggest that an understanding of whether inmates perceive their environment to be crowded depends on a number of factors, including the demographic and background characteristics of inmates as well as their institutional experiences during incarceration.

A possible theme underlying the significance of the preinstitutional variables is that inmates with characteristics that are less typical of the inmate population overall are more likely to perceive a crowded environment compared to inmates who share the characteristics of the mainstream population. Researchers of inmate social systems have suggested that inmates who undergo the prisonization process (i.e., socialization into an inmate "subculture") are better able to adapt to imprisonment because their social system provides opportunities to help lessen the pains of imprisonment (Carroll, 1974; Sykes, 1958). However, researchers have also noted that inmates with atypical characteristics may be less likely to become integrated into an inmate group either because they are unable to do so (i.e., they are not accepted as readily by other inmates because of their differences from them), or they are actually better able to avoid and/or resist the prisonization process (Clemmer, 1940). A possible consequence of remaining on the periphery of such a social system is that an inmate is alienated from those he is forced to interact with (or at least come into close proximity to) on a daily basis. Such a situation could result in perceptions of less personal space among these types of inmates and the attitude that the environment is "too crowded" (even when the facility is operating at its original design capacity).

Some inmates who perceive a crowded environment may opt voluntarily into segregation to escape the "problem," suggesting that the time an inmate spends in segregation might correlate with the perception of a crowded environment. However, the number of days an inmate spent in segregation during the 6 months prior to the survey was *not* a significant predictor of this perception. Yet many of the segregated inmates who were surveyed were being punished for committing rule infractions. One would have to examine the perceptions of only those inmates who opt voluntarily into segregation to provide an indirect test of this idea. The small number of these inmates prevented such a test in the present study.

Regarding the institutional variables examined, the finding for whether an inmate had been victimized recently may be consistent with the ideas just presented. Specifically, being victimized by other inmates may increase feelings of vulnerability and alienation on the part of the victim. This, in turn, could result in an inmate adopting a more liberal definition of personal space. It is also possible that the more likely victims of inmate crime are inmates with characteristics that are less similar to institutional offenders. Therefore, the findings for inmate victimization may actually be more consistent with those for the preinstitutional variables (i.e., inmates with atypical characteristics are more likely to perceive their environment as being too crowded).

The finding that inmates who received fewer visits the previous month were more likely to perceive a crowded environment could be a reflection of a relationship between an inmate's mental well-being overall and his attitudes toward the facility's environment. The mean and median number of visits during the previous month was equal to one visit for the entire sample. This means that a substantial number of inmates received no visitors, which is a common scenario for the types of inmate populations examined. For some inmates this could reflect an absence of ties to the outside world. If these types of social ties help some inmates to endure the pains of their incarceration, then the absence of such ties may enhance feelings of deprivation and insecurity during incarceration.

The result for the last statistically significant institutional variable, whether an inmate resided in the high-close facility with the linear arrangement of cells, is consistent with the observation of Paulus et al. (1985) who found that perceptions of crowding were reduced in facilities with architectural designs that create the illusion of more space by reducing the number of inmates in view. This is perhaps the most policy-relevant finding for the study, as it suggests that the more modern podular designs may be preferable to the more traditional linear designs found in many older facilities.

CONCLUSION

Perhaps one of the most interesting findings from the present study is that significant variation in the perception of crowding exists among inmates of facilities that operate at their design capacities. Although policies designed to force administrators to match inmate populations to design capacities are certainly worthwhile from an economic standpoint, such policies may do very little for improving perceptions of a facility's environment for some groups of inmates. The results from the logit analysis provide insight into the possible characteristics of those inmates (e.g., older inmates and sex offenders). The literature on inmate populations discusses the potential problems with mixing special offender groups (such as older inmates and sex offenders, to name just a couple) into mainstream prison populations (e.g., Allen & Simonsen, 1995). The present study provides further support to the argument that these groups of inmates should be treated separately from the mainstream population. Although this may sound politically naive, effective policies designed to reduce the unintended negative consequences of incarceration may have to consider these types of inmate characteristics.

More realistically, there may be some things that administrators can do to improve inmate perceptions of their environment. For example, the findings for the institutional variables suggest that encouraging visitation by family members as well as more effective methods of controlling inmate-on-inmate crime may help in this regard. Also, the trend toward smaller inmate populations housed in podular facilities may already be helping to improve inmate perceptions of crowding (as suggested by the findings for whether inmates were housed in the high-close linear facility or the two podular facilities).

The existence of inmate crowding has important implications for the effective control and treatment of inmates. If situations defined as being real are real in their consequences, then whether inmates *perceive* a crowded environment (despite the actual ratio of inmates to design capacity) has the same types of implications. For this reason, further research on the possible influences on such perceptions would be worthwhile.

REFERENCES

Akers, R., Hayner, N., & Gruninger, W. (1977). Time served, career phase and prisonization. In R. Leger and J. Stratton (Eds.), *The sociology of corrections: A book of readings.* New York, John Wiley.

Allen, H., & Simonsen, C. (1995). *Corrections in America.* New York: Macmillan.

Averill, J. (1973). Personal control over aversive stimuli and its relationship to stress. *Psychology Bulletin, 80,* 286–303.

Berk, B. (1966). Organizational goals and inmate organization. *American Journal of Sociology, 71,* 522–534.

Bleich, J. (1989). The politics of prison crowding. *California Law Review, 77,* 1125–1180.

Booth, A., & Cowell, J. (1976). Crowding and health. *Journal of Health and Social Behavior, 17,* 204–220.

Bonta, J., & Gendreau, P. (1990). Re-examining the cruel and unusual punishment of prison life. *Law and Human Behavior, 14,* 347–372.

Carroll, L. (1974). *Hacks, blacks, and cons.* Prospect Heights, IL: Waveland Press.

Champion, D. (1988). Some recent trends in civil litigation by federal and state prison inmates. *Federal Probation, 51,* 43–47.

Clemmer, D. (1940). *The prison community.* New York: Holt, Rinehart & Winston.

Cobb, A., Jr. (1985). Home truths about prison overcrowding. *The annals of the American Academy of Political and Social Science, 478,* 73–85.

Cox, V., Paulus, P., McCain, G., & Karlovae, M. (1982). The relationship between crowding and health. In A. Baum & J. Singer (Eds.), *Advances in environmental psychology.* Hillsdale, NJ: Lawrence Erlbaum.

Dye, T. (1978). Population density and social pathology. *Urban Affairs Quarterly, 11,* 265–275.

Ellis, D., Grasmick, H., & Gilman, B. (1974). Violence in prisons: A sociological analysis. *American Journal of Sociology, 80,* 16–43.

Freedman, J. (1979). Reconciling apparent differences between the responses of humans and other animals to crowding. *Psychological Review, 86,* 80–85.

Gaes, G., & McGuire, W. (1985). Prison violence: The contribution of crowding versus other determinants of prison assault rates. *Journal of Research in Crime and Delinquency, 22,* 41–65.

Galle, O., Gove, W., & McPherson, J. (1972). Population density and pathology: What are the relationships for man? *Science, 176,* 23–30.

Glaser, D. (1964). *The effectiveness of a prison and parole system.* Indianapolis, IN: Bobbs-Merrill.

Goodstein, L., MacKenzie, D., & Shotland, R. (1984). Personal control and inmate adjustment to prison. *Criminology, 22,* 343–369.

Gove, W., Hughes, M., & Galle, O. (1979). Overcrowding in the home: An empirical investigation of its possible pathological consequences. *American Sociological Review, 44,* 59–80.

Hanushek, E., & Jackson, J. (1977). *Statistical methods for social scientists.* New York: Academic Press.

Klofas, J., Stojkovic, S., & Kalanich, D. (1992). The meaning of correctional crowding: Steps toward an index of severity. *Crime and Delinquency, 38,* 171–188.

Levy, L., & Herzog, A. (1974). Effects of population density and crowding on health and social adaptation in the Netherlands. *Journal of Health and Social Behavior, 15,* 228–240.

Manton, K., & Meyers, G. (1977). The structure of urban mortality: A methodological study of Hanover, Germany, part II. *International Journal of Epidemiology, 6,* 213–223.

McCain, G., Cox, V., & Paulus, P. (1980a). *The effect of prison crowding on inmate behavior.* Washington, DC: National Institute of Justice.

McCain, G., Cox, V., & Paulus, P. (1980b). The relationship between crowding and manifestations of illness in prison settings. In D. Oborne (Ed.), *Research in psychology and medicine* (Vol. II). New York: Academic Press.

Paulus, P., McCain, G., & Cox, V. (1973). A note on the use of prisons as environments for the investigation of crowding. *Bulletin of the Psychonomic Society, 1,* 427–428.

Paulus, P., McCain, G., & Cox, V. (1981). Prison standards: Some pertinent data on crowding. *Federal Probation, 45,* 48–54.

Paulus, P., McCain, G., & Cox, V. (1985). The effects of crowding in prisons and jails. In D. Farrington & J. Gunn (Eds.), *Reactions to crime: The public, police, courts, and prisons.* New York: Wiley.

Porporino, F., & Zamble, E. (1984). Coping with imprisonment. *Canadian Journal of Criminology, 26,* 403–421.

Ruback, R., & Innes, C. (1988). The relevance and irrelevance of psychological research: The example of prison crowding. *American Psychologist, 43,* 683–693.

Skovron, S., Scott, J., & Cullen, F. (1988). Prison crowding: Public attitudes toward strategies of population control. *Journal of Research in Crime and Delinquency, 25,* 150–169.

Steiner, I. (1979). Three kinds of reported choice. In L. Perlmuter & R. Monty (Eds.), *Choice and perceived control.* Hillsdale, NJ: Lawrence Erlbaum.

Sykes, G. (1958). *The society of captives: A study of a maximum security prison.* Princeton, NJ: Princeton University Press.

Thomas, C. (1977). Theoretical perspectives on prisonization: A comparison of the importation and deprivation models. *Journal of Criminal Law and Criminology, 68,* 135–145.

Thomas, C. (1978). Structural and social psychological correlates of prisonization. *Criminology, 16,* 383–393.

Tittle, C. (1972). *Society of subordinates: Inmate organization in a narcotics hospital.* Bloomington: Indiana University Press.

Toch, H. (1977). *Living in prison: The ecology of survival.* New York: Free Press.

Wellford, C. (1967). Factors associated with adoption of the inmate code. *Journal of Criminal Law, Criminology, and Police Science, 58,* 197–203.

CHAPTER 11

FEAR AND LOATHING IN THE JOINT: THE IMPACT OF RACE AND AGE ON INMATE SUPPORT FOR PRISON AIDS POLICIES

Craig Hemmens and James W. Marquart

The get tough on crime movement and the war on drugs have resulted in a changing inmate demographic in this country. More people are being incarcerated for longer periods of time. Many inmates are members of groups at high risk for AIDS, such as minorities, the young, and drug users. This article examines the current correctional AIDS policies of mandatory testing, segregation, and notification. In particular, the authors focus on inmate attitudes toward these policies and the impact of race/ethnicity and age on fear of AIDS in prison and support for AIDS policies.

The popular media frequently portray maximum-security prisons as dangerous, even deadly places (Earley, 1992). Judging from media accounts alone, death comes to most inmates in the form of a shank or the executioner's needle. The reality of death in prison is not in accordance with this picture, however. Far more inmates die each year from disease than violence, and the leading cause of death in many state prisons is AIDS. *In fact, AIDS is the second leading cause of deaths in prison nationwide, behind only the catch-all* category of "natural causes" (Gilliard & Beck, 1996). In 1994, 995 inmates died of AIDS-related causes in state and federal prisons. AIDS is far more prevalent in prisons than in the free world. Currently, the per capita rate of AIDS in the United States is 27 per 100,000 persons, compared to a rate of 485 per 100,000 in prisons (Cotten-Oldenburg, Martin, Jordan, Sadowski, & Kupper, 1997). Between 1991 and 1993, 1 of 3 inmate deaths was attributable to AIDS, compared to just 1 of 10 deaths in the general population (Gilliard & Beck, 1996). Although the

An earlier version of this article was originally presented at the 1997 meeting of the American Society of Criminology, San Diego, CA.

THE PRISON JOURNAL, Vol. 78 No. 2, June 1998 133–151
© 1998 Sage Publications, Inc.

available evidence suggests that HIV transmittal in prison is rare (Chang, 1991; Hammett & Daugherty, 1991), the number of AIDS-related deaths in prison is likely to continue to increase as prison populations increasingly comprise members of groups at risk for HIV infection, such as minorities, the young, and drug users (Robles et al., 1993).

Corrections administrators have responded to the prison AIDS crisis by implementing policies intended to reduce the spread of AIDS and protect infected and healthy inmates as well as staff. These policies include mandatory AIDS testing for all inmates, segregating AIDS-infected inmates, and providing information on HIV-positive inmates to staff and other inmates. Although the Supreme Court has not spoken definitively on the constitutionality of corrections AIDS policies, lower courts have generally upheld most policies under the "deliberate indifference" standard (*Anderson v. Romero*, 1995; *Harris v. Thigpen*, 1991).

There has been a substantial amount of research on public attitudes toward individuals with AIDS (Samuels, Vlahove, Anthony, & Chaisson, 1992), as well as research on the attitudes of correctional personnel regarding AIDS policies (Marquart, Brewer, & McIntyre, in press). To date, little attention has been paid to the attitudes of those living in prison, however. This research seeks to fill this gap in the literature through an examination of the attitudes of a sample of 775 recently released Texas inmates. In particular, we focus on the relationship between race/ethnicity and age and support for common correctional AIDS policies.

THE NEW INMATE DEMOGRAPHIC AND AIDS

The war on drugs has changed the composition of the correctional population in this country. More people are being incarcerated than at any time in American history (Zimring & Hawkins, 1995). Almost 1.6 million people were incarcerated in 1995 (Gilliard & Beck, 1996). Most inmates are young, poor, minority males with a history of drug and/or alcohol abuse (Zimring & Hawkins, 1995). Although the number of individuals infected with the AIDS virus appears to be slowing in the general population (Marquart, Merianos, Cuvelier, & Carroll, 1996), it appears otherwise in the prison population, which is increasingly dominated by members of groups at high risk for HIV contraction. Significant risk factors for imprisonment, such as race, intravenous drug use, and poverty, are also related to increased risk of exposure to communicable diseases such as HIV (Burris, 1992).

Minority Offenders

It is well documented that the health conditions of minorities are worse than those of their White counterparts. Blacks have a higher incidence of diabetes, hypertension, cardiovascular disease, cancer, and sexually transmitted diseases. Hispanics also have higher rates of heart disease, cancer, and cirrhosis (Feinstein, 1993). Both Blacks and Hispanics underuse preventive health care (Marquart et al., 1996). A disproportionate number of incarcerated offenders are minority group members, and the majority of these offenders are either Black or Hispanic (Gilliard & Beck, 1996). As Blacks and Hispanics are overrepresented in correctional populations, the higher incidence of health problems among these groups naturally translates into increased health problems among correctional populations.

Minority group members are also disproportionately represented in the numbers of people infected with the HIV/AIDS virus. For young men (ages 25 to 44), AIDS is the second leading cause of death. Although Blacks and Hispanics constitute just 20% of the general population, they account for 45% of all AIDS cases (Burris, 1992). Blacks and Hispanics also represent a disproportionate number of AIDS cases attributable to injection drug use; 38% of Blacks and 40% of Hispanics contracted HIV through injection drug use, compared to only 8% of Whites infected with HIV due to injection drug use (Burris, 1992).

Drug Offenders

Much of the increase in the inmate population is attributable to the increased incarceration of drug offenders. The proportion of offenders incarcerated for drug-related offenses has increased from 29% to 61% since 1991 (Nadel, 1996). The number of drug offenders in prison is growing at a faster rate than any other category of offender (Harlow, 1993). Many of these drug offenders are also drug abusers; the result is that a large number of offenders entering prison have a history of drug abuse. In 1991, 62% of all inmates regularly used drugs prior to incarceration (Harlow, 1993).

Drug abusers, particularly those engaged in heroin and cocaine use, are more likely to be involved in a number of behaviors that increase their likelihood of contracting communicable diseases such as AIDS. These behaviors include needle sharing, sex with multiple partners, and unprotected sex (Robles et al., 1993). Consequently, the number of HIV-positive offenders is increasing. In 1993, injection drug users accounted for 70% of all AIDS cases in the general population (Frink, 1997). Injection drug-using subjects in one study were four times more likely to be HIV positive if they had shared needles in the previous year than if they had not shared needles (Chitwood, 1995).

Harlow (1993) found that less than 1% of inmates who had never used drugs were HIV positive, whereas 2.5% of those who had used drugs were HIV positive, 4.9% of those inmates who had injected drugs were HIV positive, and 7.1% of those inmates who had shared needles were HIV positive. Another study found that intravenous drug-using inmates were eight times more likely to be HIV positive than inmates who were not intravenous drug users (Vlahove, 1991).

More inmates with AIDS means more problems for correctional administrators, who must deal with these inmates often on a long-term basis, as many are receiving long sentences under mandatory sentencing structures or three strikes laws (Zimring & Hawkins, 1995). Issues include diagnosing and treating infected inmates and minimizing the risk of transmittal of the disease to other inmates or staff (Haas, 1993). Furthermore, it should be noted that costs for inmate health care rose 16% to more than $2.3 billion annually in 1994 (Wees, 1996). Clearly, then, the health of the inmate population is a concern on many levels for corrections administrators.

AIDS POLICIES AND CONSTITUTIONAL REQUIREMENTS

Although the Eighth Amendment has been interpreted by the Supreme Court to prohibit actions by correctional personnel that manifest deliberate indifference to the needs of inmates, this standard is not always easy to apply to particular issues, including inmates with AIDS (Belbot & del Carmen, 1991). In

Estelle v. Gamble (1976), the U.S. Supreme Court for the first time held that the Eighth Amendment prohibition against cruel and unusual punishment applies not only to actions that are expressly a part of the sentence (such as the method of execution) but also to deprivations experienced by inmates as a consequence of incarceration (Gutterman, 1995). The Court determined that deliberate indifference to serious medical needs constituted "unnecessary and wanton infliction of pain," in violation of the Eighth Amendment. In two subsequent cases, *Wilson v. Seiter* (1991) and *Farmer v. Brennan* (1994), the Court further delineated the deliberate indifference standard, holding that liability attaches only when there is proof that corrections officials "knowingly" disregard an "excessive risk" to the health and safety of an inmate. This is a difficult burden for most inmate plaintiffs to meet (Call, 1995; Haas, 1993).

There are essentially two ways in which a corrections department may violate the deliberate indifference standard. First, corrections officials are liable if they ignore the requests of a physician to give specific medical treatment to an inmate (Davis, 1992). According to the language of *Estelle v. Gamble* (1976), officials would have to "intentionally interfere with the treatment once prescribed." Second, corrections officials are liable if they fail to provide medical treatment that is up to the minimal standards of care established by the medical community (Belbot & del Carmen, 1991; Call, 1995). This, then, is the legal standard by which correctional polices regarding AIDS are measured.

AIDS Policies

In response to the growing numbers of inmates with AIDS and the legal requirement not to manifest deliberate indifference to the needs (medical and otherwise) of inmates, correctional administrators have instituted a variety of policies regarding AIDS. These policies include mandatory AIDS testing, segregation of AIDS-infected inmates, and notification of infected inmates for staff and/or inmates (Gutterman, 1995; Haas, 1993). Virtually all of these policies have been challenged by inmates, but in most instances, courts have upheld policies so long as a rational relationship has been demonstrated between the policy and the legitimate penological goals of safety, security, and treatment (Friedman, 1992; Gutterman, 1995). In *Harris v. Thigpen* (1991), the Eleventh Circuit Court of Appeals wrote that "it is inescapable that corrections' systems should attempt to: (1) prevent high risk behavior among inmates, (2) make reasonable efforts to protect all inmates from victimization, and (3) avoid any practices which could lead to unprotected blood exposure" (p. 1499). This, then, is what corrections departments must do—how have they gone about doing it?

Testing. Mandatory AIDS testing of all inmates is one approach that some corrections departments have taken to combat the spread of AIDS in prison. As of 1994, 16 state correctional systems have mandated AIDS testing for all inmates, and 11 other states have mandated testing for those inmates classified as members of high-risk groups (Braithwaite, Hammett, & Mayberry, 1996). For example, Texas tests only high-risk inmates who have previously tested positive or those inmates involved in incidents where there is "blood spillage."

According to a recent survey of state inmates, almost 59% of all inmates in state prisons have been tested for HIV at some point. Slightly more than 32% have never been tested, and 9% were unaware whether they had been tested.

Of those who had been tested, 2.2% admitted to being HIV positive (Beck, 1993). The percentage of those testing positive varied considerably by race, however. Only 1% of White inmates tested positive, compared with 2.5% of Black and 3.5% of Hispanic inmates. In addition, the survey revealed that among all inmates, those who had used drugs prior to incarceration were 1½ times more likely to test positive for HIV (Beck, 1993). This confirms what public health researchers on the outside have been saying for a while: Race/ethnicity and drug use, particularly intravenous drug use, are correlated with a greater likelihood of contracting HIV (Robles et al., 1993).

Inmates have filed suits both requesting and challenging mandatory AIDS testing (Belbot & del Carmen, 1991; Haas, 1993). Although a number of lower courts have recognized that exposing inmates to communicable diseases may violate the Eighth Amendment, courts have generally upheld correctional department policies that do not mandate AIDS testing (Frink, 1997). For a court to find a lack of mandatory testing violative of the Constitution, an inmate must establish that the absence of testing creates a pervasive or "excessive" risk of harm and that prison officials were aware of and were deliberately indifferent to that risk (*Anderson v. Romero*, 1995). Thus, a corrections department can support a decision not to institute mandatory AIDS testing by pointing out that institutional rules prohibiting activity by which the disease is transmitted are in place and, if followed and/or enforced, eliminate most risk. In other words, if a corrections department prohibits sexual activity and drug use, the two most common forms of HIV transmittal, then the corrections department can successfully argue that it is not being deliberately indifferent to the risk of AIDS infection in inmates.

Not only have courts refused to mandate AIDS testing, but they have upheld AIDS testing where corrections officials are able to establish a relation between such tests and some legitimate penal interest, such as safety of staff and inmates or protection of the health of inmates (Belbot & del Carmen, 1991; Frink, 1997). Lower courts have accepted the argument that the institution's legitimate interest in treating and preventing AIDS transmission outweighs the inmate's privacy interest affected by mandatory testing, so long as there is a logical connection between the policy (mandatory testing) and the goal (preventing the spread of AIDS).

Separate Facilities. Segregation of HIV-infected inmates and/or inmates with full-blown AIDS is a frequently debated policy. Advocates of segregation point out that high-risk behaviors such as needle sharing, tattooing, and unprotected sex do occur in prisons (Blumberg, 1997). Given that high-risk activity does take place, one way to protect uninfected inmates is to remove infected inmates from their presence.

Several corrections departments have created separate institutions for AIDS inmates; others have segregated AIDS inmates into specified areas within an institution. This has been done for several reasons: (a) to reduce the possibility of transmission of the virus, (b) to protect other inmates from those infected with AIDS, (c) to protect those infected with AIDS from other inmates, and (d) make health care delivery more efficient and effective (Chang, 1991). Potential consequences of segregating AIDS inmates are the damage to them that may occur, including physical isolation (Gutterman, 1995) and a lengthier period of incarceration because of a lack of opportunity to earn credits through vocational training or education (Chang, 1991).

HIV-positive inmates have challenged the constitutionality of segregation policies on two grounds (Haas, 1993). First, they have argued that segregation is unconstitutional because it implicitly reveals their HIV-positive status and thereby deprives them of a privacy right. This claim generally fails, as courts look askance at privacy claims of inmates, and segregation is easily explained as rationally related to the legitimate correctional objective of maintaining security (Haas, 1993).

Second, AIDS-infected inmates have argued that failure to segregate them is unconstitutional because it increases the risk of harm to them by other inmates who may prey on them or attack them out of fear of AIDS. These claims have also proven largely unsuccessful, as courts have noted that prison rules and polices prohibit such attacks, and so long as corrections officials are not deliberately indifferent to the possibility of such attacks, mainstreaming does not pose an excessive risk (Haas, 1993).

Conversely, inmates not infected with AIDS have argued that leaving an HIV-infected inmate in the general population constitutes cruel and unusual punishment. This claim has been turned aside by lower courts on the ground that mainstreaming does not rise to the level of deliberate indifference (Frink, 1997). Interestingly, an overwhelming majority of states now mainstream inmates with asymptomatic HIV infection. Between 1985 and 1994, the number of prison systems that segregated HIV-positive inmates declined from 8 to 2; the number of prison systems that segregated inmates with AIDS declined from 38 to 4 (Braithwaite et al., 1996). Whether this is done for security or financial reasons, it is clearly the policy of choice in today's prisons.

Notification. Although the Constitution nowhere specifically mentions a right of privacy, one has been inferred from the right to be free of unlawful searches and seizures as well as other limitations of the ability of the government to intrude on the private lives of its citizens (Domino, 1994). Historically, inmates have been accorded few privacy rights (Hemmens, 1997; Palmer, 1997). Regarding AIDS-infected inmates, the issue that arises is whether an inmate with AIDS has the right to limit disclosure of his or her status or, conversely, whether an inmate without AIDS has the right to know which other inmates have AIDS.

Although several lower courts have found a constitutionally protected privacy right of inmates to prohibit disclosure of their HIV-positive status to other inmates and/or staff (Frink, 1997), other courts have allowed corrections departments to obviate this privacy right upon demonstration of a legitimate penological interest, such as maintenance of institutional security or promotion of staff and inmate safety. Courts have held that disclosure of AIDS test results must be limited to prevent "unjustified dissemination of confidential medical information" (Olivero & Roberts, 1989). However, such test results may be made available when there is a need to know, such as when there is blood contact (Belbot & del Carmen, 1991).

Presently, the legal standard by which correctional AIDS policies are judged is deliberate indifference. According to the courts, testing, segregation, and notification are, in most instances, permissible. In addition, there is general support for these polices among correctional officers (Marquart et al., in press). The obvious question at this point, then, is how do inmates feel about these AIDS policies? In this article, we examine inmate attitudes toward these policies.

METHODS

The data for this article were obtained from a survey administered over a 6-week period to 775 men just released from incarceration in the Texas Department of Corrections–Institutional Division (TDC–ID). These former inmates, or "exmates," were interviewed at the bus station in downtown Huntsville. Although there are more than 100 prisons in TDC–ID, virtually all inmates are processed and released through one institution. Inmates are released through the front entrance of the Walls Unit, located in downtown Huntsville. They are provided with their personal belongings, a small amount of cash (in the form of a check from the state), and a voucher for a bus ticket to their destination. State law requires that persons released from prison must return to the place where they were convicted and sentenced; this requirement ensures that virtually all releasees will in fact go to the bus station on their release.

As the former inmates approached the bus station to purchase their tickets, the interviewers approached and asked them to participate in the survey. No material inducements were offered, and confidentiality was ensured. Some exmates agreed to submit to the interview at this time, others agreed to be interviewed after obtaining their bus ticket, and still others agreed to be interviewed after first going to a nearby store or restaurant. Some exmates initially refused to cooperate but later changed their mind and were interviewed while they waited for the bus to arrive. Some exmates refused to be interviewed or were not approached by the interviewers. Reasons given for refusing to participate included general disinterest in the project ("What do I care about some survey?"), suspicion of the interviewer's motives ("How do I know you don't work for the state?"), and a lack of time ("I just got out of TDC and I want to have some fun, not sit around and answer some dumb survey."). Interviewers did not approach every exmate because there were times when there were too many exmates and not enough interviewers. The selection of whom to interview was random in that interviewers simply attempted to contact as many exmates as possible, given the limited number of interviewers and the large number of exmates.

A total of 775 surveys were completed. None of the 775 completed surveys were unusable, although exmates did occasionally choose not to answer a particular question. Some exmates did, of course, elect not to participate. Still others were not contacted by the interviewers due to a lack of time and/or interviewers. According to TDC–ID data, some 1,900 inmates were released during this 6-week time period, and 775 inmates were in fact interviewed. This represents a response rate of 41%. This is an acceptable level, but the question remains whether those who did not respond are systematically different from the whole population. If so, then selection bias exists, and this would limit the generalizability and accuracy of the survey results (Maxfield & Babbie, 1995).

Interviewers noted no apparent similarity among those who refused to participate—no one racial or ethnic group or age category seemed more likely to refuse to participate. It was not possible to determine if certain groups of exmates with similar but unobservable characteristics refused to participate. However, a comparison of demographic variables of the respondents with all TDC–ID inmates reveals no appreciable difference between respondents and nonrespondents.[1] This comparison suggests that nonresponse bias is not a significant factor in this research project. Nevertheless, it must be acknowledged that there is the possibility that the inclusion of the attitudes and perceptions of the nonrespondents may have altered the findings to some degree.[2]

FINDINGS

It may be, as the adage goes, that reality is the only thing that counts, but it is also true that if a situation is perceived as real, it is real in its consequences (Lampe, 1984, citing Thomas & Thomas, 1928). In this section, we examine inmate perceptions of their risk of contracting AIDS in prison and their level of support for common correctional AIDS policies such as mandatory testing, segregation, and publicizing AIDS status to other inmates and staff. A question public health scholars have begun to study and that needs the attention of criminal justice scholars is, How well do inmates understand AIDS? The items that form the basis for this article are listed in Table 11.1.

Respondents as a Whole

Respondents were asked to indicate their level of support for the correctional AIDS policies of mandatory testing, segregation of infected inmates, and allowing other inmates to know who is infected with the AIDS virus. Respondents were also asked their opinion concerning the likelihood of contracting AIDS while in prison. Possible answers ranged from 1 = *strongly agree* to 4 = *strongly disagree.*

Examined as a whole, the exmates evince overwhelming support for correctional AIDS policies. More than 95% of all respondents believe that all inmates should be tested for AIDS. Support for separating HIV-positive inmates from other inmates was almost as high, with more than 88% of the respondents indicating agreement with such a policy. Almost 80% of the exmates agree that inmates have a right to know who has AIDS. It is worth noting that although support for notification is strong, the level of support is somewhat less than it is for either segregation or testing. A possible explanation for this is that inmates recognize the potential risk to an inmate associated with publicizing his condition.

Table 11.1
AIDS Perception Variables

Survey Item
The chances of getting the AIDS virus in the Texas Department of Corrections (TDC) are very low.[a]
All inmates should be tested for the AIDS virus.
All AIDS-infected inmates should be separate from the general population.
Inmates have the right to know which other inmates in the TDC have AIDS.

NOTE: Responses range from 1 = *strongly agree,* 2 = *agree,* 3 = *disagree,*
4 = *strongly disagree.*
[a]Reverse scored for data analysis.

Respondents were also asked whether they thought it likely that inmates could contract the AIDS virus while in prison. This question was intended to determine whether the exmates, who overwhelmingly support policies such as testing, segregation, and notification, do so out of a concern of contracting AIDS while incarcerated. Slightly less than half of the respondents, approximately 48%, believe that the chances of contracting AIDS in prison are very low. A little more than half of the respondents, approximately 52%, disagree that the chances of contracting AIDS are very low. These responses indicate that a majority of respondents perceive at least some risk of AIDS in prison.

Exactly how high is unclear, as the question asked exmates whether they agreed that the chances of contracting AIDS were very low. Disagreement with such a statement suggests there is at least some perception of risk, but it is unclear what the exact degree of risk is perceived by the exmates.

Relationship between Demographic Characteristics and Support for Policies

Examination of responses in the aggregate does not paint a complete picture, however. Analysis of responses by selected demographic characteristics, such as race/ethnicity and age, reveals that the apparent overwhelming support for AIDS policies suggested by the responses in the aggregate masks some significant variation within the exmate population.

Correctional populations in the United States as well as Texas disproportionately comprise minorities, the young, the single, and the undereducated (Pollock, 1997). Not surprisingly, the same holds true for the exmate sample. Minorities comprise almost two thirds of survey respondents. Forty-seven percent of respondents are Black, and 18% are Hispanic. Only 34% of respondents are White. Thirty-eight percent of the exmates are younger than age 30, 42% are between the ages of 30 and 39, and only 20% are age 40 or older. Less than 23% of exmates are married; the remainder are either single, divorced, or separated. More than half of the exmates lack so much as a high school diploma. Twenty-nine percent have a high school diploma or GED; 15% have at least some college or technical school education.

The typical exmate, then, is young, minority, single, and relatively undereducated. Although respondents as a whole appear to possess similar attitudes about prison AIDS policies, it remains to be seen whether race/ethnicity or age is related to perceptions of AIDS and support for AIDS policies.

Race/Ethnicity and AIDS in Prison

Respondents were asked the likelihood of contracting AIDS while in prison. For this item, a lower score means the respondent believes the chance of contracting AIDS in prison is more likely; a higher score means the respondent believes the chance of contracting AIDS in prison is less likely. The mean score for all respondents was 2.63. The mean score of each of the three dominant racial/ethnic groups varied considerably, however. Whites had a mean score of 2.50, Blacks 2.72, and Hispanics 2.62 (see Table 11.2).

The difference in mean scores indicates that White exmates perceive a greater likelihood of contracting AIDS relative to Black or Hispanic exmates, and Blacks clearly perceive the chances of contracting AIDS as less likely than

Table 11.2
Likelihood of Contracting AIDS in Prison, by Race

Group	Number of Cases	Mean Score
All exmates	711	2.63
White exmates	245	2.50
Black exmates	340	2.72
Hispanic exmates	126	2.61

Table 11.3
Mean Scores by Race/Ethnic Group on Support for Prison AIDS Policies

Age Group	AIDS Test	Segregate AIDS	Notice of AIDS
All exmates	1.73	1.76	1.98
White exmates	1.68	1.68	1.93
Black exmates	1.73	1.81	2.02
Hispanic exmates	1.77	1.75	1.93

either Whites or Hispanics. Furthermore, the difference between White and Black exmates is statistically significant at the .01 level.

The differential perception of the risk of contracting AIDS in prison carries over to exmates' perceptions of AIDS policies. Black exmates are generally less supportive of AIDS policies than Hispanic or White exmates (see Table 11.3).

Testing. When respondents were asked their level of agreement with mandatory AIDS testing, the mean score for all respondents was 1.73 on a scale from 1 = *strongly agree* to 4 = *strongly disagree*. This indicates, as stated before, that exmates as a whole strongly support AIDS testing. When responses are broken down by race/ethnicity, however, some variation emerges. White exmates had a mean score of 1.68, Black exmates 1.73, and Hispanic exmates 1.77. White exmates, then, are more supportive as a group of mandatory AIDS testing than either Black or Hispanic exmates. In addition, the difference in the mean scores of White and Black exmates is statistically significant at the .05 level. This is not surprising, given that White exmates also perceive the likelihood of contracting AIDS as higher than either Blacks or Hispanics and thus are more likely to support policies that identify inmates infected with AIDS, thereby allowing staff and other inmates to take precautions in dealing with these inmates.

Segregation. Exmates as a whole evince strong support for separating AIDS-infected inmates from the general population. The mean score for all respondents was 1.76. Scores again varied between racial/ethnic groups, however. White exmates had a mean score of 1.68, Black exmates had a mean score of

1.81, and Hispanic exmates had a mean score of 1.75. The difference between the mean scores of White and Black exmates is statistically significant at the .05 level. Again, White exmates as a group are the most supportive of the AIDS segregation policy, whereas Black exmates are the least supportive and Hispanic exmates fall between the two groups.

Notification. When asked whether inmates had the right to know which inmates had AIDS, respondents as a whole generally agreed with such a policy. The mean score for all exmates was 1.98. Broken down by race/ethnicity, however, the White and Hispanic exmate groups each had a mean score of 1.93, whereas the Black exmate group had a mean score of 2.0. Although Black exmates are somewhat less supportive of notification than White or Hispanic exmates, the difference is small and not statistically significant. This is not too surprising, given that notification was the policy with the least support among respondents as a whole.

These data indicate that there are some differences between racial and ethnic groups regarding AIDS policies, as well as the likelihood of contracting AIDS. White and Black exmates in particular have divergent attitudes and perceptions. This information in some respects mirrors what public health researchers have discovered regarding knowledge of AIDS and fear of AIDS among the general population. Minority groups are at much higher risk of contracting AIDS, and some of the blame for this has been laid because of lack of awareness among minority groups concerning how AIDS is contracted. Despite being at higher risk, minority groups engage in more high-risk behaviors, take fewer precautionary measures, and know less about the disease than Whites.

Age and AIDS in Prison

We next examined the responses to the AIDS policy questions on the basis of age. Respondents were divided into four age categories: exmates younger than age 30, those between ages 30 and 39, those between ages 40 and 49, and those age 50 or older. Not surprisingly, the majority of exmates are young. Almost 38% are younger than age 30; less than 5% are age 50 or older. The exmates ranged in age from 17 to 71 (see Table 11.4).

Significant differences between older and younger exmates exist regarding the chance of contracting AIDS in prison and the appropriateness of AIDS

Table 11.4
Exmate Age Categories

Age Group	Number of Exmates	% of Exmates
17–29	293	38
30–39	326	42
40–49	119	15.3
50–71	36	4.7

policies. As Table 11.5 indicates, the perceived likelihood of contracting AIDS in prison increases steadily, in a linear fashion, with age—the older the exmate, the greater the perception that it is possible to contract AIDS in prison. The mean for all respondents was 1.87, on a scale from 1 = *more likely* to 4 = *less likely*. The mean scores for the four age groups ranged from 2.23 to 2.74.

The differences in the mean scores of Group 1 (17–29) and Group 4 (50–71), as well as Group 3 (40–49), are statistically significant at the .05 level. The difference in the mean scores of Group 2 (30–39) and Groups 3 and 4 are also significant at the .01 level. This tells us that the younger inmates are less concerned that they will contract AIDS in prison. It is alarming to note that it is the young who are at a higher risk of contracting HIV, as they are more likely to engage in aggressive and violent behavior (McCorkle, 1993), yet they are less concerned.

When responses to AIDS policy questions are broken down by age, some interesting patterns emerge. Table 11.6 compiles the mean scores for the groups for each of the three questions regarding AIDS policies: mandatory testing of all inmates, segregation of AIDS-infected inmates, and notice to all inmates of which inmates are HIV positive. The scores are on a scale ranging from 1 = *strongly agree* to 4 = *strongly disagree*.

Testing. When respondents were asked their level of agreement with mandatory AIDS testing, the mean score for all respondents was 1.73 on a scale from 1 = *strongly agree* to 4 = *strongly disagree*. There is significant variation in the mean score of the age groups, however. The youngest exmate group had a mean score

Table 11.5
Likelihood of Contracting AIDS in Prison, by Age

Age Group	Number of Cases	Mean Score
17–29	280	2.74
30–39	304	2.65
40–49	109	2.42
50–71	35	2.23

Table 11.6
Mean Scores by Age Group on Support for Prison AIDS Policies

Age Group	AIDS Test	Segregate AIDS	Notice of AIDS
All exmates	1.73	1.76	1.98
Group 1: 17–29	1.65	1.65	1.85
Group 2: 30–39	1.76	1.81	2.04
Group 3: 40–49	1.85	1.85	2.04
Group 4: 50–71	1.75	1.83	2.17

of 1.65, whereas the 40 to 49 age group had a mean score of 1.85. This suggests that the youngest exmates are more supportive of mandatory AIDS testing than other exmates. Interestingly, support for testing does not decrease steadily with age. The oldest exmates are less supportive of AIDS testing than the youngest exmates but are more supportive than the 40 to 49 age group, which had the highest group mean, 1.85. The difference in the mean score between Group 1 and Groups 2, 3, and 4 are statistically significant at the .05 level.

Segregation. Exmates as a whole possess strong support for separating AIDS-infected inmates from the general population. The mean score for all respondents was 1.76. Scores again varied between age groups, however. The youngest age group was the most supportive of segregation of AIDS-infected inmates, with a mean score of 1.65. The other three age groups had higher mean scores, all above 1.80. The difference in mean scores between Group 1 and the other three groups was statistically significant at the .05 level.

Notification. When asked whether inmates had the right to know which other inmates had AIDS, respondents as a whole generally supported such a policy. The mean score for all exmates was 1.98. Broken down by age, however, the level of support for this policy varies. Again, the youngest exmates evince the most support for notification, with a mean score of 1.85, but the other three age groups all had mean scores above 2.0.

These data indicate that there are some differences between the age groups regarding AIDS and AIDS policies. These differences are particularly pronounced between the youngest exmate age group relative to the other three exmate age groups. The younger exmates are considerably more supportive of AIDS policies than older exmates. This is especially interesting, given that the younger exmates are also the least concerned with contracting HIV while in prison.

CONCLUSION

This research has provided additional support for the hypothesis that inmates are not of a piece. Whatever the "pains of imprisonment" may be today, and whatever their impact, it is clear that not all inmates are alike. Inmates bring a lifetime of experience with them to prison, and this life experience has an impact on how they perceive the institutional experience and how they respond to incarceration (Jacobs, 1976).

A number of studies have demonstrated that inmates vary by both race/ethnicity and age in their perceptions of the institutional experience (Goodstein & MacKenzie, 1984; Wright, 1989, 1991). This difference in perception also exists with regard to AIDS in prison. Exmates vary in how seriously they perceive the risk of HIV infection in prison, and they vary in their level of support for several currently popular correctional policies designed to reduce and/or prevent the spread of AIDS in prison. Much of this difference is age based; it is also affected by race/ethnicity. In particular, Whites are more concerned about contracting AIDS in prison than Blacks; Whites are also more supportive of correctional AIDS policies than Blacks. In addition, the older exmates are more concerned about contracting AIDS and yet are less supportive of AIDS policies than the youngest inmates.

Taken together, these findings suggest that, at least in some respects, life in the joint mirrors life on the street; an abundance of research indicates that among the public, fear of AIDS is highest among White, older Americans, the group least likely to in fact contract AIDS. Much as fear of criminal victimization is highest among some of the least victimized groups (Schmalleger, 1995), fear of AIDS is highest among groups least at risk. This is true, apparently, both in the free world and in prison.

What does it mean that young and Black inmates are less concerned about AIDS? For corrections departments, it means that individuals in these groups may be less likely to engage in risk-free behaviors. If they perceive little danger, there is no incentive to change. It also means that inmate education about AIDS is essential to remedy differential misunderstanding on the part of younger and older inmates and minority and nonminority inmates.

NOTES

1. Demographic variables compared included race/ethnicity, age, number of prior convictions, length of present sentence, marital status, and education level. The Texas Department of Corrections-Institutional Division data are on file with the authors.
2. Another potential sampling problem is selection bias. Selection bias occurs when potential respondents are systematically excluded from participation by actions of the interviewer (Babbie, 1995). Steps taken to limit selection bias in this research project included: (a) contacting inmates as soon as possible after their release, so as to contact as much of the population as possible; (b) employing interviewers of differing ages, races, and genders in an effort to match as closely as possible the demographic characteristics of the exmate population and thus foster a sense of commonality and trust; (c) employing an interviewer who could communicate with Spanish-speaking exmates, so as not to exclude any non-English-speaking members of the population; (d) reading the survey to exmates, so as not to exclude those members of the population with nonexistent or negligible reading skills; (e) making the survey short and easy to respond to, so as to encourage exmates to participate; and (f) instructing the interviewers on effective techniques and pretesting to work out any kinks in the techniques.

REFERENCES

Anderson v. Romero, 72 F.3d 518 (1995).

Babbie, E. (1995). *The practice of social research* (6th ed.). Belmont, CA: Wadsworth.

Beck, A. (1993). *Survey of state prison inmates, 1991.* Washington, DC: U.S. Department of Justice.

Belbot, B. A., & del Carmen, R. V. (1991). AIDS in prison: Legal issues. *Crime & Delinquency, 37,* 135–153.

Blumberg, M. (1997, November). *The impact of HIV/AIDS on corrections.* Paper presented at the meeting of the American Society of Criminology, San Diego, CA.

Braithwaite, R. L., Hammett, T. M., & Mayberry, R. M. (1996). *Prisons and AIDS: A public health challenge.* San Francisco: Jossey-Bass.

Burris, S. (1992). Prisons, law and public health: The case for a consolidated response to epidemic disease behind bars. *University of Miami Law Review, 47,* 291–335.

Call, J. E. (1995). The Supreme Court and prisoners' rights. *Federal Probation, 59,* 36–46.

Chang, D. S. (1991). Out of the Dark Ages and into the nineties: Prisons' responses to inmates with AIDS. *Connecticut Law Review, 23,* 1001–1027.

Chitwood, D. (1995). Risk factors for HIV-1 sereoconversion among injection drug users: A case-control study. *American Journal of Public Health, 85,* 1538–1542.

Cotten-Oldenburg, N., Martin, S., Jordan, B., Sadowski, L., & Kupper, L. (1997). Preincarceration risky behaviors among women inmates: Opportunities for prevention. *The Prison Journal, 77,* 281–294.

Davis, D. L. (1992). Deliberate indifference: An "unnecessary change?" *Houston Law Review, 29,* 923–961.

Domino, J. C. (1994). *Civil rights and liberties: Toward the twenty-first century,* New York: HarperCollins.

Earley, P. (1992). *The hot house: Life inside Leavenworth Prison.* New York: Bantam.

Estelle v. Gamble, 429 U.S. 97 (1976).

Farmer v. Brennan, 511 U.S. 825 (1994).

Feinstein, J. S. (1993). The relationship between socioeconomic status and health: A review of the literature. *Millbank Quarterly, 71,* 279–322.

Friedman, M. C. (1992). Cruel and unusual punishment in the provision of prison medical care: Challenging the deliberate indifference standard. *Vanderbilt Law Review, 45,* 921–949.

Frink, S. E. (1997). AIDS behind bars: Judicial barriers to prisoners' constitutional claims. *Drake Law Review, 45,* 527–549.

Gilliard, D. K., & Beck, A. J. (1996). *Prison and jail inmates, 1995.* Washington, DC: U.S. Department of Justice.

Goodstein, L., & MacKenzie, D. L. (1984). Radial differences in adjustment patterns of prison inmates: Prisonization, conflict, stress, and control. In D. Georges-Abeyie (Ed.), *The criminal justice system and Blacks* (pp. 271–306). New York: Clark Boardman.

Gutterman, M. (1995). The contours of Eighth Amendment prison jurisprudence: Conditions of confinement. *Southern Methodist University Law Review, 48,* 373–407.

Haas, K. C. (1993). Constitutional challenges to the compulsory HIV testing of prisoners and the mandatory segregation of HIV-positive prisoners. *The Prison Journal, 73,* 391–422.

Hammett, T. M., & Daugherty, A. L. (1991). *1990 update: AIDS in correctional facilities.* Washington, DC: National Institute of Justice.

Harlow, C. W. (1993). *HIV in U.S. prisons and jails.* Washington, DC: U.S. Department of Justice.

Harris v. Thigpen, 941 F.2d 1495 (11th Circuit, 1991).

Hemmens, C. (1997). Correctional law for the correctional officer. In D. Bales (Ed.), *The correctional officer resource guide* (pp. 15–21). Lanham, MD: American Correctional Association.

Jacobs, J. B. (1976). Stratification and conflict among prison inmates. *Journal of Criminal Law and Criminology, 66,* 476–482.

Lampe, P. E. (1984). Ethnicity and crime: Perceptual differences among Blacks, Mexican Americans, and Anglos. *International Journal of Intercultural Relations, 8,* 357–372.

Marquart, J. W., Brewer, V., & D. McIntyre, D. (in press). *Towards an understanding of HIV/AIDS-related risk among prison officers.*

Marquart, J. W., Merianos, D. E., Cuvelier, S. J., & Carroll, L. (1996). Thinking about the relationship between health dynamics in the free community and the prison. *Crime & Delinquency, 42,* 331–360.

Maxfield, M. G., & Babbie, E. (1995). *Research methods for criminal justice and criminology.* Belmont, CA: Wadsworth.

McCorkle, R. C. (1993). Living on the edge: Fear in a maximum-security prison. *Journal of Offender Rehabilitation, 20,* 73–91.

Nadel, B. A. (1996). Correctional health care: Challenges and opportunities for the future. *Corrections Compendium, 21,* 1–5.

Olivero, R., & Roberts, A. (1989). The management of AIDS in correctional facilities: A view from the federal court system. *The Prison Journal, 69,* 3–89.

Palmer, J. W. (1997). *Constitutional rights of prisoners.* Cincinnati, OH: Anderson.

Pollock, J. N. (1997). *Prisons: Today and tomorrow.* Gaithersburg, MD: Aspen.

Robles, R., Colon, H., Matos, T., Reyes, J., Marrero, C., & Lopez, C. (1993). Risk factors and HIV infection among three different cultural groups of injection drug users. In B. Brown & G. Beschner (Eds.), *Handbook of risk of AIDS* (pp. 256–274). Westport, CT: Greenwood.

Samuels, J. F., Vlahove, D., Anthony, J. C., & Chaisson, R. E. (1992). Measurement of HIV risk behaviors among intravenous drug users. *British Journal of Addiction, 87,* 417–428.

Schmalleger, F. (1995). *Criminal justice today.* Englewood Cliffs, NJ: Prentice Hall.

Thomas, W., & Thomas, D. (1928). *Child in America.* New York: Knopf.

Vlahove, D. (1991). Prevalence of antibody to HIV-1 among entrants to U.S. correctional facilities. *Journal of the American Medical Association, 265,* 1129–1132.

Wees, G. (1996). As health care commitments climb, health care budgets follow. *Corrections Compendium, 21,* 6–9.

Wilson v. Seiter, 475 U.S. 312 (1991).

Wright, K. N. (1989). Race and economic marginality in explaining prison adjustment. *Journal of Research in Crime and Delinquency, 26,* 67–89.

Wright, K. N. (1991). A study of individual, environmental, and interactive effects in explaining adjustment to prison. *Justice Quarterly, 8,* 217–242.

Zimring, F. E., & Hawkins, G. (1995). *Incapacitation: Penal confinement and the restraint of crime.* New York: Oxford University Press.

CHAPTER 12

PERSONAL PRECAUTIONS TO VIOLENCE IN PRISON

Richard C. McCorkle

Although studies have documented increased levels of violence in U.S. prisons, little attention has been given to how this violence shapes inmate behaviors and life-styles. This article presents results from a survey of 300 adult males incarcerated in a maximum-security facility, providing data on the types, prevalence, and social correlates of personal precautions to violence. A factor analysis of responses revealed two distinct dimensions of precautionary behavior. The more fearful, older, and socially isolated inmates primarily used avoidance behaviors to reduce the threat of victimization. On the other hand, younger inmates who use the inmate culture as a source of status and privilege tended to employ more aggressive or proactive techniques to deter attacks.

Since the 1960s, U.S. prisons have been plagued by high levels of violence. In 1990, 76 prison homicides were reported in state and federal facilities. The number of homicides, however, fails to convey the true scope of the problem. There were 9,552 inmate-on-inmate assaults that same year that required medical attention (Camp & Camp, 1991). As alarming as these figures may be, they undoubtedly do not represent the true incidence of prison violence. Most victims of prison violence never report their victimization, their silence maintained by a perception of staff apathy or well-placed fears of inmate reprisals. Even those assaults reported to or observed by staff may never be officially recorded, given the concern that a high assault rate would reflect poorly on the

AUTHOR'S NOTE: Funding for this research was provided by a dissertation enhancement grant from Vanderbilt University. Requests for reprints should be sent to Richard C. McCorkle, Department of Criminal Justice, University of Nevada at Las Vegas, 4505 Maryland Parkway, Las Vegas, NV 89154-5009.

CRIMINAL JUSTICE AND BEHAVIOR, Vol. 19 No. 2, June 1992 160-173
© 1992 American Association for Correctional Psychology

administration's ability to govern the prison. The fact is that violence between inmates is now so common that it is considered a "norm of the convict world" (Johnson, 1987).

There have been several studies that have attempted to document, through inmate surveys, the true levels and distribution of prison victimization (see Bowker, 1980, for a review). But little is known concerning how the climate of violence existing in prison may be affecting inmate behaviors and life-styles. Outside the prison, the efforts of citizens to deal with the threat of crime has been thoroughly researched. That literature generally shows weak relationships between victimization, fear, and precautionary behaviors (Garofalo, 1979; Gordon & Riger, 1979; Hartnagel, 1979; Lizotte & Bordua, 1980; Skogan & Maxfield, 1981; Yin, 1985). However, given the ostensibly greater risk of victimization, these logical relationships should be more pronounced in prison.

We do know that inmates are affected by the violence. Several studies have shown, for example, that victims of sexual assault frequently resort to a self-imposed solitary confinement, spending inordinate amounts of time in their cells and away from other inmates in the hope of avoiding another attack (Bartollas, Miller, & Dinitz, 1975; Huffman, 1961; Lockwood, 1980; Parisi, 1982). Fearful of any form of victimization, many other inmates attempt to escape violence by avoiding particular areas of the compound that are judged to be "risky" (Irwin, 1980). Increasing numbers of inmates, both victims and non-victims, are requesting placement in protective custody, choosing to be locked up virtually 24 hours a day rather than be exposed to the dangers of life in the general inmate population (Greenfield, 1980). Not all, however, respond to the threat in their environment with such passive maneuvers. Many believe that unless an inmate can convincingly project an image that conveys the potential for violence, he is likely to be dominated and exploited throughout the duration of his sentence. Hence violence and threats are frequently used as both general and specific deterrents–a form of preemptive self-defense (Irwin, 1980; Johnson, 1987; Lockwood, 1980). To lend credibility to that image, alarming numbers of prisoners carry crude weapons constructed from raw materials gathered from their cells or work stations (see Fleisher, 1989, for a description).

Although these general observations point to the behavioral consequences of victimization and fear in prison, what is missing in the literature is any systematic examination of this aspect of prison violence. This article presents the results of such a study, providing specificity to the types, prevalence, and social correlates of inmate precautionary behaviors.

METHOD

The Research Site

The site for this study was the Tennessee State Prison (TSP) located in Nashville. It is the state's main maximum-security facility for adult male criminal offenders. Although plagued with overcrowding in the past, compliance with federal court orders to depopulate have kept the facility slightly under capacity for the past few years. At the time of the study the inmate population was approximately 970.

According to both inmate and staff accounts, the level of violence in TSP decreased as the population was reduced. Unfortunately, evidence for this decline is anecdotal. Attempts to keep accurate data on inmate-on-inmate violence did not begin until 1986, at a time when the inmate population had already been greatly reduced. Still, records show that reducing crowding has not eradicated violence in the prison. In the 12 months prior to this study there were 14 instances of serious violence, 10 of which involved weapons. Of course, these official counts do not include undetected, unreported acts of physical or sexual violence, threats, or coercion.

Sampling and Data Collection Methodology

The sample for this study was provided by the Planning and Research Section of the Tennessee Department of Correction. A sample of 600 inmates was drawn using a computer-generated random method. Nearly one sixth (99) of those selected were discovered to have been temporary residents of the prison, having been transferred back to facilities across the state subsequent to court appearances or treatment in TSP's medical center. These inmates were excluded from the study.

Each inmate in the sample was given a packet by prison staff, containing (a) a cover letter, (b) a questionnaire, and (c) a return, stamped envelope. The cover letter described the study's purpose, the nature of the requested participation, and offered a direct incentive of $3 for the return of a completed questionnaire. The instrument itself was 13 pages in length and took, according to inmate reports, approximately 15–20 minutes to complete. A description of items included in the instrument is presented in the appendix.

During the data collection stage, one of the respondents was shot and killed on the recreational field by another inmate. Of those 500 inmates remaining in the sample, exactly 300 returned completed questionnaries for a response rate of 60%. This relatively high response rate was likely the result of the cash incentive. For most inmates, this sum represented the equivalent of three days pay in the prison's various industries.

In addition to this instrument, 25 face-to-face interviews were conducted with inmates at the prison. These interviews were semistructured and lasted approximately 45–60 minutes.

Description of Sample

Table 12.1 presents a description of the inmates who participated in the study. Respondents were generally in their mid-30s, unmarried, and from urban areas. Approximately half were White and half were Black, which closely approximates the racial composition of TSP's inmate population. Also, like that general inmate population, the majority of respondents had been incarcerated at least once prior to current sentence and were currently facing lengthy terms for primarily violent offenses.

RESULTS

Table 12.2 presents the prevalence of the eight types of precautionary behaviors among the sample.

Table 12.1
Description of Sample

	Mean	*SD*
Age	36.3	8.3
Race		
White	48.0%	—
Black	46.6%	—
Other	3.7%	—
Education	11.1 (years)	2.7
Less than 12 years	40.8%	—
High school degree	36.7%	—
Some college	22.5%	—
Marital status		
Married	13.8%	—
Widowed	3.4%	—
Divorced	32.0%	—
Separated	6.1%	—
Never married	44.8%	—
Place of origin		
Urban	60.3%	—
Rural	39.7%	—
Weight	178.6 (lbs.)	29.8
Offense		
Murder	39.4%	—
Aggravated assault	6.0%	—
Robbery	23.6%	—
Sex offenses	14.8%	—
Property offenses	16.2%	—
Years served on current sentence	8.8	35.6
Years before parole hearing	11.9	14.7
Number of times imprisoned	1.9	1.2
Total years spent in prisons	13.5	6.6

In general, most respondents (77.7%) felt they could substantially reduce their risk of a violent encounter by simply "keeping to themselves." In subsequent interviews it was found that this behavior corresponded to two tenets of the convict code: "do your own time" and "don't exploit other inmates" (Sykes, 1958). Three typical comments from inmate interviews include the following:

> You can stay out of trouble by just minding your own business. Just like the guy who got shot on the ballfield . . . lots of people saw that. When they seen that, that was just it. Don't say nothing about it . . . just keep what you seen to yourself.

Table 12.2
Prevalence of Precautionary Behaviors

Precaution	Percentage Employing
Kept more to self	77.7
Avoided certain areas of the prison	41.5
Spent more time in cell	39.5
Avoided activities	17.1
Requested protective custody	5.4
Had to "get tough" to avoid victimization	69.7
Kept a weapon nearby	25.1
Lifted weights	46.6

> I just don't do anything to make people want to victimize me. I'm not out robbing anybody. I'm not out making deals with people I can't keep. I get off of work at pest control in the afternoons, I read, write some letters, watch my little biddy black & white TV. I'm not sticking my neck out.
>
> Best way to stay out of trouble is to avoid drugs and homosexuality. Get involved in the rackets and you're asking for trouble. Just stay to yourself.

More than 40% of respondents also reported that they avoided certain areas on the prison compound as a means of reducing risks. When asked, in the context of the survey, what were the most "dangerous" places in the prison, respondents reported the chow hall, housing units, recreational areas, and the yard—areas in which large numbers of inmates preclude close supervision. Similar numbers reported spending more time in their cells as a precaution to being victimized (39.5%). However, relatively few (17.1%) stated that their fear prevented them from participating in various activities taking place in the prison, and even fewer (5.4%) had gone as far as to request placement in protective custody.

Inmates had used violence or its threat to deter aggression (Table 12.2). A majority of the sample (69.7%) stated that they had been forced to "get tough" with another inmate to avoid being victimized or exploited. Interviewees stated that such moves send signals to the aggressor, and to the wider audience of inmates, that the target is willing to use violence in defense of self. Many confessed that "getting tough" often requires more than just "tough talk." The following two inmates were representative:

> You have to show you're a man, not just talk about it. You got to bust their heads. You have to get violent with them before they'll leave you alone.
>
> Sometimes, you have to be violent to save your ass. The last time was when I was living in Unit 4. For whatever reason, there was a certain individual here that thought I looked nice, and he didn't know me and I didn't know him. Just from my appearance he assumed too much. One day I went inside to shower, and he came on the walk and said something about my ass. So, we threw down right then. You constantly have to work on your reputation. I'm not saying you got to run out every week and crack somebody's head. But you do have to be constantly aware of your dealings with other people.

Table 12.3

Factor Analysis of Precautionary Behaviors

	Passive Precaution	*Aggressive Precaution*
Kept more to self	.56	−.06
Avoided certain areas of the prison	.64	.08
Spent more time in cell	.74	−.08
Avoided activities	.63	.16
Requested protective custody	.35	.38
Had to "get tough" to avoid victimization		.76
Kept a weapon nearly	.11	.82
Lifted weights	−.19	.40

More than a quarter of respondents also reported that they kept a "shank" or some other weapons on or near them in case they were attacked. Lifting weights also appeared to be a common response to the threat of violence, with nearly one half of the sample reporting that they engaged in this type of behavior on a regular basis.

A factor analysis of these eight items revealed two distinct dimensions of precautionary behavior (Table 12.3). Keeping more to self, avoiding areas in the prison, spending more time in the cell, and avoiding activities all loaded heavily on a factor labeled "passive precaution." Having to get tough, possessing weapons, and lifting weights composed an "aggressive precaution" factor. Protective custody failed to load conclusively on either of the two dimensions and was eliminated from use in further analysis.

The items composing each factor were then summed to create indexes of passive and aggressive precautionary behaviors. The zero-order correlations between these two precautionary indexes and other study variables are presented in Table 12.4. There was a significant relationship between fear and avoidance behaviors. Such passive responses also were related to the experiences of being threatened or robbed, but not assaulted. Older inmates and those who had spent more time in prisons also tended to use these types of precautions. And, as each of the social integration measures indicate (last three items in Table 12.4), prisoners who were not integrated into the inmate subculture more frequently reported using avoidance behaviors to shield themselves from aggressors in the population.

Fear was also related significantly to the aggressive precaution index. Each of the victimization variables was significantly related to this index, with the associations being extremely strong for assaults and threats. As compared to passive behaviors, these proactive strategies were more likely to be employed by younger inmates in TSP. Smaller inmates and those who had been at TSP longer, as well as those with fewer incarceration experiences, also tended to use these types of precautions. None of the three social integration variables were significantly related to the index.

Table 12.5 presents the results of a stepwise regression of the passive precaution index. Five variables explained just over 20% of the variance in the index. The best predictor was fear (beta = .287), indicating that a concern for

Table 12.4
Zero-Order Relationships Between Prisoner Experiences/Characteristics and Precaution Indexes

Experience/Characteristic	Passive Precaution Index	Aggressive Precaution Index
Has been assaulted	.08	.42***
Has been threatened	.15**	.45***
Has been robbed	.22***	.17**
Fear index	.34***	.30***
Age	.15**	−.32***
Race (White = 1, non-White = 0)	.02	.04
Weight	−.00	−.12*
Origin (urban = 1, nonurban = 0)	−.05	.01
Offense (violent = 1, nonviolent = 0)	−.08	.08
Time served	.01	.11*
Times imprisoned	.03	−.13*
Total years imprisoned	.11*	.04
Inmate friends (yes = 1, no = 0)	−.24***	.01
Perceived aid if attacked (yes = 1, no = 0)	−.21***	.05
Presence of intimates in the prison (yes = 1, no = 0)	−.16**	−.08

*$p < .05$; **$p < .01$; ***$p < .001$.

Table 12.5
Stepwise Regression of Passive Precaution Index

	Passive Precaution Index
Fear index	.29***
Age	.21***
Has been robbed	.14**
Inmate friends	−.12*
Perceived aid if attacked	−.11*
R^2	.21

NOTE: The values represent standardized regression coefficients.
*$p < .05$; **$p < .01$; ***$p < .001$.

Table 12.6
Stepwise Regression of Aggressive Precaution Index

	Aggressive Precaution Index
Has been threatened	.24***
Age	−.27***
Has been assaulted	.20***
Total years imprisoned	.17**
Fear index	.11*
R^2	.31

NOTE: Values represent standardized regression coefficients.

*$p < .05$; **$p < .01$; ***$p < .001$.

personal safety imposed a constraint on the social behavior of many inmates living in the prison. Age also had a strong independent effect on the use of avoidance strategies. The older the inmate, the more likely he was to report avoiding activities, areas, other inmates, and so on. Having been robbed was the only victimization variable to be a significant predictor of the index after controlling for the contribution of age. Two of the three social integration measures also remained significant. Respondents who reported they had no friends in the prison, or who felt that another inmate would not help out if attacked, were more likely to use avoidance as a means of reducing risks.

The independent variables were able to explain substantially more of the variation in the aggressive precaution index ($R^2 = .311$; Table 12.6). Fear was significantly related to this index but at a lesser magnitude than its association with the passive precaution index. The best predictor of aggressive precautions was age, with younger inmates more likely to report such behaviors. When the contribution of age was controlled, total years in prison remained a significant correlate of these behavioral adaptations. Finally, those who used these measures also tended to be those who had been threatened or physically assaulted during their sentence.

DISCUSSION

Fear appeared to be shaping the life-styles of many of the men living at TSP. Indeed, the relationships between victimization and fear, on the one hand, and the use of personal precautions, on the other, were decidedly more pronounced in the prison than has been observed in the free world (for a review, see Liska, Sanchirico, & Reed, 1988). The nature of these precautionary responses did vary in predictable ways. More specifically, older inmates and the socially isolated generally reported using the more passive, avoidance techniques to decrease their risks of victimization. This strategy does, in fact, provide some limited protections. Because the most severe victimizations (i.e., physical assaults) that occur in prison typically follow challenges to machismo, strivings for status, or disreputable dealings on the sub rosa economy (Bowker, 1980), those who avoid such trappings inevitably reduce their risks of serious violence. However, because such passive behaviors are generally interpreted by aggressive inmates as signs of weakness and vulnerability, those who employ them risk being assigned to a pool of victims who can easily be robbed or more generally exploited or dominated.

On the other hand, those who assumed a more aggressive, proactive stance were generally younger offenders with long histories of institutionalization. They were also far more likely to have been the targets of weapon-related violence during their current sentences. Given Bowker's (1980) observations concerning the antecedents of serious violence in prison, one can infer that, because these inmates have experienced this form of victimization, they are more oriented toward the prison culture at TSP as a source of social, psychological, and material gratification.

It is also likely that any individual inmate uses, to some degree, both methods of dealing with the threat of violence. A "tough" inmate, for example, approaching a parole hearing will avoid confrontations with other inmates in the hopes of securing an early release. Likewise, the more passive inmate can be moved to act violently in a particular situation if avoidance has not reduced the threat and the consequences of the attack are perceived to be severe (e.g., rape). Nonetheless, the general orientation and response to perceived threats, be it passive or aggressive, probably remains consistent over the course of the incarceration experience. It is unlikely that the inmate who has cowered in the presence of aggressors would later be able to assume a credible, threatening posture. Similarly, it is doubtful that the tough inmate would relinquish a role that has provided him with status and self-esteem.

This research points more generally to the salience of violence in the inmate world today. In the "big houses" that dominated the correctional scene prior to the 1960s, prison administrators could ensure order and inmate safety through policies of strict regimentation, supervision, and discipline. This charge has proven much more difficult, however, in the wake of relaxed custodial regimes, increased inmate rights in disciplinary matters, and mushrooming prison populations. Indeed, in a very real sense, the onus of personal safety has shifted from prison staff to the inmate. As the opportunities for violence have expanded, and the risks of detection and punishment diminished, more responsibility has had to be taken by the inmate to secure his own safety. The present study has documented the extent and variety of behaviors used by inmates in one facility to attempt to make prison life safe, although the high rates of victimization reported suggest that they are largely inadequate protections.

To provide effective protections for inmates, correctional administrations must first assume responsibility for current conditions. Steps then can be taken to reduce the opportunities and motivations for aggressive behaviors. The incentives for aggression could be reduced, for example, by augmenting the reward system, installing ombudsmen to mediate disputes, and developing meaningful programs of work that would provide alternate avenues of status and material gain. The opportunities for exploitation and aggression would be greatly reduced by improved classification systems, greater restrictions on movements inside the prison, and a trained staff that would respond quickly and formally to signs of inmate aggressiveness. Of course, some level of prison violence is inevitable, despite whatever steps may be taken. But effective interventions could greatly increase inmate safety and in so doing produce an environment where something more than simply warehousing of offenders might occur.

REFERENCES

Bartollas, C., Miller, S. J., & Dinitz, S. (1975). *Juvenile victimization.* Beverly Hills, CA: Sage.

Bowker, L. H. (1980). *Prison victimization.* New York: Elsevier.

Camp, G. M., & Camp, C. G. (1991). *Corrections yearbook.* South Salem, NY: Criminal Justice Institute.

Fleisher, M. (1989). *Warehousing violence.* Newbury Park, CA: Sage.

Garofalo, J. (1979). Victimization and fear of crime. *Journal of Crime and Delinquency, 16,* 80-97.

Gordon, M., & Riger, S. (1979). Fear and avoidance: A link between attitudes and behavior. *Victimology, 4,* 395-402.

Greenfield, L. A. (1980). *Assessing prison environments: A comparative approach.* Hackensack, NJ: National Council on Crime and Delinquency.

Hartnagel, T. (1979). Perception and fear of crime: Implications for neighborhood cohesion, social activity and community affect. *Social Forces, 58,* 176-193.

Huffman, A. (1961). Problems precipitated by homosexual approaches on youthful first offenders. *Journal of Social Therapy, 7,* 216-222.

Irwin, J. (1980). *Prisons in turmoil.* Boston: Little, Brown.

Johnson, R. (1987). *Hard time: Understanding and reforming the prison.* Monterey, CA: Brooks/Cole.

Liska, A., Sanchirico, A., & Reed, M. (1988). Fear of crime and constrained behavior: Specifying and estimating a reciprocal effects model. *Social Forces, 66,* 827-837.

Lizotte, A. J., & Bordua, D. (1980). Firearms ownership for sport and protection: Two divergent models. *American Sociological Review, 45,* 229-244.

Lockwood, D. (1980). *Prison sexual violence.* New York: Elsevier.

Parisi, N. (1982). *Coping with imprisonment.* Beverly Hills, CA: Sage.

Skogan, W., & Maxfield, M. (1981). *Coping with crime: Individual and neighborhood reactions.* Beverly Hills, CA: Sage.

Sykes, G. (1958). *The society of captives: A study of a maximum security prison.* Princeton, NJ: Princeton University Press.

Yin, P. (1985). *Victimization and the aged.* New York: Charles C. Thomas.

APPENDIX

 Description of Items Included in the Survey Instrument

1. Personal precautions: Respondents were asked if they had done any of the following to reduce their chance of victimization: (a) avoided certain areas of the prison, (b) spent more time in their cell, (c) avoided prison activities, (d) asked to be placed in protective custody, (e) kept more to themselves, (f) kept a weapon on or near them, (g) "gotten tough" with another inmate to avoid an attack, (h) lifted weights to bulk up their size. All items were coded 1 = yes, 0 = no.

2. Victimization: This was measured by asking respondents "During this sentence has anyone (a) made a threat to you that you took seriously, (b) made a sexual advance toward you, (c) hit you with their fists, (d) used a knife or other weapon on you, (e) threatened to hurt you if you didn't give up your property? Items 1 and 2 were used as a threat index. Items 3 and 4 served as an assault index. Item 5 was used as an indicator of robbery.

3. Fear of victimization: Three items were used to measure fear—(a) "How safe do you feel in this prison?" (very safe, reasonably safe, somewhat unsafe, very unsafe); (b) "How much do you worry that you'll be attacked during this sentence?" (a great deal, some, very little); (c) "Would you say the chance of being attacked during this sentence is . . . ? (high, medium, low). Response categories were ordered and summed to create a fear index, with a high score reflecting a high level of fear.
4. Status variables: age; race (1 = white, 0 = non-White); weight (lbs.); place of origin (1 = urban, rural = 0).
5. Sentence variables: offense (1 = violent, 0 = nonviolent); years served on current sentence.
6. Correctional history variables: number of times previously imprisoned; total years spent in all prisons (including juvenile).
7. Social integration variables: presence of inmate friends in the prison; presence of another inmate to talk with about personal problems; perceived aid of friends if attacked. All items coded 1 = yes, 0 = no.

CHAPTER 13

THE ORGANIZATIONAL STRUCTURE OF PRISON GANGS: A TEXAS CASE STUDY

By Robert S. Fong, Ph. D.[*]

INTRODUCTION

In recent years, American courts have played an important role in the evolution of prisoners' rights. Through court litigation, prisoners have successfully defended their claims to many constitutional rights. While court-mandated changes have improved the treatment of inmates, it is argued that court intrusion has undermined the legitimate authority of correctional personnel in maintaining order and discipline among inmates (Jacobs, 1977). It is further argued that the weakening of control over inmates has created an era where inmate gangs have formed for the purpose of sharing and eventually dominating, through violent means, the power base once occupied by correctional personnel (Jacobs, 1977).

For decades, the Texas Department of Corrections, the second largest prison system in the United States, was virtually free from inmate gang disruption. This condition might be attributable to the institution of the officially approved "building tender" system. Building tenders, often referred to as inmate guards, were inmates carefully selected by prison officials to assist in the performance of staff work. With proper supervision, not only did the building tenders effectively maintain order among the inmates (frequently through the use of force), but, more importantly, they served as an intelligence network for prison officials. In fact, up until 1983, the only known inmate group in the Texas prison system was the Texas Syndicate, a self-protection gang formed by a group of prisoners who had been members of the Texas Syndicate in the prisons in California. Outnumbered and closely monitored by the building tenders, the Texas Syndicate caused no major disruption.

---

[*]Dr. Fong is assistant professor, Department of Criminal Justice, University of North Carolina. He previously served 5 years (1984–89) as a special monitor for the Texas Department of Corrections in the Federal civil action case of *Ruiz v. Estelle,* presently known as *Ruiz v. Lynaugh.* FEDERAL PROBATION, Vol. 54 No. 1, January 36–43 ©Administrative Office of the United States Courts.

Table 13.1
Breakdown of Prison Gangs in Texas (September 1985)

Name of Gang	Racial Composition	Size of Membership	Year Formed
Texas Syndicate	Predominantly Hispanic	296	1975
Texas Mafia	Predominantly White	110	1982
Aryan Brotherhood of Texas	All White	287	1983
Mexican Mafia	All Hispanic	351	1984
Nuestro Carneles	All Hispanic	47	1984
Mandingo Warriors	All Black	66	1985
Self-Defense Family	Predominantly Black	107	1985
Hermanos De Pistolero	All Hispanic	21	1985
Others		115	1985

Source: Data verbally provided by a member of the Gang Task Force of the Texas Department of Corrections.

Despite its usefulness, the building tender system, along with several other aspects of prison operations, was declared unconstitutional by Chief Federal District Judge William Wayne Justice in the historic prison lawsuit of *Ruiz v. Estelle* (1980), which involved the testimonies of 349 witnesses and consumed 161 trial days. On June 1, 1982, Judge Justice issued the *Stipulated Modification of Sections IID and IIA of Amended Decree* ordering the immediate elimination of the building tender system. The issuance of this court order created two new crises for Texas prison administrators: (1) a severe shortage of security staff as evidenced by a pre-*Ruiz* staff-inmate ratio of 1:10 (Beaird, 1986) and (2) an inability to monitor inmate illegal activities due to the lack of inmate informants. In the meantime, they were forced to implement and comply with many court orders with specific guidelines affecting various aspects of the daily operations of the prison system. As a result, a state of chaos emerged where prison administrators nearly lost control over their prisons (Beaird, 1986). It was during this period that inmates began actively to organize themselves to fill this power vacuum. Texas Department of Corrections statistics showed that in March 1983, there was only one prison gang, the Texas Syndicate, with 56 members. Two and a half years later, eight inmate gangs along with several other small groups formed, and the reported membership increased to 1,400.

As these prison gangs competed for power and dominance, the number of serious violent incidents also sharply increased. In 1982, the year the process of eliminating the building tender system began, members of the Texas Syndicate were reported to be responsible for 5 (41 percent) of the 12 inmate homicides. In 1984, 20 (80 percent) of the 25 inmate homicides were found to be gang-related. Of the 20 gang-related inmate homicides, 6 (30 percent) were committed against members of the Mexican Mafia by members of the Texas Syndicate. During the same year, 404 non-fatal inmate stabbings, an all-time high in the history of the prison system, were reported. In the first three quarters of 1985, 27 inmate homicides were recorded, of which 23 (85 percent) were gang-related.

Of the 23 gang-related homicides, 13 (48 percent) were committed against members of the Mexican Mafia by members of the Texas Syndicate, while 1 (3 percent) was committed against members of the Texas Syndicate by members of the Mexican Mafia (Buentello, 1986).

In August 1985, the Texas Syndicate declared war on the Mexican Mafia, the largest inmate gang in the Texas prison system, by fatally assaulting four Mexican Mafia members. In September 1985, after considering all available strategies, the director of the Texas Department of Corrections ordered the emergency detention of all confirmed and suspected gang members. These inmates were subsequently assigned to security detention group A (assaultive) or security detention group B (non-assaultive) on a permanent basis, subject to review for release every 90 days. The continuing process of confining group members to administrative segregation resulted in a sizeable increase in the administrative segregation population, from 1,860 on September 5, 1985, to 3,055 on January 29, 1987.

The severity of the war between the Texas Syndicate and the Mexican Mafia has not only been felt within the Texas Department of Corrections but in the free world as well. Law enforcement agencies in several metropolitan areas have identified several recent homicides committed on the streets as being directly related to this war (Buentello, 1986). Despite efforts by some members of both groups and by some public officials to propose "peace treaties," the war has continued to escalate.

The purpose of this study is to compare and contrast the Texas Syndicate and the Mexican Mafia, the two largest prison gangs in America, from an organizational perspective. Emphasis will be placed upon such characteristics as: (1) organizational structure; (2) leadership style; (3) methods of recruitment; (4) gang activities and goals; (5) operational strategies; and (6) gang activities outside the prison setting. One reason for studying the organizational characteristics of these two inmate gangs is that there is currently very limited information concerning prison gangs. Perhaps a more important reason is that without basic knowledge of these characteristics, the application of scientific research methods to seek further understanding of prison gangs will be, if not impossible, difficult and impractical.

LITERATURE REVIEW

The formation of prison gangs began in 1950 when a group of prisoners at the Washington Penitentiary in Walla Walla organized themselves to become known as the Gypsy Jokers (Camp and Camp, 1985). Thereafter, prison gangs continued to emerge in various jurisdictions.

The latest statistics show that prison gangs are present in the Federal prison system and 33 state jurisdictions. Of the 33 jurisdictions experiencing the presence of prison gangs, 29 are able to identify individual gangs by name. In those 29 jurisdictions, prison officials have identified 114 gangs with an estimated total membership of 12,634. Overall, gang members make up about 3 percent of the total Federal and state prison population (Camp and Camp, 1985).

With the emergence of prison gangs, two serious conditions have developed in prisons. The first is the increased difficulty experienced by prison offi-

Table 13.2
When and Where Prison Gangs Began in The United States

Year Formed	Jurisdiction	Name of Gang
1950	Washington	Gypsy Jokers
1957	California	Mexican Mafia
1969	Illinois	Disciples
		Vice Lords
1970	Utah	Aryan Brotherhood
		Neustra Familia
		Black Guerilla Family
1971	Pennsylvania	Philadelphia Street Gangs
1973	Iowa	Bikers
		Vice Lords
1973	Nevada	Aryan Warriors
1974	North Carolina	Black Panthers
1974	Virginia	Pagans
1974	Arkansas	KKK
1975	Arizona	Mexican Mafia
1975	Texas	Texas Syndicate
1977	Federal System	Aryan Brotherhood
		Mexican Mafia
1978	Wisconsin	Black Disciples
1980	West Virginia	Avengers
1981	Missouri	Moorish Science Temple
1982	Kentucky	Aryan Brotherhood
		Outlaws
1983	Indiana	Black Dragons

Source: Camp, G.M. and Camp, C.G. *Prison Gangs: Their Extent, Nature, and Impact on Prisons.* Washington, DC: U.S. Department of Justice, 1985.

cials in maintaining order and discipline among inmates (Jacobs, 1977; and Irwin, 1980). The second is the rapid increase in inmate violence primarily caused by the violent nature of prison gang members and of prison gang activities such as drug trafficking, extortion, prostitution, protection, gambling, and contract inmate murders (Yablonsky, 1962; Toch, 1978; Jacobs, 1974; Jacobs, 1977; and Irwin, 1980). Camp and Camp's (1987) study of prison gangs in American prisons reported that prison gangs accounted for 50 percent or more of all prison problems. However, in most jurisdictions, the absence of a gang intelligence-gathering system and the inadequate monitoring of gang activities have made it impossible to assess the exact impact of prison gangs on prison operations.

METHODOLOGY

The inability to obtain information directly from active gang members is a frustrating experience shared both by researchers and prison administrators. Thus far, the only available method for intelligence-gathering has been the sole reliance on information provided by a few voluntary former gang members who are placed on the gang "death" lists and are under maximum official protection in the prisons. The collection of data for the present study also relied, to a significant extent, on the voluntary cooperation of some former members of the Texas Syndicate and the Mexican Mafia.

With the prior approval of the deputy director for operations of the Texas Department of Corrections, extensive face-to-face interviews were conducted with four former members of the Texas Syndicate and four former members of the Mexican Mafia (N=8). In order to protect their identities and safety, the names of the eight individuals will not be disclosed in this report. These eight inmates were recommended for this study by the Gang Task Force of the Texas Department of Corrections. The basis for this recommendation was the proven credibility of these individuals as informants and the accuracy of the information they had provided to the Gang Task Force.

For each interview, no structured or standardized questionnaire was used. The researcher asked each interviewee a set of open-ended questions relating to the topic under study. Initially, the researcher had intended to tape-record each interview; however, this request was declined by each interviewee due to personal safety concerns. As an alternative, notes were taken of each interview. The longest interview lasted about 5 hours while the shortest interview lasted 2½ hours. The average length of the interviews was about four hours.

After all eight interviews were conducted, the researcher assessed and evaluated the information and arrived at a preliminary summary of findings. These findings were then verified through similar interviews with two members of the Gang Task Force and two unit wardens who have had extensive experience dealing with these two prison gangs. In the event that different responses were made to the same question, it would be so stated in the report. It was only when all responses to the same question were the same that it would be stated as a finding.

FINDINGS

Organizational Structure

Formed in 1978 by a group of inmates who previously served time in the California prison system, the Texas Syndicate, with a confirmed membership of 241, is the oldest and the second largest inmate gang in the Texas Department of Corrections. The Mexican Mafia or MEXIKANEMI (Soldiers of Aztlan), less than 2 years in existence, has a confirmed membership of 304 and is the largest inmate gang in Texas. Hierarchically, both gangs are organized along paramilitary lines. The Texas Syndicate is headed by a president and vice president who are elected by the entire membership. On the unit level, the Texas Syndicate is controlled by a chairman who oversees the vice chairman, captain, lieutenant, sergeant of arms, and soldiers.

Table 13.3
Number of Gangs and Gang Members Reported by Correctional Agencies in the United States—1984

Jurisdiction	Prisoners 1-1-1984	Number Gang	Total Members	Year Started	Percent Gang Members
Arizona	6,889	3	413	1975	6.0
Arkansas	4,089	3	184	1974	4.5
California	38,075	6	2,050	1957	5.5
Connecticut	5,042	2	—	—	—
Federal System	30,147	5	218	1977	0.7
Florida	26,260	3	—	—	—
Georgia	15,232	6	63	—	0.4
Idaho	1,095	3	—	—	—
Illinois	15,437	14	5,300	1969	34.3
Indiana	9,360	3	50	1983	0.5
Iowa	2,814	5	49	1973	1.7
Kentucky	4,754	4	82	1982	1.7
Maryland	12,003	1	100	—	0.8
Massachusetts	4,609	1	3	—	0.1
Michigan	14,972	2	250	—	1.7
Minnesota	2,228	2	87	—	3.9
Missouri	8,212	2	550	1981	6.7
Nevada	3,192	4	120	1973	3.8
New York	30,955	3	—	—	—
North Carolina	15,485	1	14	1974	0.1
Ohio	17,766	2	—	—	—
Oklahoma	7,076	5	—	—	—
Pennsylvania	11,798	15	2,400	1971	20.3
Texas	35,256	6	322	1975	0.9
Utah	1,328	5	90	1970	6.8
Virginia	10,093	2	65	1974	0.6
Washington	6,700	2	114	1950	1.7
West Virginia	1,628	1	50	1980	3.1
Wisconsin	4,894	3	60	1978	1.2
Average Totals		114	12,634		3.0

Source: Camp, G. M. and Camp, C. G. *Prison Gangs: Their Extent, Nature, and Impact on Prisons.* Washington, DC: U.S. Department of Justice, 1985.

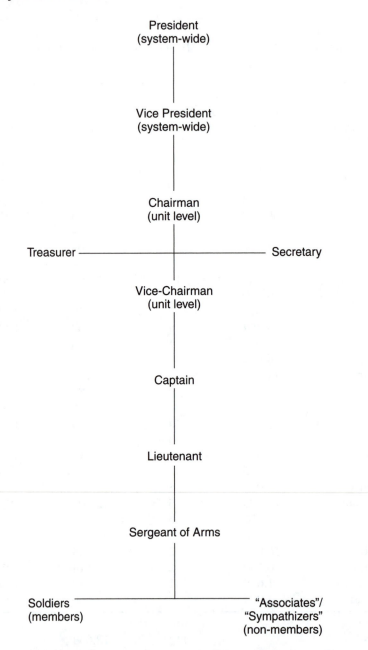

President
(system-wide)

Vice President
(system-wide)

Chairman
(unit level)

Treasurer ———————————————— Secretary

Vice-Chairman
(unit level)

Captain

Lieutenant

Sergeant of Arms

Soldiers ———————————— "Associates"/
(members)   "Sympathizers"
                             (non-members)

Figure 13.1 The General Organizational Structure of the Texas Syndicate
Source: Based on interviews.

With the exception of the president, vice president, chairman, and vice chairman, all other lower ranking positions are filled by individuals of outstanding criminal activity performance records for the gang. In order to avoid intra-gang conflict, a ranking member, other than the president and vice president, is automatically reverted to the status of a soldier when he is reassigned to a different unit by prison officials.

The Mexican Mafia is composed of a president, vice president, regional generals, lieutenants, sergeants, and soldiers.

All ranking positions in the Mexican Mafia organization, excluding the sergeants, are elected based on the individuals' leadership ability to deal harmoniously with people. There is no system designed to avoid intra-gang conflict. Leaders keep their ranks and titles upon reassignment to a different unit by prison officials.

Regardless of ranks, both inmate gangs require their members to abide by a strict code of conduct known as the "Constitution." For members of the Texas Syndicate, the constitution consists of eight rules:

1. Be a Texan.
2. Once a member, always a member.
3. The Texas Syndicate comes before anyone and anything.
4. Right or wrong, the Texas Syndicate is right at all times.
5. All members will wear the Texas Syndicate tattoo.
6. Never let a member down.
7. All members will respect each other.
8. Keep all gang information within the group (*Texas Syndicate Constitution*).

For members of the Mexican Mafia, the constitution outlines 12 rules:

1. Membership is for life—"blood in, blood out."
2. Every member must be prepared to sacrifice his life or take a life at any time when necessary.
3. Every member shall strive to overcome his weakness to achieve discipline within the MEXIKANEMI brotherhood.
4. Never let the MEXIKANEMI down.
5. The sponsoring member is totally responsible for the behavior of the new recruit. If the new recruit turns out to be a traitor, it is the sponsoring member's responsibility to eliminate the recruit.
6. When disrespected by a stranger or a group, all members of the MEXIKANEMI will unite to destroy the person or the other group completely.
7. Always maintain a high level of integrity.
8. Never release the MEXIKANEMI business to others.
9. Every member has the right to express opinions, ideas, contradictions and constructive criticisms.
10. Every member has the right to organize, educate, arm, and defend the MEXIKANEMI.
11. Every member has the right to wear the tattoo of the MEXIKANEMI symbol.

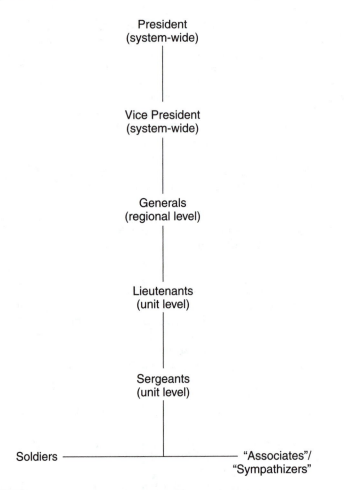

Figure 13.2 The General Organizational Structure of the Mexican Mafia
Source: Based on interviews.

12. The MEXIKANEMI is a criminal organization and therefore will participate in all aspects of criminal interest for monetary benefits (*Constitution of the Mexican Mafia of Texas*).

For both inmate gangs, the penalty for intentionally or unintentionally violating any of the established rules is death.

Leadership Style

The Texas Syndicate practices a democratic style of leadership. Each member is allowed to cast one vote, and only when an unanimous vote is obtained will a proposal become a decision. In the event that a "hit" (the task of killing a member for breaking a rule or of killing a nonmember for other reasons) is to be carried out, a volunteer will be sought. If no member volunteers to carry out the task, a number drawing is conducted. If the task requires one executioner, the member who draws the number "1" will be assigned the duty. If the task requires two executioners, the two members who draw the numbers "1" and "2" will be assigned the duty. While the Mexican Mafia emphasizes that no decision will be carried out unless an unanimous vote is reached, in actuality, unit lieutenants are known to have frequently manipulated the democratic process by issuing orders to individual members without collective consent. The reason for this abuse of power, as observed by members of the Gang Task Force and wardens interviewed for this project, is that the Mexican Mafia is a rather new organization and has not had sufficient time to become adapted to the prescribed leadership style. The system-wide lockdown of all gang leaders and members has added more confusion for the achievement of their goals.

Methods of Recruitment

The Texas Syndicate practices a comprehensive and lengthy recruiting process. Every prospective member must meet the "homeboy connection" requirement which means that he is known by one of the active members as a childhood friend. Once this first requirement is met, the prospective member is approached and socialized by that member. In the meantime, a thorough background investigation is conducted by the unit chairman through communicating with other chairmen and their members who may have knowledge of the prospective member. In the end, if the investigation reveals that the prospective member is "clean," the entire membership must cast an unanimous vote before formal admittance is granted. If the investigation reveals that the prospective member has served as a police informant or has a questionable sense of loyalty, membership will not be granted to the individual. Instead, the individual will be coerced into paying the gang for protection or be used as a prostitute by the gang.

Theoretically, the Mexican Mafia follows closely the recruiting method adopted by the Texas Syndicate. In practice, however, membership is granted to any Hispanic inmate who meets the "homeboy connection" requirement. In many instances, the prospective member has already been rejected by the Texas Syndicate. The background investigation is often poorly conducted, and new membership requires only a majority vote of the entire group. This loosely structured recruiting procedure, as observed by Texas Department of Corrections gang experts, is the major contributing factor to making the Mexican Mafia the largest inmate gang in the Texas prison system.

Gang Activities and Goals

The Texas Syndicate was originally formed for the purpose of self-protection against the "building tenders." As the "building tender" system faded away, it left behind a power vacuum. The Texas Syndicate wasted no time filling that power base and was able to control such illegal activities as drug trafficking, extortion, prostitution, protection, gambling, and contract murder. The Mexican Mafia, as it grew in size, quickly entered into competition with the Texas Syndicate in the struggle for power dominance. To date, both gangs are at war with each other for total territorial control behind the Texas prison walls and perhaps in the free world.

Operational Strategies

Both the Texas Syndicate and the Mexican Mafia operate in secretive ways in the prison environment. On the unit level, instructions and decisions are relayed through verbal communications. For inter-unit communication, however, the most commonly known method is the use of the U.S. mail. Coded messages are hidden in letters. For the Texas Syndicate, the most frequently used coded method is the number code. The following coded letter is an example of this communication strategy.

Dear Bro,

Haven't heard nothin from ya for almost 4 weeks. Thought you might have fall in the "black hole" they been talkin about in the paper. What's goin on? Not much happenin here, just want to touch base. Remember Big Al, he just got back from the hospital after spendin 3 weeks there for a major heart attack. Said it was a change. Really liked it there. The room was nice and even had a 19 inch color tv. What a lucky mother-f. . . . . . ! Said he wouldn't mind staying there for 1/2 a year.

Guess what, he said when he woke up in his room the first time, he almost had a second heart attack cause couldn't believe what he saw, a real cute nurse with Dolly Pardon's figure. Said she was taller, about 5 foot 8 inches in her early 20's. Big Al said they got to be real good friends. Said she even hugged him a dozen times or so a day. She told him will come visit in the joint. Said would divorce his old lady if things get juicy with this cutie. What a 2-timer. So much for Big Al.

I am getting a visit this weekend. My old man is bringin my son to see me cause next Monday is his B-day. Gonna to be 10 years old. Wish I could be out there with him. Been away for almost 5 years since got busted for raping that 19 year old alut down in that Motel 6. Got 3 more years to go and I'll be a free man again. As crowded as we are now, maybe those sons-of- bitches in the capital would pass a law to let us go home early. Can't wait!

Well, such is life! Like they say, life is a bitch and you die, sometimes if ya lucky, ya marry one. Gonna put the brakes on for now. Give my best to the best and f. . . the rest.

Your bro till death

In interpreting the underlying message of this letter, one must first learn the number codes. It is assumed that the number codes are broken down as follows:

A	B	C	D	E	F	G	H	I	J	K	L	M	N
8	1	7	26	18	9	13	3	19	20	14	22	5	16

O	P	Q	R	S	T	U	V	W	X	Y	Z
12	17	23	2	10	6	36	15	21	11	27	34

The number 4 in the beginning of the letter is a code indicator. Having understood the number codes, the letter reveals the following numbers:

1st paragraph - 3, 19, 6(1/2 year = 6)
2nd paragraph - 5, 8, 20, 12, 2
3rd paragraph - 10, 5, 19, 6, 3

Applying these numbers to the letter designations will reveal the following message:

	3	19	6	
	H	I	T	

	5	8	20	12	2
	M	A	J	O	R

10	5	19	6	3
S	M	I	T	H

Decoded message: "Hit Major Smith"

In order to avoid official intervention and intrusion, the number codes are changed from time to time.

The Mexican Mafia operates in ways similar to that of the Texas Syndicate. Thus far, the most intense criminal activity conducted by the Mexican Mafia appears to be drug trafficking. The major source of drugs comes from prison staff, particularly correctional officers who are young, single, and inexperienced. For those officers who are willing to bring drugs into the prisons for the Mexican Mafia, the reward is 40 percent of the profit made from the sale of drugs. Once involved, the officer is not allowed to terminate his service to the gang unless he resigns his position with the department of corrections.

For inter-unit communication, the Mexican Mafia utilizes three methods: (1) by visit with free world people; (2) by prison bus or any type of prison transportation; and (3) by U.S. mail (Scallan, 1987). When a message is to be relayed in written form, it is usually written in the form of a matrix or "Tic-Tac-Toe" code.

The Matrix Code

Since the system-wide lockdown, members of the Mexican Mafia have adopted the method of hiding coded messages in legal petitions which are sent to a free world address for someone falsely identified as an attorney at law. This so-called attorney will place the letter in an envelope (which looks like one that is used by a law firm) and mail it to the inmate to whom the letter is intended. This is an effective method of communication since prison personnel are prohibited by the courts from reading the contents of mail to and from an attorney.

Gang Activities Outside Prison

Released members of both gangs are required to stay in close contact with members in the prisons. There is indication that both gangs are engaged heavily in expanding their crime bases in the free world by participating in drug trafficking from such countries as Mexico with the assistance of nonmembers called "associates."

For those released members who can generate independent income, a percentage of that income must be surrendered to the gang. The Texas Syndicate requires a 10 percent income contribution, while the Mexican Mafia takes a 15 percent income contribution. Failure to obey this rule will result in the death of the member.

CONCLUSION

All research projects or studies share one common purpose: the exploration of new knowledge. In the understanding of criminal behavior, especially that of prison gangs, very limited information is available in the existing literature. It was for this reason that the present study was conducted.

Initially, it was predicted that the Texas Syndicate and the Mexican Mafia would differ from each other in terms of (1) organizational structure, (2) leadership style, (3) methods of recruitment, (4) gang activities and goals, (5) operational strategies, and (6) gang activities outside the prison setting. The findings, however, reveal that such is not the case. On the contrary, both groups share similar characteristics. A question that may result from this study is whether all inmate gangs in the prison environment share similar characteristics as evidenced by the Texas Syndicate and the Mexican Mafia. Clearly, the answer to this question is that further research of prison gangs is needed.

REFERENCES

Adams, N. M. America's Newest Crime Syndicate—The "Mexican Mafia." *The Reader's Digest,* 1977, pp. 97–102.

Beaird, L. H. "Prison Gangs: Texas." *Corrections Today, 18,* July 1986, p. 22.

Buentello, S. *Texas Syndicate: A Review of Its Inception, Growth in Violence and Continued Threat to the TDC.* Unpublished manuscript, Texas Department of Corrections, 1986.

Camp, G. M. and Camp, C.G. *Prison Gangs: Their Extent, Nature, and Impact on Prisons.* (Grant No. 84-NI-AX-0001). United States Department of Justice, Office of Legal Policy. Washington, DC: U.S. Government Printing Office, 1985.

Camp, G. M. and Camp, C.G. *The Correctional Year Book.* South Salem, New York: Criminal Justice Institute, 1987.

Constitution of the Mexican Mafia of Texas. Confidential gang document confiscated by Texas Department of Corrections officials, undated.

Davis, J. R. *Street Gangs: Youth, Biker and Prison Groups.* Iowa: Kendall Hunt Publishing Company, 1982.

Eckland-Olson, S. *Judicial Decision and the Social Order of Prison Violence: Evidence from Post Ruiz Years in Texas.* Unpublished manuscript, University of Texas, Department of Sociology, 1986.

Irwin, J. *Prison in Turmoil.* Boston: Little, Brown and Company, 1980.

Jacobs, J. B. *Stateville.* Chicago: University of Chicago Press, 1977.

Jacobs, J. B. "Street Gangs Behind Bars." *Social Problems, 24,* 1974, pp 395–409.

Scallan, J. H. *Prison Gang Codes and Communications.* Unpublished manuscript, Texas Department of Corrections, 1987.

Texas Department of Corrections 1986 Fact Sheet. Huntsville, Texas: Huntsville Unit Print Shop, 1987.

Texas Department of Corrections 1986 Fiscal Year Statistical Report. Huntsville, Texas: Huntsville Unit Print Shop, 1987.

Texas Department of Corrections—Prison Gang Task Force. *Prison Intelligence Report: Prison Gang Tattoos,* June 1986.

Texas Department of Corrections. *Administrative Segregation Summaries,* September 5, 1985 to January 29, 1987.

Texas Syndicate Constitution. Confidential gang document confiscated by Texas Department of Corrections officials, undated.

Toch, H. "Social Climate and Prison Violence." *Federal Probation, 42*(4), December 1978, pp. 21–25.

Yablonsky, L. *The Violent Gang.* New York: The McMillan Company, 1962.

CHAPTER 14

ULTRAMASCULINE PRISON ENVIRONMENTS AND INMATES' ADJUSTMENT: IT'S TIME TO MOVE BEYOND THE "BOYS WILL BE BOYS" PARADIGM[*]

Faith E. Lutze[**] and David W. Murphy[***]

Shock incarceration programs have become increasingly popular as an alternative to traditional prisons. Critics state, however, that such programs are characterized by ultramasculine environments which may lead to a number of negative outcomes for inmates. This study compares inmates in a shock incarceration program with inmates in a traditional minimum-security prison on the degree to which they perceive their environments as masculine, and how these perceptions relate to institutional adjustment. Inmates who describe their environment as possessing ultramasculine attributes were more likely to report negative patterns of adjustment.

*Opinions expressed here are those of the authors but not necessarily those of the Federal Bureau of Prisons or the U.S. Department of Justice. An earlier version of this paper was presented at the annual meetings of the American Society of Criminology, held in San Diego, California, in November 1997. We are thankful to the staff of the Federal Bureau of Prisons for providing the opportunity to conduct this project and to Robert Jackson, Nicholas Lovrich, Otwin Marenin, Susan Marcus-Mendoza, and the anonymous reviewers for their helpful comments.

**Faith E. Lutze, Ph.D., is an Assistant Professor in the Criminal Justice Program at Washington State University. Her current research interests include the rehabilitative nature of prison environments, the impact of ultra-masculine environments on inmate adjustment, offender adjustment to community corrections supervision, and violence toward women. She teaches courses related to corrections and to women and criminal justice. Dr. Lutze currently serves as Chair of the Corrections Section of the Academy of Criminal Justice Sciences.
***David W. Murphy, M.S., is a doctoral candidate in the Department of Political Science/ Criminal Justice Program at Washington State University. He recently completed a study on the impact of police residency requirements on public attitudes toward the police. His current research interests include comparative policing, the public's perception of law enforcement officers, and gender issues in criminal justice.

JUSTICE QUARTERLY, Vol. 16 No. 4, December 1999

Gender is universally recognized as one of the most fundamental determinants of human behavior. Criminologists consistently propose that it is one of the strongest predictors of criminal involvement (Messerschmidt 1993:1).[1] Decades of evidence indicate that men are far more likely than women to engage in nearly all types of illegal behavior, especially violent crime (Belknap 1996; Chesney-Lind and Shelden 1998; Cullen, Golden, and Cullen 1979). Although gender has been acknowledged as an important influence on behavior and is commonly used in criminological studies about female offenders and their treatment by the criminal justice system (Belknap 1996; Daly and Chesney-Lind 1988), the influence of gender on behavior is often ignored in criminal justice research on or about men (Collier 1998; Newburn and Stanko 1994).

Understanding how behaviors are influenced is a prerequisite to creating appropriate correctional institutions and effective correctional programs. Although many studies have considered gender differences in criminal offending (see Adler 1975; Belknap 1996; Chesney-Lind and Shelden 1998; Messerschmidt 1993; Simon and Landis 1991; Steffensmeier 1995) and the influences of gender-biased sex-role stereotypes on women in prison (Pollock-Byrne 1990; Rafter 1995), few studies have considered the influence of gender-stereotyped environments on all-male correctional populations (Morash and Rucker 1990; Sim 1994; Wright 1991b). With the relatively recent advent of boot camp prisons, also known as shock incarceration programs, concerns have been raised about subjecting women to a military model of corrections designed for men (MacKenzie and Donaldson 1996; Marcus-Mendoza, Klein-Saffran, and Lutze 1998; also see Hannah-Moffat 1995). Yet few observers have voiced concerns about the wisdom of subjecting men to an ultramasculine model of corrections that emphasizes aggressive interactions and male sex-role stereotypes (Morash and Rucker 1990).

In this study we explore the influence of ultramasculine prison environments on inmates' adjustment to prison. We begin by examining the meanings and significance of gender and the influence of social environments on gender formation. We further explore this influence by comparing inmates of a shock incarceration environment with those of a traditional minimum-security prison.

DEFINITIONS OF MASCULINITY AND FEMININITY

Despite the lack of general agreement on the specific definition of masculinity, certain elements of the concept appear in virtually all related discussions.[2] First, it is assumed that a general relationship exists between sex (i.e., being male or

---

[1]Theorists in psychology, feminist studies, masculine studies, and education have also analyzed the influence of gender on behavior (see Sapiro 1990 for a review).

[2]As with many concepts encountered in the social sciences, a single, agreed upon definition of masculinity does not exist. This is quite evident when we examine the variety of ways in which masculinity has been operationalized across studies (Baker and Chopik 1982; Norland, Wessell and Shover 1981; Wilkinson 1985) and defined across disciplines (e.g., psychology, feminist studies, etc.). Wilkinson (1985) explains that masculinity exists on multiple dimensions, and leaves conceptualization to the discretion of individual researchers. Consequently the validity of any analysis of masculinity depends on the appropriateness of the definition and the measurement.

female) and gender (i.e., being masculine or feminine) (Vetterling-Braggin 1982). Second, specific behavioral characteristics and personality traits tend to be associated with masculinity, specifically in contrast to femininity (Deaux 1987). These terms largely have emerged from traditional stereotypes linking femininity to "weakness and passion" and masculinity to "power and rationality" (Money 1987:13). Although the definitions of these terms continue to evolve, they still reflect similar stereotypes today.[3]

The words associated with masculine characteristics carry a sense of superiority, which is unmistakable in contrast with the terms used to describe feminine characteristics. For instance, *sissified* carries profoundly derogatory implications; being *powerful,* however, is commonly considered desirable. The influence of gender labeling is evident in instances where men and women depart from sex-role stereotypes (see Collier 1998 for a discussion). For instance, men who fail at particular tasks are often labeled with derogatory feminine terms such as being a sissy, while women who demonstrate power are often referred to as bitch. Thus sex-role labeling tends to reinforce behavioral patterns, social networks, and existing institutions of power and rewards.

Subscribing to masculine sex-role stereotypes (i.e., valuing masculinity and/or devaluing femininity), however, has been associated with a number of negative attitudes and behaviors. Although masculine attributes are not inherently bad, they have the potential of being detrimental when alternative behaviors are ignored because of stereotypical beliefs that "real" men can act only in one way (see Basow 1986; Collier 1998; Thompson, Grisanti, and Pleck 1985; Toch 1998). For instance, independence may be considered a positive attribute in some circumstances, but sometimes help from others is needed to overcome personal problems such as drug and alcohol abuse or financial difficulties. Also, although authoritative action and assertiveness may be necessary at times, they may be counterproductive if they are the only means considered acceptable for men in communicating with others. Such behavior may cause conflict in the home and in public places (Thompson et al., 1985), and may cause crime. Refusal to accept less stereotypical masculine responses inhibits the solving of problems that may be related to criminal behavior. Consequently an overreliance on masculine sex-role stereotypes may hinder prosocial behavior.

GENDER AND ENVIRONMENTAL EFFECTS ON BEHAVIOR

Historically, the apparent difference between males' and females' criminal tendencies were attributed to sex (i.e., biological traits). Modern criminological theorists, however, subscribe to the general assumption that masculinity and femininity are genderlinked characteristics which are the function of socializa-

---

[3]Common adjectives used to describe masculine and feminine characteristics include the following:

MASCULINE: virile, manly, mannish, gentlemanly, strong, vigorous, brawny, muscular, broad-shouldered, powerful, *forceful,* macho, *red-blooded, two fisted* (*Webster's* New World Thesaurus 1997; emphasis added).

FEMININE: effeminate, epicene, *sissified, sissyish,* unmanly, womanish (*Roget's II* 1997; emphasis added).

tion and the environment (see Belknap 1996). According to accepted theories of masculinity, males engage primarily in certain behaviors because those behaviors represent their masculinity effectively. In other words, masculinity is *learned,* and males use it as a means of establishing their gender identity (Franklin 1984).

Particular forms of masculinity, and the appropriate behaviors used to express them, are established not at the individual level but within a larger social group or network. Masculinities therefore are constructed, maintained, and restructured according to the relationships that exist within various social networks in a given environment (Franklin 1984). Consequently, "different types of masculinity exist in the school, the youth group, the street, the family, and the workplace," but each is subject to the influences of the patriarchal culture in which they exist (Chatterbaugh 1990; Messerschmidt 1993:84). Moreover, these types of masculinity exist in relatively specific and identifiable contexts; yet they develop systematically and are ever-changing, always unfinished products (Chatterbaugh 1990; Messerschmidt 1993). Therefore the behaviors in which men engage depend on what type of masculinity that exists in their particular environment or social setting. These settings serve as the venues in which males find support for their self-identity and in which they ultimately contribute to the identification of others (Franklin 1984).

THE GENDERED NATURE OF PRISON

Understanding how support for masculine behavior is influenced by social networks and given environments is important to the study of correctional environments. Whether prisons are meant to punish or to rehabilitate, their purpose is to change behavior and prevent future criminality. Correctional environments that support overreliance on male sex-role stereotypes may inadvertently support behaviors and attitudes that inhibit prosocial behavior by rewarding aggression and hindering the transition from prison to a law-abiding lifestyle (see Abbott 1981; Bernard and McCleary 1996; Sim 1994).

Traditional Prison Environments

Research on traditional prison environments tends to show that the institutional environment, or prison climate, influences inmate behavior and adjustment (see Ajdukovic 1990; Goffman 1959; Moos 1968, 1975; Sykes 1958; Toch 1977; Wright 1985, 1991a; Wright and Goodstein 1989; Zamble and Porporino 1988). Gender, however, is rarely considered as an environmental attribute (Sim 1994; Toch 1998). When the prison is considered as gendered or as reinforcing sex-role stereotypes, it usually is in regard to women inmates rather than men. Concern about the reinforcement of gender-biased policy and environments in women's prisons has long been considered detrimental to women and their success after prison (see Belknap 1996; Eaton 1993; Pollock-Bryne 1990; Rafter 1995). Even when issues of equality are discussed, especially when programs designed for men are provided to women, the appropriateness of subjecting women to such environments is questioned because women's needs are different from men's and because of the gendered nature of programs designed to fit men's needs (see Hannah-Moffat 1995; Marcus-Mendoza et al., 1998). Yet in spite of this history of concern about the gendered nature of women's prisons, and the long-standing gender disparity in the commission of violent crime, sex-role stereotyped prison environments for men have been called into question only recently.

Unfortunately, little research has been conducted on how masculine environments affect inmates in traditional male prisons. The literature largely provides graphic accounts of survival in maximum-security institutions permeated with personal and institutional violence and aggression (see Abbott 1981; Bernard and McCleary 1996; Sykes 1958). It appears that masculinity, along with violence and aggression, are valued in the traditional prison culture (Lockwood 1982; Toch 1998). Wright (1991b) argues that the establishment and reinforcement of a masculine identity legitimizes an inmate's use of violence and aggression. Moreover, violence appears to be most common among those inmates who have negative perceptions of (and difficulty in adjusting to) the prison environment and the effects of incarceration (Wright 1991b). Furthermore, Wilson (1986) concludes that male and female inmates differ in their adherence to the inmate code: Male inmates are less trusting of the staff than are female inmates. Wilson attributes this difference to the prison setting, not to gender differences.

Most discussions of masculine prison environments have been linked to violence in maximum-security institutions, where serious, often violent offenders are incarcerated. Few studies have considered how masculine sex-role stereotypes may be replicated or perpetuated in minimum-security institutions, where violent exchanges between inmates are less common and where the institutional environment may be considered safer and more predictable than in maximum-security institutions.

Shock Incarceration Environments

Shock incarceration programs appeared in the early 1980s as an alternative to traditional prisons and as a means of getting tough with young male offenders. Boot camp prisons mirror military boot camps in their common use of "strict discipline, physical training, drill and ceremony, military bearing and courtesy, physical labor, and summary punishment for minor misconduct" (Morash and Rucker 1990:205). The purpose of a strict, disciplined correctional environment is to scare offenders away from future criminality and to transfer prosocial behavior to the street. Soon after boot camp prisons developed, however, the severity of such an environment was strongly criticized, and its impact on inmates was questioned (Morash and Rucker 1990; Sechrest 1989).

Because of concern about the principles of military boot camps, which include the promotion of aggression, toughness, and intimidation, Morash and Rucker (1990:206) asked perhaps the most pertinent question: "Why would a method that has been developed to prepare people to go to war, and as a tool to manage legal violence, be considered as having such potential in deterring or rehabilitating offenders?" Specifically, Morash and Rucker (1990) argue that ultramasculine sex-role stereotyped environments may promote aggression and competitiveness as well as leading to isolation and helplessness; each of these outcomes may inhibit prosocial adjustment in some males. Thus an important aspect of the boot camp environment may be the extent to which it is gendered. A gendered boot camp environment generally values what is known as *ultra-*

masculinity (Morash and Rucker 1990). Such a setting supports notions of male forcefulness and strength of will and informally rewards bravado, aggression, and toughness (see Karner 1998). Morash and Rucker state that these beliefs "rest on the assumption that forceful control is to be valued" and that to succeed is to have masculine characteristics—characteristics that may be a cause of crime (1990:215).

For instance, many boot camp programs emphasize the complete dominance of staff members over inmates, confrontational modes of expression, physical fitness, and repeated verbal insults that degrade minorities, women, and homosexuals (Lutze and Brody 1999). Examples of confrontation often are displayed proudly to the media by shock administrators. Numerous newspapers have depicted staff members at boot camp prisons "in the face" of offenders, yelling commands or insults and administering discipline through demanding physical exercise (see Bohlen 1989; Brodus 1991; McDermand 1993; Stobbe 1993). Confrontation, dominance, and control are displayed without much consideration of the idea that other forms of communication (e.g., personal or group sessions, private discussions/counseling) may be more effective in initiating positive responses. Considering a less gender-stereotyped response to men in prison is important in view of recent research on male victimization. According to research (Newburn and Stanko 1994), and personal accounts (Abbott 1981; Bernard and McCleary 1996), some men victimize others to regain their "manhood" and a sense of control in their lives.

In spite of early concerns about the abusive nature of boot camp prisons, most of the work on shock incarceration programs suggests that such prison environments have a positive effect on inmates' attitudes and adjustment (Burton et al., 1993; MacKenzie and Shaw 1990; MacKenzie and Souryal 1995; McCorkle 1995) and do not tend to increase aggression (Lutze 1996a, 1996b).[4] More recent research on the nuances of inmates' attitudinal change and adjustment has yielded mixed results, however (see Lutze 1996b, 1998; Lutze and Marenin 1997). Although researchers have not yet considered empirically whether the environment in boot camp prisons is any more ultramasculine than in traditional prisons, emerging evidence suggests that the environments of boot camp prisons in fact are gendered and may influence inmates' adjustment accordingly. For instance, MacKenzie and Shaw (1990) report that inmates were well-adjusted overall and remained so over time, except for an increase in conflict. This outcome may indicate the confrontational nature of boot camp prisons and the gender-limited means of dealing with stress among inmates and between inmates and staff.

Lutze (1996a, 1996b) also reports that although shock incarceration inmates were better-adjusted and held more positive attitudes toward the program and staff than inmates in a traditional prison, inmates in the shock incarceration program reported greater feelings of isolation and helplessness over time than did the comparison group. These findings tend to support Morash and Rucker's (1990) argument that inmates in boot camp prison may be forced to deal with

---

[4]Research on aggression and boot camp prisons has focused on behavior within the institution as opposed to behavior after release. Studies on recidivism among boot camp prison graduates do not indicate increases through new violent offenses (see MacKenzie 1991; MacKenzie and Shaw 1993).

stress in predominantly masculine ways (i.e., conflict) or by withdrawing (i.e., isolation and helplessness).

As further evidence that shock incarceration programs may be ultramasculine, Lutze (1998) discovered that such programs supported rehabilitation by providing a safe, controlled environment for inmates' participation in programs, but did not offer any greater emotional feedback and support than a traditional prison. Lutze (1998:561) concludes that there is a need to explore how fully "shock incarceration programs, or other correctional settings, can be developed to increase both the external controls that inhibit negative inmate behaviors and the support and emotional feedback that promote psychological and emotional change." Psychological and emotional support may be associated with modes of coping not fostered in an ultramasculine environment.

HYPOTHESES

This study builds on prior research by exploring the relationship between inmates' adjustment and the gendered nature of the environment in a male boot camp prison. We test the following hypotheses:

> Hypothesis 1: The gendered or ultramasculine nature of the prison environment influences inmates' adjustment and perceptions of the environment.

We expect that all prison environments are gendered, and that the extent of gendering will influence how inmates adjust to prison and how they perceive their correctional environment. We expect that the more inmates define their environment as possessing strongly masculine attributes, the more they will experience feelings of isolation, helplessness, anxiety, assertive interactions, and conflict with staff members and other inmates. We also expect that inmates will perceive their environment as being less safe, and as providing less support and emotional feedback. In addition, we believe that they will report higher levels of coercion.

> Hypothesis 2: Shock incarceration programs are more gendered or more ultramasculine than traditional prisons, and influence inmates' adjustment and perceptions of the institutional environment differently than traditional prisons.

On the basis of Morash and Rucker's (1990) analysis of boot camp prisons, we expect that shock incarceration programs will emphasize ultramasculine attributes. Given these observations, we expect that shock incarceration inmates will experience more feelings of isolation, helplessness, anxiety, assertive interactions, and conflict with staff members and other inmates. They will also be likely to report less safety, support, and emotional feedback and to report being subjected to more coercion.

In spite of the heavily military environment prevailing in most of these programs, a few also include types of rehabilitation not typically geared toward males. The presence of these features may help to neutralize the otherwise ultramasculine environment at these institutions. Some shock programs emphasize family relationships, family planning, antidrug and alcohol consumption, and personal freedom (Lutze and Marenin 1997; MacKenzie 1990; MacKenzie et al., 1989; MacKenzie and Souryal 1991; Parent 1989). Many of these programs are not given as much attention or credibility in traditional male institutions (see Flanagan and Maguire 1991). Because of the dual existence of an ultramasculine environment and "feminine-like" programs in some shock incarceration facilities, it may be difficult to determine how inmates define the gendered nature of their environment.

METHODOLOGY

On the basis of survey evaluations of two all-male groups of inmates, we compare differences in the perception of the prison environment present in a shock incarceration program and in a traditional minimum-security prison. We use these comparisons to examine the influence of the prison environment on variables measuring inmates' adjustment.

Research Setting

The subjects compared in this study are a group of inmates housed at the Intensive Confinement Center (ICC) in Lewisburg, Pennsylvania and a group of inmates in the Federal Prison Camp (FPC) at Allenwood, Pennsylvania. ICC inmates typically spend up to 17 hours a day for six months in the program, which emphasizes physical activity, work, and treatment programs such as education and drug counseling. The ICC also closely regulates inmates' appearance, demeanor, and activity in accordance with strict militaristic guidelines. All staff members are male except for one teacher, one drug and alcohol specialist,[5] and two secretaries, who have limited contact with inmates.

The public areas of the ICC may be characterized as a loud, tightly structured, highly disciplined environment. Officers commonly yell orders and inmates yell responses in acknowledgment or in request for further instruction. The staff totally dominates the inmates. Inmates must request permission to proceed past each staff member they encounter, to enter the cafeteria, and to speak with staff members. Their physical appearance is under constant scrutiny, including presentation of uniforms, length of hair, amount of facial hair, posture, and body weight. Inmates who fail to conform to the rigid expectations of the program are quickly subjected to verbal reprimands and discipline in the form of physical exercise. Inmates who show weakness or who do not measure up in their athletic ability are often called sissies, girls, or mama's boys. In the private areas of the institution (classrooms and work areas), staff members still maintain a strictly disciplined environment, though communication is somewhat more relaxed. Inmates are allowed to speak with staff members more openly and without formality. Strict rules still apply to appearance and posture, however. Treatment staff members (teachers, counselors, case managers) still may discipline inmates for their behavior, and they share their progress reports with the custody staff.

---

[5]The female drug and alcohol specialist was hired toward the end of the period of study.

FPC Allenwood, on the other hand, is a traditional minimum security institution in which inmates develop their own programs. These programs typically include work; they also may include treatment and recreation. The characteristics of offenders sentenced to institutions such as FPC Allenwood are generally similar to those sentenced to the ICC. For example, inmates in both institutions tend to be less violent, to have less serious records, and to be serving shorter sentences than inmates in more secure traditional prisons. Although most of the staff at FPC Allenwood are males, women serve as correctional officers, teachers, hospital staff members, secretaries, and work supervisors.

The public areas of FPC Allenwood are less disciplined and less structured than in the ICC. Although FPC inmates are required to observe general rules and regulations governing inmate behavior, their movement through the institution is less restricted and much more relaxed than in the ICC. Although staff members maintain control of inmates, the general staff-inmate interaction is not confrontational.

Research Procedure

In this study we use data originally generated from a larger study in which self-report questionnaires were administered to the subjects. The first of two questionnaires was given within two weeks of an inmate's arrival at his institution (Time 1); inmates completed the second questionnaire approximately six months later (Time 2). All demographic data were gathered during the first phase; inmates' evaluations of their environment as well as their attitudes and personal adjustment to confinement were collected during the second phase. The first author administered confidential surveys to inmates in small groups, away from direct observation by the staff.

Sample

Intensive Confinement Center. All inmates arriving at the ICC between December 1993 and October 1994 were surveyed for this study. Of the 334 ICC inmates completing the Time 1 questionnaire, 271 (81%) also completed the Time 2 questionnaire.[6] Of the 63 inmates (19%) who were not included in the second phase, 23 (7%) withdrew voluntarily from the ICC program, 19 (6%) were removed formally by the prison staff for misconduct, 10 (3%) were released prior to graduating from the program, 9 (3%) were unable to participate because of medical conditions, and 2 (1%) inmates' sentences were commuted by the court. This study includes only those ICC inmates who completed the program by participating at both Time 1 and Time 2.[7]

---

[6]This study includes only those who completed questionnaires at both Time 1 and Time 2, because data related to the environment were collected only at Time 2. Although dropouts did not differ significantly from completers for either group on most of the demographic variables, it is not known how dropouts may have defined their environment in terms of being gendered. Thus the results should be interpreted cautiously.

[7]On the variables listed in Table 1, ICC inmates who dropped out of the study did not differ statistically from ICC inmates who completed the study.

FPC Allenwood. The comparison group used in this study consists of inmates arriving at FPC Allenwood between March 1994 and January 1995. A total of 170 of these inmates were selected to participate in the study. Comparison group selections were made according to age (less than 45 years) and sentence length (less than 60 months). Of the original 170 inmates, 106 (62%) participated fully in the study by completing questionnaires at Time 2. Of the 64 (38%) inmates who did not complete the study, 54 (32%) were released from the institution before Time 2, and 10 (6%) declined to participate at Time 2. This study includes only those FPC inmates for whom Time 1 and Time 2 measures were collected.[8]

Measures

The measures used here relate to three specific areas: demographic information, institutional environment, and adjustment to prison.

Demographics. Subjects were asked to provide information on a variety of background characteristics including age, race, marital status, occupation, education, prior arrests, and offense leading to current confinement.

Environment. The environment of each institution is measured with the Gendered Environment Scale, Wright's (1985) Prison Environment Inventory (PEI) and the Coercion Scale. We developed the Gendered Environment Scale to explore the extent to which the environment is gendered; it measures the extent to which the prison environment supports male sex-role stereotypes (see Appendix Table A1). Composed of 11 Likert-type questions, it is based on components of the male sex role specified by Brannon and Juni (1984; also see Thompson et al., 1985). Gender stereotyping in this study relates to the overgeneralization of feminine attributes, definition of feminine attributes as negative, the use of feminine descriptors as derogatory labels for men, the portrayal of men as better than women, and support for assertive interactions between men.[9] (See Appendix Table A1 for examples of scale items; the coefficient alpha for the scale is .67, and the interitem correlation is .16.)

The PEI is used to measure how inmates define their environment (Wright 1985). The PEI consists of 80 Likert-type questions that address Toch's (1977) eight situational variables: privacy, safety, structure, support, emotional feedback,

---

[8]On the demographic variables listed in Table 1, Allenwood inmates who dropped out of the study did not differ statistically from Allenwood inmates who completed the study, except on sentence length. Dropouts (M = 24.7, sd = 17.4) tended to have slightly shorter sentences than those who completed the study (M = 30.7, sd = 19.1, p < .05). These differences should not affect the generalizability of study results.

[9]Results of a varimax factor analysis for the Gendered Environment Scale produced five factors (see Lutze 1996a for detailed results). Each of the factors relates to masculine attributes defined by prior research (see Brannon and Juni 1985), and they relate conceptually to what we call the gendered environment. Therefore we combine them into a single scale for the purposes of this study. Items remaining in the scale were determined on the basis of their corrected interitem correlations and on how they affect Cronbach's coefficient alpha for the scale. Responses were measured on a five-point Likert scale ranging from "strongly agree" (= 5) to "strongly disagree" (= 1).

social stimulation, activity, and freedom. Only the scales for safety, support and emotional feedback are used in this study. The PEI safety scale measures the extent to which the institutional environment allows inmates to feel safe from being attacked by others, or from being robbed. The support scale measures the extent to which the environment provides inmates with reliable assistance from people with programs that advocate opportunities for self-improvement. The emotional feedback scale measures the extent to which the environment allows inmates to develop intimate relationships with people who care about them and the extent to which inmates are allowed to show their emotions without being ridiculed. This scale includes interactions with staff members and with other inmates. Wright (1985:268) reported the coefficient alphas for each of these scales as follows: safety, .76; support, .67; and emotional feedback, .40. The alpha coefficients reported here exceed those reported by Wright (1985) for safety (.79) and emotional feedback (.58), but not for support (.62).[10]

The Coercion Scale, another measure of institutional attributes developed for this study measures the amount of coercion that inmates perceive they experience at their correctional institution. The coefficient alpha for this scale is .74; the interitem correlation is .41 (see Appendix Table B1 for further detail concerning this scale).

Adjustment. We use six measures to assess inmates' adjustment. Isolation is measured with the Isolation Scale, which was adapted from Stratton and Lanza-Kaduce (1980) and Thomas and Foster (1972), and which was used in prison research reported by Goodstein and Hepburn (1985). Isolation, as measured by this scale, relates to the inmates' feelings that few, if any, people can be trusted and that it is better to stay away from others if one is to complete his sentence successfully. The Isolation Scale consists of six items such as "There are no *real* friends in prison" and "In the institution I keep pretty much to myself." The coefficient alpha for isolation in this study is .69, similar to the alpha of .66 reported by Goodstein and Hepburn (1985).

The state version of the State-Trait Anxiety Inventory (Speilberger, Gorsuch, and Lushene 1970) is used to measure stress. This 20-item Likert-type scale, which has been used in prior prison research (see MacKenzie, et al., 1987), consists of items such as "I feel calm" and "I am presently worrying over possible misfortunes." The measure as used in this study exceeds the coefficient alpha of .86 reported by MacKenzie et al., (1987).

An inmate's feeling of helplessness is measured by the Victim Scale, taken from MacKenzie and Shaw's (1990) 37-item Attitude Toward IMPACT Scale. (For the remainder of this study, we refer to this scale as inmates' "helplessness".) Items consist of statements such as "I do not think I can take this anymore" and "This place is unfair." MacKenzie and Shaw (1990) reported a coefficient alpha of .76 and an interitem correlation of .29 for this scale. The Victim Scale reliability scores for this study were similar to those of MacKenzie and Shaw (.70 and .23).

Conflict is measured by two Guttman scales indicating how many times an inmate has been involved in a conflict either with another inmate or with the staff (Shoemaker and Hillery 1980). The two scales each consist of seven items that measure conflict on a continuum ranging from verbal conflict to physical

---

[10]Although the reliability scores for each of these measures exceed or are similar to Wright (1985), the reliability scores for support and emotional feedback are weak. Thus the results related to these measures should be interpreted cautiously.

violence; inmates are asked if they have been in a variety of situations involving other inmates or staff members. For example, they are asked whether they have ever been in "[a] discussion in which some disagreement occurred" and "[a] situation in which some physical force was used on someone." The coefficient alpha and the interitem correlation for the scale measuring conflict with inmates is .65 and .28 respectively; on the scale measuring inmate's conflict with staff, these values are .76 and .38.

Assertiveness is measured by the Assertive Interactions Scale (Goodstein and Hepburn 1985). This scale consists of nine questions relating to the likelihood that an inmate will assert himself in a difficult situation: for example, "I try to stay out of trouble but nobody is going to push me around and get away with it." Goodstein and Hepburn (1985) reported a coefficient alpha of .70 for this scale. This study reported a similar coefficient alpha of .74 for this scale.

FINDINGS

Demographic Characteristics

We compared inmates at the ICC and the FPC to see whether the groups differed on demographic characteristics at Time 1 of the study (see Table 14.1). The groups were statistically similar in most characteristics, except that ICC inmates tended to be younger, serving shorter sentences, younger at the age of first arrest, and single.[11] These characteristics are related primarily to age and sentence; therefore we introduce these variables as controls in all multilevel analyses.[12]

Influence of Perceptions of a Gendered Environment on Inmate Adjustment

We use an independent-sample t-test to test for the difference between the two prisons regarding the presence of gendered environments. ICC inmates (*M* = 35.1) reported the environment to be significantly more gendered than did FPC inmates (*M* = 31.7).[13]

We use linear regression (OLS) to test the relationship between the inmates' assessment of the gendered nature of the environment and how they adjust to prison. Each of the adjustment measures (assertive interactions, isolation, helplessness, stress, conflict) is regressed on the nature of the gendered environment, age, sentence, and prison setting. We pool the two prison populations for these analyses.

The gendered nature of the environment relates significantly to each of the adjustment measures (see Table 14.2). As inmates defined the environment as

---

[11]ICC inmates differed statistically from FPC inmates in the following manner: age (ICC: *M* = 26.2, sd = 5.2 vs. FPC: *M* = 33.2, sd = 7.0, p < .01), sentence length, in months (ICC: *M* = 24.4, sd = 7.8 vs. FPC: *M* = 30.7, sd = 17.4, p < .01), age at first arrest (ICC: *M* = 23.5, sd = 5.7 vs. FPC: *M* = 28.8, sd = 8.3, p < .01), and marital status (chi square = 24.8, p < .01).
[12]Statistical correlations showed that age, sentence length, age at first arrest, and marital status are highly correlated. Therefore the use of age as a single control is justified.
[13]The results of the t-test are t = 5.11; df = 359; p < .001.

Table 14.1

Demographic Characteristics of the Sample

Variable	ICC (N = 271)		Allenwood (N = 106)		F	Sig.
	Mean	SD	Mean	SD		
Age	26.2	5.2	33.2	7.0	109.1	.01
Education	12.3	1.9	12.7	2.0	3.1	NS
Sentence Length (Months)	24.4	7.8	30.7	17.4	23.4	.01
Felony Convictions	.25	.89	.36	1.04	1.1	NS
Age at First Arrest	23.5	5.7	28.8	8.3	48.7	.01
Juvenile Time	.23	1.0	.08	.54	1.9	NS
	%	n	%	n	Chi-Square	Sig.
Race						
African-American	25.9	70	19.8	21	4.42	NS
Hispanic	17.8	48	12.3	13		
White	51.5	139	61.3	65		
Other	4.8	13	6.6	7		
Total	100.0	270	100.0	106		
Marital Status						
Married	40.1	107	46.2	49	24.76	.01
Single	51.7	138	29.2	31		
Divorced	8.2	22	24.6	26		
Total	100.0	267	100.0	106		
Employment						
Full-time	73.5	197	71.5	75	.18	NS
Part-time	12.7	34	13.3	14		
Unemployed	13.8	37	15.2	16		
Total	100.0	268	100.0	105		

possessing more masculine attributes, they were more likely to report greater levels of assertive interactions, isolation, feelings of helplessness, stress, and conflict with staff members and other inmates. These relationships between adjustment and the gendered nature of the environment did not differ significantly by prison setting.[14]

---

[14] The interaction term (prison x gendered environment) was introduced into each of the regression models in Table 14.2. No interaction was significant. The interaction term for assertive interactions, however, approached significance (p = .067). As the gendered nature of the environment increased, both the ICC and FPC inmates reported that they would be more likely to assert themselves in a difficult situation. The relationship between gendered environment and assertive interactions, however, was stronger for the FPC inmates.

Table 14.2

Relationship between Gendered Environment and Inmates' Adjustment

	Assertive Interaction		Isolation		Helplessness		Anxiety	
	B	t	B	t	B	t	B	t
Constant	28.042	12.81	13.869	7.79	13.098	6.37	42.978	8.43
Gender	.208	4.75***	.108	3.02**	.277	6.73***	.418	4.12***
Prison	−3.652	−5.62***	1.021	1.91	1.032	1.68	3.363	2.20*
Age	−.118	−2.74**	.066	1.87	−.020	−.47	.118	1.17
Sentence	.005	−.217	.030	1.70	.015	.73	−.040	−.780
R^2	.117		.048		.150		.083	
F(df)	11.320(4,346)***		4.375(4,348)**		15.147(4,346)***		7.588(4,340)***	
N	347		349		347		341	

	Inmate-Staff Conflict		Inmate-Inmate Conflict	
	B	t	B	t
Constant	1.307	1.95	2.267	4.512
Gender	.029	2.19*	.030	2.98**
Prison	.389	1.95*	.215	1.43
Age	−.030	−2.28*	−.014	−1.46
Sentence	.018	2.70**	−.0001	−.02
R^2	.077		.060	
F(df)	7.070(4,342)***		5.486(4,348)***	
N	343		349	

*$p < .05$; **$p < .01$; ***$p < .001$

Perceptions of Gendered Environment on Safety, Emotional Feedback, Support, and Coercion

We use linear regression to test the relationship between the inmates' assessment of the gendered nature of the environment and their perception of safety, emotional feedback, support, and coercion. Each of the environmental measures is regressed on the gendered nature of the environment, age, sentence, and prison setting.

The gendered nature of the environment significantly influences inmates' perceptions of other environmental attributes (see Table 14.3). Inmates defining their environment as more masculine were more likely to report lower levels of safety, lower levels of emotional feedback and support, and greater levels

Table 14.3
Relationship between Gendered Environment and Inmates' Perceptions of the Environment

	Emotional Feedback		Support		Safety		Coercion	
	B	t	B	t	B	t	B	t
Constant	38.219	18.53	47.497	19.86	40.979	16.925	3.722	3.27
Gender	−.211	−5.08***	−.233	−4.85***	−.191	−3.95***	.224	9.76***
Prison	.640	1.04	−.868	−1.21	6.714	9.342***	1.712	5.01***
Age	−.069	−1.70	−.167	−3.55***	.011	.230	.013	.573
Sentence	.005	.231	.014	.590	−.016	−.668	.014	1.27
R^2	.081		.102		.255		.316	
F(df)	7.443(4,340)***		9.654(4,345)***		29.132(4,344)***		39.85(4,349)***	
N	341		346		345		350	

***$p < .001$

of coercion. The relationship between the gendered nature of the environment and environmental attributes did not differ significantly by prison setting.[15]

DISCUSSION

These findings indicate that perceptions of gender are important for inmates' adjustment to the institution. In addition, they show that perceived differences in the gendered nature of the prison environment do not influence inmates' patterns of adjustment differently in the two prison populations.

Gender Matters: The Influence of Environment on Inmates' Adjustment

Regardless of institutional setting, inmates who defined the environment as possessing ultramasculine attributes were more likely to report greater levels of assertiveness, isolation, helplessness, stress, and conflict with other inmates and with the staff. They were also more likely to perceive the environment as providing less safety, support, and emotional feedback, and as more coercive.

---

[15]The interaction term (prison x gendered environment) was introduced into each of the regression models in Table 14.3. No interaction was significant. The interaction term for safety (p = .079), however, approached significance. As the gendered nature of the environment increased, both ICC and FPC inmates described the environment as less safe. The relationship between gendered environment and safety, however, was stronger for the FPC inmates.

These findings support the notion that gendered prison environments may be directly related to adjustment in ways that inhibit rehabilitation. Prior research on inmates' adjustment shows that safety, support, emotional feedback, and positive interactions with others are important to prosocial change (see Goodstein and Wright 1989; Lutze 1998). Yet it appears that these very attributes are compromised in environments that emphasize male sex-role stereotypes. It is disconcerting that ultramasculine environments may be magnified in boot camp prisons which are designed to create a more positive correctional environment; this fact calls into question new programs that basically do "more of the same" in housing male inmates.

These findings suggest that Morash and Rucker (1990) are justified in their concern about creating an environment in shock incarceration programs which actually may promote behavior related to ultramasculine stereotypes, which in turn are believed to be correlated with criminality (see Karner 1998 for a similar discussion related to the military). In this study we offer a possible explanation why inmates in prior studies of shock incarceration programs reported greater levels of conflict (MacKenzie and Shaw 1990), isolation, and helplessness (Lutze 1996b), and reported similar levels of support and emotional feedback than those in traditional prisons (Lutze 1998).

Prison as Support for Masculine Social Groups

We find mixed support for the hypothesis that inmates will perceive boot camp prison to be more masculine than traditional prison, and thus will follow different patterns of adjustment. Although ICC inmates perceived their environment as significantly more masculine than did inmates in traditional prison (in support of Morash and Rucker 1990), inmates at the ICC did not differ overall from traditional inmates in their patterns of adjustment.

A failure to find dramatic or consistent differences between prisons may be related to the general concept that prison environments are designed by men for men, and thus tend to be gendered in similar ways regardless of their design or programmatic intent (Hannah-Moffat 1995; Sim 1994). The ICC may merely reinvent the masculine nature of traditional prisons, thus generating similar outcomes related to adjustment.

The types of behavior in which men engage depend on the type of masculinity that exists in their particular environment or social setting. These environments or social settings serve as the venues in which males find support for their self-identity; ultimately they contribute to the identification of others (Franklin 1984). Therefore, in prison, just as in free society, masculinity is reinforced through social groups and networks. The social setting of prison is an arena in which ultramasculine sex-role stereotypes are promoted and must be confronted, whether or not the individual inmate or staff member subscribes to such beliefs or behavior (see Collier 1998; Toch 1998).

Male inmates and staff members may find it difficult to provide higher levels of support and emotional feedback in programs designed to accomplish rehabilitation because more personal, more caring forms of support are not perceived as acceptable masculine forms of communication. It may be that the prison environment is not "safe" enough to enable an inmate to depart from traditional male paradigms of communication. For instance, because of a lack of trust between all actors in the prison and a fear of being perceived as weak, many men may not transcend the traditional male boundaries, which inhibit the provision of emotional support. Immersion in an ultramasculine setting may hinder the opportunity to incorporate gender-diverse modes of coping; such modes may support personal changes that may enhance success after release.

Patterns of adjustment such as increased isolation, helplessness, and stress also may have negative consequences. For instance, inmates who do not contend effectively with isolation or helplessness may continue, after release, to separate themselves from others who may be helpful in providing services that support law-abiding behavior. On the other hand, inmates who internalize repeated examples of confrontation and assertive interaction as acceptable behavior for gaining control of others may experience problems after release by overasserting their position and refusing to compromise.

It may be that sex-role stereotypes are replicated when the gendered nature of the prison environment is not considered in the creation of new programs such as shock incarceration. Thus prisons are similar to each other, not only because all total institutions function to control and influence inmates' behavior in similar ways (see Goffman 1959), but also because their environments are similarly gendered; thus they reinforce behavior related to sex-role stereotypes that create division between inmates and staff. Reinforcement of ultramasculine sex-role stereotypes actually may contribute to behaviors that perpetuate criminal behavior.

Although this study contributes to the literature on gender and on inmates' adjustment to prison, it also raises many questions that need to be addressed through future research. First, masculinity is not an unidimensional construct. Individuals differ in their adherence to different dimensions of masculinity, depending on demographic characteristics, personality, socialization, and social setting (see Messerschmidt 1993). Consequently, future studies should consider how different types of individuals interact with others (male and female) and with the environment (coercive versus noncoercive settings).

Second, more complex measures should be developed and implemented to assess the gendered nature of the environment and how inmates adjust to different social climates. The environmental and adjustment measures used in this study were derived on the basis of male populations; therefore they also may be gendered so as to influence outcomes.

Finally, it is unknown how individual inmates are affected by ultramasculine prison environments. Are weaker inmates victimized, or do they become the victimizers (see Bernard and McCleary 1996; Newburn and Stanko 1994)? Are aggressive individuals rewarded, and do they become more aggressive as a result (Morash and Rucker 1990)? To more fully understand the existence of ultramasculine environments and how individuals interact with them, researchers must explore these questions more fully.

CONCLUSION

Our findings support the notion that an inmate's ability to undergo prosocial adjustment (the goal of boot camp prisons) may be inhibited if the environment emphasizes ultramasculine values. Such environments, whether located in new, creative prison programs or in traditional prisons, are limited in their ability to provide the freedom and support that inmates need to pursue rehabilitation wholeheartedly. Ultramasculine environments also may inhibit staff members from providing full support to inmates who wish to seek personal change, because they are similarly inhibited by sex-role stereotypes. It is time for criminal justice scholars and criminologists to stop viewing gender bias as applicable only to the evaluation of women, and to begin exploring how sex-role stereotypes influence men negatively and inhibit treatment attempts to change antisocial male behavior.

REFERENCES

Abbott, J. 1981. *In the Belly of the Beast: Letters from Prison.* New York: Vintage Books.

Adler, F. 1975. *Sisters in Crime: The Rise of the New Female Criminal.* New York: McGraw-Hill Book Company.

Ajdukovic, D. 1990. "Psychosocial Climate in Correctional Institutions: Which Attributes Describe It?" *Environment and Behavior* 22:420–432.

Baker, P. and K. Chopik. 1982. "Abandoning the Great Dichotomy: Sex vs. Masculinity-Femininity as Predictors of Delinquency." *Sociological Inquiry* 52:349–357.

Basow, S. 1986. *Gender Stereotypes: Traditions and Alternatives,* Monterey, CA: Brooks/Coles Publishing Company.

Belknap, J. 1996. *The Invisible Woman: Gender, Crime and Justice.* New York: Wadsworth Publishing Co.

Bernard, T. and R. McCleary. (eds.) 1996. *Life Without Parole: Living in Prison Today,* Los Angeles: Roxbury Publishing Company.

Bohlen, C. 1989. "Expansion Sought for Shock Program." *New York Times,* June 8, pp. A20.

Brannon, R. and S. Juni. 1984. "A Scale for Measuring Attitudes About Masculinity." *Psychological Documents* 14(1):6.

Brodus, M. 1991. "Guard Combines Toughness, Concern." *The Flint Journal,* Flint, Michigan.

Burton, V., J. Marquart, S. Cuvelier, L. Alarid, and R. Hunter. 1993. "A Study of Attitudinal Change Among Boot Camp Participants." *Federal Probation* 57:46–52.

Chatterbaugh, K. 1990. *Contemporary Perspectives on Masculinity: Men, Women, and Politics in Modern Society.* Boulder: Westview Press.

Chesney-Lind, M. and R. Shelden. 1998. *Girls, Delinquency, and Juvenile Justice,* (2nd ed.). Cincinnati, OH: Wadsworth Publishing Company.

Collier, R. 1998. *Masculinities, Crime and Criminology.* London: Sage Publications.

Cullen, F., K. Golden, and J. Cullen. 1979. "Sex and Delinquency: A Partial Test of the Masculinity Hypothesis." *Criminology* 17:301–310.

Daly, K. and M. Chesney-Lind. 1988. "Feminism and Criminology." *Justice Quarterly* 5:497–538.

Deaux, K. 1987. "Psychological Constructions of Masculinity and Femininity." Pp. 289–303 in *Masculinity/Femininity: Basic Perspectives,* edited by J. Reinisch, L. Rosenblum, and S. Sanders. New York: Oxford University Press.

Eaton, M. 1993. *Women After Prison.* Philadelphia, PA: Open University Press.

Flanagan, T., and K. Maguire, 1991. *Bureau of Justice Statistics Sourcebook of Criminal Justice Statistics-1991.* Albany, NY: The Hindelang Criminal Justice Research Center.

Franklin, C. 1984. *The Changing Definition of Masculinity.* New York: Plenum Press.

Goffman, E. 1959. *Asylums: Essays on the Social Situation of Mental Patients and Other Inmates.* Chicago: Aldine Publishing Company.

Goodstein, L. and J. Hepburn. 1985. *Determinate Sentencing and Imprisonment: A Failure of Reform.* Cincinnati, OH: Anderson Publishing Company.

Goodstein, L. and K. Wright. 1989. "Inmate Adjustment to Prison." Pp. 229–251 in *The American Prison: Issues in Research and Policy,* edited by L. Goodstein and D. MacKenzie. New York: Plenum Press.

Hannah-Moffat, K. 1995. "Feminine Fortresses: Woman-Centered Prisons?" *The Prison Journal* 75:135–164.

Karner, T. 1998. "Engendering Violent Men: Oral Histories of Military Masculinity." Pp. 197–232 in *Masculinities and Violence,* edited by L. Bowker. London: Sage Publications.

Lockwood, D. 1982. "Reducing Prison Sexual Violence." Pp. 257–265 in *The Pains of Imprisonment,* edited by R. Johnson and H. Toch. Newbury Park, CA: Sage Publications.

Lutze, F. 1998. "Do Boot Camp Prisons Possess a More Rehabilitative Environment Than Traditional Prison? A Survey of Inmates." *Justice Quarterly* 15:547–563.

_____ . 1996a. "Does Shock Incarceration Provide a Supportive Environment for the Rehabilitation of Offenders? A Study of the Impact of a Shock Incarceration Program on Inmate Adjustment and Attitudinal Change." Doctoral dissertation. The Pennsylvania State University.

_____ . 1996b. "The Influence of a Shock Incarceration Program on Inmate Adjustment and Attitudinal Change." A paper presented at the annual meetings of the Academy of Criminal Justice Sciences, Las Vegas, Nevada.

Lutze, F. and D. Brody. 1999. "Mental Abuse as Cruel and Unusual Punishment: Do Boot Camp Prisons Violate the Eighth Amendment?" *Crime and Delinquency* 45:242–255.

Lutze, F. and O. Marenin. 1997. "The Effectiveness of a Shock Incarceration Program and a Minimum Security Prison in Changing Attitudes Toward Drugs." *Journal of Contemporary Criminal Justice* 12:114–138.

MacKenzie, D. 1990. "Boot Camp Prisons: Components, Evaluations, and Empirical Issues." *Federal Probation* 54:44–52.

_____ . 1991. "The Parole Performance of Offenders Released from Shock Incarceration (Boot Camp Prisons): A Survival Time Analysis." *Journal of Quantitative Criminology* 7:213–236.

MacKenzie, D. and H. Donaldson. 1996. "Boot Camp for Women Offenders." *Criminal Justice Review* 21:21–43.

MacKenzie, D., L. Goodstein, and D. Blouin. 1987. "Prison Control and Prisoner Adjustment: An Empirical Test of a Proposed Model." *Journal of Applied Social Psychology* 16:109–228.

MacKenzie, D., L. Gould, L. Riechers, and J. Shaw. 1989. "Shock Incarceration: Rehabilitation or Retribution?" *Journal of Offender Counseling, Services & Rehabilitation* 14:25–40.

MacKenzie, D., and J. Shaw. 1990. "Inmate Adjustment and Change During Shock Incarceration: The Impact of Correctional Boot Camp Programs." *Justice Quarterly* 7:125–150.

_____ . 1993. "The Impact of Shock Incarceration on Technical Violations and New Criminal Activities." *Justice Quarterly* 10:463–487.

MacKenzie, D. and C. Souryal. 1991. "Rehabilitation, Recidivism Reduction Outrank Punishment as Main Goals." *Corrections Today* 53:90–96.

_____ . 1995. "Inmates' Attitude Change During Incarceration: A Comparison of Boot Camp Prison with Traditional Prison." *Justice Quarterly* 12:325–354.

Marcus-Mendoza, S., J. Klein-Saffran, and F. Lutze. 1998. "A Feminist Examination of Boot Camp Prison Programs for Women." *Women and Therapy* 12(1):173–185.

McCorkle, R. 1995. "Correctional Boot Camps and Change in Attitude: Is all This Shouting Necessary? A Research Note." *Justice Quarterly* 12:365–375.

McDermand, D. 1993. "Hard Time: Intensive Program for Female Prisoners Teaches Responsibility." *Bryan-College Station Eagle,* October 3, p. D1. College Station, Texas.

Messerschmidt, J. 1993. *Masculinities and Crime: Critique and Reconceptualization of Theory.* Lanham, MD: Rowman and Littlefield Publishers, Inc.

Money, J. 1987. "Propaedeutics of Diecious G-I/R: Theoretical Foundations for Understanding Dimorphic Gender-Identity/Role." Pp. 13–28 in *Masculinity/Femininity: Basic Perspectives,* edited by J. Reinisch, L. Rosenblum, and S. Sanders. New York: Oxford University Press.

Moos, R. 1968. "The Assessment of the Social Climates of Correctional Institutions." *Journal of Research Crime and Delinquency* 5:173–188.

_____. 1975. *Evaluating Correctional and Community Settings.* New York: Wiley.

Morash, M. and L. Rucker. 1990. "A Critical Look at the Idea of Boot Camp as a Correctional Reform." *Crime and Delinquency* 36:204–222.

Newburn, T. and E. Stanko. 1994. *Just Doing Business? Men, Masculinities and Crime.* New York: Rutledge.

Norland, S., R. Wessell, and N. Shover. 1981. "Masculinity and Delinquency." *Criminology* 19:421–33.

Parent, D. 1989. *Shock Incarceration: An Overview of Existing Programs.* Washington, DC: U.S. Department of Justice.

Pollock-Byrne, J. 1990. *Women, Prison, & Crime.* Pacific Grove, CA: Brooks/Cole Publishing Company.

Rafter, N. 1995. *Partial Justice: Women, Prisons, and Social Control.* (2nd ed.) London: Transaction Publishers.

Roget's II: The New Thesaurus, 3rd ed. 1997.

Sapiro, V. 1990. *Women in American Society: An Introduction to Women's Studies.* (2nd ed.) London: Mayfield Publishing Company.

Sechrest, D. 1989. "Prison 'Boot Camps' Do Not Measure Up." *Federal Probation* 53:15–20.

Sim, J. 1994. "Tougher Than the Rest? Men in Prison." Pp. 100–152 in *Just Doing Business? Men, Masculinities and Crime,* edited by T. Newburn and E. Stanko. New York: Rutledge.

Simon, R. and J. Landis. 1991. *The Crimes Women Commit: The Punishments They Receive.* Lexington Mass: Lexington Books.

Shoemaker, D. and A. Hillery, Jr. 1980. "Violence and Commitment in Custodial Settings." *Criminology* 18:94–102.

Speilberger, C., R. Gorsuch, and R. Lushene, 1970. *Manual for the State-Trait Anxiety Inventory.* Palo Alto: Consulting Psychologists Press.

Steffensmeier, D. 1995. "Trends in Female Crime: It's Still a Man's World." Pp. 89–104 in *The Criminal Justice System and Women: Offenders, Victims, and Workers,* edited by B. Price and N. Sokoloff. New York: McGraw-Hill, Inc.

Stobbe, M. 1993. "Camp is No Picnic for Young Men in Trouble." *The Flint Journal,* August 30, pp. A1:A6. Flint, Michigan.

Stratton, J. and L. Lanza-Kaduce. 1980. Project Report, Mt. Pleasant Medium Security Unit. Unpublished report.

Sykes, G. 1958. *The Society of Captives: A Study of a Maximum Security Prison.* Princeton, NJ: Princeton University Press.

Thomas, C. and C. Foster. 1972. "Prisonization in the Inmate Contraculture." *Social Problems* 20:229–329.

Thompson, E. Jr., C. Grisanti, and J. Pleck. 1985. "Attitudes Toward the Male Role and Their Correlates." *Sex Roles* 13:413–427.

Toch, H. 1977. *Living in Prison: The Ecology of Survival.* New York: The Free Press.

_____. 1998. "Hypermasculinity and Prison Violence." Pp. 168–178 in *Masculinities and Violence,* edited by L. Bowker. London: Sage Publications.

Vetterling-Braggin, M. 1982. *'Femininity,' 'Masculinity,' and 'Androgyny.'* New Jersey: Rowman and Littlefield.

Webster's New World Thesaurus, 3rd ed. 1997.

Wilkinson, K. 1985. "An Investigation of the Contribution of Masculinity to Delinquent Behavior." *Sociological Focus* 18:249–263.

Wilson, T. 1986. "Gender Differences in the Inmate Code." *Canadian Journal of Criminology* 24:397–405.

Wright, K. 1985. "Developing the Prison Environment Inventory." *Journal of Research in Crime and Delinquency* 22:257–277.

————. 1991a. "A Study of Individual, Environmental, and Interactive Effects in Explaining Adjustment to Prison." *Justice Quarterly* 8:217–242.

————. 1991b. "Violent and Victimized in the Male Prison." *Journal of Offender Rehabilitation* 16:1–25.

Wright, K. and L. Goodstein. 1989. "Correctional Environments." Pp. 253–270 in *The American Prison: Issues in Research and Policy,* edited by L. Goodstein and D. MacKenzie. New York: Plenum Press.

Zamble, E. and F. Porporino. 1988. *Coping, Behavior, and Adaption in Prison Inmates.* Kingston, Ontario: Queens University.

SECTION THREE: INSTITUTIONAL ADJUSTMENT FACTORS

DISCUSSION QUESTIONS

1. What, according to Wooldredge's research, are the primary institutional variables that impact on inmate perceptions of prison crowding? How does crowding affect inmates?
2. How are inmate perceptions of AIDS and the risk of being infected by HIV affected by their background? According to the research by Hemmens and Marquart, how do inmates feel about AIDS-related prison policies?
3. How, according to McCorkle, do inmates adjust to violence in prison? What factors influence inmate perceptions of the risk of violence in prison?
4. How are Texas prison gangs organized? According to Fong, what differentiates the various race/ethnic prison gangs?
5. According to the research by Lutze and Murphy, how do the perceptions of inmates in shock incarceration programs differ from the attitudes of inmates in traditional minimum security prisons?

SECTION 4

SOCIETAL ADJUSTMENT
FACTORS

The articles contained in this section, though ostensibly separated into studies of program effectiveness (education and a therapeutic community) and the circumstances experienced by special populations (the mentally retarded inmates in California, black women in pre- and post-slavery Maryland, and women on parole in a western state), are joined by the implication that it is not only the inmate who must and does adjust to incarceration in this country. Correctional institutions, programs, and practices represent societal value placed on treatment, or not, fair and decent practice, or not, of those it incarcerates and supervises. Prisons, parole, and their practices are adjusted based on who the subject is and what the cultural and historical currents are.

Vernetta Young, in her article, "All the Women in the Maryland State Penitentiary: 1812–1869," potently illustrates how race, gender, and cultural context arrange the landscape of experience for those who are disenfranchised. Her study of incarcerated Black women in Maryland before, during, and after the Civil War, illustrates the importance of historical trappings in arranging sentences, their length, and pardons. In almost all instances, Black women were disadvantaged in their contacts with the correctional system because of their race, even when compared with relatively powerless and socially outcast lower-class and immigrant White women of the time.

This social outcast status that Black women and poor White women held in the nineteenth century, and the disadvantages it created for them when they came into contact with the correctional system, is to some degree experienced by mentally retarded inmates in prison today. As Joan Petersilia finds in her study, "Justice For All? Offenders With Mental Retardation and the California Corrections System," being mentally retarded differentially affects the chances for conviction, sentencing, and sentence length of inmates. She argues for a "fairer" system that adjusts to the diminished capacity of some low-risk offenders and recognizes that alternative programming, outside of the correctional complex, might best suit their, and the community's, needs.

Of course a fairer system would require first the recognition that people experience prison and parole differently and then the concomitant adjustment in practice. In the article titled "Collateral Costs of Imprisonment for Women:

Complications of Reintegration," Mary Dodge and Mark R. Pogrebin describe how the prison and parole system for women in a western state may be regarded as less fair because of the cultural and social differences between men and women. In the course of their study, the authors find that the separation from family, particularly children, and the alienation that women in prison and on parole experience is tied to the social stigma and self-shame they are burdened with. They speculate that this stigma and shame, both culturally and self-induced, then explains the destructive behavior of the women on parole and in prison.

In the article titled "A Large-Scale Multidimensional Test of the Effect of Prison Education Programs on Offenders' Behavior," by Kenneth Adams, Katherine J. Bennett, Timothy J. Flanagan, James W. Marquart, Steven J. Cuvelier, Eric Fritsch, Jurg Gerber, Dennis Longmire, and Velmer S. Burton, the authors test the effect of education on institutional infractions and recidivism among inmates released from Texas prisons in 1991 and 1992. What they find is that the educational programs delivered in Texas during this time period were particularly effective with those who needed it most, inmates with low IQs. Moreover, the reduction in recidivism was only experienced if these inmates had at least minimal exposure and involvement in the educational programming while incarcerated.

Kevin Knight, D. Dwayne Simpson and Matthew Hiller in their article "Three-Year Reincarceration Outcomes for In-Prison Therapeutic Community Treatment in Texas" also find that duration, and in the case of TCs, completion, of the program and aftercare renders reduced recidivism of offenders. These last two articles provide evidence that the "nothing works" stranglehold on the community mindset, and the one size fits all sentencing practices that accompanied it, as translated through the new penology paradigm of the last three decades, is worth rethinking and/or abandonment.

CHAPTER 15

ALL THE WOMEN IN THE MARYLAND STATE PENITENTIARY: 1812–1869

Vernetta D. Young

This article examines the role of race in the patterns of incarceration of women in the state of Maryland during three critical periods: pre-Civil War, Civil War, and post-Civil War. Maryland, a border state, was wedged geographically and politically between the forces of slavery and abolition. In addition to race, the author identifies female offenders by examining place of birth, age, and occupation. The author supports the view that "plantation justice" was inapplicable to Blacks in Maryland. The author also suggests that the historical neglect of women in prison can be attributed to the small contribution of "native" White women to the total female prison population. Racial differences in why female offenders were incarcerated and how long they were sentenced are addressed. These differences are examined across the three time periods, noting the focus on controlling Blacks (free and slave), women, and immigrants.

The literature on the early history of prisons emphasizes the small contribution that women made to the total prison population (Pollock-Byrne, 1990; Rafter, 1985b). Historically, this was presented as a rationale for the neglect of this segment of the population. Their small numbers were also used to justify the reluctance to build separate institutions for women until much later in the 19th century.

Our history of these early institutions indicates that women suffered from harsh treatment, overcrowding, and a lack of services (Harris, 1998; Rafter, 1985b). Much of the literature describes the conditions in these institutions and the need to separate male and female inmates. There was little detailed information provided on who these early female offenders were, why they were incarcerated, and how long they were sentenced.

This article was supported in part by a grant from the Howard University Faculty Sponsored Research Program.
THE PRISON JOURNAL, Vol. 81 No. 1, March 2001 113–132 © 2001 Sage Publications, Inc.

The Maryland State Penitentiary was authorized by Resolution 15 of the 1804 Acts of the Maryland General Assembly. Adopting aspects of the Pennsylvania model implemented at the Old Walnut Street Jail in Philadelphia in 1792, the Maryland State Penitentiary was one of the earliest state prisons established in the United States (Shugg, 2000). It opened in Baltimore in 1811.

Women were admitted to the penitentiary at its initial opening, and both men and women were housed in the same institution until 1921. However, the rules governing the management of the penitentiary stipulated that prisoners were to be separated by sex (Shugg, 2000; Wade, 1964). Unlike the male inmates who were isolated from other inmates, Maryland's handling of the female inmates foreshadowed the Auburn system that was introduced several years later. Women were housed in congregate cells located in a separate ward of the dormitory wing of the penitentiary (Shugg, 2000).

Blacks and Whites were also housed in the same institution. According to Gettleman (1962) "Racial segregation was never practiced in Baltimore" (p. 278). However, Shugg (2000) reported that this practice only lasted until the 1830s when the addition of a new dormitory and new workshops made it feasible to separate male prisoners by race. Rafter (1985) indicated that this practice extended to the women: "In Maryland in the early 1930s, for example, black women were housed on one floor of the women's wing at the House of Correction 'in cells with open-grate fronts and screen tops,' whereas white women resided in a less restrictive dorm on the floor above" (p. 152). The data used in this study do not allow us to make any definitive statement as to how early in the history of the penitentiary Black and White female inmates were separated. The suggestion is that race and gender played an important role in the management and control of the penitentiary in the border state of Maryland.

At the time the penitentiary opened, Maryland was divided by industrial and agricultural interests, as well as opinions on the institution of slavery (Evitts, 1974). In addition, the state had a sizable free Black population and a sizable slave population prior to the Civil War. Maryland also geographically separated the northern states from the southern states. The characterization of the state as a border state intent on maintaining its position of neutrality is therefore understandable.

This article will examine the role of race in the patterns of incarceration of women in the state of Maryland during the period 1812 to 1869. Using prisoner records of the Maryland Penitentiary from this time period, I will examine pre- and post-Civil War crime control. The prisoner records will be used to examine demographic differences between Black and White women as well as differences in the types of charges, length of sentences, and actual time served.

PREVIOUS LITERATURE

As noted above, there has been little detailed information published on who early female offenders were, why they were incarcerated, and how long they were sentenced. Rafter (1985b) closely examined women in early-19th- to mid-20th-century New York, Ohio, and Tennessee state prisons, emphasizing the differential treatment of women by race. Rafter (1985b, p. 131) also noted that there was a disproportionate percentage of Black women held in the prisons of the Northeast and the Midwest. In the South, few Blacks, male or female, were held in state prisons before the Civil War. Incarcerated women tended to be 21 or older, unmarried, working-class, and mostly sentenced for property crimes.

Butler (1989) acknowledged the importance of studying race in this era of slavery and reconstruction. Using the prison registers of Louisiana, Texas, Kansas, Nebraska, and Montana from 1865 to 1910, Butler reported that female inmates were usually young and uneducated. She added that Black women were more likely to be sent to the state penitentiary, serve their full sentence, and be excluded from pardon procedures than White women who committed comparable crimes (pp. 34–35).

In a later work, Butler (1997) focused on women sentenced to male state prisons because of the absence of separate female penal institutions in the western United States between 1865 and 1915. She argued that the social, economic, and political disadvantages experienced by women in the larger society were reflected in their treatment in the prisons. These inequities were compounded by race and class divisions, thereby intensifying the violent nature of institutional treatment. Her earlier findings of racial differences in the sentence length, time served, and methods of release were confirmed. In addition, Butler reported that female prisoners were used to provide domestic chores for the maintenance of the institutions and sexual services for the guards and male inmates.

Much of the detail presented by Rafter (1985a, 1985b) and Butler (1989, 1997) about women in prison covers the post-Civil War period. As a result, we know little about the handling of women in state prisons prior to the Civil War. In addition, the Civil War has been viewed as pivotal in the discussion of the punishment of Blacks in America. Hindus (1976) and Ayers (1984) argued that "plantation justice," which tended to divert Blacks from the state criminal justice system prior to the Civil War, was inapplicable to free Blacks who represented a significant proportion of the Black population in the upper South. The paucity of information on women in prison prior to the Civil War and the debate over the applicability of plantation justice to the population of Maryland, a border state, challenge us to pose a number of questions:

1. Were Black women during the antebellum period in Maryland more likely than White women to be sent to the state penitentiary?
2. Did Black female offenders differ demographically from White female offenders, especially with respect to age?
3. Were Black women committed for the same crimes as White women? Were property offenses the most likely for both groups of offenders?
4. Were Black women more likely to serve their full sentences? Were Black women more likely to be excluded from the pardon procedure?

In general, do the descriptions of female offenders, the crimes that resulted in their incarceration, and the sentences and treatment they received in the state of Maryland from 1812 to 1869 present a picture of prison history that differs from studies that described women in prison primarily during the post-Civil War period?

DATA SOURCE

Prisoner records of the Maryland State Penitentiary from 1812 to 1869 were gathered from the Hall of Records in Annapolis, Maryland. The prisoner records provide inmate demographic information (place of birth, race, ethnicity, age, sex, status [free/slave], place of residence, and occupation before and during incarceration), the county of conviction, the offense charge and sentence, and data on actual time served and how discharge occurred.

WHO WERE THE FEMALE INMATES?

Race of Offenders

There were 1,203 women received at the Maryland State Penitentiary from 1812 to 1869, an average of about 21 women each year. As indicated in Figure 15.1, the number of inmates peaked at the beginning of the period under study and again during the post-Civil War period. Blacks accounted for the majority of the incarcerated population (72%), with an average of 15 Black women received each year.[1] Whites made up the remaining 28%, with an average of 6 inmates received per year.[2] White women outnumbered Black women in the state prison in only 6 years out of the total 58-year period. As in the prisons of the Northeast, the Midwest, and the West (Butler, 1989, 1997; Rafter, 1985a, 1985b), Black women were also disproportionately held in the Maryland State Penitentiary.

During the antebellum period (1812–1860), 953 female prisoners were received at the Maryland State Penitentiary for an average of about 19 women received each year. This was also 79% of the total data set. Black women outnumbered Whites in 45 of the 49 years. There were more than twice as many Black female prisoners (70%) as White female prisoners (30%). The first time that White female inmates outnumbered Black female inmates occurred early in the history of the institution, with White women accounting for 75% of the fe-

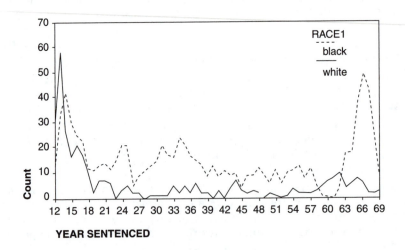

Figure 15.1 Race of Offender by Year Sentenced

male prison population in 1812 and 64% in 1813. In fact, more than one half of all White female prisoners were incarcerated early in the history of the institution, between 1812 and 1818, compared to just over 1 out of 5 or 21% of Black female prisoners.

White women again account for the largest proportion of the female prison population as we approach the beginning of the Civil War: 83% in 1859 and 100% in 1860. It is important to point out that during these 2 years, only 13 women were received in the penitentiary, 6 in 1859 and 7 in 1860. Clearly, in Maryland during the antebellum period, Black women outnumbered Whites even though Black prisoners accounted for a somewhat smaller proportion of the total number of Black prisoners (77%) than White prisoners did of the total number of White prisoners (86%) for the time period under study. Plantation justice, if it operated in Maryland, did not successfully divert Black women from the criminal justice system.

During this period, Maryland experienced a decrease in its slave population and an increase in its free Black population, resulting in a 1:1 ratio by 1860 (Walsh & Fox, 1974). With forces within the state legislating to remove Blacks from the prison and maintain control through alternative measures such as fines, public whippings, the county jail, or banishment (Laws of Maryland, 1817, 1825, 1826), the fact that a sizable number of Black women were incarcerated seems incongruous.

Black women outnumbered White women for 3 of the 5 years from 1861 to 1865, the Civil War period. The average number of women received each year increased to 23. Only 8 female inmates were received in 1861, and they were all White. In 1862, White women received at the penitentiary numbered 10, or 71% of all inmates. Two points stand out. First, most of the inmates were received later in the Civil War period. Second, as we move toward the end of the war, Black female inmates as a proportion of total female population increase.

Even though the penitentiary received just 114 female prisoners, the racial distribution was about the same as during the pre-Civil War years, with Black women accounting for 68% of the total population and White women accounting for 32%. Although Black women outnumbered White women as a proportion of total prisoners, there was not much difference in their contributions to their respective populations. More specifically, Black women incarcerated during the war accounted for 9% of all Black women incarcerated during the period under study, whereas the White women accounted for 11% of all White women incarcerated during this time.

Finally, throughout the post-Civil War period (1866–1869) covered in this study, Black female prisoners again outnumbered White female prisoners. The Maryland State Penitentiary received 136 female prisoners. This average of 34 women received per year was a significant increase from the average received in the preceding time periods. Black women accounted for 90% of the total population (123 inmates) and White women accounted for 10% (13 inmates). Black women accounted for a much larger proportion of the female prison population during the post-Civil War period (90%) than during either the antebellum period (70%) or the Civil War period (68%). Moreover, 14% of Blacks but only 4% of Whites were incarcerated after the conclusion of the war. This pattern of increased incarceration of women, especially Black women, in the post-Civil War period is similar to that reported by Butler (1997) in Texas, Kansas, and Missouri.

In summary, these data indicate that Black women outnumbered White women in the penitentiary from 1812 to 1869 as well as during the antebellum, Civil War, and post-Civil War periods. This was especially dramatic during the post-Civil War period. So, the Maryland data support Rafter's (1985a) finding that Black women often outnumbered Whites in custodial units. However, although Maryland practiced slavery, its classification as a border state rather than a southern state prevents any challenge to the statement "that during the antebellum period in the South this generalization did not hold" (p. 240).

Place of Birth of Offenders

Almost all of the female inmates (90%) sentenced to the penitentiary were born in the United States. Furthermore, most were born in Maryland (about 78%). There were significant differences in place of birth by race. Black women were much more likely to have been born in Maryland (91%) than were White women (44%). Only 9% of Black women were born outside the state of Maryland, with just 3 Black female inmates born outside the United States, in Jamaica, West Indies.

In the case of White women, 21% were born in the United States but not in Maryland. Thirty-four percent of White female inmates were born outside of the United States. The two foreign countries making the largest contribution to the White female penitentiary population were Ireland and Germany (22% and 8%, respectively).

McCaffrey (1976) reported that during this same time period, between 1818 and 1870, large numbers of Irish people entered the United States. These data suggest that a number of these women were among those incarcerated in the state of Maryland. Although the age of the offender will be discussed in more detail below, it is interesting to note that the women who were born outside of the United States were on average considerably older, a mean age of 33, than those who were born in the United States, a mean age of 25. In addition, for close to one quarter of the foreign-born female inmates, no occupation was listed.

There are any number of possible scenarios. These may have been women driven to crime as a result of being left homeless and poor due to the death of their husbands, the laws regulating property rights, and the absence of family in the United States.[3] Otherwise, these may have been women who landed in prison as a result of their lack of legitimate or marketable occupational skills.

During the pre-Civil War period, almost 70% of incarcerated White women were born in the United States (49% in Maryland), with Ireland accounting for 19% and Germany 6% of the population. This decreased to a low of only 31% of incarcerated White women reportedly born in the United States during the Civil War (11% in Maryland). Ireland accounted for 36% of the incarcerated White female population and Germany contributed 25%. During the post-Civil War period, the majority (54%) of White female inmates was again born in the United States (31% in Maryland). However, Ireland accounted for almost 39% and Germany added 8%.

Foreign-born women, especially Irish women, increased as a proportion of the total White female prison population during the Civil War. According to Smith's (1990) study of female prisoners in Ireland:

The director's reports do show a gradually aging population. These women had moved from one public or private institution to another for most of their lives. Freed from prison, unable to obtain lawful work, and knowing only other offenders, they ended up in prison again. Crofton himself argued that ex-convict women should emigrate and begin again. (p. 77)

Perhaps these are women who tried and failed in Ireland, emigrated to the United States, and ended up again in a public institution but on another shore.

A look at the race of the inmates and the place of birth indicates that the majority of the female inmate population were not native White Marylanders but were more likely to be Black or foreign born. Given the historical time period, it could be argued that the neglect of the study of women in prison was, in part, attributed to the fact that Black women and foreign women constituted the largest proportion of this segment of the prison population.

Age of Offenders

The state of Maryland did not establish a separate institution for White juvenile women until 1855. Just more than one decade later, in 1866, the Maryland Industrial School for (White) girls was incorporated (Young, 1994, pp. 249–250). Consequently, for the time period under study, there were minimal separate correctional provisions for White juvenile women and none for Black juvenile women. Therefore, Black and White juvenile women were likely to be housed with adult women.

Female prisoners ranged from 10 to 80 years of age over the time period, with both the youngest and the oldest prisoners identified as Black women. In the case of White women, the youngest prisoner was 13 years old and the oldest was 69 years old. However, young prisoners were relatively rare, with those 14 years of age or younger accounting for less than 3% of the total female prison population, either Black or White. Similarly, there were very few older female prisoners housed in the Maryland State Penitentiary. Just 7 women older than 60 were identified.

Butler (1997) noted that in the prisons of the West, "youthfulness marked the female inmate" (p. 98). This characterization aptly applies to the Maryland female prison population, especially to Black female prisoners. The 18 to 24 and 25 to 34 age groups accounted for more than 60% of the total female prison population (37% and 27%, respectively). The mean age for the women prisoners was 26. However, there were significant differences by race. The 18 to 24 age category accounted for the largest proportion of Black female prisoners (41%) followed by the 25 to 34 age group (24%), whereas for White female prisoners the reverse was the case (see Figure 15.2). The 25 to 34 age category accounted for the largest proportion of White women prisoners (35%), with the younger 18 to 24 age category adding 28%. Moreover, those younger than 18 accounted for three times as many Black prisoners (22%) as White prisoners (7%). The mean age for Black female prisoners was 24, whereas that for White female prisoners was 30. In addition, for Black women the median age was 22 with a mode of 18, whereas for White women the median age was 27 with a mode of 25. Clearly, Black women were incarcerated at a much younger age than White women.

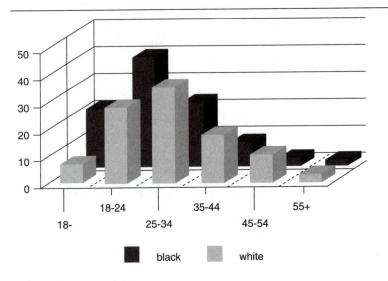

Figure 15.2 Percentage of Inmates by Age

As noted above, this 58-year time period covers the pre-Civil War, the Civil War, and the post-Civil War. However, the peak ages for Black (18–24) and White (25–34) female inmates remained constant over the three time periods. The number of Black female inmates younger than 25 increased from 59% of the total Black female incarcerated population during the pre-Civil War period to 71% during the Civil War period. During this same time period, the number of White female inmates younger than 25 decreased from 37% to 31%. The proportion of the total Black female inmate population accounted for by young Black women compared to the proportion of the total White female inmate population accounted for by young White women increased from a ratio of 1.6 to 1 in the pre-Civil War period to a ratio of 2.3 to 1 during the Civil War. The most dramatic differences were evident during the post-Civil War period. Almost three quarters of all Black inmates were younger than 25, whereas less than 8% of Whites were classified as young offenders. This is a ratio of 9.6 to 1 for young Black inmates relative to young White inmates. We must view this with caution because these data cover a very short post-Civil War period.

Place of Residence

The records provided information on the place of residence that included the 23 counties in the state of Maryland as well as the U.S. Army, the high seas, the almshouse, the penitentiary, and locales outside the state. As expected, none of the women's residences were in the U.S. Army or on the high seas. There were also no women listed as residing in the almshouse. One Black woman resided in the penitentiary, and 35 women (7 Black and 28 White) resided outside of the state. The remaining inmates lived in the counties of Maryland prior to their incarceration.

Generally, counties on both the eastern shore and the southern sector of the state were classified as rural and predominantly agricultural, whereas the western counties were viewed as rural and more industrial. Baltimore City was the major urban area in the state during the time period under study.

A look at place of residence indicated that almost three fourths (74%) of the inmates lived in Baltimore County/City prior to their incarceration. There were some interesting differences by race. Although 7 of every 10 Black female prisoners came from Baltimore, Talbot (4%), Queen Anne (3%), and Worcester (3%), all eastern shore counties, made modest contributions to the Black female prison population. White female prisoners were also most likely to reside in Baltimore (83%), with the next largest proportion (8%) from outside of Maryland.

Both Black and White women were more likely to reside in Baltimore, the more urban area of Maryland. However, it is interesting to note that a number of Black female inmates had lived in more rural and possibly more agricultural counties of the state prior to their incarceration. It is not possible to determine whether these inmates were slaves because the practice of indicating status (slave, servant, or free) was sporadic. In fact, slave status was entered for only 9 years for a total of 21 inmates.

Place of Conviction

Not surprising, the place of conviction mirrored the place of residence for the female inmates. Most (77%) were convicted in Baltimore. Talbot (3%), Queen Ann (2%), Worcester (2%), and Frederick (2%) counties accounted for an additional 10%.

Again, there were some differences by race. For Black female inmates, 72% were convicted in Baltimore, with Talbot, Queen Ann, Worcester, and Frederick, in that order, accounting for an additional 12%. However, a much larger proportion of White female inmates were convicted in Baltimore (89%), with Frederick (2%) and Washington (2%) accounting for the larger of the remaining proportions.

Occupation

Preprison occupational information was recorded for 925 or 77% of those incarcerated. Prison officials identified 99 different occupations in which inmates were employed prior to their incarceration. However, the majority of inmates were employed in just 5 areas. Most of the inmates, Black (50%) and White (33%), worked as housemaids. Black women worked as spinsters (27%), wash women (8%), seamstresses (3%), and spinners (3%), whereas White women were employed as seamstresses (18%), spinsters (16%), spinners (12%), and wash women (4%).

There were a number of interesting findings. First, the prison officials classified spinsters as an occupation. Was this a euphemism for involvement in prostitution that was not included in the listing of occupations as some have suggested? Or were the two designations separate and distinct and more in line with the argument presented by Bullough and Bullough (1987) that the predominance of men unsuitable for marriage led to both spinsterhood and prostitution? More specifically, Bullough and Bullough reported that "inevitably, a significant number of women never married, and the spinster aunt became an important institution in nineteenth-century American life. Other women, however, turned to prostitution as a temporary occupation" (p. 216). Second, White women were five times as likely to be employed in the skilled jobs, seamstresses and spinners, as were Black women. Even so, the employment history suggests that most of the women were working-class women employed in service positions. Similarly, Butler (1997) reported that the women imprisoned in the West after the Civil War had also been employed in low-paying jobs.

Rafter (1985b) reported that women in state prisons were involved in very minimal work activity. Harm (1992, p. 94) characterized the work activity of female prisoners as the making and washing of uniforms for male prisoners. According to Shugg (2000), women and men in the Maryland State Penitentiary worked in separate yards. Prison occupational information was recorded for 1,115 or 93% of those incarcerated. Prison officials identified 86 specific occupations to which inmates were assigned while incarcerated. However, the majority of inmates were assigned to just 3 areas: spinning, sewing, and washing. Most of the inmates, Black (38%) and White (45%), worked as spinners. The next largest percentage of Black women (17%) were assigned to washing, with 10% assigned to housework and an additional 10% assigned to sewing. One quarter of the White women were assigned to sewing (25%), and an additional 7% were assigned to housework.

It is interesting that almost all of the female inmates were given a work assignment. However, almost 7 out of 10 assignments were limited to three areas. The most common assignment, spinning, seemed to be more in line with industrial commitments than institutional maintenance. It is clear that the female inmates at the Maryland State Penitentiary were involved in more than the making and washing of uniforms. Although assignments were scattered over the other areas, it is difficult to attribute any meaning to the assignments because the numbers were so small. Still, the bulk of prison labor performed by the female inmates seemed to be in line with their gender roles, supporting Butler's (1997) findings of the replication of female labor evident in state prisons in the West.

In summary, the women sentenced to the Maryland State Penitentiary were young (18–24), Black or foreign born, living in Baltimore County/City, and working as housemaids. Moreover, the Black female inmate was younger, more likely to be born in the United States, and drawn from a more diverse setting than her White counterpart.

CRIME DATA

The penitentiary records contain data on the types of crime, the length of sentence, the actual time served, how prisoners were discharged, and whether the prisoner was a repeat offender. In this section, I will examine each of these criminal justice characteristics as they relate to the women offenders. I will also examine racial differences.

Why Were the Female Prisoners Incarcerated?

Forty-two specific crime categories were identified from the prisoner records. These were recoded into four general categories: felony, property, violent, and "else." The property category included larceny, arson, horse stealing, and bur-

Table 15.1
Type of Crime by Race

	Felony	Violent	Property	Else	Total
Black	10%	4%	77%	8%	863
	(87)	(38)	(667)	(71)	
White	7%	3%	54%	37%	338
	(23)	(10)	(181)	(124)	
Total	110	48	848	195	1,201

glary. The violent crime category consisted of murder in the first and second degree, manslaughter, assault to murder, cutting ears, assault to rape, rape, mail robbery, and robbery. The felony category remained. Unfortunately, I have no specific information about this category. All that one can say is that these were serious offenses. The else category was composed of 28 crimes, only 9 of which resulted in the incarceration of at least one woman.[4]

More than 7 of every 10 prisoners (71%) were imprisoned for serious property crimes, with larceny accounting for the largest proportion (67%). This supports findings from earlier studies (Harm, 1992; Rafter, 1985a, 1985b). The miscellaneous else category accounted for 16% of all convictions, with vagrancy contributing 12% to the total.

Table 15.1 indicates differences in type of crime by race. Of the Black women, 77% were imprisoned for serious property crimes (73% for larceny), 10% for an unspecified felony, 8% for the miscellaneous else, and 4% for violent crime. Property crimes also accounted for the largest proportion of White female prisoners incarcerated (54%). Of the White female prisoners, 37% were incarcerated for else.

Almost all of these prisoners were incarcerated for vagrancy. In fact, more than 80% of the White women were incarcerated either for larceny (52%) or vagrancy (32%). The remaining White female prisoners were convicted of unspecified felonies (7%) and violent crime (3%).

Serious property crime accounted for the incarceration of the largest proportion of both Black and White female prisoners. The most dramatic difference by race is evident in the else category. Almost five times as many White women as Black women were incarcerated for the miscellaneous else category. As noted above, almost all of those incarcerated for the miscellaneous else category were incarcerated for vagrancy. It has also been suggested that vagrancy cases had overtones of sexual promiscuity (Rafter, 1985b, p. 117). Earlier studies found that offenses against morality committed by Blacks were generally ignored, whereas White women were more likely to be incarcerated for these public order offenses because

these offenses either were taken more seriously and seen as a greater threat to public order when committed by White women or that these offenses were more visible to law enforcement officers and that complaints about such behavior were made more frequently by members of the White community. (Harm, 1992, p. 99)

Throughout each of the time periods under discussion, more female offenders, Black and White, were incarcerated for property crime than for any of the other types of crime. There were, however, some interesting differences. There was much more variety in the types of crimes women were incarcerated for during the pre-Civil War period than during the other time periods. This is especially true for White female offenders, with 48% incarcerated for property offenses, 42% for miscellaneous offenses, 8% for a felony, and 2% for violent crime during the pre-Civil War period.

The Maryland legislature passed a number of statutory provisions during the pre-Civil War period that may have affected the types of crimes and the length of sentences imposed on Black women. For example, in 1817 legislation was passed that provided that the minimum sentence to the penitentiary for a Black person must exceed 1 year (Laws of Maryland, 1817, chap. 72). Another example of legislation that may have affected prison admissions was the 1858 supplement that provided that free Blacks convicted of larceny and other crimes be sentenced not to prison but to public sale (Laws of Maryland, 1858, chap. 324). These data do not allow us to determine the impact of this legislation, but the passage of the legislation requires that the findings be presented with caution.

During the Civil War, White women were considerably more likely to have been incarcerated for property crimes (89%), whereas during the post-Civil War period they were more likely to be incarcerated for any of the other offenses (77%). In the case of Black women, during the pre-Civil War period, 73% were incarcerated for property crime, 13% for a felony, 10% for miscellaneous offenses, and 4% for violent crime. During both the Civil War and the post-Civil War periods, 90% of Black female prisoners were incarcerated for property crime.

How Long Were They Sentenced?

Inmates received sentences from less than 1 day to life in prison. Most inmates (68%) were sentenced to less than 3 years, with near equal proportions sentenced to between 1 and 2 years (31%) and between 2 and 3 years (31%). In fact, only 7% of the inmates received sentences longer than 5 years.

More than one half of the White women (55%) were sentenced to 1 year or less in the penitentiary. This was almost twice the proportion of Black women receiving a sentence of this length (29%). More than one third of the Black women but just about one fifth of the White women were sentenced to 2 years in the penitentiary. Only three life sentences were imposed during this time period, and they were imposed on Black women as a result of convictions for first-degree murder. No White woman was convicted of this offense. Moreover, no White woman was sentenced to more than 14 years, whereas 10 Black women were so sentenced. The 10 Black women were convicted of the following offenses: first-degree murder (4), second-degree murder (5), and aiding a runaway (1). Next to the 3 Black women sentenced to life for first-degree murder, the longest sentence was 43 years for aiding a runaway. The longest sentence meted out to a White woman was 14 years for larceny, with one other White woman receiving a sentence of 9 years for cutting off the ears of the victim. The racial differences in the types of crimes and the differential sentence lengths evident in these data were also evident in Butler's (1997) study of prisons in the American West.

Given the time period under consideration, it is interesting to note that only 1 Black woman was incarcerated for counterinsurgency (10 years) and just 4 were incarcerated for aiding a runaway. In addition, the 2 White women who were incarcerated for child slavery received sentences of 18 months and 3 years, respectively.

In summary, Black women were sentenced for longer periods of time than White women. However, Black women were also sentenced for more serious offenses than White women. These data do not allow us to determine whether this was related to a difference in the behavior of Black and White women or a difference in the treatment of these two groups by the criminal justice system.

Actual Time Served

One half of the women served 1 year or less. There were significant differences by race. As noted above, about 1 of every 4 Black women received a sentence of 1 year or less, with a little more than 4 of 10 (43%) actually serving 1 year or less. On the other hand, even though a little more than one half of the White women were sentenced to 1 year or less in the penitentiary, more than two thirds (67%) actually served 1 year or less. These data suggest that for a large number of Black women, the actual time served was significantly less than the original sentence. Still, a larger proportion of Black women served more time than White women, with the racial differences increasing as time served increased.

Throughout the time periods under study, Black women served more time in prison than White women. During the pre-Civil War period, 38% of Black female inmates served 1 year or less, 29% served 2 years, 26% served between 3 and 5 years, and 6% served 6 years or more. In the case of White female inmates, 68% served 1 year or less, 14% served 2 years, 16% served between 3 and 5 years, and 2% served 6 years or more. Over the years, the proportion of Black inmates serving 1 year or less increased from 50% during the Civil War to 63% during the post-Civil War period. However, this was also the case for White inmates, with 53% serving 1 year or less during the Civil War and 85% serving 1 year or less during the post-Civil War period.

Discharged

The methods of release for inmates at the penitentiary included the following: sentence expired, pardoned, died, or sold. Most of the prisoners had their sentences expire, meaning they served their total sentences (86%), with 7% dying during their term of incarceration and 6% receiving pardons. Blacks were just as likely to serve their full terms as Whites. However, Blacks were more likely to die in prison (9%) than Whites (2%). This difference could be attributed to older women serving long sentences or young women becoming ill after incarceration (Rafter, 1985b, p. 124). It could also be related to the nature of medical treatment of inmates, in particular of Black inmates. On the other hand, Whites were more likely to receive pardons (11%) than Blacks (4%). During the time period under study, only 9 female inmates, 8 Black and 1 White, were sold. This accounted for less than 1% of the total female prison population.

Repeat Offenders

Of the 1,203 female inmates, only 117, less than 10%, were identified as repeat offenders. Of this group, 73% were identified as two-time offenders, 21% as three-time offenders, and 6% as four-time offenders. Blacks accounted for 70% of the repeat offenders, and Whites accounted for 29%. Although most of the repeaters, Black (76%) and White (65%), were two-time offenders, a larger proportion of White (29%) than Black (18%) were three-time offenders.

The vast majority of the women sentenced to the Maryland State Penitentiary from 1812 to 1869 were sentenced for property offenses, mainly larceny. This was the case for both Black and White inmates. White inmates were more likely than Blacks to be sentenced for vagrancy. Offenders as a group were sentenced to less than 3 years; however, White female inmates received shorter sentences and served less time than Black female inmates. Black inmates were also less likely to be pardoned than White inmates. These data demonstrate the significance of race in the handling and treatment of the female inmates at the Maryland State Penitentiary.

DISCUSSION

These data have accorded us a glimpse of women in the Maryland State Penitentiary from 1812 to 1869. This study examined female inmates in a male penitentiary in a state in which throughout the pre-Civil War period Blacks occupied two opposing statuses, free and slave. We looked at those received at the institution through slavery, the Civil War, and the post-Civil War period when men and women and Blacks and Whites were housed together.

Earlier studies attributed the historical neglect of women in prison to the small contribution women made to the total prison population. The suggestion here is that this historical neglect may be attributed to the small contribution of "native" White women to the total female prison population. These data indicate that Black women were indeed incarcerated in the state during the antebellum period and beyond. They outnumbered White women throughout the time period under study. This finding provides some support for the argument presented by Hindus (1976) and Ayers (1984) that plantation justice was inapplicable to free Blacks. It was also the case that the White women who were incarcerated were likely to have been born outside the state of Maryland, with a large number from Ireland and Germany. It is instructive that Black and foreign-born women, two groups that did not fit the acceptable standard of womanhood of the time, were more likely to be incarcerated than native White women.

Previous literature about women in prison covered the post-Civil War period. This study provides information from one state on who early female offenders were, why they were incarcerated, and how long they were sentenced. I also compared female offenders across the three time periods: pre-Civil War, Civil War, and post-Civil War.

There were age differences among the female inmates by race and place of birth. As a group, the women serving time in the penitentiary were young, 18 to 24, with Black inmates tending to be younger than White inmates. However, the foreign-born White women were somewhat older than their native counterparts. The female prisoners resided and were convicted in Baltimore and worked as housemaids. Black inmates were more likely than White inmates to have been engaged in unskilled occupations.

The Maryland legislature introduced a number of provisions to control the Black population. Clearly, attempts to restrict admission to the penitentiary to Whites failed. Measures to limit the admission of Blacks and restrict the offenses they could be incarcerated for were introduced. These data indicate that Black women were admitted to the penitentiary. Of course, it is possible that without the legislation, more would have been admitted. Most of the inmates, Black and White, were committed for property offenses, namely larceny. These data cannot discern the impact of an imposed restriction on the types of offenses for which Black women could be incarcerated. The biggest difference in the type of crime by race was evident in the miscellaneous else category. White inmates were much more likely to have been committed for this category of offense, which consisted largely of vagrancy, than Black inmates. As noted above, it is possible that the charge of vagrancy was a euphemism for sex offenses that were viewed as more serious when a White woman was involved.

Although most inmates tended to serve their full sentences, Black inmates did receive longer sentences and served more time than their White counterparts. Black inmates were also less likely to be pardoned. These findings support earlier reports by Rafter (1985a, 1985b) and Butler (1989, 1997) of racial discrimination in the handling of women inmates.

The picture of the female offender presented here and that derived from earlier reports is of a young, working-class property offender. Earlier works have stressed the importance of looking at geography. These data reemphasize the importance of placing our discussions within a historical context. This is important in our discussions of racial differences as well as in our discussions of gender differences. The Maryland State Penitentiary opened when the state had a large slave population. As the free Black population of the state increased, the penitentiary was subject to the political juggernaut of a border state caught between abolitionist and slave factions. In the Maryland data, we see the impact of slavery on the differential treatment of Black and White female prisoners. In the Maryland data, we see the differential treatment of native and foreign-born women. This highlights the view that when we move to examine the impact of a movement or an event on women, it is essential that we recognize that not all women are White; that there is an intersection of race and gender and a number of other characteristics. The recognition of the differential impact of historical events on different people is crucial to our understanding of these events.

NOTES

1. In the prison records, inmates were identified by complexion rather than race: black, white, other, yellow, fair, dark, light, ruddy, and brown. Consequently, race was derived by cross-referencing complexion with place of birth and status, slave or free, as well as noting the descriptions of hair. In addition, there were many notions indicating that the prisoner was colored or mulatto.
2. There were only two cases of other women; therefore, the information presented will examine differences between Black and White female prisoners.
3. This scenario was suggested by an anonymous reviewer.

4. This listing of offenses included vagrancy, stolen goods, kidnapping, gaming, counterin-surgency, aiding a runaway, killing a horse, fraud, and child slavery.

REFERENCES

Ayers, E. L. (1984). *Vengeance and justice: Crime and punishment in the 19th-century American South.* New York: Oxford University Press.

Bullough, V., & Bullough, B. (1987). *Women and prostitution: A social history.* Buffalo, NY: Prometheus Books.

Butler, A. M. (1989). Still in chains: Black women in western prisons, 1865–1910. *Western Historical Quarterly, 20,* 19–35.

Butler, A. M. (1997). *Gendered justice in the American West: Women prisoners in men's penitentiaries 1865–1915.* Chicago: University of Illinois Press.

Evitts, W. J. (1974). *A matter of allegiances: Maryland from 1850 to 1861.* Baltimore: Johns Hopkins University Press.

Gettleman, M. E. (1992). The Maryland Penitentiary in the age of Toqueville, 1828–1842. In Eric H. Monkkonen (Ed.), *Crime and Justice in American History* (Vol. 6, pp. 271–292). New York: Saur. (Original work published 1962).

Harm, N. (1992). Social policy on women prisoners: A historical analysis. *Affilia: Journal of Women and Social Work, 7,* 90–108.

Harris, M. K. (1998). Women's imprisonment in the United States: A historical analysis of female offenders through the early 20th century. *Corrections Today, 60,* 74–78.

Hindus, M. (1976). Black justice under White law: Criminal prosecutions of Blacks in antebellum South Carolina. *Journal of American History, 63,* 575–599.

Maryland. (1817). An Act concerning crime and punishments (Chap. 72, suppl.). In *Laws of 1817: Laws made and passed by the General Assembly of the State of Maryland.*

Maryland. (1825). An Act concerning crime and punishments (Chap 93, suppl.). In *Laws of 1825: Laws made and passed by the General Assembly of the State of Maryland.*

Maryland. (1826). An Act concerning crime and punishments (Chap. 229, suppl.). In *Laws of 1826: Laws made and passed by the General Assembly of the State of Maryland.*

Maryland. (1858). An Act to modify the punishment of free negroes, convicted of larceny and other crimes in this state (Chap. 324). In *Laws of 1858: Laws made and passed by the General Assembly of the State of Maryland.*

McCaffrey, L. (1976). *The Irish diaspora in America.* London: Indiana University Press.

Pollock-Byrne, J. (1990). *Women, prison, and crime.* Pacific Grove, CA: Brooks/Cole.

Rafter, N. H. (1985a). Gender, prisons, and prison history. *Social Science History, 9,* 233–247.

Rafter, N. H. (1985b). *Partial justice: Women in state prisons, 1800–1935.* Boston: Northeastern University Press.

Shugg, W. (2000). *A monument to good intentions: The story of the Maryland Penitentiary, 1804–1999.* Baltimore: Maryland Historical Society.

Smith, B. (1990). The female prisoner in Ireland, 1855–1878. *Federal Probation, 54*(4), 69–81.

Wade, R. C. (1964). *Slavery in the cities.* New York: Oxford University Press.

Walsh, R., & Fox, W. L. (Eds.). (1974). *Maryland: A history, 1632–1974.* Baltimore: Johns Hopkins University Press.

Young, V. D. (1994). Race and gender in the establishment of juvenile institutions: The case of the South. *The Prison Journal, 74,* 244–265.

CHAPTER 16

JUSTICE FOR ALL? OFFENDERS WITH MENTAL RETARDATION AND THE CALIFORNIA CORRECTIONS SYSTEM

Joan Petersilia

California correctional agencies handle an estimated 22,000 adults and juveniles with mental retardation (MR)—or 2% of all probationers and 4% of all those in custody. MR inmates in California are not usually identified or given specialized programming. A lawsuit, Clark and Woods v. California, was recently filed against the California Department of Corrections on behalf of all MR inmates, and this suit has created renewed policy interest in this population. Studies show that MR offenders are more likely to be convicted, receive a prison sentence, and serve a greater portion of their prison term than nondisabled offenders. Sentencing low-risk MR persons to intermediate sanctions may save money and reduce recidivism rates. The Americans With Disabilities Act (ADA) requires that all corrections agencies establish screening and rehabilitation programs specifically for MR offenders. Such policies will create a fairer system—one that provides equal opportunity, protection from victimization, and appropriate treatment.

DIMENSIONS OF THE PROBLEM

Duane Silva, a 23-year-old from Tulare County, California, sits today in a California prison cell serving 25 years to life, having been convicted of stealing a VCR and jewelry in a 1994 residential burglary. Silva is mentally retarded (MR; also stands for mental retardation), with an IQ of 70, the mental age equivalent to that of a 10- or 11-year-old.[1] Silva was one of the first offenders to be sentenced under California's Three Strikes Law, having had two previous "strikes" for arson, one involving a fire he started in a trash can and another involving a fire that began in a parked truck where it appears he was playing with matches.

This research was funded by a generous gift to RAND from Irving and Muriel Cohen.
THE PRISON JOURNAL, Vol. 77 No. 4, December 1997, 358–380
© 1997 Sage Publications, Inc.

Silva and the other estimated 6,400 MR California adult and juvenile inmates represent a complex, troubling, and increasingly costly issue for the corrections system. On one hand, we do not wish to excuse the criminal behavior of criminals who are MR, but many offenders with MR are not so much lawbreakers as they are low-functioning citizens who lack training on how to function responsibly in a complex society.

MR and developmentally disabled (DD) persons are usually defined as those with less than a 70 IQ, but practically speaking, such persons can be described with fair accuracy as having a childlike quality of thinking, coupled with slowness in learning new material.[2] MR persons have little long-term perspective and little ability to think in a causal way to understand the consequences of their actions. They are usually followers, easily manipulated, and often used by others with more intelligence and/or experience.

Studies have shown that although their rates of crime are similar to those of nondisabled persons, and consist mostly of less serious felonies and property crimes, the offender with MR is disproportionately represented in correctional agencies.[3] The prevalence of MR is about 1% to 2% in the population at large, but in the criminal justice system, it is estimated to be about 4% to 10% (although prevalence rates in the literature range from 1% to 30%).[4] A number of cumulative factors explain this.

Police and Prosecution Decision Making

Offenders with MR come disproportionately from low-income minority groups, where police presence and the probability of arrest is high. MR persons cannot think quickly, often make no attempt to disguise what they have done, nor do they run from the scene. As a result, they are generally easily arrested and convicted. As one police officer put it, "They are the last to leave the scene, the first to get arrested, and the first to confess." Studies show that many MR persons cannot understand their rights when arrested (e.g., the term *waiver*), especially in the form read by the police (Edwards & Reynolds, 1997). People with MR often exhibit low self-esteem and have a heightened desire to please authority figures. As such, they often will acquiesce to the wishes of other individuals who are perceived to be more influential (delinquent peers as well as police officers).

For most offenders with MR, official justice system processing (from arrest through sentencing) will proceed without officials becoming aware of the offender's intellectual disability.[5] Most justice personnel are not trained to identify the MR (indeed, they often confuse mentally ill with MR), and there are seldom any formal procedures for identifying such persons.[6] Moreover, MR offenders, anxious to fit in, are rather clever at masking their limitations and rendering the magnitude of their disability invisible to the criminal justice system (CJS) personnel. Only when impairments become visible enough, such as when the offender acts in a bizarre or disruptive manner, are formal evaluations completed.

Even if the offender with MR is identified, special handling or programming is extremely rare. Psychological evaluations are seldom performed prior to trial or sentencing, the result being that their condition is sometimes not discovered until incarceration, when it is too late to employ special procedures to ensure a fair trial. Defendants are often simply viewed as slow and uncooperative, especially in cases involving minority defendants (McGee & Menolascino, 1992).

Incarceration Before Trial

Offenders with MR are unlikely to meet the criteria for personal recognizance or bail, because the individual is probably unemployed and living with less stable surroundings, two of the major criteria used in bail decision making. The MR defendant is usually held in the local jail prior to the case disposition, and research has shown that other factors being equal, defendants held for trial in lieu of bail are convicted more often. In addition, when convicted, they go to prison more often and receive longer sentences than those who post bail (Goldkamp, 1979; Toberg, 1992). Although it is difficult to isolate the detention factors from other variables such as the severity of the crime, research has consistently found a relationship between being held in jail pretrial and the severity of court disposition. Persons who remain in the community while their case is being adjudicated have the opportunity to assist in their defense, secure employment or training, and, generally speaking, show the court that they can "make it" in the community. The hardship of detention before trial also puts pressure on defendants to waive their rights and to plead guilty.

Plea Bargaining, Court Processing, and Sentencing

Persons with MR confess more readily, provide more incriminating evidence to authorities, and are less successful in plea bargaining. As a result, they are more likely to be convicted and receive longer sentences. The offender with MR is subjected to the same judicial procedures—confrontational, legalistic, and impersonal—as are persons having greater intellectual capacities. The result is that offenders with MR do poorly in plea negotiations. Studies show that the vast majority of MR defendants are represented by public defenders, confess to the crime, plead guilty to the original (not reduced) charge, and waive their right to a jury trial (Moschella, 1982; Santamour, 1986). When MR persons do go to trial, their ability to remember details, locate witnesses, and testify credibly is limited. Defense attorneys know they make less-than-ideal defendants and are easily manipulated by prosecutors pretending to be on their side.[7]

At sentencing, MR offenders do not often look like a good prospect for probation, which is more commonly granted to individuals with higher intelligence and greater educational and work achievement. Again, studies show that even when presentence investigations are prepared for the court to use in sentencing, the MR condition is not usually noted and the offender is evaluated similarly to the nondisabled person (Laski, 1992). Probation is less frequently granted for offenders with MR (Haskins & Friel, 1973; Santamour & West, 1979). When intermediate sanctions (e.g., boot camps) or diversion programs (e.g., work release) are available to the court, eligibility requirements often explicitly exclude those who are physically or mentally handicapped.

Recent studies show that MR offenders are most often convicted of property crimes (often arson and theft)—although a minority are convicted of violent and sex-related offenses (often assault, indecent exposure, and pedophilia).[8] Legislative changes in sentencing laws in the 1980s made it routine to send such offenders to prison for long terms. California increased its prison population by 400% between 1980 and 1993 (to 125,605 inmates), yet only 27% of the additional prison space confined people convicted of violent offenses; the remaining 73% were convicted of nonviolent crimes (Zimring & Hawkins, 1997). Recidivism rates for MR offenders are fairly high; therefore,

MR offenders are increasingly coming under mandatory sentencing laws, such as California's Three Strikes Law, which requires imprisonment for all but the first conviction.[9]

Incarceration, Parole, and Recidivism

While in prison or jail, it is estimated that less than 10% of all inmates with MR receive any specialized services, even if the system officially identifies them (Hall, 1992). California, for example, identifies some inmates as K class offenders, but they receive no special services and are mainstreamed with the general prison population. Housed with the general prison population, the offenders with MR are often cruelly abused or victimized (Sobsey, 1994). Their personal property may be stolen, they may be forced to participate in homosexual acts (increasing exposure to AIDS), or they may be used by more intelligent inmates to violate institutional rules.

The responses of MR inmates to such threatening situations are more likely to be physical than verbal or intellectual. The result is that MR inmates are more prone to getting into fights and becoming correctional management problems, both because of their outbursts and their high profile for victimization by others. The offender with MR takes up an inordinate amount of staff time, and many are eventually reclassified to a higher (and more expensive) security level and moved to maximum-security cells. Their poor institutional behavior and "overclassification" also means that they fail to earn good-time or work-time credits, are unable to participate in institutional or early release programs, and in states with parole, fail to become eligible for parole because they have not finished the programs or procedures required for parole consideration.

When inmates with MR are considered for parole release, they will likely have a poor prison record with little program participation, many infractions and violations and a very weak postdischarge plan. Also, inmates with MR generally do not do well in interviews with the parole board, because those types of intense verbal interactions are particularly difficult for them. The result is that MR offenders end up serving a greater portion of their court-imposed sentence than non-MR offenders.[10]

When released, there is usually no distinction made between MR and non-MR parolees, and the likelihood is that people with MR will be no more successful at navigating the parole supervision situation than they were at being a successful inmate within the correctional institution. Placed on regular supervision caseloads and told to abide by strict rules and procedures (e.g., report to parole officer, get a job, submit to drug testing, and pay victim restitution), they often experience technical and other rule violations. Moreover, with few rehabilitation programs suited to their special needs, they have little opportunity to participate in substance abuse, education, and/or work training programs. Now possessing a criminal record, the MR offender will have almost no possibility of getting a job. Even for nondisabled persons, studies have shown that any involvement with the criminal justice system (even an unsubstantiated arrest) significantly lowers employment prospects (Hagan, 1993). For offenders with MR, such stigmatization is likely to be devastating.

Resulting rearrest rates are correspondingly high, and the cycle described above repeats itself (New York State Office of Mental Retardation and Developmental Disabilities, 1987).

In sum, it appears that offenders with MR do more time, do harder time, get less out of their time, and are more likely to be returned to prison after release than persons who are not mentally handicapped. Clearly, this situation is intolerable. It not only raises questions of fundamental equality under the law but also offends our sense of common decency when our weakest and most vulnerable citizens are further subjected to an unduly harsh and victimizing legal system. It is not that we wish to excuse the crimes of the MR, but rather, we wish to create a fairer system—one that provides appropriate treatment, protection from victimization, and equal opportunity for rehabilitation.

THE PROBLEM IS LIKELY TO WORSEN

Although the details above may be new to some, this troubling situation is well known to corrections professionals. Interviews conducted in recent months with officials throughout the nation reveal a heightened awareness and concern for the handling (and more accurately, the mishandling) of MR persons in correctional facilities.[11] Officials realize that this group requires greater patience, assistance, and specialized programming, and yet, due to prison crowding, staff are increasingly unable to provide it. As Rowan (1976) noted more than 20 years ago, "The care and treatment of MR offenders is one of the most consistently frustrating problems that confront administrators of both correctional institutions and facilities for the retarded. Both types of facilities are geared to treat their predominant groups, and offenders with mental retardation are misfits in both settings" (p. 4).

Experts predict the problem will worsen considerably over the next several years, as the factors known to be associated with MR and DD prevalence increase. Factors related to epidemiological rates of MR and related developmental disabilities are prenatal care, low birth weight, adolescent pregnancy, and substance abuse during pregnancy (Fryers, 1993; President's Commission on Mental Retardation, 1988). Fetal Alcohol Syndrome and prenatal substance abuse are major causes of MR.

Moreover, a greater number of young people of all intellectual abilities are now under correctional control, and the rates are increasing fastest for Black minority youth living in the inner city. Mauer (1990) estimated that in 1990, 1 in 4 young Black men (ages 20 to 29) was under correctional control—meaning either in jail, in prison, on probation, or on parole. By 1995, he found a worsening situation, with 1 in 3 young Black men under correctional control (Mauer & Huling, 1995). More young persons are choosing to commit crime, and the MR are easy prey for their delinquent peers, both as victims and accomplices. As one Los Angeles police officer noted, "With the growth of gangs in urban areas of California, we are finding greater incidence of exploitation of the mentally retarded offender in criminal activities."

It is also now well established that abuse as a child increases the chances of perpetrating crime later in life by the victims themselves. One recent national study showed that being the victim of abuse and neglect as a child increases the chances of later juvenile delinquency and adult criminality by 40% (Widom, 1995). And importantly, recent studies also show that children with disabilities suffer significantly higher rates of criminal abuse than children without disabilities. Considerable research demonstrates that both children and adults with disabilities experience greater risks of criminal physical abuse and sexual assault; minimally, it is estimated that they are at least twice as likely to suffer sexual assault (Sobsey, 1994). Moreover, research shows that abuse against disabled persons is reported at a much lower rate, and results in fewer prosecutions and convictions, than crimes against nondisabled persons (Sobsey, 1994). As a result, the criminal justice system seldom intervenes, and the disabled victim often suffers repeated victimization. Sobsey and Doe (1991) found that of the 86% of women with developmental disabilities in their study who had been sexually assaulted, half of them had been sexually assaulted 10 or more times. This situation has led one author to observe that disabled persons are "invisible victims"—unnoticed and unprotected by the justice system (Sorensen, 1997).

These facts, coupled with an overall trend toward deinstitutionalizing large numbers of MR persons, have led to a rise in the number of such persons who live on the streets or in shelters. Lakin and Prouty (1996) report that in 1994, national MR institution populations were barely one third of their 1967 populations, decreasing from 194,650 to 65,735 over the time period. Ironically, of the 99 state institutions closed or planned for closing between 1970 and 2000, the majority have become state and federal correctional facilities; and the staff, laid off from the state MR institutions, are being hired to staff the new jails and prisons (Braddock, Hemp, Bacheldner, & Fajiura, 1995). For many MR offenders, the well-intentioned deinstitutionalization movement has produced disastrous effects. Many get released from state mental hospitals to community settings with few services and little support. Without services, many flounder and eventually come to the attention of the police and the courts. The result is they end up trading one institutional address for another, and the number of MR persons in correctional institutions continues to grow.

It is troubling that the size of the MR (and other low-income) populations living in the community under poor conditions and the American prison population both increased dramatically in the 1980s. The U.S. prison population quadrupled during the last decade, whereas the average rate of poverty increased 17% overall and for African American children increased an astonishing 44% (U.S. Department of Commerce, 1994). Worse, the growth of each seemed to feed off the growth of the other. This is because funding for prison expansion came largely at the expense of funding for programs designed to alleviate poor community conditions.

For example, the California state budget for 1997–1998 proposes the largest spending increase (11%) for corrections-related programs. In contrast, proposed 1997–1998 spending for social services programs declines by 7% (Legislative Analysts Office, 1997–1998). In California, this upward spending trend for corrections, coupled with a downward trend in social services spending, began in the late 1980s. Between 1988 and 1998, the state adopted a series of reductions in both grants to low-income persons in families with children under the Aid to Families With Dependent Children (AFDC), and grants to elderly, blind or disabled persons under Supplementary Security Income (SSI) (Legislative Analysts Office, 1997–1998). Programs to support employment, training, welfare, and health-related programs for the low-income and disabled persons were cut. We spend billions of dollars to lock up hundreds of thousands of people while cutting billions of dollars for programs that might provide them opportunities to avoid committing crime in the first place. In this context, an increase in the prevalence of MR and other low-income persons within the California justice system is expected.

ESTIMATING THE SCOPE OF THE CURRENT CALIFORNIA PROBLEM

No one knows the exact number of MR housed in jail or prison, or on probation or parole. Such statistics are not maintained for any of these populations, and only for the prison population have national estimates been attempted. In fact, all available data on the prevalence rates or characteristics of persons with MR or DD within the criminal justice system must be viewed with extreme caution. Despite universal agreement that individuals with MR are not handled appropriately in the justice system, little official attention has been paid to the problem, and basic statistics in every aspect of the problem are lacking.

The most recent estimate of the prevalence of MR and other disabilities in the prison population comes from a survey of all federal and state prisons by Veneziano and Veneziano (1996). Researchers asked each facility for information on inmates with the following five types of disability: visual deficits, mobility or orthopedic deficit, hearing deficit, speech deficit, and psychological disability. Administrators reported the results shown in Table 16.1, estimating that 4.2% of all prison inmates are MR and 10.7% are learning disabled.

Table 16.1
Percentages of Total U.S. Prison Populations With Disabilities

Type of Disability	Percentage Prevalence
Physical disabilities	
Visual deficit	0.2
Mobility or orthopedic deficit	0.3
Other major health problems	14.2
Cancer	0.2
Cardiovascular disease	3.4
Diabetes	3.1
Epilepsy	0.9
Hypertension	6.6
Human immunodeficiency virus (HIV)	2.4
Communicative disabilities	
Hearing deficit	0.2
Speech deficit	0.06
Psychological disabilities	
Learning disabilities	10.7
Mental retardation	4.2
Psychotic disorders	7.2
Other psychological disorders	12.0

NOTE: All figures, except for the HIV rate, are from Veneziano and Veneziano (1996). The HIV estimate is from the Bureau of Justice Statistics (1995). Neither study reports multiple conditions.

Table 16.2
Mentally Retarded Offenders in California Corrections (estimated)

	1996 Offender Population	*Percentage Mentally Retarded (MR)*
Adults		
Probation	300,000	6,300
Jail	66,358	2,654
Parole	98,013	4,116
Prison	141,017	5,923
Adult total	605,388	18,993
Juveniles		
Probation	70,000	1,470
Halls	6,400	256
Ranches and camps	4,000	160
California Youth Authority	9,000	360
Parole	6,000	240
Juvenile total	95,400	2,486
Combined total	700,788	21,479

NOTE: The population figures are from the California Department of Corrections; the California Youth Authority; the California Probation, Parole, and Corrections Association; Legislative Analysts Office; and the U.S. Bureau of Justice Statistics.

These authors had conducted a similar survey in 1987, and at that time, found that 1.8% of the prison population was MR (Veneziano, Veneziano, & Tribolet, 1987). These data suggest that the national prevalence rate of MR in prisons has more than doubled—in fact, increased by 133%—in less than a decade.[12]

If the prevalence of persons with MR in California prisons is similar to the national estimate of 4.2% (and there are reasons to believe it might be higher), then at a minimum, we estimate that the California Youth Authority (CYA) now houses about 360 MR youths and the California Department of Corrections (CDC) now houses about 6,000 MR adults. There are no national estimates of the prevalence of offenders with MR on probation, so as a conservative estimate for that population, we use half the institutional rate, or 2.1% (see Table 16.2). If we included those who are borderline retarded (defined as having an IQ of between 70 and 85) or the broader category of the developmentally disabled, the figures would be significantly higher.

Some may argue that relative to the total of 700,788 persons under correctional control in California, 21,479 persons with MR are not a high-priority problem. As Brown and Courtless noted in 1971, when the problem was much less pronounced, "the problem of the mentally retarded offender is small in absolute numbers and large in significance" (p. 77). The problem is now both large and significant!

FINDING WORKABLE SOLUTIONS

Recognizing the problem is far easier than identifying a solution. Philosophically, the issue of how to handle the MR in criminal justice matters quickly becomes mired in debates concerning *normalization*. Nirje (1969) defined normalization as "making available to the mentally retarded patterns and conditions of everyday life which are as close as possible to the norms and patterns of the mainstream of society" (p. 369). If full normalization is the goal (and to many MR advocates, it is), then, logically, it follows that people with MR are fully responsible for complying with normal laws and expectations, and violations should result in the same kinds of punishments given to those without such disabilities. Yet, MR professionals profusely debate how the normalization concept should be applied to corrections. The emerging consensus within the profession seems to be that there are highly unique aspects to the correctional environment and that the normalization goals for the MR should not fully apply in this setting (Association of Retarded Citizens, 1992).

Beyond these philosophical debates, there are also serious practical problems. Is it really beneficial to identify MR offenders? As Petrella (1992) observed, many defendants with MR are identified and then unidentified because it better serves their legal interests. The common assumption that if only individuals with MR were identified, they would be appropriately served, may not be valid. Sometimes, the MR label creates more difficulties and limits the available options more significantly than any lack of identification.

If identification is deemed desirable, how and at what point in the process should MR persons be identified? What types of additional training would criminal justice personnel need to more accurately identify and appropriately handle the MR offender? If programs were developed, which MR offenders could be successfully diverted to them: That is, what types of programs seem to work, for which offenders, and at what cost? Which agencies should be responsible for operating such programs, and what collaboration is necessary? If incarceration is warranted, what are the implications of different housing arrangements? Should the MR be segregated from the rest of the population, housed with the total inmate population, or something in between? Do specialized probation and parole caseloads make a difference to offender success and recidivism rates? What expectations are reasonable for supervising the MR offender on probation or parole? And the important unanswered questions go on and on.

It is not that these questions cannot be answered but, rather, we have not devoted the public policy attention necessary to answering them. The MR offender has never attracted the attention that other specialized populations have or that their numbers alone should warrant. For example, we spend inordinate amounts of time and energy debating programs and policies for elderly inmates, child molesters, spouse assaulters, and offenders with AIDS. Yet, often, their prevalence is less than that for offenders with MR or DD. As shown in Table16.1, for example, about 2% of federal and state prison inmates are known to be infected with the HIV virus that causes AIDS, and yet there are hundreds of articles, federal data-collection activities, and special study groups and conferences on the topic. It is not that the AIDS issue is unimportant, but rather that one wonders why there is no similar scholarly or policy attention paid to the MR offender. As Talent and Keldgord (1975) wrote, "Less effort has been expended in the US to the MR offender than any other group of offenders" (p. 23). Their statement is still true more than 20 years later.

Some believe that the lack of attention reflects a long history of callous disregard for the lives of individuals with MR and a constant devaluing of their worth. Others suggest it results from the fact that MR offenders lack a committed, well-organized and fiscally sound advocacy group. Whatever the reason, it is certainly true that the topic has garnered little scholarly, public, or policy interest.

It is not that the issue has received no attention. President Kennedy, whose sister was MR, created the President's Committee on Mental Retardation in 1962. Over the ensuing years, it tackled a number of issues related to MR and in 1989, sponsored a presidential forum on the special issues that arise when people with MR commit crimes or become crime victims. Subsequently, the papers presented at the forum were published in *The Criminal Justice System and Mental Retardation* (Conley, Luckasson, & Bouthilet, 1992), which remains the major piece of scholarly work in this field.[13] Dick Thornberg, then the attorney general of the United States, in writing the foreword to the book, called on the justice system to develop special procedures for the appropriate handling of persons with mental disabilities. Thornberg wrote the following:

> Disabled offenders must at times be treated differently from others to ensure protection of their rights and to ensure an equal opportunity to benefit from services. People with mental retardation cannot be "processed" exactly like others who come into contact with the criminal justice system because, for them, it may be a system they do not understand or a system that does not understand them. Thus, we must take care to ensure that our criminal justice system does not compound the challenges that individuals with disabilities face in other aspects of their lives. (p. xvi)

The President's Committee on Mental Retardation encouraged a major program of national reform, incorporating legal, program, and policy changes. They outlined the necessary training and agency collaboration that was needed; described exemplary program models; and encouraged a serious program of national data collection, research, and program demonstration.

Despite their good intentions and the high quality of the undertaking, the committee's report never got the attention it deserved, and most of the recommendations were never implemented. Prison crowding and budget shortfalls reached catastrophic proportions in the early 1990s, and corrections officials became singularly preoccupied with providing enough secure cells to house an increasing number of inmates. Dollars had to be allocated, and prisons and jails had to be sited and built. Concerns for individualized justice gave way to the doctrine "do the crime, do the time." The U.S. prison population exploded, increasing from 319,598 in 1980 to 1,182,169 in 1996, a 370% increase (Bureau of Justice Statistics, 1997). Probation, parole, and jail populations grew similarly, but their budgets did not increase commensurately, and in many counties, dollars to support local probation and jail services actually declined, whereas populations more than doubled (Petersilia, 1997b). Within this context, then, focusing on any one special offender population—regardless of their recognized differences—simply became impossible. And, offenders with MR do not seem to be anyone's primary responsibility. Correctional programs cannot handle the health and behavioral problems, and mental health programs cannot handle the criminal or disruptive behavior. In our interviews, we continually heard that this was a group that concerned professionals, but that it "wasn't really their problem."

However, a few jurisdictions have implemented special corrections programs for the MR offender, and their success rate appears high. Although few formal program evaluations exist, persons who operate and fund the programs believe they protect the public, teach the offender with MR to obey the law, and save tax dollars. For example,

- The Boston MassCAPP (Community Assistance Parole Program) is operated by the Massachusetts Parole Board to provide MR parolees with extra assistance on prison release. Although parolees who are MR have the same parole conditions on release as other inmates, they are given additional help in following them. MassCAPP uses volunteer community assistants to assist the parole offender by providing advocacy, positive role modeling, and guidance in use of leisure time, and academic training or tutoring. MassCAPP also provides a weekly counseling group and resource meeting led by a forensic psychologist and a social work intern. The program, funded by the state, has been operating for 15 years and is judged highly successful.
- Texas has a wide variety of programs within and outside institutions. In Fort Worth, Volunteers of America works with the Adult Probation Department in specialized programs for MR probationers. The goal of the 24-hour residential program includes eliminating drug and alcohol problems, obtaining employment, and developing basic hygiene and survival skills. All inmates entering the Texas Department of Corrections (DOC) are given group intelligence tests. Inmates identified as MR are transferred to a specified unit where they receive habilitation, social support, and help in pre- and postrelease planning.
- Cuyahoga County: Cleveland, Ohio; Tucson, Arizona; and Lancaster County, Pennsylvania, all operate exemplary programs for probationers with MR. Each of these programs incorporates a wide variety of activities designed to assist the probationer in the community with social support and vocational education, but most also involve an educational component. The educational component attempts to familiarize the person with MR with the workings of the justice system and the law.
- New York has a number of small residential halfway houses specifically for the MR offender. These programs, which accept both full-time residents and day-reporting offenders, accept referrals from corrections facilities throughout the state, and can be used as a probation alternative, a prison or jail diversion, or as a means of transitioning from prison. Individuals receive training on basic skills, as well as training on building socialization skills.
- The Association of Retarded Citizens (ARC), a voluntary national organization with chapters in every state, operates the Developmentally Disabled Offenders Program (DDOP) in New Jersey. The DDOP is one of the few programs nationwide that specifically provides alternatives to incarceration for defendants with DD and MR. The program, directed by an attorney with a background in criminal law, acts as a liaison

between the criminal justice and human services systems. DDOP, through the use of a personalized justice plan (PJP), offers the court alternatives to incarceration by identifying community supports and programs to appropriately treat and sanction disabled offenders. If the PJP is accepted by the judge, the offender is diverted to DDOP and then appropriately monitored by probation staff and ARC volunteers until the sentence is completed. The DDOP also provides training and technical assistance to professionals on matters relating to identifying and processing disabled defendants, as well as developing materials for disabled persons on what to do if they are arrested. The ARC of New Mexico operates a similar program called the Justice Advocacy Project (Reynolds & Berkobien, 1997).

The goal of all these programs is to help offenders attain the skills and discipline needed so that they can live independent, productive, and crime-free lives. Program operators say that such programs help break the cycle of crime and recidivism, and as such, end up saving taxpayers money.

THE GROWING SIGNIFICANCE OF THE MENTALLY HANDICAPPED OFFENDER TO CORRECTIONS POLICY

The MR in corrections are attracting renewed policy interest for two reasons. First, as states continue to struggle to fund the growth in prison populations, the positive experiences of specialized MR programs are attracting attention as a means of diverting low-risk inmates to community-based programs, thereby saving the state the cost of providing an expensive prison or jail cell. Second, public interest law firms have begun to file class action civil rights lawsuits against correctional facilities for their failure to apply the American with Disabilities Act (ADA) to the MR population within corrections facilities. The California DOC, housing the largest prison population in the nation, is currently the subject of such a lawsuit: *Clark and Woods v. California.*

DEVELOPING INTERMEDIATE SANCTIONS FOR OFFENDERS WITH MR

In the past decade, every state in the nation has experimented with intermediate sanction programs (ISPs). ISPs are community-based programs that are tougher than traditional probation, but less stringent and expensive than prison. The most popular intermediate sanctions are intensive probation supervision, house arrest, electronic monitoring, substance abuse treatment, and boot camps. All these programs are considerably cheaper to operate than prison because they do not require the state to provide secure structures, guards, food, or the other round-the-clock expenses of prison. Hundreds of programs have been implemented, primarily in the hopes of saving money, and the evaluation evidence is in: they have not saved the dollars that program proponents had hoped for (Tonry and Lynch, 1996).

The problem is basically one of "target group." ISPs will only save prison funds if those who would have otherwise served a significant time in prison are diverted to them. But, those sentenced to longer than average prison terms are likely to have been convicted of serious property or person offenses or have lengthy criminal records (hence, the longer sentence), and that is exactly the group that the public wants to remain in prison. As such, intermediate sanction programs have ended up serving as a prison diversion program only for very low-risk prisoners, usually those returned to prison for a technical violation of their probation or parole conditions, rather than the commission of a new offense. But because such persons serve only a few months' prison time, diverting them to the community may serve justice goals, but the prison cost savings are negligible. Recent California analysis by Petersilia (1997a) reveals that technical violators and other lower risk inmates serve, on average, about 4 months in prison, at a state (operational) cost of about $7,300 per inmate. (The average time served in CDC is now 21 months.) Diverting these persons to community-based ISP programs, which often last for 1 year, may actually end up costing the state more, especially if the programs employ more intensive surveillance that detects a higher rate of violations and thus results in increased recommitments to prison.

The system is caught in a catch-22: To realize true cost savings through intermediate sanctions, one must identify segments of the prison population who are both nonserious (so that the public and judiciary will support their diversion, and public safety is not compromised) and who now spend a significant time in prison (so that true cost savings are realized).

The offender with MR represents an ideal target group for ISPs. As discussed above, the MR offender is usually convicted of less serious offenses but spends a longer than average term in prison due to institutional behavior and an inability to participate in early release programs or to put together an acceptable prerelease plan. Because of poor prison behavior, this inmate requires greater attention and therefore larger staffing. Eventually, the MR inmate may be reclassified to a higher security status, and as a medium or maximum inmate, he or she is occupying a more expensive prison cell. California estimates that the construction costs alone for a maximum-security cell average $113,000 each, whereas a minimum-security cell costs $60,000 each. The 2:1 cost differential between maximum- and minimum-security inmates also applies to operational costs that now average about $21,000 per year per inmate (Lasley, Hooper, & Dery, 1997). These cells could be more appropriately reserved for violent, repeat offenders.[14]

Finally, there is emerging evidence that the offenders with MR can be safely supervised in intermediate sanctions given the right support, and importantly, that recidivism can be reduced—meaning that the costs of subsequent incarcerations are also avoided. The Lancaster County, Pennsylvania, intensive probation or parole program for MR offenders reports maintaining a 5% recidivism rate, compared to the often-cited national rate of 60% (White & Wood, 1986).

Importantly, there is also likely to be widespread public support for handling the MR offender outside of an institution. Officials interviewed during the past several months continually voiced their concern over the mishandling of this population and often noted that sending these persons to prison or jail was not out of malevolence but rather because of a lack of options. As one person observed, "Nine out of the ten times, it is the lack of alternatives, not the nastiness of the court, that sends the mentally retarded to miserable incarceration."

Offenders with MR, Corrections, and the Americans with Disabilities Act (ADA)

The ADA, signed into law July 26, 1990, bans discrimination based on disability and guarantees equal opportunity for individuals with disabilities in employment, transportation, state and local government services, and public accommodations. It is generally conceded that the ADA is probably the most sweeping civil rights legislation passed since the enactment of the Civil Rights Act of 1964. Of importance, the ADA has provided the foundation for court intervention on the operations of correctional agencies on behalf of MR inmates. Significant litigation has already begun and will likely accelerate in the near future. There is no doubt that such litigation will profoundly affect the manner in which corrections identifies and treats MR inmates. The ADA significantly expands the requirements previously defined in *Ruiz v. Estelle* (1980), which, until the ADA was passed, represented the most comprehensive attempt by the federal judiciary to intervene in the operation of a correctional agency. It profoundly affected how Texas handles MR offenders, establishing the first statewide correctional screening process for their identification and programming specifically targeted toward their specialized needs.

Two recent Department of Justice reports have been written to assist states in interpreting the implications of the ADA for corrections. The reports by Rubin and McCampbell (1994, 1995) make clear that states are no longer able to mainstream MR offenders, with little or no recognition of how their disability affects their corrections experience. ADA requires that all corrections agencies (including probation, parole, jail, and prisons) establish screening and rehabilitation programs specifically for offenders with MR. The ADA further requires that each correctional facility and program evaluate each program, service, and activity in such a way so that, when viewed in its entirety, the program service or activity is readily accessible to and usable by eligible inmates with disabilities. Legally, corrections must now examine all programs—including work release, parole hearings, education, recreation, substance and alcohol abuse, boot camps, halfway houses, community service, and visitation—and facilities to assure that procedures do not eliminate eligible inmates from programs and services on the basis of a mental disability. In short, the ADA (1990) requires that all corrections programs be "readily accessible and usable" by inmates with MR.

As the ADA mandates have become clearer, so too has the fact that most corrections systems are not in compliance. In April of 1996, the Prison Law Office (PLO) and two private law firms filed a class action civil rights suit on behalf of all MR inmates in California against Governor Pete Wilson, the director of the CDC, and various state officials. Believed to be the first statewide, class action civil rights suit filed on behalf of MR prison inmates since the passage of the ADA, the case was filed in the U.S. District Court in San Francisco under the ADA and for violations of the Sixth, Eighth and Fourteenth Amendments of the U.S. Constitution.

The suit, *Clark and Woods v. California,* alleges that Derrick Clark and Ambrose Woods, two CDC inmates with mental retardation, and others similarly situated cannot "obtain necessary and adequate accommodations, protection, and services necessitated by their disabilities as required by the US Constitution and federal law." Furthermore, because they cannot adapt to prison without such accommodations, protection and services, they are more likely to be "beaten or raped than non-disabled prisoners, to be manipulated by other prisoners, are less able to comprehend and to comply with prison rules and procedures than non-developmentally disabled prisoners, and do not have access to the full range of services and privileges available to non-developmentally disabled prisoners" (p. 2). The suit asserts that Clark has been continually abused by other inmates and has not been separated from the general prison population, despite staff recommendations that he be removed. Woods has been denied access to prison work and education programs as a result of his disability, and was rejected from a reading class because he was "too stupid."

Clark and Woods v. California is now proceeding through the U.S. District Court, Northern District of California, but, a resolution is not expected quickly. There is no doubt that the case—and those that will undoubtedly follow in other states—will mandate that the DOC implement revised procedures for the special handling of the MR within corrections. Debate will likely center on the desirability of one of three policy positions: segregation and the use of special facilities; normalization and mainstreaming within the general prison populations; or the use of alternatives to incarceration. But, without empirical data on characteristics of MR inmates, the kinds of crimes they commit, and what programs and procedures work best, in what settings, and for whom, changes are likely to be ill informed and misguided.

ANSWERING THE IMPORTANT QUESTIONS

There is a serious need for more and better information on offenders with MR. At a minimum, we need to know the following:

- What is the prevalence of MR offenders coming into contact with various correctional agencies—probation, parole, jail, and prison—in different states? How does their mental handicap affect their interactions with justice agencies?
- What training is now provided correctional personnel regarding the characteristics, behavior, and handling of MR offenders? Do corrections agencies make any distinctions between mentally ill, MR, and DD offenders?
- What systems are used, in different states, to identify the MR offender at different points in the correctional system? If identified or more information on the offender's disability is known—or known at different stages in the process—what difference does it make in decision making?
- What have been the demonstrated and perceived effects of alternative approaches to correctional handling of MR inmates—on costs, system management, and offender performance?

There are no simplistic solutions to the problem of the mentally handicapped offender in corrections. For one thing, there are a multitude of local jails, probation, parole, and prisons throughout the nation, each of which operates rather independently when it comes to these issues, and most are already over-burdened in dealing with their "dominant" populations. The author does believe, however, that more knowledge and analysis could significantly influence the priority the nation places on this topic and the program and policy changes that are considered. In short, the issue of the MR offender needs to be brought to the forefront of corrections policy attention.

There will probably always be some persons who, like Silva, continue to sit in prison and jail cells bewildered and unable to comprehend and negotiate correctional rules and conditions. But, hopefully the numbers will decrease, and it should not be because we have "swept these persons" under the rug or failed to devote sufficient energy and analysis to considering alternative options. If a culture is measured by how it treats its weakest members, then the handling of the mentally handicapped in corrections reveals an American justice system at its basest. As Sobsey (1994) put it, "We must strive to make right what is currently so very wrong" (p. 370). Our respect for the human rights of *all* persons and our system of justice demands no less.

NOTES

1. The most widely accepted definition of mental retardation (MR; also stands for mentally retarded) is that developed by the American Association on Mental Deficiency (AAMD). This definition states that MR is based on "significant subaverage general intellectual functioning existing concurrently with deficits in adaptive behavior" (AAMD, 1983, p. 1). An IQ level below 70 is the criteria for measuring the deficit in intellectual function for retardation.
2. A developmental disability (DD) may be defined as a severe chronic disability attributable to a mental or physical impairment that manifests before age 22 and is likely to continue indefinitely. DDs may consist of epilepsy, MR, and/or severe learning disabilities. The California Department of Developmental Services estimates that 86% of those served by the state system for those labeled DD, are MR.
3. Despite the common perception that the MR population commits many violent crimes, studies show that the majority of offenses committed by MR persons are less serious offenses (although data on the subject is rare and affected by selection biases). See Illinois Retarded and Mentally Ill Offender Task Force (1988) and White and Wood (1986).
4. The earliest reported estimate of the MR of offenders appears to have been made by Zeleny (1933), who examined the intelligence tests of more than 60,000 inmates and reported that the number of retarded offenders was close to 30% of the inmate population. A more comprehensive effort was conducted by Brown and Courtless (1971) who reported that 9.5% of the inmate population was MR (IQ below 70). Texas reported a rate of 10% for adult offenders and 12% to 16% for juvenile offenders, Georgia estimated its figure to be 27% for prison inmates, and the South Carolina Department of Corrections reported a figure of 8% (Santamour & Watson, 1982). The varying estimates result from different testing instruments and methods, and underlying differences in the prevalence rates across the nation.
5. See McAfee and Gural (1988) who found that 75% of MR offenders were not identified at arrest, and more than 10% were not identified until they were in prison.
6. MR and mental illness (MI) are quite distinct conditions. MR refers to subaverage intellectual functioning; MI has nothing to do with IQ. A person with MI may be a genius or subaverage. MR refers to impairment in social adaptation; a person with

MI may be very competent socially but have a character disorder. MR is usually present at birth; MI may strike at any time. The intellectual impairment of MR is permanent; MI is often temporary and in many cases reversible. An MR person can be expected to behave rationally at his or her operational level; a person with MI may vacillate between normal and irrational behavior. MR persons are unlikely to be violent except in those situations that cause violence in non-MR persons; a person with MI may be erratic and violent (see Montgomery, 1982). There is no accurate count of the number of the mentally ill in correctional institutions, but it has been estimated that 5% to 10% of incarcerated inmates reveal serious psychopathology, and more than half could be diagnosed as having some type of psychiatric problem, most commonly a personality disorder. See McShane (1996) for a complete discussion.

7. The President's Committee on Mental Retardation (1991) noted that MR persons are in a uniquely damned position before the courts. If their disability remains undetected, the chances of receiving special court handling are impossible. But if the impairment is recognized, he may receive a long, institutional commitment without a trial for the alleged offense, because very often laws make no distinction between MI—where a lengthy civil commitment is possible without a criminal conviction—and MR.

8. It is important to point out that selection biases seriously affect our ability to know the distribution of crime types committed by MR or DD offenders or their personal characteristics. Criminal justice agencies do not routinely test or record the MR or DD condition unless some unusual behavior on the part of the offender brings it to their attention. This selection bias means that those who are IQ tested do not represent the MR or DD population at large but rather a biased subpopulation (e.g., those who are "acting out"). Much of the literature inappropriately uses such data to describe the general characteristics of MR or DD offenders. For example, it is asserted that a high proportion of MR offenders are dual diagnosed as MI (Rockowitz [1986] estimates the figure to be as high as 40%). Clearly, this high prevalence rate is due to selection biases in the population studied. Offenders often do not get IQ tested unless they are exhibiting unusual behavior, which is more characteristic of persons with MI. Therefore, those who get IQ tested have a higher probability of having both the MR and MI conditions, whereas the prevalence rate of dual diagnosis in the overall MR or DD population would be much lower if all (not just a select group) of MR persons were IQ tested. Such selection biases influence much of the data we have on MR and DD offenders, making them appear more handicapped and seriously criminal than they are.

9. Frank Zimring's 1997 analysis of the increase in California's prison population showed that "the greatest impact of the growth in the California prison population since 1980 has been on convictions for burglary and thefts, two nonviolent offenses that have experienced 366% and 635% increases" (p. 23). In 1996, about 59% of inmates incarcerated in California prisons were convicted of nonviolent offenses (Legislative Analysts Office, 1997–1998). The same is true with the growth in the U.S. prison population—fully 84% of the increase in state and federal prison admissions since 1980 was accounted for by nonviolent offenders (Bureau of Justice Statistics, 1996). These crimes are exactly the ones MR offenders are usually convicted of.

10. Lampert (1987) observed that in a sample of Texas prisoners, inmates with MR served a significantly longer portion of their sentence when contrasted to inmates with normal intelligence.

11. As part of this RAND research project, informal telephone and personal interviews were conducted by the author with about two dozen persons interested in the issue of the developmentally disabled offender. These persons represented criminal justice and mental health agencies, citizen advocacy groups, and national associations for the MR. All interviews were conducted in the spring and summer of 1997.

12. It is also important to note that estimates of MR incarcerated youth are much higher than those for adults and have been estimated to be as high as 40% (Wolford, Nelson, & Rutherford, 1997). The higher rate is probably because legal mandates require correctional agencies to test for the MR condition so that required special education services can be provided according to the Education of the Handicapped Act (PL 94-142) and its amendments (PL 101-476, the Individuals With Disabilities Education Act of 1990).

13. The other major treatise of the topic is published in Santamour and Watson (1982).

14. There is also evidence that adopting special procedures for the MR while in jail or prison reduces the number and severity of disciplinary infractions and reduces staff time necessary to supervise such inmates (Hall, 1992).

REFERENCES

American Association on Mental Deficiency (AAMD). (1983). *Manual on terminology and classification in mental retardation.* Washington DC: Author.

Americans With Disabilities Act (ADA). (1990). 42 USC § 12101.

Association of Retarded Citizens (Arc). (1992). *Access to justice and fair treatment under the criminal law for people with mental retardation: Position statement.* Arlington, TX: Arc National Headquarters.

Braddock, D., Hemp, R., Bacheldner, L., & Fujiura, G. (1995). The state of the states in developmental disabilities. Washington DC: American Association on Mental Retardation.

Brown, B. S., & Courtless T. F. (1971). *The mentally retarded offender* (DHEW Publication No. 72-90-39). Washington, DC: Government Printing Office.

Bureau of Justice Statistics. (1995). *HIV in prisons and jails, 1993* (Bulletin NCJ-152765). Washington, DC: Department of Justice.

Bureau of Justice Statistics. (1996). *Correctional populations in the United States, 1994* (Bulletin NCJ-1600091). Washington, DC: Department of Justice.

Bureau of Justice Statistics. (1997). *Prisoners in 1996* (Bulletin NCJ-164619). Washington, DC: Department of Justice.

Clark and Woods v. California, No 12153529, U.S. Dist. April 1996.

Conley, R. W., Luckasson, R., & Bouthilet, G. N. (Eds.). (1992). *The criminal justice system and mental retardation.* Baltimore, MD: Brooks.

Edwards, W., & Reynolds, L. A. (1997). Defending and advocating on behalf of individuals with "mild" mental retardation in the criminal justice system. *IMPACT, 10*(2) 12–13.

Fryers, T. (1993). Epidemiological thinking in mental retardation: Issues in taxonomy and population frequency. In N. W. Bray (Ed.), *International review of research in mental retardation.* Novato, CA: Academic Therapy.

Goldkamp, J. (1979). *Two classes of accused.* Cambridge, MA: Ballinger.

Hagan, J. (1993). The social embeddedness of crime and unemployment. *Criminology, 31*(4).

Hall, J. N. (1992). Correctional services for inmates with mental retardation: Challenge or catastrophe? In R. W. Conley, R. Luckasson, & G. N. Bouthilet. (Eds.), *The criminal justice system and mental retardation* (pp. 167–190). Baltimore, MD: Brooks.

Haskins, J., & Friel, C. (1973). *Project CAMIO: The mentally retarded in an adult correctional institutions.* Huntsville, TX: Sam Houston State University Press.

Illinois Mentally Retarded and Mentally Ill Task Force. (1988). *Mentally retarded and mentally ill offender task force report.* Springfield, IL: Illinois Mentally Retarded and Mentally Ill Task Force, Department of Social Services.

Lakin, C. K., & Prouty, R. (1996). Trends in institution closure. *IMPACT, 9*(1) 4–5.

Lampert, R. O. (1987). The mentally retarded offender in prison. *Justice Professional,* *2*(1), 60–69.

Laski, F. J. (1992). Sentencing the offender with mental retardation: Honoring the imperative for intermediate punishments and probation. In R. W. Conley, R. Luckasson, & G. N. Bouthilet. (Eds.), *The criminal justice system and mental retardation.* Baltimore, MD: Brooks.

Lasley, J. R., Hooper, M., & Dery, G. M. (1997). *The California criminal justice system.* Upper Saddle River, NJ: Prentice Hall.

Legislative Analysts Office. (1997–1998). *California budget analysis: Perspective on state expenditures—an overview of state expenditures.* http://www.lao.ca.gov/part_4a_expenditures_pi97.html.

Mauer, M. (1990). *Young Black men and the criminal justice system: A growing national problem.* Washington, DC: The Sentencing Project.

Mauer, M., & Huling, T. (1995). *Young Black Americans and the criminal justice system: Five years later.* Washington, DC: The Sentencing Project.

McAfee, J., & Gural, M. (1988). Individuals with mental retardation and the criminal justice system: The view from the state attorney's general. *Mental Retardation, 6,* 5–12.

McGee, J., & Menolascino, F. (1992). The evaluation of defendants with mental retardation in the criminal justice system. In R. W. Conley, R. Luckasson, & G. N. Bouthilet. (Eds.), *The criminal justice system and mental retardation.* Baltimore, MD: Brooks.

McShane, M. D. (1996). Mentally ill prisoners. In M. D. McShane & F. P. Williams III, (Eds.), *Encyclopedia of American prisons.* New York: Garland.

Montgomery, R. H. (1982). Curriculum for use in training criminal justice personnel. In M. B. Santamour & P. S. Watson (Eds.), *The retarded offender.* New York: Praeger.

Moschella, S. (1982). The mentally retarded offender: Law enforcement and court proceedings. In M. B. Santamour & P. S. Watson (Eds.), *The retarded offender.* New York: Praeger.

New York State Office of Mental Retardation and Developmental Disabilities. (1987). *Mentally retarded offenders: Considerations for public policy.* Albany, GA: Author.

Nirje, B. (1969). The normalization principal and its human management implications. In R. B. Kigel & W. Wolfensberger (Eds.), *Changing patterns in residential services for the mentally retarded.* Washington, DC: President's Committee on Mental Retardation.

Petersilia, J. (1997a). Diverting nonviolent prisoners to intermediate sanctions: The impact on California prison admissions and corrections costs. In E. Rubin (Ed.), *Minimizing harm as a goal for crime policy in California: A CPS Crime Policy Project Report.* Berkeley, CA: California Policy Seminar.

Petersilia, J. (1997b). Probation in the United States. In M. Tonry (Ed.), *Crime and Justice: A Review of Research* (vol. 22, pp. 149–200). University of Chicago Press.

Petrella, R. (1992). Defendants with mental retardation in the forensic services system. In R. W. Conley, R. Luckasson, & G. N. Bouthilet. (Eds.), *The criminal justice system and mental retardation.* Baltimore, MD: Brooks.

President's Commission on Mental Retardation. (1988). *Preventing the new morbidity: A guide for state planning for the prevention of mental retardation and related disabilities associated with socioeconomic conditions.* Washington DC: Department of Health and Human Services.

President's Committee on Mental Retardation. (1991). *Citizens with mental retardation and the criminal justice system: Report to the president* (DHHS Publication No. 91-21046). Washington DC: Department of Health and Human Services.

Reynolds, L. A., & Berkobien, R. (1997). The Arc: Tackling criminal justice issues at the national, state and local levels. *IMPACT, 10*(2): 8–9.

Rockowitz, R. J. (1986). Developmentally disabled offenders: Issues in developing and maintaining services. *Prison Journal, 66*(1), 19–23.

Rowan, B. (1976). Corrections. In M. Kindred et al. (Eds.), The mentally retarded citizen and the law. New York: Free Press.

Rubin, P. N., & McCampbell, S. W. (1994). *The Americans With Disabilities Act and Criminal Justice: Providing inmate service.* Washington DC: Department of Justice.

Rubin, P. N., & McCampbell, S. W. (1995). *The Americans With Disabilities Act and Criminal Justice: Mental Disabilities and Corrections.* Washington DC: Department of Justice.

Ruiz v. Estelle. (1980). 503 F. Supp. 1265, S.D. Texas, cert.denied, 103 Ct. 1438.

Santamour, M. B. (1986). The offender with mental retardation. *Prison Journal,* (7) 3–18.

Santamour, M. B., & Watson, P. S. (1982). *The retarded offender.* New York: Praeger.

Santamour, M. B., & West, B. (1979). Retardation and criminal justice: A training manual for criminal justice personnel. Washington DC: President's Committee on Mental Retardation.

Sobsey, D. (1994). *Violence and abuse in the lives of people with disabilities.* Baltimore, MD: Brooks.

Sobsey, D., & Doe, T. (1991). Patterns of sexual abuse and assault. *Journal of sexuality and disability, 9*(3), 243–259.

Sorensen, D. (1997). The invisible victims. *IMPACT, 10*(2): 1–2.

Talent, A., & Keldgord, R. (1975, September). The mentally retarded probationer. *Federal Probation, 2,* 39–46.

Toberg, M. A. (1992). *Pretrial release: A national evaluation of practice and outcomes.* McLean, VA: Lazar Institute.

Tonry, M., & Lynch, M. (1996). Intermediate sanctions. In Crime and Justice: A Review of Research (vol. 20). University of Chicago Press.

U.S. Department of Commerce. (1994, March). *Current population report.* Washington DC: Government Printing Office.

Veneziano, L., & Veneziano, C. (1996). Disabled Inmates. In M. D. McShane & F. P. Williams III (Eds.), *Encyclopedia of American prisons.* New York: Garland.

Veneziano, L., Veneziano, C., & Tribolet, C. (1987). The special needs of prison inmates with handicaps: An assessment. *Journal of Offender Counseling, Services, and Rehabilitation, 12:* 61–72.

White, D., & Wood, H. (1986). The Lancaster County, Pennsylvania Mentally Retarded Offender's Program. *The Prison Journal, 66*(1): 77–84.

Widom, C. S. (1995). *Victims of childhood sexual abuse—later criminal consequences* (National Institute of Justice). Washington, DC: Department of Justice.

Wolford, B., Nelson, M., & Rutherford, R. (1997). Developmentally disabled offenders. In M. D. McShane & F. P. Williams III (Eds.), *Encyclopedia of American prisons.* New York: Garland.

Zeleny, L. D. (1933). Feeblemindedness in criminal conduct. *American Journal of Sociology, 139:* 564–576.

Zimring, F., & Hawkins, G. (1997). Distinguishing crime from violence. In E. Rubin (Ed.), *Minimizing harm as a goal for crime policy in California: A CPS crime policy project report.* Berkeley, CA: California Policy Seminar.

CHAPTER 17

COLLATERAL COSTS OF IMPRISONMENT FOR WOMEN: COMPLICATIONS OF REINTEGRATION

Mary Dodge and Mark R. Pogrebin

This article examines issues of family separation and community isolation as experienced by women on parole. Qualitative data, based on unstructured, in-depth interviews with 54 former inmates, offer retrospective reflections and current accounts that delineate many of the unintended costs of imprisonment. The narratives portray the difficulties these women experienced in parenting, relationships, and community reintegration. Social stigma and self-shame are important definitional and reactional elements of their efforts to reestablish social bonds. The collateral costs of imprisonment are related to diminished investment in self and others that is created by continued internal and external shaming.

Women in prison, once considered the forgotten population, have become the focus of considerable research. Incarceration rates for women have increased threefold over the past decade and created a wide range of individual and social concerns (Bloom & Chesney-Lind, 2000). This study gives voice to former women inmates who explore their experiences, feelings, and thoughts on the obstacles that they endured in prison and now face in the community. Their retrospective reflections and current accounts portray conflicted emotions about children and relationships both in and out of prison and the difficulties of community reintegration. Their narratives identify and expand on the often over-looked consequences of being an incarcerated female offender.

The stigmatization that imprisoned and paroled women experience carries great costs. The stigma (Goffman, 1963) associated with criminality becomes what Becker (1963) referred to as one's master status. Women who are labeled as criminals find confirmation of their deviant master status as they undergo the process of community reintegration with few social bonds (Braithwaite, 1989). The difficulty, if not impossibility, of attempting to disavow one's deviant label

THE PRISON JOURNAL, Vol. 81 No. 1, March 2001 42–54

is a formidable task for many women offenders. Once released into the community, women on parole may be treated as outcasts, excluded from the job market, and judged for their past criminal behavior. According to Braithwaite (1989), stigmatizing shaming inhibits reintegration and furthers criminal behavior. As a consequence of society's labeling and the mechanisms of self-shaming, it appears that women offenders often experience a degradation process (Garfinkel, 1956). Female inmates and parolees who have low self-esteem (Fox, 1982) and suffer from feelings of powerlessness and vulnerability (Bill, 1998) are likely to experience increased levels of shame in their relationships.

Punishment is compounded for many women inmates when they are separated from their children. The majority of incarcerated women are mothers—estimates range from 60% to 80% (Bloom & Steinhart, 1993; Henriques, 1996). Most women inmates were living with their children and providing the sole means of family support prior to incarceration (Baunach, 1985; Chesney-Lind, 1997; Datesman & Cales, 1983; Greenfeld & Minor-Harper, 1991; Henriques, 1982, 1996). Imprisoned mothers rank estrangement from children as their primary concern (Baunach & Murton, 1973; Glick & Neto, 1977; Henriques, 1996; Stanton, 1980; Ward & Kassebaum, 1965). Rasche (2000) noted that the harshest single aspect of being imprisoned may be the separation of mother and child. The secondary costs of imprisonment to children have been acknowledged but are largely incalculable (Henriques, 1996; McGowan & Blumenthal, 1978).

Women in prison experience an unparalleled sense of isolation. Added to the pains of women's imprisonment (Sykes, 1958) are the frustration, conflict, and guilt of being both separated from and unable to care for their children (Barry, 1987). According to Crawford (1990), as a result of imprisonment, female parents often experience feelings of despair and depression. Crawford further stated that these emotions appear to be widespread, even on the part of women inmates who believe that they were inadequate as parents when they were living with their children at home. Furthermore, anxiety arises over fear of losing custody (Bloom, 1995; Fletcher, Shaver, & Moon, 1993; Knight, 1992; Pollock-Byrne, 1990).

Divorce, another contributing factor to the loneliness of separation, is a common occurrence for imprisoned women. Rafter (1985) noted that, unlike men in prison, women are unable to count on a spouse or significant other to provide a home for their children. Because of this, female parents in prison suffer more anxiety about the type of care their children are receiving. Stanton (1980) found that a great many women prisoners report being divorced by their husbands or deserted by men with whom they lived before coming to prison. Three out of four women in prison leave children, and only 22% say that they can depend on the fathers of their children to care for them while they are incarcerated (Bloom & Steinhart, 1993). Overall, women inmates, because of their primary parental role, are not, to any great degree, receiving child care help from spouses or fathers of their children.

The obstacles imprisoned women must overcome in order to maintain a relationship with their children can be extremely frustrating (Bloom & Steinhart, 1993). Loss of contact, coupled with an inability to meet social service contract requirements resulting from a lack of visitations by the children via foster parents, places inmates at considerable risk of losing parental custody (Gabel & Johnston, 1995). Bloom and Steinhart (1993) reported results from a national study that more than 54% of the children with mothers in prison never visited them during their incarceration, despite research findings that frequent contact promotes ongoing custody and family reunification (Martin, 1997).

Reestablishing relationships and social ties often represents a barrier to successful reintegration. A majority of incarcerated female mothers expect to take responsibility for their children once they are released and rarely receive any financial or emotional support from the fathers (Prendergast, Wellisen, & Falkin, 1995). Reunification is an important although somewhat unrealistic goal for released mothers (Browne, 1998; Hairston, 1991; Harris, 1993; Henriques, 1982; Jones, 1993). If the child has been placed in foster care or state custody, it is even more difficult for a released female prisoner to show that she is able to take care of and provide for her child adequately (Pollock-Byrne, 1992). Women on parole often have to overcome many barriers in order to maintain their parental rights (Barry, 1995).

Prison is a difficult experience for most women, and the subsequent hardships that they endure upon release are no less significant. Internalized self-shame, whether derived from embarrassment or guilt, along with stigmatizing social shame from the community often constitute punishment well beyond the actual time women offenders serve and may contribute to further deviance.

METHOD

Qualitative data were collected from female parolees who were incarcerated at the same correctional facility located in a western U.S. state. The prison was constructed in 1968 and has a mixed classification of inmates. The prison population at the time of this study was approximately 300 women, with 61 correctional officers (37 female and 24 male). The ethnic and racial composition of the prison population was 45.6% Anglo-American, 31.5% Black, 18.4% Hispanic, 1.7% Native American, 0.4% Asian, and 2.4% unknown.

Women on parole were contacted at the time they had appointments to see their parole officers. The participants in this study were not chosen at random, but, according to a representative case sampling method, their experiences provide examples that are indicative of the issues women on parole confront (Shontz, 1965). Each person volunteered to participate and gave informed consent. A total of 54 women agreed to interviews over a 3-month period. Their ages ranged from 23 to 55 (median = 36), and their length of incarceration ranged from 1 to 12 years (median = 4.8) for all classes of offense. Seventy percent of the women interviewed were mothers.

Interviews were conducted at the parole offices in private conference rooms. Each interview lasted approximately 60 minutes and was tape recorded with the participant's consent. All women parolees were guaranteed confidentiality and told that they could choose not to tape the interview. Three women requested not to be taped, and notes were taken during those sessions. The former inmates were cooperative and seemed willing to discuss their prior prison life. We found those interviewed to be open and quite frank in relating their personal experiences, although at times the process was emotionally painful. We used a semistructured interview format, which relied on sequential probes to pursue leads provided by participants. This approach allowed the women parolees to identify and elaborate on important domains that they perceived to characterize their prison experiences retrospectively (rather than the researchers' eliciting responses to structured questions).

The interview tapes were transcribed for qualitative data analysis, which involved a search for general relationships between categories of observations using grounded theory techniques similar to those suggested by Glaser and Strauss (1967). The data were categorized into conceptual domains as portrayed by our participants. The experiences of these women may not be reflective of all women who have served time, but the narratives add depth to our understanding of the issues (Ragin, 1994; Seidman, 1991).

FINDINGS

Separation Concerns

For female inmates in this study, being separated from their children provoked considerable stress and threatened their self-esteem. Women who violate the law are not only viewed as social outcasts but are often perceived by the community as inadequate parents. The most difficult aspect of being in prison was voiced by one respondent who seemed to portray a representative opinion for most of the women who left their children behind:

> It was so long. I missed my kids. I missed my freedom. I went to bed every night and woke up in a tiny cell. I just wish it was all a bad dream and I would wake up and I would still be there.

Often, inmates with children begin to perceive themselves as bad people, as expressed by one parent whose child has grown up not knowing her:

> Being away from my daughter affected me a lot. She is only 6, so that means that I have been in the system almost her entire life. I haven't been there for her. I feel like a horrible person because of this.

Another great concern for women in this study was the degree to which the fathers of their children took responsibility for them during the mother's incarceration. There are cases in which the husband does take responsibility for the children but leaves his imprisoned spouse for another woman. Obviously, this circumstance causes great distress for incarcerated women. There is little they can do about the situation from behind bars, and feelings of abandonment become intense. One woman stated:

> My husband chose to go to another woman. He cheated on me. It's so much to go through. You lose your husband, you lose your kids, your kid's gonna always love you, but someone else takes care of your kids, another woman, it's so much to go through. It's tragic. It's a terrible thing that you wake up and say I want to go home.

Abandonment by a husband or partner is one matter, but the additional problem of displaced children seemed insurmountable to many of these women. In the following case, one woman expressed her feelings about her husband remarrying and taking custody of her daughter. Her feeling of helplessness is apparent:

> My daughter ended up with her dad. He got married, and they took her in. He is a pretty good guy. I was upset at first when I knew he was involved with someone

cause I always thought when I got out we would be together. I guess I was just young and dumb. When I first found out, I spent many nights crying over him. At first, he wrote and visited me once, but then it just stopped. Then he wrote and told me he met someone and they were getting married and were going to raise Meg. It was hard. I was so hurt. I mean I'm glad Meg is with her dad and has a family, but she is my daughter and I just wish she was with me.

As painful as having others taking one's place as the child's primary parent, nothing, it seems, can be as emotionally difficult as giving up a newborn infant while incarcerated. A respondent explained:

The hardest part about being in prison was being away from my kids. I was pregnant when I just got in. It hurts so bad; I mean I had my daughter here. I didn't even get to hold her. I mean she was my baby. I didn't even know how she is doing or if she is alive or anything. For all I know, she could be living right by me, but I'll never know because they won't tell me, and I'll never forgive myself for getting into trouble and losing her.

In this instance, the state took custody of the newborn child and placed her in a foster home. The child was later put up for adoption. This is not an uncommon occurrence for incarcerated women.

Mothers who are in prison often find their children transferred to foster homes when there are no relatives who will be responsible for them. If multiple children are involved, they frequently are placed in different homes and separated, making it difficult for incarcerated mothers to locate them. Not being able to see one's children for a long period of time is a reality for many inmate parents. One respondent explained:

I talked to my daughter when she was with my family and I wrote her but I never got to see her and I wasn't able to talk to her after she moved in with her dad.

Information about where their children are, who they are with, and their general welfare is not always forthcoming from state departments of social services. One parent related the difficulty she experienced:

I wrote and stuff but they won't tell me where they are. My social worker said once I get on my feet and keep a job for 6 months we can see about visitation. What she doesn't understand is for the past year I have been trying to find a job, but no one wants to have someone who was in prison for 6 years. They [my children] are the only good thing that has ever happened to me, and I want them back. I didn't even know where they are.

In some cases, women in prison lose custody of their children. A woman related her story:

My children, there isn't much to say. I had three boys and I lost them when I went in. I haven't seen them since I violated my probation, it's been about 5 years. I get letters from a social worker telling me how they are doing, but I can't see them or talk to them or anything. I talked to someone from social services about it, but I will never get them back. I really miss them.

Having one's children placed in foster care while incarcerated frequently is related to the financial circumstance of the female prisoner's relatives who are taking responsibility for the children. In many cases, children are being cared for by grandparents or other relatives who often cannot afford the financial burden. In these instances, family members would like to seek financial aid from the state but often are reluctant to do so. Many female prisoners do not seek government funds for relatives who are responsible for their children for fear of losing custody. This is what occurred in the following case when the inmate's mother applied for agency funding from the state to help her care for the children:

> I wanted my kids to be with my mom, but she didn't have much money, so she tried to get help and the state came in and took my kids. They helped all right. I haven't seen them since.

Problems of Reunification

The paroled women in this study had been out of prison for a period of 14 to 24 months, and many were involved in drug and alcohol rehabilitation programs. Some resided in halfway houses, whereas others were living on their own or with relatives. Most told of extreme difficulties in their attempts to regain custody of their children. A woman on parole who wishes to regain custody must meet the criteria of state social services agencies. For example, if she had an alcohol or drug abuse problem prior to her incarceration, she must show that she has actively participated in a rehabilitation program and has been off drugs and/or alcohol for a period of time. A woman on parole must show that she has sustained employment, can financially support her children, has a permanent and appropriate residence, and is no longer involved in any criminal activity. Obviously, these criteria, along with additional discretionary demands that the paroling authorities impose, present difficult obstacles to women who wish to regain custodial rights of their children.

Part of the dilemma paroled parents face is convincing child service workers that they have become responsible adults who are capable of providing adequate care for their children who remain in foster homes. Once paroled to the community, this particular parent summarized the problems she faced in proving she was a mature, responsible adult. She talked about her daughter:

> I get visits. I am trying to get her back. It is hard. The social worker had a hearing set, but I had to take a bus cause I'm not allowed to drive, but the bus never showed up, so I was late. I know that didn't look good, but I guess I'll keep trying. It's hard. I didn't even know where she is at. When I see her, we go to social services. I don't even know how she is treated or anything.

Another case clearly illustrates the conflict women on parole face between wanting their children back and not having the financial resources to adequately provide for them. One woman commented:

> I visit and we can spend the day together. It is hard cause part of me feels I should just leave her alone. She is 7 and she is doing good in school and has a lot of friends, but I just can't do it, she's my little angel and I know it might not be the best thing, but I need her.

When asked whether it was possible in the future to get custody of her daughter, the woman commented:

> No, I've tried. It's hard enough to get visits. I know I fucked up big time, but I paid the price and I screwed up, but now I am ready to move on.

Impediments to Reintegration

Once out of prison and on parole, women in this study reported the many difficulties they experienced in adjusting to living in the community. The one factor common to the experience of all the interviewees was the distrust community members communicated. The women constantly felt they had to prove themselves as worthy citizens to others who had knowledge of their criminal backgrounds. One respondent explained:

> I am doing very well. I have a place to live, but it's hard getting your kids back because nobody will believe that I have changed and I'm a different person now. No matter how much time we do, everyone always thinks it's like once a criminal always a criminal and that is how people see me and it's very hard to deal with.

When interacting with others in the community who have no knowledge of their past criminal background and imprisonment, the respondents reported being treated in a "normal" manner. One study participant, however, explained the change in attitudes when parents of her child's friends learned of her background:

> I became friends with some other mothers at my kid's school. They were really nice. I joined the PTA and it was going good. Then I told someone, I don't know how it came up, that I was in prison. Now, some of them won't talk to me, and they won't let their kids play with mine. So I learned my lesson. I don't really care what people think of me. Well, I kind of do, but I just don't want my kids to suffer.

The consequences of the criminal label and the stigma attached to it were experienced by another woman in a religious environment:

> It's been tough, my sister is great letting me live with her, and all at once when people find out I was in prison they look down on me. I was going to church cause I really found God and everyone was so nice. Then, someone found out I was in prison and everything changed, no one would talk to me anymore. Now I don't go, I just pray at home.

One of the biggest problems faced by the parolees was finding well-paying employment. Often, women on parole have few job skills. This, coupled with their past criminal history, leads to low-paying, dead-end employment. The negative reactions of potential employers toward their past criminal lifestyle make attaining meaningful employment with future growth potential nearly impossible for these women. A respondent said:

> I was lucky cause I had a place to live. I know a lot of people end up not having anywhere to go. When you're getting out, you are just so excited to have your

freedom again. Once I got out, I couldn't find a job. It is hard. Nobody will give you a break. I could be such a good worker, but they can't see it cause I was in prison. I mean it is a lot worse in prison, and I'm glad I'm not still there, but it's been very hard for me out here.

Importance of Family Support

Close ties to families during incarceration are crucial in maintaining connections in the community. Visits from relatives, sustained correspondence, phone calls, or any type of communication serves to maintain a support system for inmates. Family contacts let the woman know that she is not forgotten and that there are people who care about her. For women returning to the community, the assistance of family is crucial to success. Family support for women on parole may mean a place to live, money for necessities, transportation, food, and a host of short-term needs until they become financially independent.

Support from relatives also enhances emotional survival. Families often provide love and a sense of caring that lifts a newly released woman's self-esteem. One example of how meaningful family support is was related by the following respondent:

My family was great. I know that I was lucky. A lot of people in prison do not have any support, and that is what helps you get through the rough times. I don't know why my family stuck by me. My husband could have given up on me. He could have got custody of the kids and left. He must really love me, and I thank God every day that he stayed in the relationship. My family offered me the support I needed. I never would have got through it without them.

In contrast, we also found that almost half of the women had lost touch with their families. They tried several times to contact family members but never received any type of communication in return. After a while, the women stopped attempting to contact relatives: such a void of a family support system means female prisoners released to the community must function pretty much on their own. This makes for greater adjustment problems in reintegrating into the community. To illustrate the rejection by family members, one woman explained the type of response she received when she attempted to make contact while imprisoned:

My sisters live out east and have their own lives with nice houses and kids. I am just an embarrassment to them. They won't have anything to do with me. I wrote them each a couple of times cause when you're in a place like this, you realize how important your family really is, but they sent the letters back, and I've never heard from them.

For women without family support, being released from prison appears to be even more frightening. In these circumstances, women on parole have to become their own support system. Yet, success in the community is very much dependent on the belief that they will be accepted in society.

DISCUSSION

Women on parole experience the pain of social and self-imposed punishment that manifests from feelings of shame or guilt connected to external and internalized norms (Cochran, Chamlin, Wood, & Sellers, 1999; Grasmick & Bursik, 1990). Although the distinction between guilt and shame is equivocal, shame is an internalized emotion that arises from public disapproval, whereas guilt is related to a specific behavior (Gehm & Scherer, 1988; Tangney, 1995). Shame for paroled women develops from being unable to live up to societal definitions of what it means to be a woman, a good parent, and a responsible citizen. Ex-offenders rarely view themselves as blameless, but continued societal alienation accentuates feelings of guilt and hinders successful reunification and reintegration. Women on parole are likely to experience "guilt with an overlay of shame" that leads to rumination and self-castigation (Tangney, 1995, p. 1142). The "bad mother" label, identified by Burkart (1973), is a painful and enduring stigma. Women in this study appear to engage in continued self-deprecation over the loss of their children, families, and relationships.

Community members often are reluctant to accept female ex-offenders and seem to engage in harsh moral judgments. Consequently, few efforts are made to reconcile the offender's presence in the community, and the person, not the deed, is labeled as bad (Braithwaite, 1989). The narratives in this research show that many of the women believe that once they are identified as a criminal, they remain a criminal in the eyes of others. Women on parole also experience disapproval from a variety of social organizations, which promotes further alienation.

Negative labels may lead to limited employment opportunities. Many parolees also lack relevant job training. Vocational education and training programs for women in most corrections facilities are limited (Moyer, 1992). Training programs for clerical jobs, food services, and cosmetology, although cost-effective for the prison, fail to prepare women to be self-supporting upon release (Durham, 1994). The lack of job training, coupled with the label of being a female criminal, results in fewer employment opportunities.

This research represents a starting point for identifying the additional costs of imprisonment associated with displacement and the loss of significant others. The narratives, although based on women from one prison, emphasize the need for alternative sanctions, parenting programs, and community education. The collateral costs of prison and parole can be reduced by increasing opportunities that emphasize reentry into the job market, reintegration into the community, and reunification with children and families.

REFERENCES

Barry, E. (1987). Imprisoned mothers face extra hardships. *National Prison Journal, 14,* 1–4.

Barry, E. (1995). Legal issues for prisoners with children. In K. Gabel & D. Johnston (Eds.), *Children of incarcerated parents* (pp. 147–156). New York: Lexington Books.

Baunach, P. J. (1985). *Mothers in prison.* New Brunswick, NJ: Transaction Books.

Baunach, P. J., & Murton, T. O. (1973). Women in prison: An awakening minority. *Crime and Corrections, 1,* 4–12.

Becker, H. (1963). *Outsiders: Studies in the sociology of deviance.* New York: Free Press.

Bill, L. (1998). The victimization and revictimization of female offenders: Prison administrators should be aware of ways in which security procedures perpetrate feelings of powerlessness among incarcerated women. *Corrections Today, 60*(7), 106–108.

Bloom, B. (1995). Public policy and the children of incarcerated parents. In K. Gabel & D. Johnston (Eds.), *Children of incarcerated parents* (pp. 271–284). New York: Lexington Books.

Bloom, B., & Chesney-Lind, M. (2000). Women in prison: Vengeful equity. In R. Muraskin (Ed.), *It's a crime: Women and justice* (pp. 183–204). Upper Saddle River, NJ: Prentice Hall.

Bloom, B., & Steinhart, D. (1993). *Why punish the children? A reappraisal of the children of incarcerated mothers in America.* San Francisco: National Council on Crime and Delinquency.

Braithwaite, J. (1989). *Crime, shame and reintegration.* Cambridge, UK: Cambridge University Press.

Browne, D. C. (1998). Incarcerated mothers and parenting. *Journal of Family Violence, 4*, 211–221.

Burkart, K. (1973). *Women in prison.* Garden City, NY: Doubleday.

Chesney-Lind, M. (1997). *The female offender: Girls, women and crime.* Thousand Oaks, CA: Sage.

Cochran, J. K., Chamlin, M. B., Wood, P. B., & Sellers, C. S. (1999). Shame, embarrassment, and formal sanction threats: Extending the deterrence/rational choice model to academic dishonesty. *Sociological Inquiry, 69*, 91–105.

Crawford, J. (1990). *The female offender: What does the future hold?* Washington, DC: American Correctional Association.

Datesman, S., & Cales, G. (1983). I'm still the same mommy. *The Prison Journal, 63*, 142–154.

Durham, A. (1994). *Crisis and reform: Current issues in American punishment.* Boston: Little, Brown.

Fletcher, B., Shaver, L., & Moon, D. (1993). *Women prisoners: A forgotten population.* Westport, CT: Praeger.

Fox, J. (1982). Women in prison: A case study in the reality of stress. In R. Johnson & H. Toch (Eds.), *The pains of imprisonment* (pp. 205–220). Beverly Hills, CA: Sage.

Gabel, K., & Johnston, D. (1995). *Children of incarcerated parents.* New York: Lexington Books.

Garfinkel, H. (1956). Conditions of successful degradation ceremonies. *American Journal of Sociology, 61*, 420–424.

Gehm, T. L., & Scherer, K. R. (1988). Relating situation evaluation to emotion differentiation: Nonmetric analysis of cross-cultural questionnaire data. In K. R. Scherer (Ed.), *Facets of emotion: Recent research* (pp. 61–77). Hillsdale, NJ: Lawrence Erlbaum.

Glaser, B. G., & Strauss, A. L. (1967). *The discovery of grounded theory: Strategies for qualitative research.* London: Weidenfeld and Nicholson.

Glick, R., & Neto, V. (1977). *National study of women's correctional programs.* Washington, DC: Government Printing Office.

Goffman, E. (1963). *Stigma: Notes on the management of spoiled identity.* Englewood Cliffs, NJ: Prentice Hall.

Grasmick, H. G., & Bursik, R. J. (1990). Conscience, significant others, and rational choice: Extending the deterrence model. *Law and Society Review, 24*, 837–861.

Greenfeld, L. A., & Minor-Harper, S. (1991). *Women in prison* (Bureau of Justice Statistics special report). Washington, DC: U.S. Department of Justice.

Hairston, C. F. (1991). Mothers in jail: Parent-child separation and jail visitation. *AFFILIA, 6*(2), 9–27.

Harris, J. W. (1993). Comparison of stressors among female vs. male inmates. *Journal of Offender Rehabilitation, 19*, 43–56.

Henriques, Z. W. (1982). *Imprisoned mothers and their children.* Washington, DC: University Press of America.

Henriques, Z. W. (1996). Imprisoned mothers and their children: Separation-reunion syndrome dual impact. *Women & Criminal Justice, 8,* 77–95.

Jones, R. R. (1993). Coping with separation: Adaptive responses of women prisoners. *Women & Criminal Justice, 5,* 71–91.

Knight, B. (1992). Women in prison as litigants: Prospects for post prison futures. *Women & Criminal Justice, 4,* 91–116.

Martin, M. (1997). Connected mothers: A follow-up study of incarcerated women and their children. *Women & Criminal Justice, 8,* 1–23.

McGowan, B., & Blumenthal, K. (1978). *Why punish the children? A study of the children of women prisoners.* Hackensack, NJ: National Council on Crime and Delinquency.

Moyer, I. L. (1992). *The changing roles of women in the criminal justice system, offenders, victims, and professionals.* Prospect Heights, IL: Waveland Press.

Pollock-Byrne, J. M. (1990). *Women, prison, and crime.* Pacific Grove, CA: Brooks/Cole.

Pollock-Byrne, J. M. (1992). Women in prison: Why are their numbers increasing? In P. J. Benekes & A. V. Merlo (Eds.), *Corrections: Dilemmas and directions* (pp. 79–95). Cincinnati, OH: Anderson.

Prendergast, M., Wellisen, J., & Falkin, G. (1995). Assessment of and services for substance-abusing women offenders in community and correctional settings. *The Prison Journal, 75,* 240–256.

Rafter, N. (1985). *Partial justice: Women in state prisons, 1800–1935.* Boston: Northeastern University Press.

Ragin, C. C. (1994). *Constructing social research.* Thousand Oaks, CA: Pine Forge Press.

Rasche, C. (2000). The dislike of female offenders among correctional officers. In R. Muraskin (Ed.), *It's a crime: Women and justice* (pp. 237–252). Upper Saddle River, NJ: Prentice Hall.

Seidman, T. E. (1991). *Interviewing as qualitative research: A guide for researchers in education and the social sciences.* New York: Teachers College Press.

Shontz, F. (1965). *Research methods in personality.* New York: Appleton Crofts.

Stanton, A. (1980). *When mothers go to jail.* Lexington, MA: Lexington Books.

Sykes, G. M. (1958). *The society of captives: A study of a maximum security prison.* Princeton, NJ: Princeton University Press.

Tangney, J. P. (1995). Recent advances in the empirical study of shame and guilt. *American Behavioral Scientist, 38,* 1132–1145.

Ward, D., & Kassebaum, G. (1965). *Women's prisons.* Chicago: Aldine.

CHAPTER 18

A LARGE-SCALE MULTIDIMENSIONAL TEST OF THE EFFECT OF PRISON EDUCATION PROGRAMS ON OFFENDERS' BEHAVIOR

Kenneth Adams, Katherine J. Bennett,
Timothy J. Flanagan, James W. Marquart,
Steven J. Cuvelier, Eric Fritsch, Jurg Gerber,
Dennis R. Longmire, and Velmer S. Burton, Jr.

This study examined the prison behavior and postrelease recidivism of more than 14,000 inmates released from Texas prisons in 1991 and 1992. Comparisons were made between participants and nonparticipants in prison education programs on a variety of behavioral outcomes. The findings suggest that these programs may be most effective when intensive efforts are focused on the most educationally disadvantaged prisoners. Implications for correctional education policy and correctional program research are discussed.

Inmate education programs have been a central feature of state correctional systems since the 1930s (Clemmer, 1958). Beginning with "training schools" for delinquents, the provision of academic and vocational education programs has become almost a universal element of incarceration. These programs address the glaring educational deficits that offenders present on admission (Glaser, 1969). They also reinforce deeply held cultural beliefs about the importance of education for achieving a productive and satisfying life.

Education programs within prisons also have several attributes that make them attractive to correctional administrators. They provide incentives to inmates in surroundings that are otherwise devoid of constructive activities; they provide exposure to positive civilian role models; and they engage inmates for many hours in quiet, productive activity in an otherwise monotonous institu-

Viewpoints or opinions expressed in this article are those of the authors. They do not represent the official position or policies of the Texas Department of Criminal Justice or of the Windham School System.

THE PRISON JOURNAL, Vol. 74 No. 4, December 1994 433–449

tional environment. Education programs are a key component of what has been called "dynamic security" within prisons.

In addition to these presumed benefits of educational programs for institutional management, corrections leaders hope that upgrading offenders' educational levels will increase their opportunities to lead crime-free lives after release. Investments in correctional education programs are thought to bring rewards in the form of lower recidivism rates (Sharp, 1993). This research examines these assumptions in a large, multiservice state prison education system.

Education, Inmates' Behavior, and Recidivism in the Research Literature

In the most widely known assessment of correctional programs, Lipton, Martinson, and Wilks (1975) reported that "offenders are amenable to training and education . . . [and] can generally improve basic educational skills, given the teacher's real concern, personal interest, and dynamic instruction" (p. 363). The researchers observed that these findings were "useful in dispelling Lombrosian notions concerning the inherent genetic incapacities of criminal offenders" (p. 363). By 1975, however, this research seemed "superfluous;" the bottom line, according to Lipton, et al. (1975), was a need for "evidence concerning the differential effects of educational programs on postrelease behavior" (p. 363).

Twenty years after the publication of *The Effectiveness of Correctional Treatment,* concerns about the effectiveness of correctional programs and the focus on the "bottom line" of recidivism reduction have increased. Dramatic and unprecedented increases in prisoner populations have stretched correctional agency budgets despite huge increases in state appropriations. Public officials, the media, and citizens demand that the practical payoff of correctional programs be demonstrated.

We reviewed the empirical literature on the impact of correctional education programs through summer 1993 (Gerber & Fritsch, in press). We included empirical studies that incorporated (a) a control group; (b) random assignment, documented matching of experimental and control subjects, or methods of statistical control of intergroup differences; and (c) tests of statistical significance between experimental and control groups.

The findings of these 90 studies can be summarized briefly. Of 14 studies that examined participation in *precollege* education programs and postrelease recidivism, 9 found that participation in programs was related significantly to lower recidivism rates. Also, 3 of 4 studies of precollege programs found a significant relationship with postrelease employment, and both of the studies that examined postrelease participation in education found that offenders who participated in precollege education programs were more likely to continue their education after release. Participation in *college* programs in prison was associated with lower recidivism rates (10 of 14 studies), higher rates of postrelease employment (3 of 3 studies), and higher rates of participation in education programs after release. Research showed that involvement in prison-based *vocational education* programs was linked with lower recidivism (10 of 13 studies) and higher rates of postrelease employment (5 of 7 studies). Finally, we reviewed the sparse literature on prison-based "life skills" programs; only 1 study, however, investigated the postrelease behavior of life skills participants.

Our review of the literature also examined the relationship between participation in educational programs and involvement in prison disciplinary violations. Three studies examined this issue among participants in college programs: one study found lower rates of disciplinary involvement among prisoner college students, and two found no significant relationship between college programs and disciplinary activity. Two studies of participation in vocational education programs, however, found significantly lower rates of disciplinary violations among program participants.

On balance, our review of the scientific literature supports the view that adult academic and vocational correctional education programs may be associated with fewer disciplinary violations during incarceration, reductions in recidivism, and increased rates of employment and participation in education programs on release. These findings, however, are based on studies that often observed small samples, employed widely varying definitions of concepts, used varying follow-up periods, and applied differing definitions of recidivism.

This study is part of a larger research project that examines the impact of prison education programs in Texas and extends and expands the line of research described previously. The Prison Education Research Project (PERP) was designed to address questions about the effectiveness of educational programs offered by the Windham School System (Windham), the educational programs division of the Texas Department of Criminal Justice-Institutional Division (TDCJ-ID).

METHODOLOGY

Ideally, a study of the effects of prison education programs on inmates' behavior would involve needs assessment of inmates entering prison; random allocation of inmates to programs that are matched to each inmate's needs; collection of detailed information on the inmates' performance from teachers' ratings and educational test scores; collection of detailed information on other aspects of the inmates' prison experience based on prison records and interviews with the inmates; and extended observation of the inmates' postrelease behavior with regard to criminal activity, employment, and further involvement in educational programs. Obviously, such a study would be extremely expensive and time consuming. In addition, postrelease follow-up findings would be unavailable for many years because of the nature of the data collection. Our approach was directed by the need for more timely information, and so we employed a design that involved a naturally occurring intact comparison group (Rezmovic, 1979).

We selected a cohort of 14,411 inmates who were both admitted and released from the TDCJ-ID between March 1991 and December 1992. The sample included all inmates released on parole, mandatory supervision, and expiration of sentence. Released parole violators were not included in the sample. The sample was limited to inmates who entered the prison after March 1991 because accurate records on inmate participation in educational programs are not available before this time. Inmates had to be released from prison by December 1992 to allow for an adequate follow-up period.

The strategy of studying a release cohort offers a number of advantages. The sample is relatively large, capturing inmates in different Windham programs as well as inmates who did not participate in any educational programs. Also, the inmates in the sample had completed their sentences, and so their educational and disciplinary experiences throughout their prison stays could be investigated. Finally, the sample provides a contemporary picture of the prison system while allowing adequate time for a follow-up of criminal behavior in the community.

Having designated the release cohort, we obtained computerized information maintained by the TDCJ-ID and Windham. The TDCJ information covered social and demographic variables (e.g., age, race, sex, marital status, educational achievement), criminal history and current offense variables (e.g., conviction offense, sentence length, time served, prior incarcerations), and disciplinary involvement (e.g., major and minor infractions). We used background information to describe the sample and to identify differences between Windham and non-Windham inmates. The information on major and minor disciplinary infractions represents an important outcome variable in the analyses. Windham provided information on educational test scores and program involvement regarding both the type of program and the number of hours of participation.

We used return to prison as the primary outcome variable for the community follow-up. This information was provided by TDCJ-ID on a computer tape of prison admissions from January 1991 through March 1994. By matching identification numbers of the released inmates against the admissions file, we identified inmates in the sample who had been returned to prison and calculated elapsed time to readmission for recidivists. We used this information to supplement the standard recidivism variable, return to prison, by examining whether Windham participation delayed the return to prison for those inmates who recidivated.[1]

Because the follow-up information was collected with regard to a fixed point in time (March 1994) and because inmates have different release dates, the length of the follow-up period varied among inmates. The follow-up period for the sample varied from 14 to 36 months depending on when an inmate was released. This variation could be a problem if inmates in Windham programs were systematically exposed to shorter or longer follow-up periods than were non-Windham inmates, but examination of the distribution of follow-up periods for groups of inmates by service delivery category showed that the distribution was nearly identical for all groups. The average follow-up period was 25 months for non-Windham inmates, inmates in Windham academic programs, and inmates in Windham vocational programs; it was 24 months for inmates in both Windham programs. Thus the variations in length of follow-up should not bias comparisons of groups by type of service delivery.

FINDINGS

Sample Characteristics

Table 18.1 displays the social, criminal, and educational characteristics of Windham and non-Windham inmates. We compared groups of inmates who did not participate in Windham, inmates who participated only in academic programs, inmates who participated only in vocational programs, and inmates

Table 18.1

Social, Criminal, and Educational Characteristics of Windham and Non-Windham Inmates (in percentage)

	No Windham Participation (n = 7,793)	*Academic* (n = 5,130)	*Vocational* (n = 208)	*Both Academic and Vocational* (n = 1,280)
Conviction offense				
Homicide/kidnap	1.7	1.6	4.1	2.3
Sex offense	2.0	2.1	0.0	2.5
Robbery/assault	9.5	10.0	13.3	14.8
Burglary/larceny	39.6	38.2	44.1	42.2
Forgery/fraud	6.8	5.0	5.1	3.0
Drugs	32.9	35.8	28.2	30.0
Traffic	6.1	5.3	4.1	3.2
Other	1.5	2.0	1.0	2.1
Violent offense				
Yes	25.5	27.4	24.4	32.8
No	74.5	72.6	75.6	67.2
Prior adult incarcerations				
None	63.8	65.2	59.2	64.3
One or two	34.1	33.5	38.3	34.8
Three or more	2.1	1.4	1.5	0.8
Age (in years)				
16-21	17.1	22.3	28.8	27.4
22-27	25.1	27.1	24.5	28.2
28-35	32.3	31.1	29.8	28.2
36+	25.5	19.6	16.8	16.2
Mean	30.5	29.1	27.7	27.6
Standard deviation	9.1	9.0	7.5	7.9
Gender				
Male	85.7	79.8	87.5	87.3
Female	14.3	20.2	12.5	12.7
Race				
Black	45.3	44.9	30.8	38.8
White	19.6	29.6	23.1	27.7
Hispanic	34.9	25.2	46.2	33.3
Other	0.3	0.3	0.0	0.2
Marital status				
Married	29.9	32.0	35.1	34.4
Single	70.1	68.0	64.9	65.6
IQ test score				
60 to 79	19.0	29.0	8.6	19.2
80 to 100	51.7	53.7	57.4	56.2
101 to 135	29.2	17.3	34.0	24.6
Mean	86.3	78.8	90.3	85.9
Standard deviation	26.6	28.9	24.4	24.3

Table 18.1
Continued

	No Windham Participation (n = 7,793)	Academic (n = 5,130)	Vocational (n = 208)	Both Academic and Vocational (n = 1,280)
Educational achievement (grade level)				
Less than 6.0	31.8	58.8	17.1	41.8
6.0 to 7.4	15.4	16.3	16.5	17.9
7.5 or higher	52.8	24.9	66.5	40.3
Mean	4.6	4.6	6.4	5.8
Standard deviation	4.5	3.3	3.3	3.6
Mandatory education status				
Yes	44.1	59.8	29.3	41.8
No	55.9	40.2	70.7	58.2

who participated in both academic and vocational programs. The major findings in this table pertain to the IQ and educational achievement test scores of inmates in academic programs and to the effects of time served on participation in both academic and vocational Windham programs. The comparisons reveal that *inmates in the academic programs had substantially lower IQ and educational achievement test scores than did inmates in other categories.* That is, Windham academic programs enroll educationally and intellectually disadvantaged inmates.

We also examined the extent to which Windham delivers services to inmates who are required by statute to participate in educational programs because they have less than a sixth-grade educational achievement test score and lack a high school degree or its equivalent. The data show that 59.8% of the inmates who participated in academic programs fit the criteria for mandatory education whereas 40.2% did not. Among inmates who did not participate in any Windham programs, 44.1% met the criteria for mandatory education. There are many reasons why inmates who are mandated to participate in education programs do not receive services—for example, program resources vary by institution and inmates differ in classification status, motivation, cooperation, and length of sentence. Similarly, there are many reasons why prison academic programs should reach beyond the most disadvantaged group of inmates. From the standpoint of program evaluation, however, the findings suggest that the assignment process for participation in prison academic programs does not correspond with official policy goals.

Time Served and Exposure to Windham Programs

Length of prison stay was related strongly to hours of service delivery. Overall, non-Windham inmates served an average of 4.5 months in prison, Windham academic participants served 5.6 months, Windham vocational participants served 6.7 months, and Windham inmates participating in both programs served 7.6 months. The data also showed that time served was related to total hours of participation in Windham programs. For example, among Windham academic inmates with 300 or more hours of academic programs, more than two-thirds served more than 9 months in prison. By contrast, fewer than 11% of non-Windham inmates served more than 9 months.

The fact that inmates in academic programs serve an average of only 5.6 months should not be overlooked in assessing the performance of these programs because time served relates directly to Windham's opportunity to work with inmates. Hudson (1977) described a common characteristic of correctional programs, namely that offenders are not exposed to the "treatment" for a long enough time. He referred to such diluted treatment efforts as "puny interventions" (p. 80). When the average time-served figures are considered in connection with the low IQ and low educational achievement test scores discussed previously, the predicament faced by prison academic programs becomes even more difficult to resolve. These data suggest strongly that the "window of opportunity" available to Windham programs is very small. In other words, the dosage effect of prison education programs in a revolving-door correctional system is very limited (Marquart et al., 1994).

Program Participation, Accomplishments, and Outcome Measures

Tables 18.2 through 18.6 compare the non-Windham inmates to the Windham inmates with regard to measures of program participation and accomplishment. We examined the type of program, mandatory participation, hours of participation, and achievement in the program in relation to prison disciplinary infractions and return to prison.

Program participation, prison disciplinary infractions, and return to prison. Table 18.2 shows that participation in academic and vocational programs, when measured in a straightforward yes/no manner, bore no relation to reincarceration. For all practical purposes, the percentage of inmates who were returned to prison did not vary across groups of Windham and non-Windham inmates; between 21% and 25% of inmates in the various groups were returned to prison. The data also show that participation in Windham academic and vocational programs was not related to the number of months to return for reincarcerated inmates. In general for the various inmate groups, 14 to 17 months passed between release and reincarceration.

Table 18.2 also distinguishes, in the non-Windham group, between inmates who were and were not eligible for academic programs. (In general, inmates with a high school diploma or the GED, its equivalent, are not eligible for school programs.) This distinction provides a clearer assessment of Windham's performance by comparing actual clients (the Windham group) to potential clients (Windham-eligible with no service) and thus controls for prior educational experience to a modest extent. Among the no-service group, the noneligible inmates had a considerably lower reincarceration rate (19.1%) than did the eligible inmates (25.1%).

Windham participation had a strong relationship to involvement in major and minor disciplinary infractions. Of non-Windham inmates, 24.1% were

Table 18.2

Prison and Community Outcomes, by Windham Eligibility and Type of Education Program Participation (percentage)

Windham Participation	Prison		Community	
	Minor Disciplinaries	*Major Disciplinaries*	*Return to Prison*	*Months to Return*[a]
None (*n* = 8,001)	24.1	5.7	23.7	15.7 (mean)
				6.7 (*SD*)
Windham eligible	22.5	5.8	25.1	15.5 (mean)
				6.6 (*SD*)
Windham ineligible	23.8	5.7	19.1	16.7 (mean)
				6.5 (*SD*)
Academic (*n* = 5,051)	34.1	8.4	23.0	16.5 (mean)
				6.5 (*SD*)
Vocational (*n* = 422)	29.9	7.8	20.9	14.2 (mean)
				6.1 (*SD*)
Both academic and vocational (*n* = 1,359)	44.7	12.4	21.6	15.6 (mean)
				6.1 (*SD*)

[a]Applies only to those inmates who are reincarcerated.

involved in minor infractions during their prison stays compared to 34.1% of inmates in academic programs, 29.9% in vocational programs, and 44.7% in both programs. Corresponding figures for involvement in major infractions were 5.7% (non-Windham), 8.4% (Windham academic), 7.8% (Windham vocational), and 12.4% (both). These findings are surprising because they are opposite of what would be predicted on the basis of the prison management literature. Possibly the figures are biased because inmates in Windham programs served more time in prison and therefore had more opportunity to violate prison rules or a greater risk of exposure to violations. This issue is discussed subsequently.

Mandatory education and outcomes. Table 18.3 examines the outcomes of the mandatory service inmates (generally those with less than a sixth-grade education) by whether the inmates actually received service. About half of the mandatory service group did not enroll in Windham programs. Recidivism rates varied little among groups of inmates, ranging from 22.2% to 25.3%. Among inmates in the mandatory service group, those who received services had lower reincarceration rates than did those who did not although the difference was very small (25.3% vs. 23.1%). We obtained similar findings with regard to the number of months to reincarceration for those inmates who failed while in the community. Thus, according to these data, the policy of mandating

Table 18.3
Prison and Community Outcomes, by Mandatory Participation in Windham
Programs and Actual Service Delivery (percentage)

Windham Participation	Prison		Community	
	Minor Disciplinaries	*Major Disciplinaries*	*Return to Prison*	*Months to Return*[a]
Not mandatory, no service (*n* = 4,503)	24.8	5.7	22.3	16.4 (mean) 6.9 (*SD*)
Not mandatory, service (*n* = 2,807)	37.9	9.7	22.2	16.4 (mean) 6.5 (*SD*)
Mandatory, no service (*n* = 3,498)	22.2	6.0	25.3	15.3 (mean) 6.5 (*SD*)
Mandatory, service (*n* = 3,603)	33.3	8.7	23.1	16.6 (mean) 6.6 (*SD*)

[a]Applies only to those inmates who were reincarcerated.

participation in educational programs, although admirable, does not reduce recidivism. Table 18.3 also shows that participation in academic programs was related to prison misbehavior: Windham inmates again displayed higher rates of involvement in both minor and major disciplinary infractions.

Hours of participation in educational programs and outcomes. Table 18.4 examines the relationship between the number of hours in Windham programs and the outcome variables. Because of the relatively short time served in the Texas prison system during the period examined here, we must take into account the quantity of services actually received. Hours of participation are a more discriminating measure of program exposure that indicates participation more precisely than does the simple yes/no measure of participation used thus far in the analyses.

The data show that the number of hours of participation in both academic and vocational programs was related negatively to recidivism and positively to prison misbehavior. Inmates with fewer than 100 hours in academic programs had a reincarceration rate of 25.0% compared to 16.6% for inmates with more than 300 hours in academic programs and 23.6% for inmates who did not participate in academic programs. Similarly, inmates with fewer than 100 hours in vocational programs had a recidivism rate of 22.8%, inmates with more than 300 hours in vocational programs had a rate of 18.3%, and inmates who did not participate in vocational programs had a rate of 22.4%. The data suggest that

Table 18.4
Prison and Community Outcomes, by Number of Hours in Windham
Programs (percentage)

Windham Participation	Prison		Community	
	Minor Disciplinaries	*Major Disciplinaries*	*Return to Prison*	*Months to Return*[a]
Participation in academic programs				
None	22.8	5.7	23.6	15.7 (mean) 6.6 (*SD*)
100 hours or fewer	31.2	7.3	25.0	16.5 (mean) 6.6 (*SD*)
101 to 200 hours	39.8	8.5	20.7	16.0 (mean) 6.5 (*SD*)
201 to 300 hours	42.7	12.5	21.8	16.9 (mean) 6.4 (*SD*)
301 hours or more	48.5	18.2	16.6	15.2 (mean) 5.5 (*SD*)
Participation in vocational programs				
None	27.1	6.7	22.4	16.1 (mean) 6.2 (*SD*)
100 hours or fewer	35.8	9.8	22.8	15.2 (mean) 6.3 (*SD*)
101 to 200 hours	45.2	12.4	22.6	15.8 (mean) 6.6 (*SD*)
201 to 300 hours	47.6	10.7	18.2	15.0 (mean) 5.5 (*SD*)
301 hours or more	48.8	14.8	18.3	14.9 (mean) 5.5 (*SD*)

[a]Applies only to those inmates who were reincarcerated.

participation in academic and vocational programs has discernible dosage or exposure features; recidivism rates declined only after 200 hours of program participation. Our decision to categorize service delivery in blocks of 100 hours was somewhat arbitrary, but the data show that academic and vocational programs exhibit a dose-response curve such that relatively brief periods of participation had little or no effect.

Finally, the data show that extended participation in academic and vocational programs was associated with *increased* violations of prison rules. With each 100-hour increase in program participation, the rate of minor and major rule violations increased. Inmates with more than 300 hours of Windham participation had a minor infraction rate about two times greater and a major infraction rate about three times greater than did non-Windham inmates. In part, this finding reflects the influence of time at risk because inmates who participated more in prison programs also spent more time in prison and therefore had more opportunity to commit infractions. We examine this issue subsequently. It also is possible that inmates in academic and vocational programs were charged with program-related infractions (e.g., tardiness, classroom misbehavior). A recently completed study of TDCJ disciplinary cases clarifies this issue. A study of disciplinary charges written between November 1993 and February 1994 showed that "Windham areas" of prisons accounted for 8.5% of systemwide disciplinary charges. However, 80% of the charges identified as in the Windham area indicated "some aspect of students failing to attend class" (TDCJ, 1994).

Educational achievement and outcomes.   We also sought to examine the relationship of *achievement* in academic and vocational programs to outcomes. For inmates in academic programs, we measured achievement in terms of change in educational achievement test scores and; for vocational programs, in terms of a certificate of program completion. In principle, these achievement measures offer the most accurate indicator of program exposure for evaluation because they translate directly into change on the part of inmates. Unfortunately, our investigation was hampered by the fact that only a small proportion of inmates were tested more than once for educational achievement. Nearly all inmates had an educational achievement score, presumably measured at intake, but only about 1,200 inmates in academic programs, or about 20%, were tested again. Given the large amount of missing data (roughly 80% of the inmates in academic programs), we have little confidence in the reliability and validity of the findings for academic programs.

With this important caution in mind, we found that academic achievement, measured directly, was not related to recidivism or disciplinary involvement. Inmates who increased by half a grade level or more had roughly the same recidivism rates as did inmates who made no progress in the academic program when progress was measured in terms of standardized test scores. Among the recidivists, however, inmates who increased at least half a grade level stayed out of prison almost 3½ months longer than did inmates who made no academic progress. In view of the conflicting findings and the large proportion of missing data, the relationship between academic achievement and recidivism should be targeted for future study.

Prison disciplinary infractions and monthly participation in educational programs.   Table 18.5 investigates the relationship between monthly participation in academic and vocational programs and prison rule violations. The analysis deals only with inmates who participated in Windham academic programs and examines whether inmates who participated in Windham programs during a given month were likely to be written up for a violation of prison rules during that month. By examining program and disciplinary involvements monthly, we standardize the time at risk for infractions. Further, because inmates who participate in programs often do so intermittently, the analysis addresses directly

Table 18.5
Disciplinary Involvement, by Monthly Participation in Windham
Programs (percentage)

	Minor	*Major*
Monthly participation in academic programs		
None	9.4	2.3
1 to 39 hours	15.3	3.4
40 or more hours	15.5	1.5
Monthly participation in vocational programs		
No	10.5	2.2
Yes	18.2	3.1

NOTE: The data pertain only to inmates who participated in Windham programs and describe the inmates' month-by-month program and disciplinary involvements.

the issue of program participation and rule violations by taking into account the temporal concordance of the two events.

The data show that participation in Windham academic programs was related positively to prison rule violations when we took into account the number of hours of program participation. We found that among Windham inmates who were not in academic programs, 9.4% were charged with prison infractions compared to 15% of those who participated in programs. The figures for major disciplinary infractions suggest that violation rates rise when inmates are involved only slightly with programs and decrease when inmates are involved more heavily. Yet because major rules violations are relatively infrequent, small fluctuations in rates can be difficult to interpret. A similar pattern existed for vocational programs.

These findings are counterintuitive in that they are opposite to those predicted by the observations of correctional managers and by findings in the relevant literature. As mentioned previously, it may be that Windham inmates are more likely to be written up for program-related rule violations; this would be the case if Windham teachers were relatively strict. This issue could be explored in future analyses by studying the type and circumstances of prison rules violations by inmates engaged in academic and vocational programs.

Does the program work better for some inmates than for others? That is, are some inmates more amenable to treatment and, therefore, do they show greater success than less amenable inmates who also participated in a program? We explored this issue by examining the outcome variables for various categories of inmates using the social, educational, and criminal history information displayed in Table 18.1. *In general, we found that social and criminal history variables were not related to Windham program outcomes.* There was some suggestion that young first-time offenders benefited most from academic programs, but we found no great differences in outcomes by prison segregation class (which is based on a combination of age and prior incarcerations). By contrast, the educational variables showed a substantial interaction with participation in Windham academic programs, as discussed subsequently.

Initial grade levels, participation in education, and outcomes. Table 18.6 displays the outcome variables by initial grade level and hours of participation in Windham academic programs. Inmates with lower educational levels at intake and inmates who received fewer than 200 hours of academic programs were more likely to recidivate. The data also indicate a significant interaction effect such that the benefits of academic programming were confined largely to inmates with the lowest academic achievement. In other words, significant participation in academic programs (more than 200 hours) apparently reduced recidivism, but this benefit was limited mainly to inmates at the low end of the academic achievement scale.

For example, among inmates with an initial grade level of 1.0 to 3.9, 26.6% of the non-Windham inmates were reincarcerated in contrast to 25.7% of the inmates who received fewer than 200 hours of academic programs and 18.1%

Table 18.6

Prison and Community Outcomes, by Initial Grade Level and Hours of Participation in Academic Programs (percentage)

	Prison		Community	
Initial Grade Level	*Minor Disciplinaries*	*Major Disciplinaries*	*Return to Prison*	*Months to Return (mean)*
1.0 to 3.9				
No participation	21.4	7.0	26.6	14.2
200 hours or fewer	30.0	7.6	25.7	16.8
More than 200 hours	41.0	11.5	18.1	17.0
4.0 to 5.9				
No participation	29.2	7.7	27.9	15.9
200 hours or fewer	33.5	8.5	22.8	16.5
More than 200 hours	46.3	17.8	20.7	16.6
6.0 to 8.9				
No participation	25.5	6.6	26.2	16.0
200 hours or fewer	35.1	7.6	24.7	16.1
More than 200 hours	52.5	19.3	20.5	15.5
9.0 to 11.9				
No participation	23.0	5.7	21.4	17.5
200 hours or fewer	38.9	7.3	19.8	17.7
More than 200 hours	46.5	12.7	16.9	15.3
12.0 or higher				
No participation	26.6	5.4	15.3	14.4
200 hours or fewer	39.5	5.7	13.2	14.1
More than 200 hours	40.6	9.4	12.5	14.0

of the inmates who received more than 200 hours. The difference represents approximately a one-third reduction in the recidivism rate for the intensive service group; this is the largest effect of Windham academic programs in Table 18.6. Other inmates benefited from substantial participation in academic programs but less so than did inmates at the lowest grade level. For example, among inmates with an initial grade level of 4.0 to 5.9, the recidivism rate was 27.9% for non-Windham inmates and 20.7% for Windham inmates with more than 200 hours of programs, a one-quarter reduction in the recidivism rate. Similarly, among inmates with an initial grade level of 6.0 to 8.9, the recidivism rate was 26.2% for non-Windham inmates and 20.5% for Windham inmates with at least 200 hours of service, a reduction of about one-fifth. Inmates with an initial grade level of 9.0 to 11.9 also show roughly a one-fifth reduction in recidivism rates when non-Windham inmates were compared to inmates receiving at least 200 hours of service (21.4% vs. 16.9%). Overall, these findings show that the *most substantial reductions in recidivism are found among inmates at the lowest educational level who receive a relatively substantial amount of academic programming.* Inmates above a 12.0 educational level also benefit from participation in academic programs but less than do those at the lowest level.

CONCLUSION

This research assessed the impact of Windham programs on disciplinary infractions and recidivism rates, but we should not lose sight of other educational goals. Providing all individuals with educational services is a fundamental value in the American society. Discipline and education has been the mainstay of prison programs for inmates since the early years of our penal history.

In terms of correctional goals, we examined involvement in prison discipline (both major and minor offenses) along with reincarceration; we used the latter as a measure of criminal recidivism. We expected that participation in programs would be associated with lower rates of disciplinary infractions and lower rates of recidivism. Windham participation was examined in several ways: simple yes/no participation, the type of program in which inmates participated (academic and/or vocational), hours of participation, and educational achievement. The findings emphasized the importance of measuring such participation in various ways. Hours of program participation surfaced as the most discriminating measure of program exposure; the binary (yes/no) measure of program participation was not discriminating, and use of the achievement variable was hindered by missing data.

Two major findings emerged from our analysis; we believe that they are relevant for discussions of correctional education policy and for consideration in further research. First, the data show that inmates at the lowest levels of educational achievement benefit most (as indicated by lower recidivism rates) from participation in academic programs. Second, some minimum level of program exposure or involvement is necessary if differences in outcomes are to materialize. *When these two factors are combined, the data suggest that the recidivism rate can be reduced by about one-third if extensive services are targeted at inmates at the lowest level of educational achievement.* This is not to suggest that other inmates cannot benefit; in fact, evidence suggests that recidivism is reduced through the 12th grade. Yet, if one is looking for the greatest return on programming investment, the payoff is clearly greatest for inmates at the low end of the educational spectrum.

The present research cannot explain exactly why inmates at lower educational levels seem to benefit most from educational service. It may be that participating in educational programs improves the self-image of the educationally disadvantaged and gives them new skills.

Findings on hours in programming are critical because of the relatively short amount of time served. If programs are to have an impact, some minimum level of services must be delivered. Length of time served, however, constrains an inmate's opportunity to participate in education programs. It might be possible to work within these constraints by identifying clients as early as possible and offering them more intensive services. On the other hand, it might be more practical simply to consider sentence length and expected time served in deciding how to allocate scarce program resources.

In this study, participation in vocational programs showed smaller effects on reincarceration rates, but important information was missing from the analysis. It is crucial to examine postrelease employment availability and to determine whether that employment corresponds to the vocational training received in prison.

This study used data from a period during which Texas corrections suffered major internal and external pressures. Average time served plummeted in Texas during the late 1980s and 1990s but has increased since 1992 as prison capacity has begun to expand. As capacity increases, time served will increase as well, thus widening the window of opportunity for Windham and other programs. A more suitable approach to addressing offenders' educational deficits would integrate the efforts of community and institutional resources. An integrated correctional case management system would assess an offender's educational needs in community programs and would begin to deliver academic and vocational programs while the offender was on probation. If the offender were subsequently incarcerated, professional correctional educators could continue his or her schooling in prison and then could arrange for continuing educational services on release. Public education in the wider society has failed these offenders, and so professional correctional educators must assume the burden. In return, a successful correctional education program may offer the promise of reducing recidivism and the associated victimization.

This study further calls into question the often-repeated dictum that "nothing works in corrections"—that unfortunate belief born as a result of the work of Lipton, Martinson, and Wilks (1975). As in numerous studies of correctional effectiveness conducted during the past 20 years, these findings suggest that correctional intervention works best when programs are matched with offenders' needs and are delivered in a concerted, purposeful manner. This point implies that correctional program administrators must be more successful in assigning inmates to programs so as to maximize the use of resources and minimize the prospect of recidivism.

NOTE

1. It would have been desirable to use rearrest as a criterion variable in the community follow-up because arrest is a more sensitive measure of criminal activity than is reincarceration. In fact, we obtained some arrest information on the sample of released inmates from the Texas Department of Public Safety. Yet because prison records and arrest records could not be matched accurately on the basis of a unique identifier, we used names to match inmates with arrest records. This procedure proved to be inefficient and yielded only a relative small number of arrest records. On the basis of our judgment that the procedures for identifying arrest records generated an appreciable amount of error, we used only reincarceration information in the follow-up. Because this less discriminating measure of criminal activity was used, subtle differences between Windham and non-Windham clients may have gone undiscovered.

REFERENCES

Clemmer, D. (1958). *The prison community.* New York: Rinehart. (Originally published 1940).

Gerber, J., & Fritsch, E. (in press). Adult academic and vocational correctional education programs: A review of recent literature. *Journal of Offender Rehabilitation.*

Glaser, D. (1969). *The effectiveness of a prison and parole system* (abridged ed.). Indianapolis, IN: Bobbs-Merrill.

Hudson, J. (1977). Problems of measurement in criminal justice. In L. Rutman (Ed.), *Evaluation research methods: A basic guide* (pp. 75–100). Beverly Hills, CA: Sage.

Lipton, D., Martinson, R., & Wilks, J. (1975). *The effectiveness of correctional treatment.* New York: Praeger.

Marquart, J., Cuvelier, S., Burton, V., Adams, K., Gerber, J., Longmire, D., Flanagan, T., Bennett, K., & Fritsch, E. (1994). A limited capacity to treat: Examining the effects of prison population control strategies on prison education programs. *Crime and Delinquency, 40*(4), 516–531.

Rezmovic, E. (1979). Methodological considerations in evaluating correctional effectiveness: Issues and chronic problems. In L. Sechrest, S. White, & E. Brown (Eds.), *The rehabilitation of criminal offenders: Problems and prospects* (pp. 163–209). Washington, DC: National Academy of Sciences.

Sharp, J. (1993). *Schools behind bars: Windham school system and other prison education programs: A performance review.* Austin, TX: Comptroller of Public Accounts.

Texas Department of Criminal Justice. (1994). *Report on disciplinary cases in Windham* (mimeo). Huntsville: Texas Department of Criminal Justice.

CHAPTER 19

THREE-YEAR REINCARCERATION OUTCOMES FOR IN-PRISON THERAPEUTIC COMMUNITY TREATMENT IN TEXAS

Kevin Knight, D. Dwayne Simpson, and Matthew L. Hiller

Longer term in-prison therapeutic community (ITC) outcome studies are needed, along with more attention on who benefits most from these programs. This study examined reincarceration records for 394 nonviolent offenders during the 3 years following prison. Those who completed both ITC and aftercare were the least likely to be reincarcerated (25%), compared to 64% of the aftercare dropouts and 42% of the untreated comparison groups. Furthermore, high-severity aftercare completers were reincarcerated only half as often as those in the aftercare dropout and comparison groups (26% vs. 66% and 52%). The findings support the effectiveness of intensive treatment when it is integrated with aftercare, and the benefits are most apparent for offenders with more serious crime and drug-related problems.

In-prison therapeutic communities (ITCs) have been credited with reducing short-term recidivism rates among drug-involved offenders. For example, an evaluation of the Stay'n Out program in New York—the first largescale, federally funded evaluation of in-prison drug treatment in the United States—found that ITC participants were less likely than several comparison groups to be rearrested during the first few months following release from prison (Wexler,

This project was supported in part by Grant No. 96-IJ-CX-0024 awarded by the National Institute of Justice, Office of Justice Programs, U.S. Department of Justice. Points of view in this document are those of the authors and do not necessarily represent the official position or policies of the U.S. Department of Justice. Special appreciation is expressed to Kirk Broome, Ph.D., for his analytic advice and to the TDCJ-PSD and Kyle New Vision staff, particularly Shirley Livingston and Cathy Sturrock, for their invaluable support and assistance. Correspondence should be addressed to the Institute of Behavioral Research, Texas Christian University, TCU Box 298740, Fort Worth, TX 76129; e-mail: ibr@tcu.edu. More information is available on the Internet at http://www.ibr.tcu.edu.

THE PRISON JOURNAL, Vol. 79 No. 3, September 1999 337–351
© 1999 Sage Publications, Inc.

Falkin, & Lipton, 1990). These results have been replicated by more recent and scientifically rigorous evaluations, including studies of treatment programs in the Federal Bureau of Prisons (Pelissier et al., 1998), Delaware (Inciardi, Martin, Butzin, Hooper, & Harrison, 1997), California (Wexler, De Leon, Kressel, & Peters, 1999), and Texas (Knight, Simpson, Chatham, & Camacho, 1997). Nonetheless, additional research is needed to determine the sustained impact these types of correctional drug treatment programs have on longer term follow-up outcomes, which is the central purpose of the studies included in this special issue of *The Prison Journal.*

To achieve favorable outcomes, research also suggests that offenders need to participate in a community-based residential aftercare program following ITC treatment. Previous findings from the Delaware Key/Crest program show that offenders who completed both the ITC and aftercare programs were significantly less likely to be rearrested within 18 months following prison than were those who only completed the ITC and those in an untreated comparison group (Inciardi et al., 1997). Similarly, offenders who participated in a community-based aftercare program following their release from the California Amity program, located in the Donovan Prison in San Diego, had better 2-year follow-up outcomes than the untreated comparison and aftercare dropout treated groups (Wexler et al., 1999). Following the same pattern, our previous assessment of the Texas ITC program found that inprison treatment, especially when followed by aftercare treatment, was effective for reducing postrelease rearrest rates within 2 years after prison (Hiller, Knight, & Simpson, 1999).

Furthermore, intensive ITC programs might be optimally effective or appropriate for certain drug-involved individuals. For example, the Risk Principal implies that intensive services should be reserved for higher risk offenders (e.g., those with more severe crime and drug-related problems) to maximize treatment effectiveness (see Gendreau, Cullen, & Bonta, 1994). Some evidence suggests that these offenders often respond best to more, rather than less, intensive intervention, whereas offenders with lower problem severity seem to respond about as well (or sometimes better) to less intensive intervention (Andrews, Bonta, & Hoge, 1990). Similar findings were reported recently in a national study of community-based programs treating cocaine dependence (Simpson, Joe, Fletcher, Hubbard, & Anglin, 1999). Also, in their evaluation of an ITC program in California, Wexler et al. (1999) noted that "one of the reasons that the Amity program performed so well may be the high-risk level of the population it served" (p. 163).

Given that demand typically exceeds the limited number of intensive treatment slots available within the criminal justice system (National Center on Addiction and Substance Abuse, 1998), choosing who is most appropriate for treatment is a practical necessity. In addition to eligibility criteria that often are used to make these decisions (such as being classified as having a drug problem and having sufficient time left to serve), an inmate's level of problem severity also may need to be considered. Further research is needed to determine if in fact these types of programs will benefit primarily high-severity offenders.

When Texas began its statewide criminal justice treatment initiative in the early 1990s (for details, see Eisenberg & Fabelo, 1996), it presented an opportunity for these issues to be examined. The current study extends our previous evaluations of the first and largest Texas ITC program by examining 3-year reincarceration rates and how they are differentially related to participation in ITC and aftercare treatment, as well as an offender's problem severity level.

METHOD

Description of the Treatment Continuum

The Texas ITC, based on the New York Stay'n Out model, became operational in May 1992. The first unit that opened was a 500-bed, 9-month, modified therapeutic community. The treatment program still operates in Kyle, Texas, where it is both operationally and physically separate from the general prison system. Shortly after completion of ITC treatment, Texas offenders are paroled and transferred to a community-based residential aftercare program, typically 3 months in length and located nearest to the city where they had lived prior to prison. These transitional programs are designed to reintegrate the offender back into the community using a work-release model. The initial residential aftercare phase is followed by required participation in up to 12 months of outpatient counseling.

In addition to the aftercare program requirements, graduates of the inprison program meet regularly with their assigned parole officer and submit to urine testing on a routine (usually monthly) basis. Also, graduates meet with an assigned case manager periodically to review personal progress and deal with ongoing problems.

Measures

Sociodemographic information. Sociodemographic information was abstracted for all study participants from the Texas Department of Criminal Justice Institutional Division (TDCJ-ID) database and included gender, age, ethnicity, education level, criminal history, and the Salient Factor Score (described below).

Severity level. The Salient Factor Score (SFS) (Hoffman & Beck, 1974) used by TDCJ-ID assesses the severity of an inmate's crime and drug-related problems and provides an estimate of the relative probability of recidivism after release from prison. It was developed originally by the U.S. Parole Commission and has been used widely in making parole decisions because of its good predictive validity (see Hoffman, 1983, 1994; Hoffman & Beck, 1976, 1980, 1985). It includes nine items—five focus on criminal history and the other four are based on drug dependence, education level, previous employment, and plans for postrelease employment. The TDCJ-ID version of the original classification scheme increases the emphasis on prior criminal involvement items by expanding their response ranges. Some items, such as the assessment of drug dependence, have a 0 = history, 1 = no history response option. Other items, particularly those related to criminality, such as number of prior convictions, range from 0 (*3 or more*) to 3 (*none*). The SFS used by TDCJ-ID is the sum of the item responses and ranges from 0 (*lowest risk/severity*) to 15 (*highest risk/severity*). Severity level is based on a cutoff score used in determining intensive parole supervision, with 0 to 7 reflecting an individual with a need for intensive supervision because of their relatively severe crime and drug-related problems (referred to as high-severity in this study) and 8 to 15 denoting a need for less intensive supervision because of less severe problems (referred to as low-severity in this study).

Reincarceration. Postrelease reincarceration records were obtained from the TDCJ-ID centralized database and used to identify individuals returned to a Texas prison. Most parolees had been released from prison for at least 4 years by the time institutional records were assessed for this study, which allowed sufficient time for complete record processing in regard to the first 3 years following prison release. The database included offenders returned to a TDCJ prison because of a newly convicted first-degree felony (e.g., burglary of a habitation), second-degree felony (e.g., robbery), or third-degree felony (e.g., forgery). It also included those returned to prison because of repeated parole violations. However, it did not include those who were convicted of a jail felony (e.g., burglary of a building) or a misdemeanor offense (e.g., criminal trespass); instead of prison, they typically were sentenced to a city, county, or state-run jail. Records for those who committed these lesser offenses usually were kept at the local level and were not part of the TDCJ-ID database. Because the numerous local databases could not be accessed (and there were inconsistencies across them), this study focused strictly on TDCJ-ID database records.

As a result of their prior drug-related offenses, ITC participants were subject to frequent urine tests as part of their intensive parole supervision. Graduated sanctions were used for positive results, including being sent to a state-run residential drug treatment program as an alternative to incarceration. In contrast, untreated comparisons who violated their parole because of drug use typically were jailed or sent to a county-run drug treatment program (but these records were not included in the TDCJ-ID database). To reduce the impact of these systematic records variations, referrals to drug treatment to state-run facilities in the TDCJ-ID database were not counted as reincarceration in this study.

Sample

Initial ITC treatment eligibility in Texas during the time of this study was determined by a brief drug use screening instrument given at prison intake as well as by other classification criteria (such as excluding those with severe mental problems and those with certain aggravated offenses). After meeting eligibility requirements, each case was reviewed by correctional staff and those identified as having a drug problem were, in turn, forwarded to the parole board. The board then made final selection decisions based on staff recommendations and its own assessment of treatment need and suitability for parole (Eisenberg & Fabelo, 1996).

For implementation of this study, our initial sampling efforts (beginning in 1994) focused on selecting ITC treated and untreated comparison samples from a list of TDCJ inmates recommended for ITC placement. The original treatment sample pool included 482 ITC inmates admitted to the Kyle New Vision treatment program between June 10, 1993, and January 31, 1994 (thereby eligible to graduate 9 months later, between March 10, 1994, and October 31, 1994).

Of our original sample on which the present study is based, 14 of the 482 ITC admissions had not been paroled, and another 27 had been paroled beyond their expected release date and did not have a 3-year follow-up window (and therefore had not been at-risk for at least 3 years); in addition, 2 had died, 1 had been deported, and 1 had moved out of state. Of the remaining 437 ITC offenders who were paroled and had been out of prison for at least 3 years, 382 were graduates of the ITC, another 39 had been terminated from the ITC program for noncompliance, and 16 were transferred to another facility (primarily for medical reasons or inappropriate classification of drug problems). Of the 382 ITC graduates, 291 (76%) agreed to participate in the study.

The treatment sample in the present study, therefore, was based on the 291 follow-up eligible parolees who completed the ITC program. Those who had been out of prison for at least 3 years but had been terminated ($n = 39$) or transferred ($n = 16$) from the ITC program were not included, primarily because of their small sample sizes. Our untreated comparison sample (comparisons) included 103 inmates from the general prison population who, although recommended by institutional staff to be sent to the ITC during the same timeframe, did not receive treatment because they had less than 10 months remaining on their sentence or because of other parole board considerations. As illustrated in Table 19.1, we found no significant differences between the ITC and untreated comparison groups on average age, ethnicity, average education level, and previous criminal offense for robbery, burglary, or larceny (see also Knight et al., 1997; Hiller et al., 1999). However, the groups differed significantly according to the percentage with a previous drug offense (ITC = 38% and untreated comparison = 27%; $\chi^2 = 4.00$, $p < .05$) and the percentage classified as being at a high-severity level (ITC = 77% and untreated comparison = 56%; $\chi^2 = 15.97$, $p < .01$). Although the treated and untreated groups were drawn from the same

 Table 19.1
In-Prison Therapeutic Community (ITC) Graduates and Comparisons: Background Characteristics (in percentages)

Variable	ITC (n = 291)	Comparisons (n = 103)
Ethnicity		
African American	45	46
White	32	38
Age		
18 to 25	12	13
26 to 30	22	28
31 to 35	24	18
36 to 40	22	25
Over 40	20	16
Previous criminal offense		
Robbery	11	17
Burglary	27	23
Larceny	7	9
Possession/selling drugs*	38	27
High severity (SFS = 0–7)*	77	56

NOTE: SFS = Salient Factor Score, Average age = 34, Average grade completed = 10.
*$p < .05$.

pool of ITC eligible inmates, these findings indicate that the Parole Board tended to select more severe cases for treatment.

To examine outcomes in relation to participation in community-based aftercare treatment, the ITC sample was divided into two groups. These represented the 169 who completed the ITC and the aftercare treatment program (aftercare completers), and the 122 who completed the ITC but failed to complete the aftercare program (aftercare dropouts). Technically, the latter group included aftercare program dropouts as well as expulsions and those whose aftercare treatment stay was extended beyond 6 months because of rules violations. These subsamples did not differ significantly from each other or from the comparisons with respect to average age, ethnicity, average education level, and previous criminal offense for robbery, burglary, or larceny. However, aftercare completers (73%) and aftercare dropouts (83%) did differ significantly from comparisons (56%) according to the percentage classified as being at a high-severity level, $F(2, 391) = 10.15$, $p < .01$; the aftercare completer and aftercare dropout groups were not statistically different from each other on severity level. These differences in problem severity between the treatment and comparison groups imposed special demands on our analytic strategy.

Analytic Plan

First, 3-year reincarceration rates were calculated for the entire sample, followed by a disaggregation of rates into follow-up intervals (i.e., postrelease Years 1, 2, and 3). Next, outcomes within treatment groups and severity level were analyzed. Because reincarceration rates were related both to back-ground severity and treatment group, and because ITC participants had a significantly greater percentage of high-severity offenders than did the comparisons, the subsequent set of analyses were designed to examine the combined effect of treatment group and severity level on reincarceration. Although assessing all possible main and interaction effects based on a 3 (treatment group) $\times 2$ (severity level) analysis of variance model would have been ideal, this approach was not feasible because the statistical power to detect significant differences was diminished greatly as a result of the number of effects tested in relation to relatively small cell sizes (e.g., for low-severity aftercare dropouts, $n = 21$). Therefore, the number of effects to be tested was reduced by conducting a series of planned comparisons of treatment groups within each severity level. Because we determined that those who received in-prison treatment were placed under more intensive supervision and thus more likely to be returned to prison for a technical violation, the final set of analyses focused on group differences in reincarceration rates resulting from newly convicted offenses.

RESULTS

Overall, 41% of the entire sample ($n = 394$) was returned to custody within 3 years after leaving prison. Of this total, 7% were reincarcerated during the first year after release, followed by an additional 20% during the second year and another 14% during the third year (see Table 19.2).

Table 19.2
Reincarceration Rates by Year Following Prison Release (in percentages)

Offender Group	n	Reincarcerated Year 1	Year 2	Year 3	Total
Low severity	112	3	12	15	30
Aftercare completers	46	2	9	11	22
Aftercare dropouts	21	10	32	10	52
Comparisons	45	2	13	14	29
High severity	282	9	13	24	46
Aftercare completers	123	1	11	14	26
Aftercare dropouts	101	18	32	17	66
Comparisons	58	10	30	12	52
Total sample (*N*)	394	7	20	14	41

Treatment Groups and Severity Level Differences

Return rates for ITC treated and untreated offenders were not significantly different (41% vs. 42%, respectively). However, when aftercare participation was considered, it was found that 25% of the aftercare completers were returned to custody, significantly less than the rate for the comparison group (42%), and rates for both these groups were significantly lower than for aftercare dropouts (64%), $F(2, 391) = 24.97$, $p < .01$.

As already noted, however, an offender's problem severity level also was related to outcomes. An examination of reincarceration rates by severity level revealed that 46% of all high-severity prison inmates were returned to prison during the 3-year follow-up, compared to 30% of low-severity inmates ($\chi^2 = 7.83$, $p < .01$). This is important because it suggests that the simple comparisons of reincarceration rates between the ITC graduates (41%) and untreated comparisons (42%) are confounded. That is, the ITC sample had a significantly higher proportion of high-severity offenders than did the comparisons (77% vs. 56%, respectively; $\chi^2 = 15.97$, $p < .01$). The resulting selection bias represented a type of handicap when making unadjusted outcome comparisons, favoring the untreated group because of their overall lower severity level. To show positive outcomes from unadjusted group comparisons, treatment effects would have to overcome these sampling handicaps. Therefore, further analyses were needed to examine outcomes in relation to differences between treatment groups within each severity level.

Comparisons of Treatment Groups within Severity Level

Using an analysis of variance model, a series of planned comparisons of treatment groups within each severity level were conducted (see Figure 19.1).

Within the low-severity sample, specific contrasts between treatment groups revealed that the only statistically significant difference was between

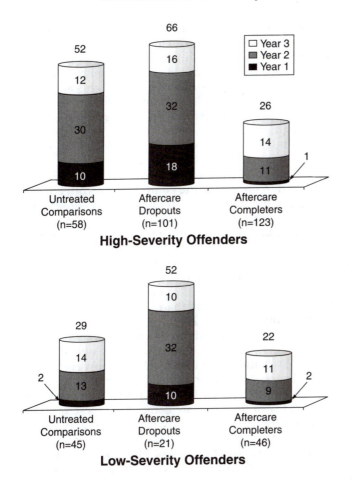

Figure 19.1 Percentage of Treatment Groups in the High- and Low-Severity Offender Categories Reincarcerated during the 3 Years Following Release from Prison

the aftercare completers and aftercare dropouts (22% and 52%, respectively), $F(1,382) = 6.33$, $p < .05$. The rates for low-severity aftercare completers and aftercare dropouts did not significantly differ from the comparisons (29%). Within the high-severity sample, specific contrasts between treatment groups indicated that the aftercare completers had a significantly lower return rate (22%) than did the aftercare dropouts (66%), $F(1,382) = 42.14$, $p < .01$, and the comparisons (52%), $F(1,382) = 12.17$, $p < .01$; the difference in return rates for the high-severity aftercare dropouts and comparisons was not significantly different. Thus, the greatest effect of treatment on outcome was realized for the high-severity offenders who completed both the ITC and aftercare treatment.

Reincarceration for Newly Convicted Offenses

In the course of examining these files, we determined that another important consideration was whether an offender was returned to prison for a newly convicted offense or because of a technical parole violation. For example, of those reincarcerated within 3 years, 35% of the low-severity versus 73% of the

rity offenders ($\chi^2 = 3.42$, $p = .06$) were returned to prison because of a
~iolation. As noted earlier, the ITC graduates had a significantly
~ortion of high-severity offenders than did the comparisons (77% vs.
~ively; $\chi^2 = 15.97$, $p < .01$), and therefore may have been reincarcer-
~cause of a technical violation. By definition, of course, the aftercare
~ropouts technically violated the conditions of their parole by failing to complete their assigned aftercare. In general, we suspected all ITC graduates may
have been at greater risk for a technical violation to be detected (e.g., positive
drug screen) because they were under more intensive supervision. For example, parole records showed that ITC graduates averaged nearly 9 (8.6) urine
tests within the first 6 months after leaving prison (aftercare completers = 9.4,
aftercare dropouts = 7.3), compared to only 3 for the comparisons. Indeed, the
ITC graduates did have significantly higher revocation rates; among those reincarcerated, the return rates due to parole revocation were 76% for aftercare completers, 65% for aftercare dropouts, and 53% for the comparisons, $F(2,160) =$
2.44, $p = .09$.

The final set of analyses, therefore, examined the relative contribution of
only newly convicted offenses (i.e., excluding parole revocations) to reincarceration rates. Overall, results showed that 6% of aftercare completers were
reincarcerated for a new offense, significantly less than the rate of 22% for aftercare dropouts and 19% for the comparisons, $F(2,391) = 9.26$, $p < .01$. A series
of planned comparisons of treatment groups within each severity level revealed
that among the low-severity offenders, there was no difference in outcome between the aftercare completers (11%) and comparisons (20%); however, rates
for both groups were significantly less than the rate for the aftercare dropouts
(38%), $F(1,382) = 9.06$, $p < .01$, and $F(1,382) = 3.98$, $p < .05$, respectively. Among
the high-severity offenders, only 4% of the aftercare completers were reincarcerated due to a newly convicted offense, significantly less than the 19% rate
for both the aftercare dropouts and comparisons, $F(1,382) = 10.43$, $p < .01$, and
$F(1,382) = 7.42$, $p < .01$, respectively. Again, the greatest effect of treatment on
outcome was realized for the high-severity offenders who completed both the
ITC and aftercare treatment.

DISCUSSION

Consistent with prior findings of the Texas ITC (see Knight et al., 1997) and
with other ITC evaluations (e.g., Inciardi et al., 1997; Wexler et al., 1999), this
study showed that offenders who completed both in-prison and community-
based aftercare treatment (aftercare completers) were the least likely to be
returned to prison. Specifically, only 25% of the aftercare completers were reincarcerated, compared to 65% of the sample that dropped out of aftercare (aftercare dropouts) and 42% of the untreated comparison sample (comparisons).
Also similar to results from previous evaluations (Hoffman, 1994), this study
found that offenders with more severe crime and drug-related problems had a
higher rate of reincarceration than did offenders with less severe problems
(46% vs. 30%, respectively).

When comparisons of treatment groups on reincarceration rates were calculated within severity level, the strongest treatment effects were found with
the high-severity aftercare completers. Their 3-year reincarceration rate was
26%, versus 66% for the aftercare dropouts and 52% for the comparisons.

Among low-severity offenders, 22% of the aftercare completers, 52% of the aftercare dropouts, and 29% of the comparisons were returned to prison. These
findings agree with the Risk Principle of effective correctional treatment delineated by Gendreau and colleagues (1994) that suggests treatment services
should be matched with offender risk (i.e., problem severity) levels. It also is
supported by data recently reported by Simpson et al. (1999) showing that cocaine users with more severe problems had better outcomes from community-
based programs that provided intensive services, and they had poorer outcomes
when treated in lower intensity (including outpatient and short-term) programs. Thus, ITC treatment appears to benefit primarily high-severity offenders but should be followed by mandated participation in a community-based
aftercare treatment program. Intensive programs in prison that treat low-severity
offenders and treatment protocols that do not include an aftercare component
may not be optimally effective and an unnecessary drain on valuable resources.
By implication, then, initial assessment procedures are needed that identify and
give priority in ITC assignment to offenders with higher problem severity.

Furthermore, when reincarceration is used as an outcome measure for treatment effectiveness, the results from this study suggest that an offender's supervision level and potential for parole revocation also should be considered. As
Petersilia and Turner (1993) note, parole violations are more likely to be noticed
by criminal justice authorities when offenders are placed under intensive supervision. In Texas, mandated participation in aftercare treatment coupled with
frequent drug testing placed graduates of the ITC program at a substantially
higher risk for detection of technical violations and for subsequent returns to
prison for not meeting conditions of their parole (see Fabelo, 1999). Indeed, our
review of parole officer records indicated that ITC graduates were under more
intensive supervision. For example, they were required to provide an average
of nearly 9 urine tests within the first 6 months after leaving prison (aftercare
completer = 9.4, aftercare dropout = 7.3), compared to only 3 for the untreated
comparison group. Furthermore, of those who were incarcerated, ITC offenders
were more likely than the untreated comparison group to be reincarcerated due
to a technical parole violation (76% for the aftercare completer, 65% for the aftercare dropout, and 53% for the comparison groups).

Because of the differences between groups in parole revocations, 3-year reincarceration rates were recalculated based strictly on newly convicted offenses.
Results indicated that the aftercare completers again had a lower return rate than
the aftercare dropouts and comparisons (6% vs. 22% and 19%, respectively).
Also note that reincarceration rates for new offenses were very similar between
the comparison and aftercare dropout groups (22% vs. 19%), compared to the
rates that included technical revocations (64% vs. 42%). Because failing to complete aftercare is technically a violation of parole, it is not surprising that parole
revocations accounted for the aftercare dropout group's relatively high reincarceration rate, and that it was not significantly different from that of the comparison group when only newly convicted offenses were considered.

Accounting for group dissimilarity, such as on measures of problem severity and intensity of supervision, is important because critics of ITC program
evaluations correctly assert that differential outcomes may be the result of
problems associated with selection bias rather than treatment effects (e.g.,
Pelissier et al., 1998). Although the aftercare completers and dropouts in this
study were equivalent on a variety of background measures (including motivation for treatment; Hiller et al., 1999), one of the limitations of this study is the

y that unidentified group differences may have accounted for the fa-
incarceration rates of aftercare completers. Ideally, a randomized
dy is needed to provide stronger evidence for the effectiveness of
itment. Randomized assignments to treatment groups in a classical
ntal design is often held up as the ultimate evaluation needed, but as
Leon, Inciardi, and Martin (1995) have noted, there are many difficulties
with control group designs that include ethical, political, and legal dilemmas
in withholding treatment. What is important, these authors argue, is that field-
based studies take into account individual differences when predicting outcomes.
When differences do exist between groups (such as on treatment motivation),
they should be considered a fundamental and important part of the recovery
process and not as an inherent weakness in study design (De Leon et al., 1995;
Simpson, 1997). Indeed, imposing strict experimental controls on treatment
conditions for studying a complex process like treatment and recovery for drug
abuse is illusory, and even if possible the design would potentially restrict the
study of the very dynamics that promote recovery.

In summary, this study helps clarify conditions under which in-prison drug
abuse treatment is effective and who can benefit most from it. First, the results
reaffirm that community-based aftercare is an integral part of correctional treatment. Failure to provide adequate treatment after releasing offenders from ITCs
undermines any positive changes that occurred during in-prison treatment.
Second, intensive ITC treatment was most effective for high-severity inmates,
and the treatment effect appears to be sustained up to 3 years after prison. On
the other hand, providing intensive treatment to low-severity offenders had
limited benefits in reducing reincarceration rates, particularly with respect to
newly convicted offenses, and may be an unnecessary drain on limited treatment resources. Better tools and utilization strategies for drug use assessments
are therefore indicated for matching needs and resources (Broome, Knight, Joe,
& Simpson, 1996).

CONCLUSION

Incarceration presents a unique opportunity to provide intensive treatment to
drug-involved offenders with relatively severe crime and drug-related problems.
Unfortunately, treatment in this setting is becoming the best (and sometimes the
only) access chronic drug users have to the long-term and uninterrupted care
needed for recovery. To optimize and demonstrate its effectiveness, the referral
process (including judges, prisons, and parole boards) must become systematic
and disciplined, and evaluations should improve by focusing on issues that
translate into policy decisions. These include cost effectiveness or benefit studies as well as attention to particular interventions and strategies that improve
therapeutic engagement in primary treatment and subsequent phases of continuing care. Failure to do so will likely lead to politicized interpretations that correctional treatment does not work and to the widespread erosion of this system
under pressures from the next reversal of the national economic pendulum.

REFERENCES

Andrews, D. A., Bonta, J., & Hoge, R. D. (1990). Classification for effective
rehabilitation: Rediscovering psychology. *Criminal Justice and Behavior,* 17(1), 19–52.

Broome, K. M., Knight, K., Joe, G. W., & Simpson, D. D. (1996). Evaluating the dru‚ abusing probationer: Clinical interview versus self-administered assessment. *Criminal Justice and Behavior, 23*(4), 593–606.

De Leon, G., Inciardi, J. A., & Martin, S. S. (1995). Residential drug abuse treatment research: Are conventional control designs appropriate for assessing treatment effectiveness? *Journal of Psychoactive Drugs, 27*(1), 85–91.

Eisenberg, M., & Fabelo, T. (1996). Evaluation of the Texas correctional substance abuse treatment initiative: The impact of policy research. *Crime & Delinquency, 42*(2), 296–308.

Fabelo, T. (1999). *Three year recidivism tracking of offenders participating in substance abuse treatment programs.* Austin, TX: Criminal Justice Policy Council.

Gendreau, P., Cullen, F. T., & Bonta, J. (1994). Intensive rehabilitation supervision: The next generation in community corrections. *Federal Probation, 58,* 72–78.

Hiller, M. L., Knight, K., & Simpson, D. D. (1999). Prison-based substance abuse treatment, residential aftercare and recidivism. *Addiction, 94*(6), 833–842.

Hoffman, P. B. (1983). Screening for risk: A revised Salient Factor Score. *Journal of Criminal Justice, 11,* 539–547.

Hoffman, P. B. (1994). Twenty years of operational use of a risk prediction instrument: The United States Parole Commission's Salient Factor Score. *Journal of Criminal Justice, 22,* 477–494.

Hoffman, P. B., & Beck, J. L. (1974). Parole decision-making: A Salient Factor Score. *Journal of Criminal Justice, 2,* 195–206.

Hoffman, P. B., & Beck, J. L. (1976). Salient Factor Score validation: A 1972 release cohort. *Journal of Criminal Justice, 4,* 69–76.

Hoffman, P. B., & Beck, J. L. (1980). Revalidating the Salient Factor Score: A research note. *Journal of Criminal Justice, 8,* 185–188.

Hoffman, P. B., & Beck, J. L. (1985). Recidivism among released federal prisoners: Salient Factor Score and five-year follow-up. *Criminal Justice and Behavior, 12,* 501–507.

Inciardi, J. A., Martin, S. S., Butzin, C. A., Hooper, R. M., & Harrison, L. D. (1997). An effective model of prison-based treatment for drug-involved offenders. *Journal of Drug Issues, 27*(2), 261–278.

Knight, K., Simpson, D. D., Chatham, L. R., & Camacho, L. M. (1997). An assessment of prison-based drug treatment: Texas' in-prison therapeutic community program. *Journal of Offender Rehabilitation, 24*(3/4), 75–100.

National Center on Addiction and Substance Abuse. (1998). *Behind bars: Substance abuse and America's prison population.* New York: Columbia University.

Pelissier, B., Rhodes, W., Gaes, G., Camp, S., O'Neil, J., Wallace, S., & Saylor, W. (1998). *Alternative solutions to the problem of selection bias in an analysis of federal residential drug treatment programs.* Washington, DC: Federal Bureau of Prisons.

Petersilia, J., & Turner, S. (1993). Intensive probation and parole. In M. Tonry (Ed.), *Crime and justice: An annual review of research* (pp. 281–335). Chicago: University of Chicago Press.

Simpson, D. D. (1997). Effectiveness of drug-abuse treatment: A review of research from field settings. In J. A. Egertson, D. M. Fox, & A. I. Leshner (Eds.), *Treating drug abusers effectively* (pp. 41–73). Cambridge, MA: Blackwell Publishers of North America.

Simpson, D. D., Joe, G. W., Fletcher, B. W., Hubbard, R. L., & Anglin, M. D. (1999). A national evaluation of treatment outcomes for cocaine dependence. *Archives of General Psychiatry, 56,* 507–514.

Wexler, H. K., De Leon, G., Kressel, D., & Peters, J. (1999). The Amity prison TC evaluation: Reincarceration outcomes. *Criminal Justice and Behavior, 26*(2), 147–167.

Wexler, H. K., Falkin, G. P., & Lipton, D. S. (1990). Outcome evaluation of a prison therapeutic community for substance abuse treatment. *Criminal Justice and Behavior, 17*(1), 71–92.

FOUR: SOCIETAL ADJUSTMENT FACTORS

DISCUSSION QUESTIONS

1. How does race affect the patterns of incarceration of women in Maryland? Is Young's research generalizable to other states and/or time periods?
2. According to Petersilia, what problems do mentally retarded offenders face during and after incarceration? How might the criminal justice system (and corrections in particular) alter its approach to mentally retarded offenders?
3. According to the qualitative research by Dodge and Pogrebin, what are the collateral costs of imprisonment for female offenders? How are these collateral costs borne by these women?
4. According to the research by Adams et al., what impact do prison education programs have on inmate behavior? What is the impact on recidivism?
5. What does the research by Knight et al., indicate about the effectiveness of in-prison therapeutic community treatment programs? Who is most and least likely to successfully complete such a program, and why?